THINKING THROUGH SHAKESPEARE

Thinking Through Shakespeare

DAVID WOMERSLEY

PRINCETON UNIVERSITY PRESS
PRINCETON & OXFORD

Published by Princeton University Press
41 William Street, Princeton, New Jersey 08540
99 Banbury Road, Oxford OX2 6JX
press.princeton.edu

GPSR Authorized Representative: Easy Access System Europe - Mustamäe tee 50, 10621 Tallinn, Estonia, gpsr.requests@easproject.com

ISBN: 978-0-691-15410-7
ISBN (e-book): 978-0-691-28836-9
ISBN (web PDF): 978-0-691-28372-2

Library of Congress Control Number: 2025946557

British Library Cataloging-in-Publication Data is available

Editorial: Ben Tate, Josh Drake
Production Editorial: Elizabeth Byrd, Kathleen Cioffi
Jacket Design: Heather Hansen
Production: Danielle Amatucci
Publicity: Jodi Price (US), Carmen Jimenez (UK)

Jacket image: Heritage Image Partnership Ltd / Alamy Stock Photo

This book has been composed in Arno

Printed in the United States of America

10 9 8 7 6 5 4 3 2 1

For Adrian Poole

CONTENTS

ACKNOWLEDGMENTS

WITHOUT WISHING TO IMPLICATE any innocent bystander in what follows, when writing this book I profited from conversations with and advice from Fabian Brandt, David Dwan, James Harris, Phillip Koralus, Heinrich Meier, Derek Morris, Adrian Poole, Galen Strawson, Adam Tomkins, Conrad Williams, and Brian Young. Participants at the 'Image' seminar that I codirected with Thomas Pfau at the National Center for the Humanities in North Carolina and the Wissenschaftskolleg in Berlin and those who over the years have attended my Oxford lectures where some of these ideas were tried out have provided constructive challenges and encouraging responses. I should also give grateful mention to those other acquaintances, academic and otherwise, upon whom fragments of the book's broad argument were tested for plausibility (not always successfully).

Oxford, February 2024

ABBREVIATIONS

Ayers, *Locke*	Michael Ayers, *Locke: Epistemology and Ontology*, 2 vols. (London: Routledge, 1991)
Bacon, *Essayes*	Sir Francis Bacon, *The Essayes or Counsels, Civill and Morall*, ed. Michael Kiernan (Oxford: Clarendon Press, 1985)
Bagehot, *Constitution*	Walter Bagehot, *The English Constitution*, ed. Miles Taylor, Oxford World's Classics (Oxford: Oxford University Press, 2001)
Boccalini, *Parnasso*	Trajano Boccalini, *I Ragguagli di Parnasso, or, Advertisements from Parnassus: In Two Centuries*, trans. Henry Earl of Monmouth, 3rd ed. (1674)
Bullough, *Sources*	Geoffrey Bullough, ed., *Narrative and Dramatic Sources of Shakespeare*, 8 vols. (London: Routledge and Kegan Paul, 1957–1975)
Burckhardt, *Renaissance*	Jacob Burckhardt, *The Civilization of the Renaissance in Italy* (London: Phaidon, 1944)
Burke, *Writings*	Edmund Burke, *The Writings and Speeches of Edmund Burke*, gen. ed. Paul Langford, 9 vols. (Oxford: Clarendon Press, 1981–2015)
Carlyle, *Chartism*	Thomas Carlyle, *Sartor Resartus, Lectures on Heroes, Chartism, Past and Present* (London: Chapman and Hall, 1890)
Coetzee, *Barbarians*	J. M. Coetzee, *Waiting for the Barbarians* (London: Vintage, 2000)
Coleridge, *Biographia*	Samuel Taylor Coleridge, *Biographia Literaria*, ed. James Engell and W. Jackson Bate, 2 vols., The Collected Works of Samuel Taylor Coleridge, vol. 7 (Princeton, NJ: Princeton University Press, 1983)

Coleridge, *Lectures*	Samuel Taylor Coleridge, *Lectures on Literature*, ed. R. A. Foakes, 2 vols., The Collected Works of Samuel Taylor Coleridge, vol. 5 (London: Routledge Kegan Paul, 1987)
Coleridge, *Table-Talk*	*Coleridge's Table-Talk* (London, 1899)
Colish, *Stoic Tradition*	Marcia L. Colish, *The Stoic Tradition from Antiquity to the Early Middle Ages: Stoicism in Christian Latin Thought Through the Sixth Century*, 2nd ed. (Leiden: E. J. Brill, 1990)
Conrad, *Lord Jim*	Joseph Conrad, *Lord Jim*, ed. J. H. Stape and Ernest W. Sullivan II, The Cambridge Edition of the Works of Joseph Conrad (Cambridge: Cambridge University Press, 2012)
Corelli, *Wormwood*	Marie Corelli, *Wormwood: A Drama of Paris*, ed. Kirsten MacLeod (Peterborough, ON: Broadview Press, 2004)
Eliot, *Essays*	T. S. Eliot, *Selected Essays*, 3rd ed. (London: Faber and Faber, 1972)
Fagles, *Oresteia*	Aeschylus, *The Oresteia*, trans. Robert Fagles (Harmondsworth, UK: Penguin, 1977)
Figgis, *Divine Right*	John Neville Figgis, *The Divine Right of Kings*, 2nd ed. (Cambridge: Cambridge University Press, 1914)
Forbes, *Politics*	Duncan Forbes, *Hume's Philosophical Politics* (Cambridge: Cambridge University Press, 1975)
Freud, *Civilization*	Sigmund Freud, *Civilization and Its Discontents* (1929–1930), ed. Albert Dickson, The Penguin Freud Library, vol. 12 (London: Penguin Books, 1991)
Fugger	*The Fuggers News-Letters*, ed. Victor von Klarwill, trans. Pauline de Chary (New York: Knickerbocker Press, 1925)
Gibbon, *Decline*	Edward Gibbon, *The History of the Decline and Fall of the Roman Empire*, ed. David Womersley, 3 vols. (London: Allen Lane, 1994)
Goethe, *Elective Affinities*	J. W. von Goethe, *Elective Affinities: A Novel*, trans. David Constantine (Oxford: Oxford University Press, 1994)

Goguet, *Origine*	Antoine-Yves Goguet, *De l'Origine des loix, des arts, et des sciences*, 3 vols. (Paris, 1757)
Greenblatt, *Swerve*	Stephen Greenblatt, *The Swerve: How the Renaissance Began* (London: Bodley Head, 2011)
Hall, *Barbarian*	Edith Hall, *Inventing the Barbarian: Greek Self-Definition Through Tragedy* (Oxford: Clarendon Press, 1989)
Harrington, *Works*	James Harrington, *The Political Works of James Harrington*, ed. J.G.A. Pocock (Cambridge: Cambridge University Press, 1977)
Harrison, *Greeks*	Thomas Harrison, ed., *Greeks and Barbarians*, Edinburgh Readings on the Ancient World (Edinburgh: Edinburgh University Press, 2001)
Hobbes, *Behemoth*	Thomas Hobbes, *Behemoth; or, The Long Parliament*, ed. Ferdinand Tönnies, intro. Stephen Holmes (Chicago: University of Chicago Press, 1990)
Hobbes, *Leviathan*	Thomas Hobbes, *Leviathan*, ed. Richard Tuck (Cambridge: Cambridge University Press, 1996)
Hume, *Enquiry*	David Hume, *An Enquiry Concerning the Principles of Morals*, ed. Tom L. Beauchamp, The Clarendon Edition of the Works of David Hume (Oxford: Oxford University Press, 1998)
Hume, *Essays*	David Hume, *Essays Moral, Political, and Literary*, ed. Eugene F. Miller, rev. ed. (Indianapolis, IN: Liberty Fund, 1985)
Hume, *Letters*	*The Letters of David Hume*, ed. J.Y.T. Greig, 2 vols. (Oxford: Clarendon Press, 1932)
Hume, *Treatise*	David Hume, *A Treatise of Human Nature*, ed. David Fate Norton and Mary J. Norton, The Clarendon Edition of the Works of David Hume, 2 vols. (Oxford: Clarendon Press, 2007)
James I and VI, *Political Writings*	James I and VI, *Political Writings*, ed. Johann P. Somerville (Cambridge: Cambridge University Press, 1994)
Johnson, *Shakespeare*	*Samuel Johnson on Shakespeare*, ed. H. R. Woudhuysen (Harmondsworth, UK: Penguin Books, 1989)

Jonson, *Works*	Ben Jonson, *Ben Jonson*, ed. C. H. Herford and P. and E. Simpson, 11 vols. (Oxford: Clarendon Press, 1925–1952)
Kant, *Critique*	Immanuel Kant, *Critique of Pure Reason*, trans. and ed. Paul Guyer and Allen W. Wood, The Cambridge Edition of the Works of Immanuel Kant (Cambridge: Cambridge University Press, 1998)
Kant, *Groundwork*	Immanuel Kant, *Groundwork of the Metaphysics of Morals*, ed. Mary Gregor and Jens Timmermann, intro. C. M. Korsgaard, rev. ed. (Cambridge: Cambridge University Press, 2012)
Kant, *Metaphysics*	Immanuel Kant, *The Metaphysics of Morals*, ed. Lara Denis, trans. Mary Gregor (Cambridge: Cambridge University Press, 2017)
Kantorowicz, *Two Bodies*	Ernst H. Kantorowicz, *The King's Two Bodies: A Study in Mediaeval Political Theology* (Princeton, NJ: Princeton University Press, 1957)
Locke, *Essay*	John Locke, *An Essay Concerning Human Understanding*, ed. P. H. Nidditch (Oxford: Clarendon Press, 1975)
Locke, *Two Treatises*	John Locke, *Two Treatises of Government*, ed. Peter Laslett, Cambridge Texts in the History of Political Thought (Cambridge: Cambridge University Press, 1988)
Machiavelli, *Works*	*The Works of the Famous Nicolas Machiavel, Citizen and Secretary of Florence* (1675)
Malcolm, *Reason of State*	Noel Malcolm, *Reason of State, Propaganda, and the Thirty Years' War: An Unknown Translation by Thomas Hobbes* (Oxford: Clarendon Press, 2007)
Mann, *Essays*	Thomas Mann, *Essays of Three Decades*, trans. H. T. Lowe-Porter (London: Secker and Warburg, n.d.)
Mann, *Reflections*	Thomas Mann, *Reflections of a Nonpolitical Man*, ed. Mark Lilla (New York: NYRB Books, 2021)
Mauss, *Gift*	Marcel Mauss, *The Gift*, ed. Jane I. Guyer (1925; Chicago: Hau Books, 2016)
Mill, 'Civilization'	John Stuart Mill, 'Civilization', first published in the *London and Westminster Review* (April 1836), as reprinted in *The Collected Works of John Stuart*

	Mill, vol. 18, *Essays on Politics and Society*, Part 1, ed. J. M. Robson and Alexander Brady (Toronto: University of Toronto Press, 1977), pp. 117–147
Mill, *Utilitarianism*	John Stuart Mill, *Utilitarianism* (London: Parker and Son, 1863)
Monod, *Power of Kings*	Paul Kléber Monod, *The Power of Kings: Monarchy and Religion in Europe 1589–1715* (New Haven, CT: Yale University Press, 1999)
Montaigne, *Œuvres*	Montaigne, *Œuvres completes*, ed. Albert Thibaudet and Maurice Rat (Paris: Gallimard, 1962)
Moore, *Principia*	G. E. Moore, *Principia Ethica*, ed. Thomas Baldwin, rev. ed. (Cambridge: Cambridge University Press, 1993)
Nietzsche, *Tragedy*	Friedrich Nietzsche, *The Birth of Tragedy and the Genealogy of Morals*, trans. Francis Golffing (New York: Doubleday Anchor Books, 1956)
NLS	National Library of Scotland
Norbrook, '*Macbeth*'	David Norbrook, '*Macbeth* and the Politics of Historiography', in *Politics of Discourse: The Literature and History of Seventeenth-Century England*, ed. Kevin Sharpe and Steven N. Zwicker (Berkeley: University of California Press, 1987), pp. 78–116
Norbrook, *Republic*	David Norbrook, *Writing the English Republic: Poetry, Rhetoric and Politics, 1627–1660* (Cambridge: Cambridge University Press, 1999)
OED	*Oxford English Dictionary*
Paine, *Political Writings*	Thomas Paine, *Political Writings*, ed. Bruce Kuklick, Cambridge Texts in the History of Political Thought (Cambridge: Cambridge University Press, 1989)
Philo, *Livy*	John-Mark Philo, *'An Ocean Untouched and Untried': The Tudor Translations of Livy* (Oxford: Oxford University Press, 2020)
Pocock, *Barbarism*	J.G.A. Pocock, *Barbarism and Religion*, 6 vols. (Cambridge: Cambridge University Press, 1999–2015)
Rawls, *Justice*	John Rawls, *A Theory of Justice*, rev. ed. (Cambridge, MA: Belknap Press of Harvard University Press, 2003)

Rousseau, *Discours*	Jean-Jacques Rousseau, *Discours qui a remporté le prix de l'academie de Dijon* (Geneva, 1750)
Rousseau, *Inegalité*	Jean-Jacques Rousseau, *Discours sur l'origine et les fondemens de l'inegalité parmi les hommes* (Amsterdam, 1755)
Schopenhauer, *World*	Arthur Schopenhauer, *The World as Will and Idea*, trans. R. B. Haldane and J. Kemp, vol. 1 (Boston: Ticknor and Co., 1888)
Scruton, *Parsifal*	Roger Scruton, *Wagner's Parsifal: The Music of Redemption* (London: Allen Lane, 2020)
Shaw, *Wagnerite*	George Bernard Shaw, *The Perfect Wagnerite* (London: Constable and Co., 1911)
Sidgwick, *Ethics*	Henry Sidgwick, *The Methods of Ethics*, 2nd ed. (London: Macmillan, 1877)
Skinner, *Forensic*	Quentin Skinner, *Forensic Shakespeare* (Oxford: Oxford University Press, 2014)
Skinner, *Visions*	Quentin Skinner, *Visions of Politics*, 3 vols. (Cambridge: Cambridge University Press, 2002)
Smith, *Essays*	Adam Smith, *Essays on Philosophical Subjects*, ed. W.P.D. Wightman and J. C. Bryce (Oxford: Clarendon Press, 1980)
Smith, *Sentiments*	Adam Smith, *The Theory of Moral Sentiments*, ed. D. D. Raphael and A. L. Macfie (Oxford: Clarendon Press, 1976)
Smith, *Wealth*	Adam Smith, *The Wealth of Nations*, ed. R. H. Campbell and A. S. Skinner, 2 vols. (Oxford: Clarendon Press, 1976)
Swift, *Gulliver*	Jonathan Swift, *Gulliver's Travels*, ed. David Womersley, The Cambridge Edition of the Works of Jonathan Swift (Cambridge: Cambridge University Press, 2012)
Thiel, *Subject*	Udo Thiel, *The Early Modern Subject: Self-Consciousness and Personal Identity from Descartes to Hume* (Oxford: Oxford University Press, 2011)
Tuck, *Hobbes*	Richard Tuck, *Hobbes* (Oxford: Oxford University Press, 1989)

Vendler, *Sonnets*	Helen Vendler, *The Art of Shakespeare's Sonnets* (Cambridge, MA: Belknap Press of Harvard University Press, 1997)
Womersley, *Divinity*	David Womersley, *Divinity and State* (Oxford: Oxford University Press, 2010)
Worden, *Instruments*	Blair Worden, *God's Instruments: Political Conduct in the England of Oliver Cromwell* (Oxford: Oxford University Press, 2012)

THINKING THROUGH SHAKESPEARE

Introduction

JOHNSON ON SHAKESPEARE

> We hear many speeches and read many books praising the unity of Western civilization. . . . But I am afraid this unity of Western civilization is spurious. Nor would I say this is a bad thing that we do not have unity in our civilization. The West, it seems to me, owes its glory and its dignity to the antagonism of its constituent elements. It owes to this antagonism its vitality.
>
> —LEO STRAUSS[1]

SAMUEL JOHNSON KNEW why Shakespeare's plays were so widely and enduringly popular. To him, the general principle of literary popularity was clear: 'Nothing can please many, and please long, but just representations of general nature.' For Johnson, Shakespeare's popularity rested on the fact that his writings embodied that principle more richly and more fully than did those of any other author:

> Shakespeare is above all writers, at least above all modern writers, the poet of nature; the poet that holds up to his readers a faithful mirror of manners and of life. His characters are not modified by the customs of particular places, unpractised by the rest of the world; by the peculiarities of studies or professions, which can operate but upon small numbers; or by the accidents of transient fashions or temporary opinions: they are the genuine progeny of common humanity, such as the world will always supply and observation will always find.[2]

1. Laurenz Denker, Hannes Kerber, and David Kretz, 'Leo Strauss's "Jerusalem and Athens" (1950): Three Lectures Delivered at Hillel House, Chicago', *Journal for the History of Modern Theology* 29 (2022): 138.

2. In the preface to his edition of Shakespeare; Johnson, *Shakespeare*, p. 122.

For over two hundred years after Johnson wrote those words in 1765, that view of the foundation of Shakespeare's greatness as a writer more or less prevailed. Of course, Shakespearean criticism did not remain static during those centuries. Romantic critics reacted against Johnson and were reacted against in their turn by the Victorians. The character-based criticism associated with A. C. Bradley was challenged by the rise in the mid-twentieth century of a criticism that put poetic coherence above psychological realism. But these successive critical phases had in common an acceptance of the implications of Johnson's repeated word 'always': namely, the assumption that Shakespeare's plays addressed human questions of perennial importance and the belief that it was the task of the critic to explain how they did so by revealing what the plays seemed to say about those questions. So when Derek Traversi wrote in the conclusion to his once-influential *An Approach to Shakespeare* that 'Shakespeare's "problem" (if we may use so self-conscious a word) is that of imparting order and poetic significance to the keenly felt but separate elements of human experience', it is easy to see how that very twentieth-century formulation nevertheless reached back to Johnson, by way perhaps of the Arnoldian notion of poetry as a 'criticism of life'.[3]

However, the migration of high theory from the social sciences to the literary humanities which occurred in the second half of the twentieth century temporarily drove from the field of literary criticism that well-established way of thinking about how and why great literature holds and rewards our attention. Suddenly all the common-sensical ideas about language and literature which had seemed so unproblematic that one could safely treat them as axioms—for instance, the belief that works of literature had discoverable (albeit often very complex) meanings or the idea that language was a system of signification which referred to things outside itself—were denounced as mere prejudices. In fact, both limbs of Johnson's memorable phrase—'just representations of general nature'—were put under devastating pressure by this new variant of literary theory. Theoretical critiques took pleasure in unmasking the idea of a 'just representation' as a delusion. According to these theorists, literature could do nothing more than point mournfully and repetitiously to its own impotence as representation. Delusional, too, was the concept of a

3. D. A. Traversi, *An Approach to Shakespeare*, 2nd ed. (London: Sands & Co., 1957), p. 286; Matthew Arnold, 'The Study of Poetry' (1880), in *English Literature and Irish Politics*, The Complete Prose Works of Matthew Arnold, vol. 9 (Ann Arbor: University of Michigan Press, 1973), p. 163.

'general nature'. Politically-minded theorists contended that what we had been offered as the 'natural' tended, when examined more closely and less sympathetically, to reveal itself as a socially-constructed fiction dictated by dominant, oppressive, usually male, western European, and white interests. And since those interests were themselves not timeless, no more timeless were the fictions of the natural that they had been used to create. So a 'just representation' was impossible for two reasons. Literary representation was itself a fallacy, and even if it were not, it could not be 'just' in either sense of that complex word, since it could be neither precise nor fair.

No doubt some of the Shakespearean criticism published before the arrival of theory was bland, conservative paraphrase and deserved a degree of rough handling. But the theoretical challenge to traditional ways of thinking about literature went well beyond simply the spring-cleaning of our critical notions. It raised the more profoundly sceptical prospect of all approaches to literature which sought to relate its content to matters of enduring human importance—what we might call 'ethical criticism'—being ruled out of court on the double grounds that, even if literature were able to engage with such issues (which given its nullity as representation, it was not), there were in the first place no such permanent and naturally human issues for literature to address.

Was there not something hyperbolical about theory's scepticism? Did it not topple over into a modern form of Pyrrhonism? It sometimes seemed as if literature's powers of subtlety of signification were being over-read as evidence of the impossibility of signification. On the subject of human nature, the constructivists who denied that such a thing existed began to be answered by those less *parti-pris* philosophers who remembered that, a few years before the composition of Johnson's preface to his edition of Shakespeare, that truly sceptical philosopher David Hume had found a way to hold in a single thought both his experience of the variably-patterned surface of human behaviour and his faith in constant principles of human nature: 'The internal principles and motives [*of human nature*] may operate in a uniform manner, notwithstanding these seeming irregularities; in the same manner as the winds, rain, clouds, and other variations of the weather are supposed to be governed by steady principles; though not easily discoverable by human sagacity and enquiry.'[4] As

4. David Hume, *An Enquiry Concerning Human Understanding* (1748), sect. 8, part 1, para. 68. Cf. also the comparison between the Rhine and the Rhone in 'A Dialogue', appended to *An Enquiry Concerning the Principles of Morals* (1751). For a helpful exploration of Hume's position on the possibility of sympathetic understanding, see Jennifer A. Herdt, 'Artificial Lives,

Marx commented in the *Grundrisse*, hunger is hunger, and the hunger of the savage who tears at raw meat and the hunger of the modern European who eats cooked food with cutlery are merely different expressions of what is nevertheless an enduring appetite.[5]

Although the fortunes of theory as a practice waned, its impact was lasting. In particular, critics who were not committed to theory nevertheless showed little desire to revive the ethical criticism the theoreticians had attacked. As the theoretical tide ebbed, three strong currents moved through Shakespearean criticism. Firstly, there was a turn to history, in the form of the 'New Historicism'. Historically-grounded readings of Shakespeare's plays revived the flavour of the old ethical criticism, without being so vulnerable to the powerful corrosives which theory had deployed to impressive effect.[6] Secondly, there was a revival of interest in theatre history and in locating Shakespeare within the dramatic archive.[7] Thirdly, a measure of critical energy was directed towards authorship studies, particularly towards the early-modern phenomenon of collaborative composition.[8]

These developments all marked at once an advance and a retreat. They showed an impressive gain in various forms of technical power and scholarly accomplishment (historical contextualisation; the study of early modern theatrical institutions; the textual analysis of authorship). At the same time, however, they revealed the academy turning in on itself and retreating further from the possibility of addressing a general educated readership.

Providential History, and the Apparent Limits of Sympathetic Understanding', in *David Hume: Historical Thinker, Historical Writer*, ed. Mark C. Spencer (University Park: Pennsylvania State University Press, 2013), pp. 37–59. For a recent re-statement of the constructivist position on human nature, see Joseph Henrich, Steven J. Heine, and Ara Norenzayan, 'The Weirdest People in the World?', *Behavioral and Brain Sciences* 33, nos. 2–3 (2010): 61–83. For a temperate and rational rejoinder, see Galen Strawson, *Selves: An Essay in Revisionary Metaphysics* (Oxford: Oxford University Press, 2009), pp. 34–36.

5. Karl Marx, *Grundrisse*, trans. Martin Nicolaus (Harmondsworth, UK: Allen Lane, 1973), p. 92.

6. Classically, Stephen Greenblatt, *Shakespearean Negotiations* (Oxford: Clarendon Press, 1988).

7. Most recently and interestingly, Simon Palfrey and Tiffany Stern, *Shakespeare in Parts* (Oxford: Oxford University Press, 2007); and Bart van Es, *Shakespeare in Company* (Oxford: Oxford University Press, 2013).

8. For instance, Brian Vickers, *Shakespeare, Co-Author* (Oxford: Oxford University Press, 2002).

The vividly contrasting social backdrop to these movements in Shakespearean criticism is the extraordinary phenomenon of world-wide attendance at performances of Shakespeare's plays. For theory, hospitable as it was to a constructivist account of human nature and hostile to any idea of essence, the fact of Shakespeare's popularity could be easily explained away as a consequence of the 'Shakespeare Establishment'. No doubt the entrenched position of Shakespeare in the British school curriculum and the existence of so culturally potent an entity as the Royal Shakespeare Company may both have played such a role, at least in Great Britain. But enthusiasm for Shakespeare is confined neither to Great Britain nor even to the West. It flourishes in cultures where no 'Shakespeare Establishment' exists or could possibly take root.[9] The recent critical preoccupations of the academy—historical explication, theatrical antiquarianism, and authorship studies—may of course yield important findings. But they will always be 'second-order' findings. These critical and scholarly modes cannot, even in their own terms, find a way of addressing—let alone of explaining—the vast, primary fact of the enduring human appetite for Shakespeare's drama.[10] Stephen Greenblatt has pleaded that 'it is not necessary to choose between an account of Shakespeare as the scion of a particular culture and an account of him as a universal genius who created works that continually renew themselves across national and generational boundaries'.[11]

9. In this connection is it worth reflecting on the experiences of Paul Stebbings, whose TNT (The New Theatre) company performs Shakespeare (but not just Shakespeare) all over the world, and frequently in China. He observes that 'TNT is not bringing Shakespeare to China. We are finding him there.' And the Chinese appetite for Shakespeare, which of course relies on no state support and indeed is of relatively recent date (the first translation of a Shakespeare play into Mandarin was made less than a century ago), eclipses that of other European authors who might be expected to travel well: 'Having filled the National Centre for Performing Arts in Beijing for "Romeo and Juliet" we were disappointed to see half empty houses at the same theatre one week later for our highly accessible "Gulliver's Travels"'. Stebbings recognises that an important element in the success of TNT has been the 'worldwide explosion of interest in Shakespeare' (Paul Stebbings and Phil Smith, *TNT: The New Theatre* [Axminster, UK: Triarchy Press, 2020], pp. 137, 138, and 240).

10. 'Shakespeare . . . quite simply not only is the Western canon; he is also the world canon. That his appeal is equal to audiences of all continents, races, and languages . . . seems to me an absolute refutation of our currently fashionable views, prevalent particularly in Britain and America, that insists upon a Shakespeare culture-bound by history and society' (Harold Bloom, *The Anxiety of Influence*, 2nd ed. [New York: Oxford University Press, 1997], p. xv).

11. Stephen Greenblatt, 'Introduction', in *The Norton Shakespeare*, ed. Stephen Greenblatt, Walter Cohen, Jean E. Howard, Katharine Eisaman Maus, and Gordon McMullan, 3rd ed. (New

Not necessary, indeed. But in recent decades, that choice has repeatedly been made in the academy, and always to the advantage of a Shakespeare who is the 'scion of a particular culture'. The universal Shakespeare has, of late, gone missing.

This book is an attempt to write once more about Shakespeare as a man whose plays reflect on deep questions of enduring human importance and to resist the modern academic trend of retreating from the central human preoccupations which animate his drama. In part, this is a matter of Shakespeare's comprehensiveness. 'What did not the man see?', Thomas Mann reports Wagner as exclaiming on one of those Venetian evenings in the Vendramin Palace, after the composer had immersed himself once more in Shakespeare's plays at the very end of his life.[12] But Shakespeare's universality was not simply a matter of the accumulation of insight. It was also, and more importantly, a matter of severe selection and concentration, of recurrent penetration to a core of central and perennial human concerns.

However, the contention of this book is emphatically not that Shakespeare possessed any timeless esoteric wisdom that he wished to impart through a theatrical medium. It is rather that, in his hands, drama itself became a forensic instrument whereby such issues might be probed and rival views about them set in motion. So this book is called *Thinking Through Shakespeare*, rather than (for example) *Shakespeare's Thought*, because I wish to place the emphasis on a process rather than on a conclusion.[13] Indeed, I don't believe that Shakespeare (unlike other great dramatists such as Ben Jonson or John Dryden or a great poet such as John Milton) either reached, or was interested in reaching, any *final* conclusions on the enduring questions his plays confront.[14] Coleridge remarked that, in every poem of Milton, it is Milton himself that you see.[15] By

York: Norton, 2016), p. 2. All references to Shakespeare that follow are to this deservedly popular edition.

12. 'Was hat der Mann *gesehen*!' (Thomas Mann, 'Richard Wagner and the *Ring*', in Mann, *Essays*, p. 355).

13. That said, this book clearly has certain limited points of contact and co-ordination with Tony Nuttall's *Shakespeare the Thinker* (New Haven, CT: Yale University Press, 2007).

14. As Coleridge saw: 'He [Shakespeare] is of no age—nor, I may add, of any religion, or party, or profession' (Coleridge, *Table-Talk*, p. 6).

15. 'In the *Paradise Lost*—indeed in every one of his poems—it is Milton himself whom you see; his Satan, his Adam, his Raphael, almost his Eve, are all John Milton; and it is a sense of this intense egotism that gives me the greatest pleasure in reading Milton's works': cf. 'There is a subjectivity of the poet, as of Milton, who is himself before himself in everything he writes'

contrast, in every poem and play of Shakespeare's, Shakespeare himself is, not utterly absent to be sure, but nevertheless elusive and sometimes hard to detect.[16] And Shakespeare's authorial escapology is related to the particular way in which his plays deploy and address ideas.

One of the great comments about literature, ideas, and the artist was made in 1918 by T. S. Eliot in an issue of *The Little Review* devoted to the recently-deceased Henry James.[17] Eliot contributed two pieces to the journal: a brief study of James's relationship to Hawthorne and a more general assessment entitled 'In Memory'. The second piece begins by reflecting on James's limitations as a literary critic, which Eliot then adroitly turns into the basis of admiration for James's skill as a novelist. For, on this account, James was not really a literary critic but rather 'a critic who preyed not upon ideas, but upon living beings.'[18] Eliot then moves on to consider the question of literature and ideas more generally, as exemplified in the special virtue of James's fiction:

> James's critical genius comes out most tellingly in his mastery over, his baffling escape from, Ideas; a mastery and an escape which are perhaps the last test of a superior intelligence. He had a mind so fine that no idea could violate it. Englishmen, with their uncritical admiration (in the present age) for France, like to refer to France as the Home of Ideas; a phrase which, if we could twist it into truth, or at least a compliment, ought to mean that in France ideas are very severely looked after; not allowed to stray, but preserved for the inspection of civic pride in a Jardin des Plantes, and frugally dispatched on occasions of public necessity. England, on the other hand, if it is not the Home of Ideas, has at least become infested with them in about the space of time within which Australia has been overrun by rabbits. In England ideas run wild and pasture on the emotions; instead of thinking with our feelings (a very different thing) we corrupt our feelings with ideas; we produce the political, the emotional idea, evading sensation and thought. George Meredith (the disciple of Carlyle) was fertile in ideas; his

---

(Coleridge, *Table-Talk*, pp. 17 and 76). Note also: 'Shakespeare's poetry is characterless; that is, it does not reflect the individual Shakespeare; but John Milton himself is in every line of *Paradise Lost*' (ibid., p. 5).

16. Again, Coleridge is acute: 'How well we seem to know Chaucer! How absolutely nothing do we know of Shakespeare!' (Coleridge, *Table-Talk*, p. 2).

17. T. S. Eliot, 'In Memory', *The Little Review* 5, no. 4 (August 1918) (Henry James special number), pp. 44–47.

18. Eliot, 'In Memory', p. 45.

> epigrams are a facile substitute for observation and inference. Mr. Chesterton's brain swarms with ideas; I see no evidence that it thinks. James in his novels is like the best French critics in maintaining a point of view, a viewpoint untouched by the parasite idea. He is the most intelligent man of his generation.[19]

The brilliant and memorable phrase 'a mind so fine that no idea could violate it' is sometimes misconstrued as a feline insult, or even as (in Gore Vidal's deliberately unsympathetic word) a 'wisecrack'.[20] But so to construe Eliot's aphorism reveals a failure of reading and a deafness to the distinction Eliot insists on between genuine thinking and the mere brandishing of ideas. Ideas are certainly the coin of thought. Yet they may turn up in the pockets of those who are unable to do anything more than fumble with them.

Once that phrase, 'a mind so fine that no idea could violate it', is restored to its original setting in the full paragraph where it occurs, it is clear that Eliot intended it as the highest praise. Of course, what Eliot is emphatically not saying is that James's mind was incapable of thought—incapable, that is, of entertaining, revolving, and, eventually, dismissing ideas. The mere temporary presence of an idea in the mind is not a *violation*; for what purpose does the mind have but to entertain and assess ideas? But 'violate' is an appropriate word for the permanent seizure, or rape, of the mind by an idea, which might then enjoy a parasitic and dominant life in this newly-colonised host. As Eliot's tart remark on Chesterton makes clear, the simple presence of an idea was for him no indisputable evidence of thought. Indeed, a chaotic profusion of ideas, those fossilised remnants of the act of thinking, may be *prima facie* evidence of an incapacity for genuine and sustained thought. And still less was Eliot saying that Henry James did no thinking: that would be absurd. Rather, Eliot admires the way in which James's thinking, of which he plainly did a very great deal, nevertheless left him unviolated and therefore free still to go on thinking. For the great writer, Eliot implies, thinking is a permanent activity, not a teleological process which will cease once a conclusion has been arrived at.

Nearly ten years later, Eliot would return to the question of the relation between ideas and great literature in 'Shakespeare and the Stoicism of Seneca', and once more he would launch a powerful attack on the Siren-notion that,

19. Eliot, 'In Memory', p. 46. Typographical errors have been silently corrected.
20. Gore Vidal, 'Lessons of the Master', *New York Review of Books*, 6 November 1986.

insofar as literature is good, it is the expression of a single coherent and compelling philosophy or system of ideas.[21]

The essay begins by reviewing, with what seems like mild commendation, recent publications claiming to have discovered Shakespeare's philosophy: 'Whether Mr. Strachey, or Mr. Murry, or Mr. Lewis, is any nearer to the truth of Shakespeare than Rymer, or Morgann, or Webster, or Johnson, is uncertain; they are all certainly more sympathetic in this year 1927 than Coleridge, or Swinburne, or Dowden.'[22] These publications, Eliot says with disarming blandness, have provoked him to pursue 'a number of reflections on literary criticism and its limits, on general aesthetics, and on the limitations of the human understanding.'[23]

The glancing mention of Coleridge, however, is of particular interest, because (to lapse for a moment into the idiom of Harold Bloom) Coleridge is the 'strong predecessor' with whom Eliot is wrestling in this essay.[24] Coleridge, himself wrestling with arguably an even stronger predecessor in Milton, had put forward a general view about the relation between poetry and philosophy and had exemplified that view in the case of Shakespeare. In 'L'Allegro', Milton had described Shakespeare as 'fancy's child', warbling 'his native wood-notes wild.'[25] Coleridge, first in his *Lectures on Literature*, then later in a more finished and elaborated form in *Biographia Literaria*, had attacked this position (the phrase 'mere child of nature' serving to key Coleridge's remarks to Milton's poem):

> No man was ever yet a great poet, without being at the same time a profound philosopher. For poetry is the blossom and the fragrancy of all human knowledge, human thoughts, human passions, emotions, language. . . . What then shall we say? even this; that Shakspeare, no mere child of nature; no automaton of genius; no passive vehicle of inspiration possessed by the spirit, not possessing it; first studied patiently, meditated deeply, understood minutely, till knowledge become habitual and intuitive wedded itself to his habitual feelings, and at length gave birth to that stupendous power, by which he stands alone, with no equal or second in his

21. First published in 1927. Quoted here as reprinted in Eliot, *Essays*, pp. 126–40.

22. Eliot, *Essays*, p. 126.

23. Eliot, *Essays*, p. 127.

24. See, classically, Harold Bloom, *The Anxiety of Influence* (New York: Oxford University Press, 1973).

25. John Milton, 'L'Allegro', ll. 133–34.

> own class; to that power, which seated him on one of the two glory-smitten summits of the poetic mountain, with Milton as his compeer not rival. . . . All things and modes of action shape themselves anew in the being of MILTON; while SHAKSPEARE becomes all things, yet for ever remaining himself.[26]

Eliot's purpose in 'Shakespeare and the Stoicism of Seneca' is to loosen, maybe even to untie, the knot in which Coleridge had attempted to bind together poetry and philosophy. Eliot's tone is, at the outset, whimsical:

> My own frivolous opinion is that Shakespeare may have held in private life very different views from what we extract from his extremely varied published works; that there is no clue in his writings to the way in which he would have voted in the last or would vote in the next election; and that we are completely in the dark as to his attitude about prayer-book revision.[27]

His own essay, ostensibly offered to the reader as a discovery of yet another Shakespearean philosophy, is in fact intended as a stealthy vaccine against all such approaches: 'I propose a Shakespeare under the influence of the stoicism of Seneca. But I do not believe that Shakespeare was under the influence of Seneca. . . . I wish merely to disinfect the Senecan Shakespeare before he appears. My ambitions would be realized if I could prevent him, in so doing, from appearing at all.'[28] However, behind this astringent playfulness lies a serious proposition about how poets or dramatists stand in relation to their ideas. Unlike philosophers, who use their writings to propagate and recommend their ideas, poets and dramatists use their ideas to populate their writings. Shakespeare's intellectual sagacity took the form of an instinctive gift for detecting in an idea or a philosophy 'something of theatrical utility': 'I cannot see in Shakespeare either a deliberate scepticism, as of Montaigne, or a deliberate cynicism, as of Machiavelli, or a deliberate resignation, as of Seneca. I can see that he *used* all of these things, for dramatic ends.'[29] In the essay's final pages, Eliot turns to John Donne and makes a very similar point about the poet's opportunistic relationship to ideas:

26. Coleridge, *Biographia*, 2:25–28. Cf. Coleridge, *Lectures*, 1:68–70.
27. Eliot, *Essays*, p. 127.
28. Eliot, *Essays*, pp. 128–29.
29. Eliot, *Essays*, pp. 129 and 134.

> In making some very commonplace investigations of the 'thought' of Donne, I found it quite impossible to come to the conclusion that Donne believed anything. It seemed as if, at that time, the world was filled with broken fragments of systems, and that a man like Donne merely picked up, like a magpie, various shining fragments of ideas as they struck his eye, and stuck them about here and there in his verse. . . . I could not find either any 'medievalism' or any thinking, but only a vast jumble of incoherent erudition on which he drew for purely poetic effects.[30]

Helen Vendler has suggested that the drama of lyric forms is verbal. That is to say, the 'true "actors" in lyric are words or vocabularies, not "dramatic persons"; and the drama of any lyric is constituted by the successive entrances of new sets of words, or new stylistic arrangements (grammatic, syntactical, phonetic) which are visibly in conflict with previous arrangements used with reference to the "same" situation'.[31] In drama, the same may be said of ideas or philosophies. By ideas and philosophies, Shakespeare could be temporarily attracted without being permanently captured. Ideas and philosophies were part of the raw material upon which his 'universal and all-accepting nature' drew, which he deployed, and which he set in motion for purposes of 'dramatic utility', just as he did his characters, before finally giving them—ideas, philosophies, and characters—permission to depart from the theatre of his mind.[32]

I wish to rehabilitate the idea of Shakespeare as a poet of general nature, but this does not entail a commitment, on either his part or mine, to an idea of human nature that is either immobile or unchanging. Rather, it invites us to reflect on a set of durable preoccupations, which have been raised in different ways in different places and at different times but which nevertheless provide threads of continuity across the centuries of recorded human experience. It is also striking that Shakespeare tended to explore these preoccupations from quite different standpoints, relying in different plays on very different presuppositions, pursuing very different angles of vision, and thus generating very different outcomes. A repeated feature of Shakespeare's drama is that we often see him (to borrow a phrase from Emilia in *Othello*) turning his wit 'the seamy-side without' and doing so, moreover, often in plays composed either

30. Eliot, *Essays*, pp. 138–39.

31. Vendler, *Sonnets*, p. 3.

32. The first quoted phrase was applied to Shakespeare by Thomas Mann: 'die universale und allbejahende Natur' ('Goethe and Tolstoy', in Mann, *Essays*, p. 115).

concurrently or successively.[33] Examples of this include *King Lear* and *Measure for Measure*, or *Antony and Cleopatra* and *Coriolanus*, or *Timon of Athens* and *The Tempest*. It is impossible to imagine even so great a playwright as Ben Jonson doing something similar to this—for instance, writing a wholeheartedly festive comedy immediately after writing the brilliant satiric demolition of festive comedy which is *Bartholomew Fair*. Jonson, like most writers—indeed, like almost all human beings—was imprisoned within his opinions. Shakespeare, on the other hand, seems to have had no settled opinions, despite overflowing with ideas. 'Others abide our question. Thou art free', as Arnold put it, with detectable feelings of envy, admiration, and bafflement (and with the silent and affronted ghost of Old Hamlet in the opening scene of that play powerfully in mind).[34]

This book is divided into four chapters, each of which takes for its theme a fundamental aspect of human life: the question of personal identity, the distinction between civilisation and barbarism, the purpose and character of political institutions, and the tangle of ethical questions surrounding the stubborn difficulty we encounter in deciding between the good and the right, and between means and ends. Too often invocations of Shakespeare and general human nature have been airy and vacuous, as if the content of the idea of general human nature did not need to be spelled out, even in the incomplete and cursory way I do here. No doubt other people would have selected different issues upon which to focus—for instance, gender or the wavy and permeable line that separates humans from other animals or race. Nevertheless, what is offered in the following pages at least makes a start on colouring in some of the larger provinces of Shakespeare's—and our—general nature.

Despite that diffidence, I would make one strong claim for the four great problems around which I have organised this book. They all raise issues on which it is impossible honestly to be of only one mind, and hence they are

33. *Othello*, IV.ii.145. Cf. two apposite remarks, the first by Tony Nuttall: 'His [Shakespeare's] thought is never still. No sooner has one identified a philosophical "position" than one is forced, by the succeeding play, to modify or extend one's account' (*Shakespeare the Thinker*, p. 24); and the second by Helen Vendler (of which the wording may contain a glance at Emilia's phrase): 'He [Shakespeare] was a master subverter of the languages he borrowed, and the point of *literary* interest is not the fact of his borrowings but how he turned them inside out' (Vendler, *Sonnets*, p. 2).

34. Matthew Arnold, 'Shakespeare', l. 1. Cf. *Hamlet*, I.i.44–51.

intrinsically dramatic.[35] It is true that Christ warns us that no man can serve two masters.[36] But it is also true that Christ rarely warns us against things to which we are not drawn. Do we not from day to day constantly experience the tug of contending intellectual loyalties and commitments? Are we not perpetually drawn by the allure of rival goods, neither of which we are willing entirely to relinquish? In our mundane dealings we rely on the solidity of the concept of personal identity, but when we reflect upon that concept, we can see a myriad of powerful arguments against it. We both benefit from the affordances of civilisation and yet also chafe against the constraints civilisation imposes upon us in order to deliver those benefits. We both see our political institutions as utilitarian, man-made contrivances assembled to deliver practical benefits to the governed and recognise that those institutions need also to be hedged about with an artificial aura of, if not necessarily supernatural, then certainly of a more than natural potency and authority if they are to function effectively. We readily denounce the immorality of treating other people as instruments, while at the same time availing ourselves of other people in countless ways every day. However vehemently we may renounce one or other of them, in practice (as the writings of even the greatest philosophers demonstrate) we remain snared by the rival considerations of expediency (or the *utile*) and right (or the *honestum*).

Henry Sidgwick asserted that the 'common sense of men cannot acquiesce in conflicting principles'.[37] Nevertheless, it is our daily experience that, though we may struggle, we are indeed at every turn enmeshed by conflicting principles. Moreover, there is a wide interval between not acquiescing in a situation and being in fact able to escape from it. Indeed, it is precisely the tension between our refusal to acquiesce and our inability to discover some means of escape that keeps these conflicts of principle active and makes them enduringly constitutive of our human nature.

Edmund Burke, in his great speech *American Taxation*, memorably censured the political character of Charles Townshend as 'a candidate for contradictory honours', whose 'great aim was to make those agree in admiration of

35. 'An allegory is never quite consistent except when it is written by someone without dramatic faculty, in which case it is unreadable' (Shaw, *Wagnerite*, p. 30).

36. Matthew 6:24; Luke 16:13.

37. Sidgwick, *Ethics*, p. 6. Cf. ibid., p. 10: 'two conflicting rules of action cannot both be reasonable'.

him who never agreed in any thing else.'[38] But is it not the case that, to the extent that we are fully human, we will tend always to be candidates for contradictory honours? And might this not be especially true of the very greatest writers? As one of them has observed, 'Authorship itself has always seemed to me to be a witness to and an expression of ambivalence, of here and there, of yes and no, of two souls in one breast, of an annoying richness in inner conflicts, antitheses, and contradictions.'[39] That is why people with normal moral constitutions so often recoil from successful politicians. In order to succeed in their cartoon-like world, politicians seem often to have willingly amputated some part of their humanity, and in so doing have implicitly disparaged a valuable, and finally indelible, inward dividedness which they ought to have acknowledged and respected.[40]

Let me acknowledge at the very outset that my intellectual contexts are drawn from only the Western tradition and my examples (particularly in, for instance, chapter 3) are very frequently British or even more narrowly English, while the human appetite for, and understanding of, Shakespeare is, as I have suggested, much broader than that. But this limitation in my own intellectual equipment should not be taken as necessarily indicating a weakness in my general argument. For one could argue that the philosophical, historical, ethical, and political themes around which I have organised this book are simply particular instantiations of deeper and more widespread human instincts and impulses which make themselves felt in other cultures too, albeit under altered appearances. It seems hard to believe, for example, that any human group, at any time or in any place, has been perfectly uninterested in questions of the

38. Burke, *Writings*, 2:455.

39. 'Schriftstellertum selbst erschien mir vielmehr von jeher als ein Erzeugnis und Ausdruck der Problematik, des Da und Dort, des Ja und Nein, der zwei Seelen in einer Brust, des schlimmen Reichtums an inneren Konflikten, Gegensätzen und Widersprüchen' (Mann, *Reflections*, p. 14).

40. This humane receptiveness to contradiction is not, by the way, anything like its evil twin, Orwell's 'doublethink', which in *Nineteen Eighty-Four* Emmanuel Goldstein defines as 'the power of holding two contradictory beliefs in one's mind simultaneously, and accepting both of them'. The difference is that, while doublethink is brazenly confessed to be 'a vast system of mental cheating', the contradictions to which I refer are not a way of letting yourself off an ethical or political or historical hook but rather of remaining on the hook (however painful it may be) in order precisely to avoid being cheated or short-changed with something inadequately simple-minded (George Orwell, *Nineteen Eighty-Four*, ed. Peter Davison [London: Secker and Warburg, 1987], pp. 223 and 224).

distinction between self and other, of the concept of personal identity, of the principle that confers or withholds legitimacy and authority within a group and of the proper purposes of such authority, and of the discrimination of a good action from a bad or selfish one. Of course, the various *responses* to these perennial and ubiquitous problems that arise in different human communities have varied, sometimes dramatically, and will no doubt continue to do so in the future. The areas of concern, however, seem to be as universal as anything human ever can be.[41]

Each of the book's four chapters begins with an examination of the large issue at its heart, before proceeding, in the first place, to explore how that issue is taken up in one of the four great Shakespearean tragedies and, after that, to show how those plays, like whirlpools, drew into themselves material from earlier plays, before spinning this material outwards, often in markedly altered forms, into the plays which followed. Thinkers and artists born after Shakespeare (such as Hume, Freud, Nietzsche, Wagner, Verdi, Rousseau, Adam Smith, Conrad, Kant, Thomas Mann, G. E. Moore, Goethe, or John Rawls) figure in the discussion, as do writers and thinkers born before Shakespeare whom there is no reason to believe he had ever read (such as Orosius or St. Ambrose). Such undisguised ahistoricism is intended, in part, to serve as a standing reminder that this book is no historical study of Shakespeare in an early-modern setting, much as I recognise the value of such scholarship.[42]

In this book I am trying to do something different. I am trying to reconnect Shakespeare's plays to the abiding concerns of thoughtful people—concerns which, in a variety of shapes, seem to have formed part of our 'general nature' since the earliest antiquity. I am trying to renew, to refresh, and to re-introduce

41. Let me underline that I am emphatically not trying to resuscitate the fatally-wounded concept of 'perennial and unchanging "unit ideas" which it [is] the task of the intellectual historian to uncover and trace' (Skinner, *Visions*, 1:176). Rather, my assertion is that our general humanity comprises, at one level, some fundamental and large-scale preoccupations (nothing so definite as ideas) which change, if at all, at only a glacial speed. These preoccupations are part of 'what we bring to the world in our efforts to make sense of it' (ibid.); and it seems to me not to endanger my position if I readily concede that the menu of second-order questions (let alone answers) that these recurrent areas of preoccupation precipitate in different societies or groups may vary greatly. That said, I nevertheless do take the force of Hume's exclamation towards the end of his essay 'Idea of a Perfect Commonwealth': '*Man and for ever!*' (Hume, *Essays*, p. 528). Hume alludes to Pope, *Second Epistle of the Second Book of Horace Imitated*, l. 252.

42. And, indeed, I have written some of it: e.g., *Divinity and State* (Oxford: Oxford University Press, 2010).

what Thomas Carlyle said narrowly and possessively about Shakespeare and the English, and in so doing to broaden his remarks into a claim about both the central place of Shakespeare in the human and the central place of the human in Shakespeare: 'Yes, this Shakespeare is ours; we produced him, we speak and think by him; we are of one blood and kind with him.'[43]

As far as I can tell, these words seem, extraordinarily and quite exceptionally, to apply to all of us, in all places, and at all times.

43. Thomas Carlyle, 'The Hero as Poet', in Carlyle, *Chartism*, p. 270.

1

Selves and Others

OTHELLO

'Tis certain there is no question in philosophy more abstruse than that concerning identity, and the nature of the uniting principle, which constitutes a person.

—DAVID HUME

'Who's there?'

'Ah, the hard questions first, eh?'

—THE GOONS (ALLUDING TO *HAMLET*)

'PROOF OF IDENTITY': three words which announce one of the most banal bureaucratic hurdles of modern life. A grainy photograph which looks a little like you did a few years ago, together with an official letter bearing your name and address—it rarely takes more than this to supply what we are, for all practical purposes, pleased to call 'proof'. As it happens, I am writing this in Munich, where I am living for a few months. Before I could open a German bank account, I had to present myself at the Kreisverwaltungsreferat in order to register myself. I needed a passport and a letter from the owner of the flat in which I am living stating who I was, why I was in Munich, and how long I would be staying. All this was more inconvenient than really demanding or difficult. It could surely be easily, even amusingly, circumvented. The most absorbing section of Frederick Forsyth's *The Day of the Jackal* (1971) was not the formulaic chase of the would-be assassin across rural France but the detailed description at the beginning of the novel of the surprisingly straightforward steps one would have to go through in order to obtain a false passport and thus (for all practical purposes, such as assassination) a new identity.

The threshold for demonstrating proof of identity is necessarily low because the need to establish personal identity is so necessary an element in our daily existence. It lies at the root of our political and legal life, to the point where some have argued that the concept of personal identity itself is nothing more than 'a creature of society, an abstract consideration of man, necessary for the mutual benefit of him and his fellows; i.e. a mere forensick term.'[1] But the utility of the concept demands, in consequence, a certain casualness about its use. The common-sense notion that, when we are born, a new identity comes into existence which endures, albeit through physical and psychological changes, until our bodies die, at which point it too ceases to exist and will never return, is the unspoken and usually unexamined, but nevertheless official and everywhere relied upon, philosophy (if that is not too lofty a term) of personal identity which informs our public life. For instance, can one imagine a claim of ownership of property that rested on the assertion that the claimant was the same person who had owned that property in the nineteenth century? Or a plea of not guilty being given serious consideration on the grounds that the person in the dock, despite all appearances to the contrary, was in fact not, in the fullest sense, the same person who had beyond all doubt committed the crime in question a month beforehand? In such matters of practical judgement, we have no difficulty in putting aside the reservations roused by our more subtle reflections. Personal identity exists, is individual, endures, and is stable. And that (in our day-to-day world, at least) is all there is to it.

However, really to supply *proof* of identity—in the first place, proof that the general concept of identity itself makes sense, quite apart from the question of *personal* identity;[2] next, proof that there is such a thing as personal identity; then, proof that you (and only you) are the person you claim to be and that you are so to the exclusion of all other possibilities, or in other words, that you

1. Edmund Law, *A Defence of Mr. Locke's Opinion Concerning Personal Identity* (Cambridge, 1769), p. 10. See ibid., pp. 18–20, for Law's distinction between our colloquial way of using the word 'person' to refer to the 'whole aggregate of a rational Being' and the more precise use of the term to denote 'one especial property of that thing or Being', namely, the rationality that 'makes him capable of knowing what he does and suffers, and on what account, and thereby renders him amenable to justice for his behaviour.'

2. 'The problem of identity in general—that is, the problem of what constitutes the identity of any object—is the historical as well as the systematic basis of the special issue of the identity of persons' (Thiel, *Subject*, p. 18).

are you, that *only* you are you, and that you are *only* you; and, finally, as if that were not enough, that this unique and separate self which is you endures through time notwithstanding the evident changes it undergoes: all of this is, in philosophical terms, far from trivial. Even in the case of inanimate objects, where one imagines that the difficulties will be at their most manageable, on closer inspection, identity is elusive. I may believe that the Mont Blanc I recently saw when flying over the Alps is the same as the Mont Blanc that inspired Shelley to write a poem in 1816. But have two centuries of weathering not brought about *any* significant changes? Maps inform me that there is still today a large piece of stone in the same place as there was then. But is that piece of stone, in every respect, the same stone that Shelley saw? When it comes to identity, we are, it seems, trapped between Scylla (the rock of the practical necessity of accepting the reality of personal identity) and Charybdis (the whirlpool of the stubborn doubts about the reality and durability of identity that even casual reflection on the subject will swiftly set running).

The history of the philosophy of identity has been shaped by precisely this enduring tension between necessity and doubt; and it demonstrates how the pressure of external, practical exigencies (sometimes religious, sometimes legal) have exerted a distorting, if occasionally salutary, constraint over the free play of the philosophical mind. The precise form taken by that perennial tension between necessity and doubt has varied over time, as different ancillary considerations and demands have seemed more or less relevant. But the tension itself has endured and remains with us.

Hume had worried about these questions in the late 1730s. When he thought seriously and rigorously about personal identity, all he could discern was plurality and change. Human beings 'are nothing but a bundle or collection of different perceptions, which succeed one another with an inconceivable rapidity, and are in a perpetual flux and movement.'[3] Such ideas Hume found (or at least professed to find) depressing and isolating. But luckily the ordinary distractions of daily life came to the rescue: 'I dine, I play a game of back-gammon, I converse, and am merry with my friends; and when after three or four hours' amusement, I wou'd return to these speculations, they appear so cold, and strain'd, and ridiculous, that I cannot find it in my heart to enter into them any further.'[4] So it surely is with us. We can puzzle ourselves about identity by pursuing our doubts further than is either natural or useful.

3. Hume, *Treatise*, I.iv.6, 1:165.

4. Hume, *Treatise*, I.iv.7, 1:175.

But in practical life we assume the reality and stability of personal identity, and no bad consequences seem to ensue. When all is said and done, we have no choice but to do so. It may in some sense be true that, as Thomas Reid said, 'no man is the same person any two moments of his life'.[5] But it is impossible to carry on the business of life upon that footing.

To rest the claim for identity on physical continuity works better for inanimate objects, such as Mont Blanc, than it does for plants or animals (though even in the case of inanimate objects a determined sceptic might still raise doubts, in the spirit of Heraclitus's famous remark that one can never step into the same river twice).[6] But in the case of plants and animals, not only do they grow, decay, and die, but, over the course of that process, their constituent matter will change many times. This is a well-known philosophical problem, for which the common shorthand is the 'Ship of Theseus'.[7] Hobbes would refer to this as an illustration of the 'great controversy among philosophers about the *beginning of individuation*. . . . Some place *individuity* in the unity of *matter*; others in the unity of *form*'.[8] As Hume would express it, resting his faith in form rather than matter, 'A ship, of which a considerable part has been chang'd by frequent reparations, is still consider'd as the same; nor does the difference of the materials hinder us from ascribing an identity to it.'[9]

Hume had been a late-comer to this rich subject. The question of personal identity had unsurprisingly caught the attention of ancient philosophers and

5. Reid is stating what he takes to be an implication of Locke's resolution of identity into consciousness, which, however, he believes Locke would have 'rejected with abhorrence' had he been aware of it (Thomas Reid, *Essays on the Intellectual Powers of Man* [Edinburgh, 1785], p. 336). For an argument that Reid misunderstands Locke's views of personal identity (which turns on the precise forensic meaning of *persona*), see Galen Strawson, *Locke on Personal Identity: Consciousness and Concernment* (Princeton, NJ: Princeton University Press, 2011).

6. Quoted by Ammonius in Plutarch, *De E apud Delphos*, 392 B–C.

7. Plutarch, *Life of Theseus*, XXIII. Cf. Thiel, *Subject*, pp. 24–25.

8. Hobbes, *De Corpore*, II.xi.7.

9. Hume, *Treatise*, I.iv.6, 1:168. Swift, however, found this line of argument so trite that he included it in his anthology of empty talk, *Polite Conversation*, where Lady Smart says that her watch has been 'twenty Years in my Lord's Family, but *Quare* lately put a new Case and Dial-Plate to it', and Mr. Neverout replies, 'Why, that's for all the World like the Man, who swore he kept the same Knife for forty Years, only he sometimes change the Haft, and sometimes the Blade' (Jonathan Swift, *Polite Conversation*, in *Parodies, Hoaxes, Mock Treatises*, ed. Valerie Rumbold [Cambridge: Cambridge University Press, 2013], p. 426). Swift may have in mind, as his immediate satirical target, a passage from Locke's *Essay Concerning Human Understanding*, II.xxvii.5 (Locke, *Essay*, p. 331).

would continue to fascinate many philosophers after Hume.[10] Aristotle, for instance, had argued for personal identity partly in terms of bodily continuity. His comments on this question are scattered through a number of his works (*Metaphysics, Nicomachean Ethics, Eudemian Ethics*), but a crucial passage occurs in his treatise *On the Soul*:

> We describe one class of existing things as substance; and this we subdivide into three: (1) matter, which in itself is not an individual thing; (2) shape or form, in virtue of which individuality is directly attributed, and (3) the compound of the two. Matter is potentiality, while form is realization or actuality, and the word actuality is used in two senses, illustrated by the possession of knowledge and the exercise of it. Bodies seem to be preeminently substances, and most particularly those which are of natural origin; for these are the sources from which the rest are derived. But of natural bodies some have life and some have not; by life we mean the capacity for self-sustenance, growth, and decay. Every natural body, then, which possesses life must be substance, and substance of the compound type. But since it is a body of a definite kind, viz., having life, the body cannot be soul, for the body is not something predicated of a subject, but rather is itself to be regarded as a subject, i.e., as matter. So the soul must be substance in the sense of being the form of a natural body, which potentially has life. And substance in this sense is actuality. The soul, then, is the actuality of the kind of body we have described. But actuality has two senses, analogous to the possession of knowledge and the exercise of it. Clearly actuality in our present sense is analogous to the possession of knowledge; for both sleep and waking depend upon the presence of soul, and waking is analogous to the exercise of knowledge, sleep to its possession but not its exercise. Now in one and the same person the possession of knowledge comes first. The soul may therefore be defined as the first actuality of a natural body potentially possessing life; and such will be any body which possesses organs.[11]

10. Though not all philosophers have seen the concept of personal identity as problematic. Schopenhauer, for instance, was untroubled by it: 'Just as a sailor sits in a boat trusting to his frail barque in a stormy sea, unbounded in every direction, rising and falling with the howling mountainous waves; so in the midst of a world of sorrows the individual man sits quietly, supported by and trusting to the *principium individuationis*, or the way in which the individual knows things as phenomena' (Schopenhauer, *World*, § 63, p. 455).

11. Aristotle, *On the Soul*, II.i, 412a.

Aristotle's idea of personal identity has a number of important features. In the first place, evidently it can accommodate the observed reality of material growth, change, and decay. Secondly, for Aristotle, personal identity is a 'compound type' in which the natural body is given form and identity over time by the soul. Hence, he argues that 'The soul may therefore be defined as the first actuality of a natural body potentially possessing life; and such will be any body which possesses organs'. So for Aristotle, the natural, material body, although not the primary element, is nevertheless a crucial and indispensable element in identity. His philosophy would prevent him from arguing (as Descartes would later do in his 'Second Meditation') that the material body was no part of the true self because of its changeability:

> What else am I? I will use my imagination. I am not that structure of limbs which is called a human body. I am not even some thin vapour which permeates the limbs—a wind, fire, air, breath, or whatever I depict in my imagination; for these are things which I have supposed to be nothing. Let this supposition stand; for all that I am still something.[12]

For Aristotle, however, identity could not be so easily abstracted from its material embodiment.[13]

In framing this argument, Aristotle gave systematic form to what appear to have been long-standing Greek beliefs about identity. Sophocles wrote his Theban plays in the century preceding the birth of Aristotle,[14] but the moral vision of *Oedipus Tyrannus* is compatible with Aristotle's philosophy, in that it finds materiality to be at the centre of identity. Although there are plenty of extenuating circumstances for Oedipus's polluting crimes of killing his father and sleeping with his mother (parental cruelty and neglect when he was newborn; entrapment by the gods; taking all conceivable precautions to avoid

12. René Descartes, 'Second Meditation', in *Meditations on First Philosophy*, ed. and trans. John Cottingham (Cambridge: Cambridge University Press, 2013), pp. 36–37. 'Descartes places much less importance on the bodily part of man than do the Scholastics. According to Descartes, the soul constitutes the essence of the self, whereas the body is something which the self merely "has", to which it is "very closely joined". . . . Descartes argues that the self is the same, with or without the body' (Thiel, *Subject*, p. 37; cf. René Descartes, *Discours*, pt. IV, in *René Descartes: Philosophical Writings*, ed. J. Cottingham et al., vol. 1 [Cambridge: Cambridge University Press, 1984–91], p. 127).

13. See Joseph Owens, 'The Self in Aristotle', *Review of Metaphysics* 41 (1988): 707–22.

14. Aristotle, 384–322 BC; Sophocles, ca. 497–ca. 406 BC (*Oedipus Tyrannus*, ca. 429 BC; *Oedipus at Colonus*, ca. 406 BC).

fulfilling the prophecy), Oedipus does not appeal to them. Rather, his moral grandeur flows from his robust assumption that, if he truly did those deeds, then he is guilty of the sins those deeds entail:

> And it was none other than I myself who laid upon myself these curses. And I am polluting the bed of the dead man with the hands by which he perished. Am I a criminal? am I not altogether unholy, if I must leave my country, and in my exile never see my dear ones, nor set foot upon my native land, or else be joined in marriage with my mother and slay my father Polybus, him who brought me up, him who begot me?[15]

When the truth of the matter is put beyond doubt by the relation of the shepherd, who has been found as a result of Oedipus's heroic determination to understand the full truth about himself, Oedipus again does not enter any pleas of mitigation: 'Oh, oh! All is now clear! O light, may I now look on you for the last time, I who am revealed as cursed in my birth, cursed in my marriage, cursed in my killing!'[16] Finally, once he has discovered the corpse of Jocasta, Oedipus again proclaims without reservation or qualification the fact of his guilt:

> For now I am discovered to be evil and sprung from evil ancestors. O three roads, hidden glade, coppice and narrow path where three ways meet, ways that drank my own, my father's blood shed by my hands, do you still remember what deeds you saw me do and what deeds I did when I came here? Marriage, marriage, you gave me birth, and after you had done so you brought up the selfsame seed, and displayed fathers who were brothers, children who were fruit of incest, brides who were both wives and mothers to their spouses, and all things that are most atrocious among men.[17]

In an act of misguided generosity, Hume would attempt to make the extenuating case that Oedipus himself refuses to make (at least in this play):

> Hence the great difference between a mistake of fact and one of right; and hence the reason, why the one is commonly criminal and not the other. When Œdipus killed Laius, he was ignorant of the relation, and from

15. Sophocles, *Oedipus Tyrannus*, ll. 819–27.

16. Sophocles, *Oedipus Tyrannus*, ll. 1182–85. For Oedipus's determination to know the truth, see ibid., l. 1065.

17. Sophocles, *Oedipus Tyrannus*, ll. 1397–1408.

> circumstances, innocent and involuntary, formed erroneous opinions concerning the action which he committed. But when NERO killed AGRIPPINA, all the relations between himself and the person, and all the circumstances of the fact, were previously known to him: But the motive of revenge, or fear, or interest, prevailed in his savage heart over the sentiments of duty and humanity.[18]

Tragedy was not Hume's strong suit, however, as his well-intentioned but hapless essay 'Of Tragedy' sufficiently shows.[19] Oedipus's idea of personal identity was simpler than Hume's, and his moral sense was sterner. One aspect of the appropriateness of the punishment of self-blinding that Oedipus inflicts on himself is that it exacts retribution on the physical body, as related by the attendant:

> For he broke off the golden pins from her raiment, with which she was adorned, and lifting up his eyes struck them, uttering such words as these: that they should not see his dread sufferings or his dread actions, but in the future they should see in darkness those they never should have seen, and fail to recognise those he wished to know. Repeating such words as these he lifted up his eyes and not once but many times struck them; the bleeding eyeballs soaked his cheeks, and did not cease to drip.[20]

When Oedipus finally reaches the end of his quest for the fullest possible understanding of who he truly is,[21] his actions show that, for him, the material body is no Cartesian accident to be airily discounted. Rather, the body is essential to Oedipus's conception of his personhood, and his moral robustness rests on his conviction of the continuity through time of his personal identity.[22] For Oedipus, this continuity is evidently more a matter of durable

18. Hume, *Enquiry*, appendix 1, pp. 86–87. In *Oedipus at Colonus*, however, Oedipus will offer extenuations of his conduct (ll. 270–74, 521–23, and 547–49) and will now say that the retribution he enacted on himself was exorbitant (ll. 433–54). Given the interval between the composition of *Oedipus Tyrannus* and *Oedipus at Colonus* (see p. 22, n. 14), this discrepancy may indicate a shift in Sophocles's own understanding of the underlying moral issues.

19. David Hume, 'Of Tragedy', in Hume, *Essays*, pp. 216–25.

20. Sophocles, *Oedipus Tyrannus*, ll. 1268–78.

21. 'You will never persuade me not to find out the truth!' (Sophocles, *Oedipus Tyrannus*, l. 1065).

22. A 'fundamental feature of the human subject is that it thinks of itself as identical through time. For example, we assume such identity when we talk of a person's responsibility for past actions' (Thiel, *Subject*, p. 1).

embodiment than of consciousness, because when he killed his father and slept with his mother he was of course *un*conscious of what he was doing (in the sense of being unaware of the full reality of his actions), even though now, in his painfully enlightened state, he can indeed remember committing those crimes. But for Oedipus, such considerations clearly make no difference. This flesh committed Oedipus's crimes in the past; and therefore, on this flesh must punishment be inflicted in the present. These eyes were metaphorically blind then; and therefore, they must be made literally blind now.

The advent of Christianity both suppressed and stimulated the philosophical topic of personal identity. For centuries, Christian doctrines concerning the soul dogmatically constrained, yet also energised and refocused, these debates. Nakedly heterodox opinions, such as the Pythagorean doctrine of the transmigration of souls (or metempsychosis), now dwindled into private imaginative playthings for those of a speculative disposition, rather than serious rivals to the teaching of the church. In the trial scene of *The Merchant of Venice*, when Graziano says what follows to the inflexible Shylock, he speaks hyperbolically to convey the extent of his disbelief in Shylock's inhumanity:

> Thou almost mak'st me waver in my faith—
> To hold opinion with Pythagoras
> That souls of animals infuse themselves
> Into the trunks of men.[23]

In *Twelfth Night*, the Puritan Malvolio, even in the depths of his torments, cannot be brought to endorse 'the opinion of Pythagoras concerning wild fowl', even though he seems to know perfectly well what it is: 'I think nobly of the soul and no way approve his opinion.'[24]

The teaching of the church—that each person has a separate and unique soul created at birth by God and that the individuality of that soul would survive the death of the body, either to be united with God eternally in heaven or to be damned for eternity in hell—claimed the final word on these matters.[25] At the same time, however, a range of Christian doctrines developed over the first few centuries of the existence of the church (principally the doctrines of the Resurrection, the Last Judgement, and the Trinity) heaped up materials and raised problems that would go on to shape the philosophical conversation

23. *Merchant of Venice*, IV.i.130–33.
24. *Twelfth Night*, IV.ii.46–52.
25. Tertullian, *De Anima*.

about personal identity and would lead that conversation into areas of great and stubborn complexity.[26] The problematic doctrine of the Trinity stimulated philosophical reflection on individuation (exemplified in the late-seventeenth-century debate between William Sherlock and Robert South), while the doctrines of transubstantiation, the Resurrection, and the immortality of the soul seemed to hold implication for the concept of diachronic identity, that is, the duration of selfhood over time.[27] If the debate about personal identity in the West takes the enduring form of a dialogue between, on the one hand, a rough-and-ready but necessary and practical assumption that identities are synchronously distinct (i.e., individuated) and diachronically stable, and on the other, a recurrent difficulty in framing arguments that will establish that assumption beyond reasonable doubt, then the arrival of Christianity served only to raise the stakes on both sides of the argument.

Locke was a devout Christian, but nevertheless, when he addressed the question of personal identity in the second edition of his *Essay Concerning Human Understanding* (1694),[28] he did not simply fall back on Christian orthodoxy, even though he was at great pains to make his argument compatible with it. Instead, he chose to ground his argument for the reality of personal identity (to which, however, he attached a very particular definition which distinguished it from mere animal being or existence) on the continuity of consciousness. Why was he drawn to do so?

Locke inserted his theory of identity into a conceptual and discursive landscape shaped by both earlier philosophical discussion and also theological doctrines (principally the Resurrection and the Trinity) which, as we have seen, hold important implications for our ideas of personal identity. In so doing, Locke had a number of different objectives, the achievement of all of which in the same argument required from him considerable philosophical finesse: finesse in the definition of concepts, in the choice of language, and in the handling of argument. What were those objectives?

In § 12 of the chapter 'Of Identity and Diversity', Locke pointed clearly towards his principal philosophical adversaries. On the one hand, he wished to separate himself from pure materialists ('who place Thought in a purely material, animal, Constitution, void of an immaterial Substance'). On the other, he wished equally to separate his theory from Cartesian arguments that

26. Ayers, *Locke*, 2:281.

27. Thiel, *Subject*, pp. 18–19 and 98.

28. Locke, *Essay*, II.xxvii, pp. 328–48.

had rested the idea of personal identity on the soul ('those, who place thinking in an immaterial Substance only').[29] Finally, Locke needed also to make the argumentative course he was about to chart between materialism and immaterialism compatible with the Christian doctrine of a personal resurrection. This was difficult, because the Bible is explicit that the Resurrection will be a bodily event.[30] But how can that be, when the matter that makes up my body changes many times over the course of my lifetime and may also at different times have been part of the bodies of others who may themselves expect to be raised from the dead on the Great Day? As Hamlet sourly observes, 'a king may go a progress through the guts of a beggar.'[31] Locke gets round this difficulty by making his theory accommodate the possibility of spirit associating itself with different matter while yet retaining its personal identity. This means that he can avoid the equal and opposite absurdities that, in his view, went hand in hand with both simple materialism and Cartesian immaterialism.[32] The crucial move Locke made that allowed him to do this was to refresh the traditional concept of 'the person' which he had inherited from the legal philosophy of antiquity (principally Cicero) and furthermore to make a very careful discrimination of that concept from the more basic concept of 'man'.

Locke begins by stating the most simple ideas of identity and diversity. But at the end of his opening paragraph, he suggests that these fundamental propositions lead to different conditions of identity when applied to different things

29. Locke, *Essay*, p. 337.

30. I Corinthians 15:12–53; I Thessalonians 4:15–18. The Bible says that the resurrected body will be renewed but not utterly changed. Christ's resurrected body still bore the wounds of crucifixion (John 20:25–27), and Christ's resurrection is the pattern for all Christian resurrections (Philippians 3:20–21; 1 Corinthians 15:49).

31. *Hamlet*, III.vi.29–30. At moments in II.xxvii, Locke seems to have half a memory of this passage of *Hamlet*: cf. 'should the Soul of a Prince, carrying with it the consciousness of the Prince's past Life, enter and inform the Body of a Cobler' (Locke, *Essay*, p. 340, § 15); and cf. also 'that, which a moment since was part of our *selves*, is now no more so, than a part of another Man's *self* is a part of me; and 'tis not impossible, but in a little time may become a real part of another Person' (ibid., p. 346, § 25); also relevant is, 'there can from the Nature of things, be no Absurdity at all, to suppose, that the same Soul may, at different times be united to different Bodies, and with them make up, for that time, one Man; As well as we suppose a part of a Sheep's Body yesterday should be a part of a Man's Body tomorrow, and in that union make a vital part of *Melibœus* himself as well as it did of his Ram' (ibid., p. 347, § 27).

32. 'Personal Identity can by us be placed in nothing but consciousness . . . without involving us in great Absurdities' (Locke, *Essay*, p. 343, § 21).

(i.e., to substance, living substance, man, and person).[33] For Locke, the imprecision of our normal way of speaking is the source of our confusion of ideas about identity: 'That which has made the Difficulty about this Relation, has been the little care and attention used in having precise Notions of the things to which it is attributed.'[34] But 'to conceive, and judge of it [identity] aright, we must consider what *Idea* the Word it is applied to stands for: It being one thing to be the same *Substance,* another the same *Man,* and a third the same *Person,* if *Person, Man,* and *Substance,* are three Names standing for three different *Ideas;* for such as is the *Idea* belonging to that Name, such must be the *Identity.*'[35]

In the case of living bodies (animal or vegetable), the principle of identity is not material stability:

> In the state of living Creatures, their Identity depends not on a Mass of the same Particles; but on something else. For in them the variation of great parcels of Matter alters not the Identity: An Oak, grown from a Plant to a great Tree, and then lopp'd, is still the same Oak: And a Colt grown up to a Horse, sometimes fat, sometimes lean, is all the while the same Horse: though, in both these Cases, there may be a manifest change of the parts: So that truly they are not either of them the same Masses of Matter, though they be truly one of them the same Oak, and the other the same Horse. The reason whereof is, that in these two cases of a Mass of Matter, and a living Body, *Identity* is not applied to the same thing.[36]

In organic entities, it is the durable, vital organisation of the entity that is the criterion of identity, even though the constituent matter may change radically, perhaps even completely, over time. In these cases, identity consists of 'a participation of the same continued Life, by constantly fleeting Particles of Matter, in succession vitally united to the same organized Body'.[37] For an animal 'is a living organized Body; and consequently, the same Animal, as we have observed, is the same continued Life communicated to different Particles of Matter, as they happen successively to be united to that organiz'd living Body.'[38]

33. Locke, *Essay,* p. 328.

34. Locke, *Essay,* p. 328. It is a point to which Locke will return at the end of the chapter: 'the difficulty or obscurity, that has been about this Matter, rather rises from the Names ill used, than from any obscurity in things themselves' (ibid., p. 348).

35. Locke, *Essay,* p. 332.

36. Locke, *Essay,* p. 330.

37. Locke, *Essay,* pp. 331–32.

38. Locke, *Essay,* pp. 332–33.

This definition of identity in living entities allows Locke to push back against the Cartesian location of identity in the immaterial soul:

> For if the *Identity* of Soul alone makes the same Man, and there be nothing in the Nature of Matter, why the same individual Spirit may not be united to different Bodies, it will be possible, that those Men, living in distant Ages, and of different Tempers, may have been the same Man: Which way of speaking must be from a very strange use of the Word *Man*, applied to an *Idea*, out of which Body and Shape is excluded.

And he goes on to offer a witty illustration of the plausibility of his view of the matter: 'I think no body, could he be sure that the Soul of *Heliogabalus* were in one of his Hogs, would yet say that Hog were a *Man* or *Heliogabalus*.'[39] Identity in man thus cannot (*pace* Descartes) be a question simply of soul; it must also take into account material substance. The anecdote Locke next relates, concerning a talking parrot that belonged to Prince Maurice, further underlines that the identity of a man is bound up with the notion of a particular material body: 'For I presume 'tis not the *Idea* of a thinking or rational Being alone, that makes the *Idea* of a *Man* in most Peoples Sense; but of a Body so and so shaped joined to it; and if that be the *Idea* of a *Man*, the same successive Body not shifted all at once, must as well as the same immaterial Spirit go to the making of the same *Man*.'[40]

Although we may colloquially use the terms 'man' and 'person' interchangeably, Locke is very careful to distinguish them.[41] For Locke, as we have seen, the concept 'Man' involves a material body. 'Person', however, does not, as Locke's definition makes clear: '[Person is] a thinking intelligent Being, that has reason and reflection, and can consider it self as it self, the same thinking thing in different times and places; which it does only by that consciousness, which is inseparable from thinking, and as it seems to me essential to it.'[42] 'Person' for Locke is a 'Forensick Term appropriating Actions and their Merit; and so belongs only to intelligent Agents capable of a Law, and Happiness and Misery.'[43] Note that this identity of Person is explicitly asserted to be

39. Locke, *Essay*, p. 332.

40. Locke, *Essay*, p. 335.

41. 'I know that in the ordinary way of speaking, the same Person, and the same Man, stand for one and the same thing' (Locke, *Essay*, p. 340, § 15).

42. Locke, *Essay*, p. 335, § 9.

43. Locke, *Essay*, p. 346.

compatible with 'divers Substances': 'For it being the same consciousness that makes a Man to be himself to himself, personal Identity depends on that only, whether it be annexed only to one individual Substance, or can be continued in a succession of several Substances.'[44] This allows Locke to argue for the diachronic stability of personal identity, notwithstanding the changes in the material constitution of the body, which (in his view) therefore hold no implication for the reality or otherwise of the concept of personal identity.

Locke now proceeds with quiet satisfaction to unfold the beneficial implications of this theory. In § 10, for example, he explains why lapses in the continuity of consciousness (failures of memory, or episodes of sleep, for instance) do not undermine the concept of personal identity, as defined in relation to Locke's forensic definition of 'Person':

> The Question being what makes the same Person, and not whether it be the same Identical Substance, which always thinks in the same Person, which in this case matters not at all. Different Substances, by the same consciousness (where they do partake in it) being united into one Person; as well as different Bodies, by the same Life are united into one Animal, whose Identity is preserved, in that change of Substances, by the unity of one continued Life.[45]

Locke can now explain why his theory is resistant to heresies, such as the Pythagorean doctrine of the transmigration of souls.[46] More importantly, however, he is also now in a position to demonstrate that his theory of personal identity (and perhaps *only* his theory) is compatible with the biblical doctrine of the bodily resurrection: 'And thus we may be able without any difficulty to conceive, the same Person at the Resurrection, though in a Body not exactly in make or parts the same which he had here, the same consciousness going along with the Soul that inhabits it.'[47] For if '*personal Identity* consists not in the Identity of Substance but, as I have said, in the Identity of *consciousness*', then 'it matters not whether this present self be made up of the same or other Substances.'[48] The benefits of this account are then summarised with a detectable (and understandable) degree of triumph:

44. Locke, *Essay*, pp. 335 and 336.
45. Locke, *Essay*, p. 336.
46. Locke, *Essay*, pp. 338–40, § 14.
47. Locke, *Essay*, p. 340, § 15. Cf. ibid., pp. 346–47, § 26.
48. Locke, *Essay*, pp. 341–42, § 16.

> This every intelligent Being, sensible of Happiness or Misery, must grant, that there is something that is *himself*, that he is concerned for, and would have happy; that this *self* has existed in a continued Duration more than one instant, and therefore 'tis possible may exist, as it has done, Months and Years to come, without any certain bounds to be set to its duration; and may be the same *self*, by the same consciousness, continued on for the future. And thus, by this consciousness, he finds himself to be the *same self* which did such or such an Action some Years since, by which he comes to be happy or miserable now. In all which account of *self*, the same numerical Substance is not considered, as making the same *self*: But the same continued consciousness, in which several Substances may have been united, and again separated from it, which, whilst they continued in a vital union with that, wherein this consciousness then resided, made a part of that same *self*.[49]

Locke's point is that only his theory of personal identity can both salvage the rough-and-ready sense of identity on which the organisation of society practically depends and at the same time address the subtle difficulties arising in the fields of theology and philosophy that have infested and conditioned that subject matter. Locke's whole account of personal identity, therefore, bears eloquent witness to the difficult position in which this question catches us. We are constrained by, on the one hand, the practical need to consider identity as individuated and diachronically continuous, and on the other, by the need to reflect on, and if possible dispose of, the difficult thoughts raised by our abstract, uninstrumental, thoughts about the subject.

Taking half a step backwards, one can see that, irrespective of the force or weakness of the particular arguments Locke advanced, the introduction of the chapter on identity and diversity into the second edition of the *Essay Concerning Human Understanding* is eloquent evidence both of the need for a serviceable account of personal identity and of the difficulty of supplying such an account. It is the confrontation between the strength of the need and the stubbornness of the difficulty that has kept the question of personal identity towards the forefront of philosophical questions since antiquity, even if since Locke, the conversation has perhaps not developed strikingly.[50] Today, the state

49. Locke, *Essay*, pp. 345–46, § 25.

50. 'Many of the issues that were raised in the debates about Locke's theory continue to occupy present-day philosophical discussions about personal identity. . . . The central philosophical issue in the debates about the identity of the resurrection-body—the Lockean distinction

of the art seems (at least to a bystander) to be a stalemate between neo-Aristotelians, for whom questions of personal identity cannot and should not be separated from considerations of physical embodiment (e.g., David Wiggins), and neo-Lockeans, for whom, notwithstanding the deficiencies of the account of the matter Locke offered in the *Essay Concerning Human Understanding,* he was essentially on the right track when he sought to rest questions of personal identity on consciousness rather than on embodiment (e.g., Derek Parfit).[51]

Narrative art, responding with even-handedness to both our unassuageable need to be reassured about personal identity and our ineradicable doubts about it, has always to some extent played fast and loose with personal identity, at one moment affirming and at the next questioning. At the most fundamental level, literature is heavily invested in the concept of personal identity. The implicit contract between the writer and the reader demands that the author not be irresponsible in the matter of identity—for example, capriciously to assert that X at the beginning of the play was also Y at the end. Virtually the whole of the later nineteenth-century novel, at least after the publication of *David Copperfield* in 1849, can be viewed as an investigation—and, ultimately, as a vindication—of the reality of underlying identity: for its recurrent and hegemonic subject is the friction between an inner life (which is typically upheld) and an outer social world (which is typically relinquished or discarded). Anagnorisis—the literary device of recognition, present in European literature from Homer onwards—turns on the underlying continuity of identity, in defiance of misleading appearances.[52] In later decadent versions, such as

between person and man—continues to be discussed in present-day debates' (Thiel, *Subject,* pp. 153 and 167).

51. 'Interest in the issues of self-consciousness and personal identity is certainly characteristic and even central to early modern thought. And . . . this is an interest that continues to this day, in a form still strongly influenced by the conceptual frameworks of early modern thought on these issues. . . . Self-consciousness and personal identity in the form in which they are so widely discussed today originate in the rich debates of the seventeenth and eighteenth centuries and are significantly informed by the latter' (Thiel, *Subject,* pp. 1–2). David Wiggins, *Sameness and Substance Renewed* (Cambridge: Cambridge University Press, 2001); Derek Parfit, *Reasons and Persons* (Oxford: Clarendon Press, 1984; corr. ed., 1987). An interesting minority position is occupied by Galen Strawson, who might be described as a Lockean rather than a neo-Lockean, since he finds what Locke says in the *Essay Concerning Human Understanding,* II.xxvii, satisfactory: Galen Strawson, *Locke on Identity* (Princeton, NJ: Princeton University Press, 2011).

52. The classic study is Terence Cave, *Recognitions: A Study in Poetics* (Oxford: Clarendon Press, 1988).

The Importance of Being Earnest, the device is trivialised and almost scandalised into the banal stage property of the handbag. But in the *Odyssey*, when Odysseus is recognised by only his dog Argus and his nurse Eurycleia (not, importantly, by either his son or his wife), Homer tells us something wise and profound.[53] Fidelity, simplicity, and long-standing familiarity are what reassure us about the reality and continuity of personal identity. Sophistication and refinement can only endanger our natural and unmisgiving confidence in its solidity and durability.

Such affirmations, however, exist alongside less confident literary explorations, in which an attention to the finer shades of experience troubles any simple faith in the singleness of personal identity. It is in literature that we can see sceptical and puzzled pressure being put on the concept of identity—not in order to destroy it, necessarily, but rather to see where it frays or buckles. Two aspects of literature's interrogation of the general problem can be distinguished. The first is diachronic identity, or the stability of identity across time. The second is individuation, or the definiteness of identity at any single moment.

Diachronic personal identity lies at the obscure heart of Joseph Conrad's *Lord Jim* (1899–1900). The novel, narrated by Marlow, tells the story of Jim, an officer on the steamer *Patna* in the Far East, who abandons his ship full of pilgrims in the mistaken belief that the ship is about to sink. The steamer, however, somehow stays afloat and is towed to port, and Jim's shameful action in abandoning ship comes to light. Stripped of his certificate and tormented by 'exquisite sensibility', Jim then moves ever further eastward in an attempt to find a society in which his lapse is unknown and in which he can begin life anew.[54] Eventually he finds such a place in the remote island of Patusan, and in a moment of extreme trial, he is able there to demonstrate a firmness before mortal danger that, perhaps, expunges or redeems his earlier failing.

Marlow's narrative explicitly engages with questions of identity and character by relating one of 'those events of the sea that show in the light of day the inner worth of a man, the edge of his temper and the fibre of his stuff; that reveal the quality of his resistance and the secret truth of his pretences not only to others but also to himself.'[55] Marlow describes Jim telling his story as 'an

53. *Odyssey*, bk. XIX, ll. 361–502 (Eurycleia); bk. XVII, ll. 290–327 (Argus).
54. Conrad, *Lord Jim*, p. 10.
55. Conrad, *Lord Jim*, p. 14.

individual trying to save from the fire his idea of what his moral identity should be.'[56] The marine service emerges in the novel as an environment in which identity is severely examined and sometimes tested to destruction. For instance, Brierly, a captain who presides at the inquiry into the abandonment of the *Patna*, commits suicide shortly after the inquiry is concluded. The surmise is that his own past contained a similar instance of culpable failure.

Jim's identity is both flawed and elusive. Marlow recalls his first sight of Jim and the conflict between healthy appearance and compromised reality that it embodied, as first innocent impressions were overlaid with later, painful knowledge:

> This was my first view of Jim. He looked as unconcerned and unapproachable as only the young can look. There he stood, clean limbed, clean faced, firm on his feet, as promising a boy as the sun ever shone on; and, looking at him, knowing all he knew and a little more too, I was as angry as though I had detected him trying to get something out of me by false pretences. He had no business to look so sound.[57]

For Marlow senses 'some infernal alloy in [Jim's] metal' and dwells on 'the mist in which he moved and had his being.'[58] Jim's occludedness of character is a recurrent emphasis: 'He was not—if I may say so—clear to me. He was not clear. And there is a suspicion he was not clear to himself either.'[59] He was 'an apparition, a wraith, a portent', whom it was 'impossible to see . . . clearly', 'a mere white speck at the heart of an immense mystery . . . always mute, dark—*under a cloud*'—a phrase which combines both obscurity and, in its colloquial sense, moral compromise; and it is a phrase to which Marlow will return at the end of the novel when he says that Jim passed 'away *under a cloud*, inscrutable at heart'.[60] Gentleman Brown, the itinerant criminal whose arrival in Patusan precipitates Jim's death, agrees: 'I could not make him out. Who was he?'[61] Jim remains 'a cruel and insoluble mystery', a man marked by 'deep inexpressible wonder, . . . the touch of an inscrutable mystery' and whose power to baffle comprehension is caught in the cacophony of the

56. Conrad, *Lord Jim*, p. 66.
57. Conrad, *Lord Jim*, p. 36.
58. Conrad, *Lord Jim*, pp. 40 and 100. Cf. Acts 17:28.
59. Conrad, *Lord Jim*, p. 135.
60. Conrad, *Lord Jim*, pp. 191, 256, 258, and 312; emphases added.
61. Conrad, *Lord Jim*, p. 290.

exclamations of Jewel, his lover, and Stein, his patron: 'He was false. . . . Not false! True! true! true!'[62]

Why is Jim so difficult to understand? Gentleman Brown is, at moments, not puzzled at all: 'He a man! Hell! He was a hollow sham'—a vigorous denunciation which perhaps, given Gentleman Brown's evident criminal corruption, is intended by Conrad to dissuade the reader from being tempted towards similar simplicities.[63] The difficulty in reading Jim turns on the question of whether or not Jim's identity has in fact inflected in his ultimate moment of firmness. Facing his final trial, Jim does not flinch, and so in that sense one might say that he has indeed buried and escaped from his earlier flawed self, the self that jumped off the *Patna*. But at the same time, it is only Jim's unerasable memory of having jumped that makes him eventually able, at the moment of supreme trial, not to flinch. The continuity of Jim's consciousness (expressed through memory) with the earlier self who had jumped creates a paradoxical surface of discontinuity. Is he, in the end, the same man or a new one? Jumping from the *Patna* was a turning point in Jim's life, one which arguably made him a different man, one who eventually would not flinch from mortal danger. But it was the memory of that earlier failure of nerve that gave him the firmness not to succumb later. There is surely identity over time (in the sense of a Lockean continuity of consciousness). But the character of what endures has also surely changed. Marlow is even unsure whether Jim's ever-eastward movement is flight or fight: 'It might have been flight and it might have been a mode of combat.'[64]

So had Jim changed in Patusan, or had he remained somehow the same? Marlow finds it impossible to say.[65] And when Marlow tells Cornelius that in Patusan Jim has 'saved himself', 'saved' hovers undecidedly between the contradictory meanings of 'redeemed' (implying that Jim's identity has changed away from its earlier defectiveness) and 'conserved' (implying that it has remained the same).[66] When Jim confronts his destiny in the court of the Rajah of Allang, he is both transformed—'He appeared like a creature not only of another kind but of another essence'—yet also trapped in the compulsive repetition of his original weakness: 'Strange, this fatality that would cast the

62. Conrad, *Lord Jim*, pp. 296 and 264.
63. Conrad, *Lord Jim*, p. 259.
64. Conrad, *Lord Jim*, p. 149.
65. Conrad, *Lord Jim*, pp. 170–71.
66. Conrad, *Lord Jim*, p. 246.

complexion of a flight upon all his acts, of impulsive unreflecting desertion—of a jump into the unknown.'[67] The shape of Jim's life, and the undecidability of whether or not his biography reveals reformation or recidivism, both shades and illuminates the question of diachronic identity.

Turning now to the question of individuation, this is an aspect of identity brought into focus most obviously by novels that include *doppelgängers*: novels such as James Hogg's *Private Memoirs and Confessions of a Justified Sinner* (1824) or Mary Shelley's *Frankenstein* (1818). But perhaps the richest and strangest literary treatment of individuation is to be found in Goethe's *Elective Affinities* (1809).[68]

Elective Affinities tells the story of the adulterous entanglements that arise between four people living in close proximity to one another in a single house: Eduard, a German nobleman; Charlotte, his wife; Eduard's friend, the Captain; and Charlotte's niece, Ottilie. Against Charlotte's inclination, Eduard invites the Captain to live with them on their estate. Charlotte in her turn then invites Ottilie to join them, a young girl who is not flourishing at school and who has hitherto made no impression on Eduard.[69] When these four people have been brought together, the materials have been assembled for the experiment on human individuation at which the title of the novel hints. For *Die Wahlverwandtschaften* is a technical term drawn from chemistry. There it refers to the natural inclination in certain elements or substances, when juxtaposed with certain other elements or substances, to join with them and so to form new substances.

The physical principle is explained at some length within the novel itself, in a chapter that exposes the terrible blindness of the characters to the process which is about to draw them in. The Captain intends to pursue some chemical experiments while he is staying with Eduard and Charlotte. One evening, before the arrival of Ottilie, the Captain touches on the principle of affinity that he will demonstrate once his chemistry set has arrived. Certain substances combine avidly, he explains:

> Alkalis and acids, although opposed to one another and perhaps precisely because they are so opposed, will in a most decisive way seek out, take hold

67. Conrad, *Lord Jim*, p. 174.

68. *Die Wahlverwandtschaften*.

69. 'I am not aware that she made the least impression [den mindesten Eindruck] on me' (Goethe, *Elective Affinities*, p. 13).

> of, and modify one another and form, in so doing, a new substance together. We have only to think of lime, which manifests towards all acids a strong inclination, a decided wish for union.[70]

In so doing, these appetitive substances abandon a pre-existing union in pursuit of a new one:

> For example, what we call limestone is a more or less pure oxide of calcium tightly combined with a weak acid known to us in gaseous form. If a piece of that rock is placed in dilute sulphuric acid this combines with the calcium to form gypsum; the gaseous weak acid, on the other hand, escapes. A separation and a new combination have come about and one even feels justified in using the term 'elective affinity', because it really does seem as though one relationship were preferred to another and a choice made for one over the other.[71]

Charlotte is both troubled and, in one respect, unpersuaded by what the Captain has said. In the first place, she dissents from the implications of the term 'elective': 'I would never call that a choice [eine Wahl], rather a necessity in Nature, and scarcely even that since in the end it is perhaps only a matter of opportunity. . . . The only choice lies in the hands of the chemist himself, who brings them together.'[72] But, more gravely, she is disturbed by the application of this chemical language, and the process to which it refers, to human relations. Eduard immediately makes such an application, and he does so with an insouciance that is grotesquely mistaken, in the light of what will transpire in a few weeks: 'Admit it! I suppose in your view I am the lime—seized by sulphuric acid in the person of the Captain, torn from your agreeable company and transformed into an unco-operative [refraktären] gypsum.'[73] 'Everyone likes playing with analogies', replies Charlotte, before turning the conversation in a more sombre direction: 'Alas, I know of enough cases in which a close and, as it seemed, indissoluble relationship was annulled by the casual arrival of a third party, and one of the pair, previously joined so beautifully, driven out

70. Goethe, *Elective Affinities*, p. 32.

71. Goethe, *Elective Affinities*, p. 33.

72. Goethe, *Elective Affinities*, p. 33.

73. Goethe, *Elective Affinities*, p. 33. For the time taken by the action, see Nicholas Boyle, 'What Really Happens in "Die Wahlverwandtschaften"', *The German Quarterly* 89, no. 3 (2016): 298–312, esp. p. 299, where he calculates the duration of the events of the novel as 'about eighteen months from the April of one year to the autumn of the year following'.

into empty space.'[74] Eduard replies flippantly but with unconscious prophetic accuracy: 'Chemists are much more gallant. They add a fourth party, so that nobody goes without.'[75] The Captain responds to the hint with alacrity:

> Those cases are the most significant and the most remarkable in which the attraction and the affinity, the desertion and the uniting, can be seen, so to speak, crosswise: when four substances, united until that moment two by two, are brought into contact, desert their previous union, and unite afresh. In this letting go and seizing hold, this fleeing one thing and seeking another, one is really inclined to discern some higher prescription; one ascribes to such substances a sort of volition and power to choose and the technical term 'elective affinities' [das Kunstwort Wahlverwandtschaften] seems perfectly justified.[76]

The Captain then schematises such an interaction with letters:

> Imagine an A closely bound to a B and by a variety of means and even by force not able to be separated from it; imagine a C in a similar relationship with a D; now bring the two pairs into contact; A will go over to D, C to B, without our being able to say who first left the other, who first with another was united again.[77]

With a ghastly joviality, Eduard then applies this chemical process to the relationships amongst those living in his house:

> We shall think of these formulae as a sort of parable, out of which we can abstract a lesson for our own immediate use. You are the A, Charlotte, and I am your B: for do I not depend on you and come after you as the B does the A? The C is quite obviously the Captain, who for the time being has to some extent taken me away from you. Now it would be right and proper, to prevent you from departing into the void [ins Unbestimmte], to provide you with a D, and quite without question that must be the amiable young lady Ottilie, and you must not now make any further objection to her joining us.[78]

74. Goethe, *Elective Affinities*, pp. 33 and 34.
75. Goethe, *Elective Affinities*, p. 34.
76. Goethe, *Elective Affinities*, p. 34.
77. Goethe, *Elective Affinities*, p. 35.
78. Goethe, *Elective Affinities*, p. 35.

At which point Charlotte reveals that, notwithstanding her earlier misgivings, she had decided that afternoon to invite Ottilie to be with them.

The human experiment is thus set up. Eduard is right that the principle of elective affinities will take effect, but he is wrong about the new pairings that will result. For he and Ottilie will fall in love, as will Charlotte and the Captain; and the result will be death and misery. 'Affinities are only really interesting when they bring about separations [wenn sie Scheidungen bewirken]', says Eduard blithely, ignorant of the extent to which the lives of all four protagonists will be devastated (albeit in an 'interesting' manner) by the ensuing events.[79] For, in the end, all four will be in some sense 'separated' from one another, since they will all be either discarded or dead.

The resulting process of involuntary (though also elective) separation and recombination is played out with agonising slowness against a backdrop of human delusions about the singleness and impermeability of personal identity and of human desires for uncompromised agency. Early in the narrative we learn that one of Eduard's foibles is that he cannot tolerate anybody looking over his shoulder as he reads aloud, and the reason he gives for this aversion is significant: 'Somebody reading over my shoulder always makes me feel I'm being torn in two [in zwei Stücke gerissen].'[80] The intolerableness of any infraction of, or incursion within, the perimeter of identity is also reflected in the Captain's political principles, which endorse an unqualified autocracy: 'Anything which is really for the common good will be done by the unrestricted exercise of sovereign power, or not at all.'[81]

Charlotte, too, shares these delusions of boundedness and participates in these unassuageable desires for control that seem to be their natural accompaniment. When the Captain carries her ashore after a rowing expedition on the lake and takes the opportunity to kiss her, Charlotte attempts to halt and even to reverse the formation of a new bond that is clearly now well-advanced:

> We cannot prevent this moment from marking an epoch in our lives; but whether it be one worthy of us, that we can still decide. You must leave, my dear friend, and you will leave. . . . I can forgive you and forgive myself only

79. Goethe, *Elective Affinities*, p. 32.
80. Goethe, *Elective Affinities*, p. 29.
81. Goethe, *Elective Affinities*, p. 44.

> if we have the courage to alter our situation, since it is not within our power to alter our feelings.[82]

This brittle and impotent attempt at control is quickly followed by an even more ambitious, and even more futile, plan to rewind time:

> Charlotte hoped she would quickly restore her own relationship with Eduard, and in her thinking she arrived at such a rational settlement of everything that she became more and more confirmed in the illusion that a return to an earlier and more restricted condition would be possible, that a thing now violently released could be brought back into confinement.[83]

Charlotte therefore speaks from the heart of her delusional character when she affirms that 'We are our own responsibility, nobody else's; we must ourselves be friends and mentors to ourselves.'[84] And it is accordingly deeply unsurprising when she characterises her own social experience in terms of an absence of interaction, even when she is enmeshed in a process which at every moment is whispering the contrary:

> If we think how many people we have seen and known, and admit how little we have been to them and how little they to us, what a strange feeling that is! We meet a witty man and have no conversation with him, a learned man and learn nothing from him, a well-travelled man and find nothing out, and one full of love and do nothing that would have pleased him.[85]

Eventually, however, even Charlotte is brought to understand that her convictions about control and boundedness are unfounded. The human sense of agency is an illusion, she belatedly realises:

> As life hurries us along . . . we suppose ourselves to be the authors of our actions [glauben wir aus uns selbst zu handeln], and that what we undertake and how amuse ourselves are matters of our own choosing; but looked at closely, of course, they are only the plans and tendencies of the times, in

82. Goethe, *Elective Affinities*, pp. 83–84.

83. Goethe, *Elective Affinities*, p. 87.

84. Goethe, *Elective Affinities*, p. 99.

85. Goethe, *Elective Affinities*, p. 121.

> whose execution we are obliged to co-operate [die wir mit auszuführen genötigt sind].[86]

Fate and natural process, Charlotte eventually sees, will prevail 'however we may wish to behave.'[87]

Against the backdrop of these delusions about personal boundedness and agency, Goethe unfolds a plot in which individuation and autonomy are steadily more compromised. A hint that the four protagonists are in fact not so well individuated as they at least initially believe is contained within their names. Eduard and the Captain are both called Otto, as is Eduard and Charlotte's baby: 'the child must be called Otto; he could have no other name but the name of the father and the friend.'[88] Moreover, the names of both Charlotte and Ottilie echo the shared name of their male counterparts.

As the four begin to live together, their sense of time and space begins to alter and weaken. Charlotte abandons her landscaping projects, and the more ambitious surveying undertaken by the Captain produces little practical result. Old but significant habits are abandoned, as the four insensibly surrender themselves to 'new affection' and 'developing passion': 'Then it turned out that the Captain, for the first time in many years, had forgotten to wind his watch; and they began to suspect, if not already actually to feel, that time was becoming unimportant [gleichgültig] to them.'[89] Soon the Captain realises that he is 'only drifting along in a state of semi-idleness.'[90]

Goethe presents this uneasy but seductive slide into new alignments as a tendency 'towards boundlessness [eine Richtung gegen das Unermeßliche]'.[91] As the transgressive passions strengthen between the four, so too their feelings and interactions are more insistently characterised in terms of this drift towards boundlessness. After Eduard's *éclaircissement* with Ottilie, 'knowing that he loved and was loved drove Eduard into boundlessness [treibt ihn ins Unendliche]'.[92] A little later, we are told that '[Eduard] would have liked to make everyone happy, his own happiness seemed so boundless [ohne

86. Goethe, *Elective Affinities*, p. 170.
87. Goethe, *Elective Affinities*, p. 212.
88. Goethe, *Elective Affinities*, p. 173.
89. Goethe, *Elective Affinities*, p. 173.
90. Goethe, *Elective Affinities*, p. 173.
91. Goethe, *Elective Affinities*, p. 49.
92. Goethe, *Elective Affinities*, p. 86.

Grenzen].'[93] When Eduard leaves the estate to travel and engage in military adventuring, Ottilie 'suffered boundlessly [unendlich]'.[94]

To a certain extent, this erasure or infraction of boundaries is a familiar and even innocent consequence of socialising. As Goethe remarks towards the end of the novel, 'Even people who are entirely strange and indifferent to one another will exchange confidences if they live together for a while, and a certain intimacy [Vertraulichkeit] is bound to develop.'[95] In Ottilie's diary, however, she sees the social acculturation of individuals as something that detracts from individuality: 'How may a person be well-mannered and yet preserve his character and his peculiarity [Eigentümlichkeit]?'[96] Quite early on, the Captain 'was already beginning to feel that a process of irresistible habituation was threatening to bind him to Charlotte.'[97]

Socialising may entail the erosion of the previously hard edges of identity, and in *Elective Affinities*, Goethe puts a series of mildly uncanny moments before us in which this compromising of individuation seems to be a literal and disconcerting reality, rather than merely a manner of speaking. These confusions of identity begin mildly and metaphorically. When Ottilie proposes a site for the new Hall that the others had overlooked, 'Eduard could not conceal his delight that it was Ottilie's idea. He was as proud as if he had thought of it himself.'[98] But they very quickly assume a more substantial form. For instance, when Ottilie accompanies Eduard (who is a very bad flautist and unable to keep time) on the piano, the accompaniment displays not so much the pianist tactfully accommodating the flautist as a curious blending of identities:

> Those listening noticed and were amazed how completely Ottilie had learned the piece for herself, but what amazed them even more was how she managed to accommodate it to Eduard's manner of playing. 'Managed to accommodate' is not the right expression; for whereas Charlotte skilfully

93. Goethe, *Elective Affinities*, p. 97. In respect of bounds (Grenzen), Luciane is a chimerical blend of her mother's commitment to boundaries and her step-father's willingness to infringe: 'she held other people within the strictest bounds of decency towards herself, whilst seeming at every moment to transgress those bounds in her dealings with them' (Goethe, *Elective Affinities*, p. 142).

94. Goethe, *Elective Affinities*, p. 104.

95. Goethe, *Elective Affinities*, p. 204.

96. Goethe, *Elective Affinities*, p. 150.

97. Goethe, *Elective Affinities*, p. 56.

98. Goethe, *Elective Affinities*, p. 53.

> and of her own free will held back to suit her husband when he hesitated and kept up with him when he raced ahead, it seemed that Ottilie, who had heard them play the sonatas on a number of occasions, had only learned them in the way that belonged to the man she was accompanying. She had made his faults so much her own that in the end something whole and alive came out of them that did not keep proper time, it is true, but was extremely agreeable and pleasing to listen to nevertheless.[99]

When Eduard is separated from Ottilie, she is still somehow present to him in an entanglement of persons: 'Everything that happens to me with her gets confused and transposed. We might be signing a contract: her hand is there and so is mine, her name and mine, they erase one another, they intertwine.'[100] In this respect, the glass with the intertwined initials of Ottilie and Eduard is a concrete embodiment of this ever more intricate recombination of originally separate human substances.[101]

An additional character, the Architect, enters the novel and undertakes the restoration of a neglected chapel in the local church. Ottilie assists him with the chapel murals, taking charge of the backgrounds and the drapery of the figures, while the Architect assumes responsibility for the more demanding work of the faces. But as the work proceeds, something uncanny emerges:

> Now they made rapid progress and the azure heavens were soon populated with fit inhabitants. Through sustained practice Ottilie and the Architect attained to a greater freedom in the last pictures; they grew markedly better. The faces too, which were left to the Architect to paint, gradually began to manifest a quite peculiar quality [eine ganz besondere Eigenschaft]: they all began to look like Ottilie. The presence of the beautiful child must doubtless have made such a lively impression upon the soul of the young man, who had no preconceptions as to faces, either from art or life, that gradually in passing from the eye to the hand nothing was lost, indeed by the finish both worked wholly in harmony. Enough, one of the last faces succeeded perfectly so that it seemed as if Ottilie herself were looking down out of the heavenly regions.[102]

99. Goethe, *Elective Affinities*, p. 55.
100. Goethe, *Elective Affinities*, p. 111.
101. Goethe, *Elective Affinities*, p. 113.
102. Goethe, *Elective Affinities*, p. 128.

A naturalistic explanation for this convergence of the painted faces with the actual face of Ottilie is offered. However, this instance of possibly natural infatuation on the part of the Architect prepares the ground for a much more disconcerting instance of an imaginary influence breaching the perimeter of identity and expressing that intrusion on a person's physiognomy.

When Charlotte and Eduard have both acknowledged to themselves their transgressive feelings for the Captain and Ottilie but have so far not declared those feelings to each other, Eduard goes to Charlotte's room at midnight, and they make love. However, on both their sides, it is the absent beloved who most deeply engages their emotions and arouses their fantasies, rather than the physically present spouse: 'By lamplight then, in a twilight, the heart's desires and the imagination at once asserted their rights over reality. Eduard held Ottilie in his arms; now closer, now receding, the Captain hovered before Charlotte's soul; and thus absent and present in the queerest fashion were intermingled, in excitement and delight.'[103] The fruit of this compromised act of congress is baby Otto, whose appearance attests to the strange circumstances of his conception. At Otto's christening, Ottilie and Mittler, a friend of the family, are taken aback by what they see:

> Prayers had been said, the child laid in Ottilie's arms, and looking down fondly at him she was more than a little startled by his open eyes, for she seemed to be looking into her own. Anyone would have been astonished by such likeness. Mittler, taking the child next, was similarly shocked, for he saw in its features a resemblance, but to the Captain, that was more striking than anything he had ever seen of the kind before.[104]

This double resemblance to the objects of his parents' adulterous longings strengthens as Otto grows:

> They thought him a wonderful child, indeed a wonder, in his size and shapeliness, his strength and good health, a delight to behold, and even more astounding was that double likeness which developed more and more. In his features and in the whole shape of his body the child more

103. 'In der Lampendämmerung sogleich behauptete die innre Neigung, behauptete die Einbildungskraft ihre Rechte über das Wirkliche. Eduard hielt nur Ottilien in seinen Armen; Charlotte schwebte der Hauptmann näher oder ferner vor der Seele, und so verwebten, wundersam genug, sich Abwesendes und Gegenwärtiges reizend und wonnevoll durch einander'; Goethe, *Elective Affinities*, p. 78.

104. Goethe, *Elective Affinities*, p. 173.

> and more resembled the Captain, and his eyes were less and less distinguishable from Ottilie's.[105]

In one respect, this shows Goethe adopting the widespread early modern superstition that the imagination had the power to imprint an image on the embryo.[106] But in *Elective Affinities*, this popular (but also, by 1809, surely rather antiquated) belief is being made to tell a different story; a story which foregrounds not the power of the imagination so much as the plasticity of personal identity.

That the edges of identity are pliable is suggested also by an episode of depersonalisation that overcomes Ottilie. She has been looking at the Architect's restoration of the neglected chapel:

> She stood, walked to and fro, looked and looked again; finally she sat down in one of the stalls, and it seemed to her, as she looked up and around, as though she existed and did not exist, as though she had feelings and had none, as though everything might vanish even as she looked; and only when the sun went from the window, which until then it had illuminated very brilliantly, did Ottilie wake and come back to herself, and hurry away to the Hall.[107]

This temporary extinguishing of the sense of concernment (one of the pillars of Locke's theory of personal identity) marks a moment when Ottilie's sense of her own identity weakens almost to the point of annihilation.[108]

Elective Affinities is perhaps unparalleled in the richness and subtlety with which it puts before us instances when personal identity is compromised or breached. But Goethe also suggests how this vulnerability in one crucial aspect of personal identity—individuation—can lead to ruptures in the other crucial aspect of personal identity, namely, diachronic continuity. Although Ottilie has not been very successful at school, nevertheless one anecdote from her history lessons has stuck in her mind, as she explains to Charlotte:

105. Goethe, *Elective Affinities*, pp. 196–97. The resemblances are later confirmed by Eduard (ibid., p. 206) and the Captain (now Major; ibid., p. 211).

106. On which, see Dennis Todd, *Imagining Monsters: Miscreations of the Self in Eighteenth-Century England* (Chicago: University of Chicago Press, 1995).

107. Goethe, *Elective Affinities*, pp. 129–30.

108. On the importance of concernment to Locke's theory of personal identity, see Galen Strawson, *Locke on Personal Identity: Consciousness and Concernment* (Princeton, NJ: Princeton University Press, 2011), ch. 4, 'Concernment', pp. 22–30.

> When Charles I of England stood before his so-called judges the gold knob of the little staff he carried fell to the floor. Accustomed, if ever such a thing happened, to having everyone bustling to help he seemed to look around him and to expect that on this occasion too someone would do him this small service. Nobody moved; he bent down himself and picked up the knob. Rightly or wrongly, I thought this such a painful thing—I don't know whether I should have done—that since then I have never been able to see anyone drop anything without bending down for it.[109]

It is surely characteristic of Ottilie to sympathise with afflicted majesty. But what the anecdote also displays is how diachronic identity can be interrupted, because what the immobility of the bystanders reveals is that Charles's identity has changed—for he has ceased to be a king.

In the case of Charles I, that break in diachronic identity is the result of external force. But, so Goethe suggests, it may equally result from a loss of sharp individuation. One of the strangest instances of the blurring of individuation in *Elective Affinities* occurs when Ottilie volunteers to be Eduard's amanuensis and to make a copy of a lengthy legal contract for him in a short space of time.[110] When she produces the fair copy,

> He [Eduard] looked at her, he looked at the copy. The first pages were written with the greatest care, in a delicate female hand; then the writing seemed to change, to become easier and freer; but how great was his astonishment when he ran his eyes over the final pages. 'In heaven's name!' he cried. 'What is this? That is my handwriting.' He looked at Ottilie, and again at the pages. Especially the ending was as if he had written it himself. Ottilie said nothing, but she was looking into his eyes with the greatest satisfaction. Eduard raised his arms. 'You love me!' he cried. 'Ottilie, you love me!' And they held one another in a tight embrace. It would not have been possible to say who first seized hold of the other.[111]

Impossible to say who seized whom first, surely, because the separation of persons that such a discrimination of priority would require is already unavailable. And the immediate result of this striking instance of breached individuation is a rift in the diachronic identities of both Eduard and Ottilie:

109. Goethe, *Elective Affinities*, p. 43.
110. Goethe, *Elective Affinities*, pp. 63–64.
111. Goethe, *Elective Affinities*, p. 81.

'Thereupon Eduard's world was turned around: he was no longer what he had been [er nicht mehr, was er gewesen], the world no longer what it had been'; while for Ottilie, the departure of Eduard 'was a terrible moment. . . . When she found herself again it seemed to her a meeting with a different being [ein anderes Wesen anzutreffen].'[112] The break in Eduard's personal identity is caught in a striking detail. As we have seen, initially he cannot tolerate anyone looking over his shoulder as he reads. But he allows Ottilie to do so, as Charlotte and the Captain both notice.[113] By the end of the novel, Eduard even sits 'in such a way that she could read over his shoulder, indeed he was uneasy, distracted, if she were not doing so, if he were not certain that she was following the words with her eyes.'[114] When the novel begins, Eduard cannot tolerate being overlooked, which he likens to being torn in two.[115] As the novel ends, unless Ottilie is looking over his shoulder, he feels incomplete.

Novelists and dramatists, then, have often reverted to those uncanny but perhaps revealing moments when our experience of identity, a concept to which they are necessarily to some extent committed (insofar as they invent and deploy characters), seems to weaken or inflect, as a result either of compromised individuation or of fractured or disrupted diachronic continuity. In this, the nature of the interest of the writer differs from that of philosophers such as Aristotle or Descartes or Locke. The subtlety of the philosopher's mind is focused on conceptual clarity and the consistent use of language. For the philosopher, as Locke pointed out, 'the difficulty or obscurity, that has been about this Matter, rather rises from the Names ill used, than from any obscurity in things themselves'.[116] For the philosopher, identity is not in itself puzzling; the illusion of being in the presence of something puzzling arises from our bewitchment by language. But for the novelist or the dramatist, identity, at its outer reaches, is intrinsically puzzling, and the only way to register that is by casting the net of language widely and using words with a justified freedom—think, for instance, of the range of words for which Goethe reached when evoking the boundlessness that the dissolving individuation of his characters placed at the centre of *Elective Affinities* ('Unermeßliche', 'Unendliche',

112. Goethe, *Elective Affinities*, pp. 82 and 104. It is important to register the full, broad force of 'Wesen', as opposed to its near, but narrower, synonym, 'Leben'.

113. Goethe, *Elective Affinities*, p. 55.

114. Goethe, *Elective Affinities*, p. 230.

115. See above, p. 39.

116. Locke, *Essay*, p. 348.

'ohne Grenzen', 'grenzenlos', 'unbedingt') or the way Conrad pressed on a *cliché* like 'under a cloud' to release from it an unexpected way of talking about Jim's obscurity of identity.

And Shakespeare himself had not been blind to this power in language to evoke the fragility of identity, as we can see in *Othello*.

———

Drama presents identity to us through dialogue. So it makes sense to begin with an example of men talking to one another. It comes from the beginning of act I, scene iii of *Othello* and is a conversation between the Duke and two senators which is interrupted twice by messengers.

DUKE. There is no composition in this news,
    That gives them credit.
FIRST SENATOR.   Indeed, they are disproportioned:
    My letters say a hundred and seven galleys—
DUKE. And mine a hundred and forty—
SECOND SENATOR.   And mine two hundred.
    But though they jump not on a just account—
    As in these cases where the aim reports,
    'Tis oft with difference—yet do they all confirm
    A Turkish fleet, and bearing up to Cyprus.
DUKE. Nay, it is possible enough to judgment:
    I do not so secure me in the error,
    But the main article I do approve
    In fearful sense.
SAILOR. [*within*]   What ho! What ho! What ho!
    Enter SAILOR.
OFFICER.   A messenger from the galleys.
    Enter SAILOR.
DUKE.   —Now, what's the business?
SAILOR.   The Turkish preparation makes for Rhodes:
    So I was bid report here to the state,
    By Signor Angelo.
DUKE. [*to* SENATORS] How say you by this change?
FIRST SENATOR.   This cannot be
    By no assay of reason: 'tis a pageant

To keep us in false gaze. When we consider
Th'importancy of Cyprus to the Turk,
And let ourselves again but understand
That as it more concerns the Turk than Rhodes,
So may he with more facile question bear it,
For that it stands not in such warlike brace,
But altogether lacks th'abilities
That Rhodes is dressed in. If we make thought of this,
We must not think the Turk is so unskillful
To leave that latest which concerns him first,
Neglecting an attempt of ease and gain
To wake and wage a danger profitless.

DUKE. Nay, in all confidence, he's not for Rhodes.

OFFICER. Here is more news.

Enter a MESSENGER.

MESSENGER. The Ottomites, reverend and gracious,
Steering with due course toward the isle of Rhodes,
Have there injointed them with an after fleet.

FIRST SENATOR. Ay, so I thought. How many, as you guess?

MESSENGER. Of thirty sail. And now they do restem
Their backward course, bearing with frank appearance
Their purposes toward Cyprus.[117]

Since this is taken from a seventeenth-century verse drama, it has a degree of artistic formality which would make it implausible if we were to cite it as an instance of how men really speak to one another now or even of how they really spoke to one another then. But allowing for that, we can nevertheless see that this conversation reflects at least one aspect of normal, daily speech, in that it is an exchange between individuals. That is to say, it represents an encounter between a number of persons, each of whom has a discrete perspective on the world and each of whom recognises that the perspective of others whom they meet and to whom they talk is just as discrete as their own. They know that they can give voice to their own understanding of reality, and they are aware that they can find out about the understandings of others, by framing questions and listening to answers. In a conversation such as this, language is

117. *Othello*, I.iii.1–39.

the medium for the exchange of opinions which have been already formulated within the privacy of individuality.

Something very different, however, is happening in this conversation between Othello and Iago in act IV, scene i:

IAGO. Will you think so?
OTHELLO. Think so, Iago?
IAGO. What,
To kiss in private?
OTHELLO. An unauthorized kiss!
IAGO. Or to be naked with her friend in bed
An hour or more, not meaning any harm?
OTHELLO. Naked in bed, Iago, and not mean harm?
It is hypocrisy against the devil.
They that mean virtuously, and yet do so,
The devil their virtue tempts, and they tempt heaven.
IAGO. If they do nothing, 'tis a venial slip;
But if I give my wife a handkerchief—
OTHELLO. What then?
IAGO. Why, then 'tis hers, my lord, and, being hers,
She may, I think, bestow't on any man.
OTHELLO. She is protectress of her honor, too.
May she give that?
IAGO. Her honor is an essence that's not seen:
They have it very oft that have it not.
But for the handkerchief—
OTHELLO. By heaven, I would most gladly have forgot it!
Thou said'st—oh, it comes o'erm memory
As doth the raven o'er the infectious house,
Boding to all—he had my handkerchief.
IAGO. Ay, what of that?
OTHELLO. That's not so good now.
IAGO. What if I had said I had seen him do you wrong?
Or heard him say—as knaves be such abroad,
Who, having by their own importunate suit,
Or voluntary dotage of some mistress,
Convinced or supplied them, cannot choose
But they must blab—

OTHELLO. Hath he said anything?
IAGO. He hath, my lord, but be you well assured,
No more than he'll unswear.
OTHELLO. What hath he said?
IAGO. Why, that he did—I know not what he did.
OTHELLO. What? What?
IAGO. Lie.
OTHELLO. With her?
IAGO. With her, on her, what you will.
OTHELLO. Lie with her? Lie on her? We say 'lie on her' when they
belie her. Lie with her? That's fulsome![118]

We can see why this conversation differs from the dialogue between the Duke and the senators by reflecting on an apparently slight, but recurrent and also very important, aspect of Shakespeare's use of dialogue in *Othello*. In this play, Shakespeare's verbal imagination was captured by 'iterance,' that is to say, the exact repetition of a word, either by the same character or by two characters. In act III, scene iii, Othello reveals that Cassio often acted as go-between during his courtship of Desdemona, to which Iago responds:

IAGO. Indeed?
OTHELLO. Indeed? Ay, indeed! Discern'st thou aught in that?
Is he not honest?
IAGO. Honest, my lord?
OTHELLO. Honest? Ay, honest.
IAGO. My lord, for aught I know.
OTHELLO. What dost thou think?
IAGO. Think, my lord?
OTHELLO. 'Think, my lord?' Alas, thou echo'st me
As if there were some monster in thy thought
Too hideous to be shown.[119]

And again, in act V, scene ii, when Emilia is dazedly repeating the phrase 'My husband' as she begins to understand what Iago has been up to in the course of the play, Othello is eventually moved to expostulate, 'What needs this

118. *Othello*, IV.i.1–34.
119. *Othello*, III.iii.99–107.

iterance?'[120] There are, I think, good reasons why Shakespeare is preoccupied with 'iterance' in this play. They are reasons to do with identity, with tragedy, and with the relation between the two.

As we commonly observe, iterated language becomes weakened and with every repetition becomes progressively more emptied of meaning. And the same is true of the users of language which comes to be repeated. As we have seen in the conversation between the Duke and the senators, when well-distinguished individuals speak to one another, what we hear is an encounter between separate points of view conducted in differentiated language. By contrast, the repetition of language may be a sign of a porousness of character and hence of a certain breaching of identity. If we look more closely at the language of the conversation between Iago and Othello in act IV, scene i, one of its particularly striking features is the way in which words are passed between the two men: from Iago's phrase 'think so' to 'kiss' to 'naked' and 'abed' to 'harm' to 'handkerchief' to clusters of smaller words such as 'may', 'hath', until we reach the final and climactic instance of iteration:

> IAGO. Lie.
> OTHELLO. With her?
> IAGO. With her, on her, what you will.
> OTHELLO. Lie with her? Lie on her?

So the exchange of language between Iago and Othello is the verbal record of an episode quite different in kind from the exchange of opinions between the Duke and the senators. Whereas there what we had was an interaction between separate entities which proceeded dialectically, in the conversation between Iago and Othello, the strange dynamics of the language suggest not so much a collision of distinct perspectives and personalities as a certain fusing of identities. Like a duet in an opera, the fragmentary utterances of Iago and Othello blend and run into one another—indeed, mutually *require* one another—to the point where it becomes hard to say cleanly where one character begins and the other ends.

This compromising of individuation is, in a variety of ways, central to *Othello*, which of all Shakespeare's tragedies is the most preoccupied with the various ways, both benign and harmful, in which we undertake the dangerous process of qualifying our separateness from others, whether it be with

120. *Othello*, V.ii.137, 141, 145.

lieutenancy or with friendship or (most centrally) with marriage.[121] But the assertion and subsequent compromising of individuality seem also from the first to have been central to tragedy as a dramatic form.

We don't know exactly how tragedy began. The etymology directs us, possibly unhelpfully, to the ancient Greek word for a goat (*tragos*). A more promising lead is supplied by Aristotle, who in his *Poetics* says that tragedy originated in the improvisations of the leader of the dithyramb, or chorus, at the festivals of Dionysus.[122] It is an insight which was elaborated over two thousand years later and with great brilliance by Friedrich Nietzsche. In *The Birth of Tragedy* (1872), Nietzsche saw tragedy as the product of a contest in ancient Greek culture between two antagonistic but also complementary principles. On the one hand, there was the Dionysiac, which was orgiastic, intoxicated, and violent and yet which also had the power to release men from the imprisonment of their individuality and return them to an awareness of the essential oneness of nature:

> Not only does the bond between man and man come to be forged once more by the magic of the Dionysiac rite, but nature itself, long alienated or subjugated, rises again to celebrate the reconciliation with her prodigal son, man. The earth offers its gifts voluntarily, and the savage beasts of mountain and desert approach in peace. The chariot of Dionysos is bedecked with flowers and garlands; panthers and tigers stride beneath his yoke. . . . Now the slave emerges as a freeman; all the rigid, hostile walls which either necessity or despotism has erected between men are shattered. Now that the gospel of universal harmony is sounded, each individual becomes not only reconciled to his fellow but actually at one with him—as though the veil of Maya had been torn apart and there remained only shreds floating before the vision of mystical Oneness. Man now expresses himself through song and dance as the member of a higher community; he has forgotten how to walk, how to speak, and is on the brink of taking wing as he dances. Each of his gestures betokens enchantment; through him sounds a supernatural

121. 'Therefore shall a man leave his father and his mother, and shall cleave unto his wife: they shall be one flesh' (Genesis 2:24). Cf. Ephesians 5:28–33. Cf. Tolstoy's Marya on love's power to fuse or compromise identities: 'All my thoughts and feelings at that time were his, not mine; but by becoming mine they went to make up my life and fill it with light. . . . And every thought was his thought, every feeling his feeling' (Leo Tolstoy, *Family Happiness* [1859], ch. 2, in *The Kreutzer Sonata and Family Happiness* [London: Scott, n.d.], pp. 21 and 24).

122. Aristotle, *Poetics*, 1449a.

> power, the same power which makes the animals speak and the earth render up milk and honey. He feels himself to be godlike and strides with the same elation and ecstasy as the gods he has seen in his dreams. No longer the *artist*, he has himself become a *work of art*: the productive power of the whole universe is now manifest in his transport, to the glorious satisfaction of the primordial One.[123]

Against the Dionysiac stood the Apollonian, which was rational, lucid, dreamlike rather than intoxicated, and the embodiment of individuality—embodying what Nietzsche, borrowing a phrase from Schopenhauer, called the *principium individuationis*:

> This deep and happy sense of the necessity of dream experiences was expressed by the Greeks in the image of Apollo. Apollo is at once the god of all plastic powers and the soothsaying god. He who is etymologically the 'lucent' one, the god of light, reigns also over the fair illusion of our inner world of fantasy. . . . But the image of Apollo must incorporate that thin line which the dream image may not cross, under penalty of becoming pathological, of imposing itself on us as crass reality: a discreet limitation, a freedom from all extravagant urges, the sapient tranquillity of the plastic god. His eye must be sunlike, in keeping with his origin. Even at those moments when he is angry and ill-tempered there lies upon him the consecration of fair illusion. . . . One might say that the unshakeable confidence in that principle [the *principium individuationis*] has received its most magnificent expression in Apollo, and that Apollo himself may be regarded as the marvellous divine image of the *principium individuationis*, whose looks and gestures radiate the full delight, wisdom, and beauty of 'illusion'.[124]

Informed by this opposition of powerful principles, Nietzsche's speculative account of the origin of tragedy goes as follows. The worshippers of Dionysus celebrate their god in a dance. At some point, the leader of the chorus or dithyramb steps apart and sings a different tune, in which his individuality is asserted. At that point he is dismembered, literally torn in pieces (as Pentheus will be in Euripides's *The Bacchae*). This is an act of what the ancient Greeks called *sparagmos*, in which the guilt incurred by the leader in asserting his separateness is expunged, and he himself is resumed into the original oneness

123. Nietzsche, *Tragedy*, pp. 23–24.

124. Nietzsche, *Tragedy*, pp. 21–22. For Schopenhauer's use of the phrase, see p. 21, n. 10.

from which he had rashly distinguished himself. It is a process which Nietzsche suggests is, in essence and notwithstanding its violence, consolatory. Now, it is clear that Nietzsche's sympathies in this process lie more with the Dionysiac than with the Apollonian, and in terms of the development of his thought, and of his own turbulent and eventually pathological psychology, there are plausible reasons why this should have been so.

However, we shall see that in *Othello*, Shakespeare holds the balance more evenly and is more wary of the dangers involved in losing identity than Nietzsche either was or would allow himself to be. We can understand why this is so if we consider how the Venice of this play relates to both other imaginings of Venice by Shakespeare and the historical Venice of Shakespeare's time.

The physical setting for act I of *Othello*, and its cultural context even after the action has moved in act II to Cyprus, is Venice. The historical Venice had been founded in the fifth century, when the population of north-east Italy had sought refuge from the depredations of the Huns in the low-lying islands which fringe the northern extremity of the Adriatic. Here they had discovered a precarious political independence, to which they added the financial strength which flowed from their eventual stranglehold on the trade between western Europe and the lands of the eastern Mediterranean: with Greece, with Egypt, and with the Levant. From the first, therefore, Venice was a border state. It was founded in the no-man's-land between earth and sea, as well as between the provinces of the Roman empire in the West and its sister, the Eastern empire; and it began to flourish at a time when the pretensions of both empires were being trimmed in the light of fiscal and military weakness. As the tide of empire retreated, so the scope for Venetian prosperity and strength increased.

Politically, too, Venice was amphibious. Its original constitution was a blend of monarchy and democracy. The doge was elected by the people and ruled as a prince for as long as he was successful and popular. But it is in the nature of popular elective monarchy to be unstable, and the first doges were frequently deposed by the tumults of the people. It was only in the twelfth century that Venice was gradually transformed into an aristocratic republic. Through the instrument of an elaborate and complex constitutional design, the senatorial aristocracy laid hold on power, reducing the people to impotence and the doge to a cipher. This constitution had endured with little change for so long that, at the time when Shakespeare was writing *Othello*, and as a result of Venice's recent successful defence of its territory against the most powerful mainland powers of western Europe, which in 1508 had formed the League of Cambrai with the specific purpose of reducing Venetian power, Venice had acquired fame as a real-life solution to a text-book problem in the realm of political theory: namely, the problem of how to overcome the instability which seemed inherent in republics and to imbue them with the stability which (in the opinion of some) was the only practical advantage enjoyed by monarchies over free governments.

Works such as Gasparo Contarini's *De Magistratibus et Republica Venetorum* (1543), translated into English as *The Commonwealth and Government of Venice* by Lewes Lewkenor in 1599 (just before the likely date of composition of *Othello*), gave powerful expression to the 'myth of Venice' which had resulted. In Ben Jonson's *Volpone,* a play written a few years later than *Othello,* the ridiculous Sir Politick Would-be travels to Venice. It was the natural destination for the aspiring politician, because, as James Howell would assert later in the seventeenth century, 'Were it within the reach of humane brain to prescribe Rules for fixing a Society and *Succession* of people under the same Species of Government as long as the World lasts, the Republic of *Venice* were the fittest pattern on Earth both for direction and imitation.'[125]

Finally, in addition to its status as a political paradigm, Venice also enjoyed a reputation for sexual dissoluteness. This lack of sexual restraint had been encouraged by the twin Venetian conditions of material prosperity and a policy of religious toleration. This latter amounted in the eyes of some almost to religious indifference.[126] But, at the very least, Venice displayed the undogmatic religious disposition which was both required and reinforced by its strong trading links with Islamic states. In *Volpone,* Lady Politick Would-be is startled to hear that her husband has been seen in a gondola 'With the most cunning curtizan, of *Venice*'.[127] She had little reason to be surprised. As the seventeenth-century traveller to Italy Richard Lassels wittily remarked, '*Others desire* to go into *Italy,* only because they heare there are fine *Curtisanes* in *Venice*. . . . And thus by a false ayming at breeding abroad, they returne with those diseases which hinder them from breeding at home.'[128] This is the context for Othello's suspicion that Desdemona is 'that cunning whore of Venice / That married with Othello.'[129]

125. James Howell, *A Survay of the Signorie of Venice* (1651), sig. C1[r].

126. Gabriel Naudé reported the Venetian maxim '*somo Venetiani dopo Chrestiani*' in his *Considérations politiqves sur les covps d'estat* (Rome, 1639), p. 67.

127. Ben Jonson, *Volpone,* III.v.18–21.

128. Richard Lassels, *The Voyage of Italy* (1670), sig. ev[r]; italic and roman reversed.

129. *Othello,* IV.ii.88–89.

Shakespeare's conception of Venice draws on this menu of contextual possibilities but also adds something to them. For *Othello* was not the first Shakespearean play to be set in Venice. Some seven or eight years earlier, in 1596 or 1597, he had written *The Merchant of Venice*. In *Othello*, Venice is primarily the military power which had reached out into the eastern Mediterranean in order to protect its trade routes. In *The Merchant of Venice*, however, Venice is presented primarily as a trading power, and its military capabilities receive no emphasis. Shakespeare's image of Venice was neither inflexible nor static, then.

However, notwithstanding that variation of outward emphasis, at a deeper level there is common structural ground between the Venice of *The Merchant* and the Venice of *Othello*. In both plays, Shakespeare associated Venice with a particular kind of social formation: a formation in which an intensely proud and self-aware culture admits carefully-chosen others to be in, yet not of, it, in order that they might perform some of the host culture's vital functions. In *The Merchant*, the chosen other is Shylock, the Jewish financier who supplies the capital without which Venice's commercial expansion would be impossible. In *Othello*, it is Othello himself, the Moorish soldier whose prowess safeguards the military hegemony without which the prosperity of the state would founder.

Both Othello and Shylock are essential to the normal functioning of the subtly different cities, both going under the name of Venice, in which Shakespeare placed them. At the same time, they are both outsiders, peripheral to its institutions, and existing in the city on quite different terms from the native Venetians. For instance, Shakespeare subtly registers the significant fact that Othello is an employee of the state when the First Senator addresses Othello in the unadorned vocabulary of simple command: 'You must away tonight'.[130] In *The Merchant of Venice*, the gulf which separates Shylock from the Venetians is captured most vividly in what is almost a logical puzzle inherent in the trial scene (act IV, scene i), in which Shylock intends to use the law to extract the pound of flesh from Antonio. In Portia's famous speech on mercy in that scene, she tells us at the outset that the defining quality of mercy is that it is not 'strained', by which she means (as we would more naturally say) that it is not *con*strained, that it is freely given.[131] The conundrum is, with this definition of mercy, how can Shylock ever act mercifully? Of course, Shylock can forgive Antonio the bond which promises him the pound of flesh. But would that

130. *Othello*, I.iii.275.

131. *Merchant of Venice*, IV.i.182.

forgiveness be, in the fullest sense, a merciful act, when the Duke has opened the scene by reproaching Shylock for his 'malice' and 'strange apparent cruelty' and concluded with the barely-concealed menace, 'We all expect a gentle answer, Jew'?[132] The Duke has already warned Antonio that Shylock is 'void and empty / From any dram of mercy.'[133] But how could it be otherwise? In this trial, whatever Shylock does, whether he insists on his bond or capitulates to the Duke's intimidation, he will surely have been constrained. In other words, however Shylock responds to the demand for mercy, he cannot satisfy the full condition of mercifulness, which is precisely that it should *not* be 'strained'. For Shylock, to comply is to be compelled, and to resist is to be defiant. And the logical bind in which Shylock is caught arises directly from his equivocal status within Venice. It arises, that is, from the fact that Shylock, alone of all the characters in this scene, is a tolerated outsider and hence is the only character onstage that is the object of coercion from the Duke. In the same way, Shylock's counterpart, the Moorish general, is also the sole object of command from the First Senator in *Othello*.

The outward condition of Othello's imperfect or qualified inherence in Venice is the fact that he is employed. But his foreignness goes deeper than this, goes deeper even than the colour of his skin, which is an outward marker of an inward foreignness. For Othello has been bred in a quite different environment from that of Venice, and this has produced in him a different *mentalité*. If we go back to the conversation between the Duke and the senators in act I, scene iii with which we began, we can glimpse something of the mental aspect of the Venetian world as Shakespeare imagines it in this play. In the first place, it is worth noting that the first fifty or so lines of this scene (that is, the first section of the scene, before the entry of Brabantio, Othello, and the rest) do nothing to drive the plot forwards. All that they establish is that the Turks are heading for Cyprus. But this could have been done much more economically with a simple announcement from the Duke later in the scene. Nevertheless, these opening lines are very important for our understanding of the play. As we see and hear the Venetians receiving reports, sifting information, and applying tests of probability to what they are told, we learn that the mental culture of Venice is rational, probabilistic, and adept at the interpretation of the behaviour of others, which they understand as feints or signs which require

132. *Merchant of Venice*, IV.i.17, 21, 34.
133. *Merchant of Venice*, IV.i.5–6.

to be construed, not as the transparent expression of inner intent. They are instinctively game-theorists, as the speech of the First Senator shows:

> FIRST SENATOR. This cannot be
> By no assay of reason: 'tis a pageant
> To keep us in false gaze. When we consider
> Th'importancy of Cyprus to the Turk,
> And let ourselves again but understand
> That as it more concerns the Turk than Rhodes,
> So may he with more facile question bear it,
> For that it stands not in such warlike brace,
> But altogether lacks th'abilities
> That Rhodes is dressed in. If we make thought of this,
> We must not think the Turk is so unskillful
> To leave that latest which concerns him first,
> Neglecting an attempt of ease and gain
> To wake and wage a danger profitless.[134]

The Venetians, then, impute skill to others, and they assume until they have evidence to the contrary that those others, like the Venetians themselves, are motivated by the twin considerations of 'ease' and 'gain'. With these as their premises, the Venetians can dissolve the 'pageant' of appearances thrown up by those who would outwit or entrap them and arrive at a solid understanding of other people's true objectives.

The instrument they use to achieve this is the 'assay of reason'. 'Assay' here is a metaphor. It refers literally to the process of testing for the purity of metals—a meaning preserved today in the title of the body still charged with determining metallic purity, the Assay Office.[135] In Shakespeare's day, the process of assaying involved the application of corrosives. These chemicals would remove base metal or impurities, leaving only the noble metal behind, which could then be weighed and hence the percentage it had formed of the original sample ascertained. As the First Senator applies the metaphor, it is the faculty of reason which performs this corrosive function, burning away the 'pageant' which would otherwise produce a 'false gaze' in the observer. In this world of signs and inferences, which is also a secondary world of report rather than of direct experience, the native Venetian picks his way with a fastidious caution,

134. *Othello*, I.iii.17–30.
135. *OED*, 'assay', *n.*, II 6a.

taking nothing on trust, alert always to the possibility of deception, bleakly persuaded that the motives of the others whom he meets are likely to be as narrowly instrumental as his own.

The utterly different world in which Othello was raised, and in which as a soldier he has existed, is evoked in the speech later in the same scene when he explains how he came to win the love of Desdemona:

Her father loved me, oft invited me,
Still questioned me the story of my life
From year to year: the battles, sieges, fortune,
That I have passed.
I ran it through, even from my boyish days
To th'very moment that he bade me tell it,
Wherein I spoke of most disastrous chances;
Of moving accidents by flood and field;
Of hairbreadth scapes i'th'imminent deadly breach;
Of being taken by the insolent foe
And sold to slavery; of my redemption thence,
And portance in my traveler's history;
Wherein of antres vast and deserts idle,
Rough quarries, rocks, hills whose head touch heaven,
It was my hint to speak—such was my process—
And of the cannibals that each other eat—
The Anthropophagi—and men whose heads
Grew beneath their shoulders. These things to hear
Would Desdemona seriously incline; . . .[136]

Othello's life as a soldier has been passed in 'disastrous chances', 'moving accidents', and 'hairbreadth scapes'. Before that, his 'traveler's history' had taken him through a domain of the marvellous, the singular, and the enormous. With this experience, the concept which stands at the centre of the mental world of Venice—namely, the probable—has had no opportunity to establish itself in Othello's mind. This is why Othello is a stranger in Venice and why he has so few defences against Iago's manipulations, which shrewdly exploit this vulnerability in Othello's intellectual armour. Coleridge saw this clearly, in challenging the common reading of Othello as a jealous man:

136. *Othello*, I.iii.128–46.

> I do not think there is any jealousy, properly so called, in the character of Othello. There is no predisposition to suspicion, which I take to be an essential term in the definition of the word. . . . Iago's suggestions, you see, are quite new to him; they do not correspond with anything of a like nature previously in his mind. . . . He could not act otherwise than he did with the lights he had.[137]

So the question of colour here is only secondary. The Moorish embassy which visited London in the years just before the composition of *Othello*, and which Shakespeare and some of the play's first audiences may have seen, were in any case North African, even Arabian, in the colour of their skin and the formation of their features. When Shakespeare calls Othello a Moor, it would be an image such as that of the portrait of the leader of the Moorish embassy which the term would probably summon up in the minds of his contemporaries.[138]

Othello is an alien amongst the Venetians, not because he is Black but because his mental world has no point of contact with theirs. In its exoticness, its colour, its alarming reversals of fortune, its capacious embracing of the opposites of 'flood and field', 'antres vast and deserts idle', and in the directness of its engagement with action: in all this, Othello's world is the very antithesis of the aloof, probabilistic, indirect, monochrome, and carefully-sifted world of the Venetians. This is confirmed by what we learn later of Othello's family background, when he explains to Desdemona the significance of the handkerchief she has mislaid:

> That's a fault. That handkerchief
> Did an Egyptian to my mother give:
> She was a charmer, and could almost read
> The thoughts of people. She told her, while she kept it,
> 'Twould make her amiable, and subdue my father
> Entirely to her love; but if she lost it,
> Or made a gift of it, my father's eye
> Should hold her loathed, and his spirits should hunt
> After new fancies. She, dying, gave it me,

137. Coleridge, *Table-Talk*, pp. 10–11.

138. Cf. Coleridge again: 'Othello must not be conceived as a negro, but a high and chivalrous Moorish chief' (*Table-Talk*, p. 10). The portrait of the Moorish ambassador is held in the collections of the University of Birmingham. It is reproduced as plate 1 in the Arden edition of *Othello* by E. A. J. Honigmann (1997).

And bid me, when my fate would have me wived,
To give it her. I did so, and take heed on't;
Make it a darling like your precious eye;
To lose't or give't away were such perdition
As nothing else could match.[139]

The elements of superstition, of magic, and of the talismanic which ran strongly in the home-life of the young Othello have no counterpart in the strictly naturalistic world of Venice.

This estrangement of background explains why Brabantio and Desdemona are so eager to hear Othello's story, why Brabantio 'oft invited me, / Still questioned me the story of my life / From year to year', and why Desdemona would 'with a greedy ear / Devour up my discourse.'[140] This is the hunger of opposites, and it is the basis of the marriage of Othello and Desdemona, as Othello himself remarks: 'She loved me for the dangers I had passed, / And I loved her that she did pity them.'[141] In this marriage, both parties are drawn to what they have not experienced, Desdemona to the 'dangers' from which she has been carefully sheltered, Othello to the 'pity' which, in its mildness, could not exist in his harsher, brighter, and more violent world. It is an attachment as precarious as it is ardent.

We can now pause and consider the play in terms of these two worlds. When, in act II, the action of the play is transferred to Cyprus, and the tragic process gets under weigh, the fact that the expected engagement with the Turks does not take place transforms Cyprus from what Othello calls 'the tented field'—namely, a setting for the masculine, military life in which he is at home—to a version of Venice itself. That is, Cyprus becomes a mixed and civil society of conversation, leisure, and surmise.[142] In the vacancy of warfare, the potential for tragedy ripens. In the place of the expected direct engagement with a known and declared enemy, Othello is made to inhabit a secondary, Venetian, world of ambivalent signs and surrogate identities which he and Iago create together. It is a world in which both men will perish.

At this point, it might be objected that when I say this is a world which Iago and Othello create together, I am giving insufficient weight to the fact that it

139. *Othello,* III.iv.52–65.
140. *Othello,* I.iii.138–30 and 149–50.
141. *Othello,* I.iii.167–68.
142. *Othello,* I.iii.85.

is surely Iago who entraps Othello. This is indeed a common and in some ways attractive understanding of the play: that it shows us the corruption of a noble Black man by a white barbarian. However, it is not, I think, a view which sits easily alongside Shakespeare's characterisation of Iago, the nuances of which come into focus if we compare it with one earlier and one later version of this character: that of the Ensign in the work which was Shakespeare's source for *Othello*, the seventh story in the third decade of Giraldi Cinthio's *Hecatommithi* (Venice, 1566); and that of Jago in Boito's libretto for Verdi's *Otello* (1887).

There are many significant differences between *Othello* and the short story by Cinthio which is its source. One of the most important concerns the motivation of the Ensign (who in Cinthio is given no other name). In Cinthio's story, the Moor and Disdemona, who have been happily married for some time, have left Venice for Cyprus, where the Moor is to be commandant of the Venetian garrison. In his entourage is 'an Ensign of handsome presence but the most scoundrelly nature in the world':

> The wicked Ensign, taking no account of the faith he had pledged to his wife, and of the friendship, loyalty and obligations he owed the Moor, fell ardently in love with Disdemona, and bent all his thoughts to see if he could manage to enjoy her; but he did not dare openly show his passion, fearing that if the Moor perceived it he might straightway kill him. He sought therefore in various ways, as deviously as he could, to make the Lady aware that he desired her. But she, whose every thought was for the Moor, never gave a thought to the Ensign or anybody else. And all the things he did to arouse her feelings for him had no more effect than if he had not tried them. Whereupon he imagined that this was because she was in love with the Corporal [i.e., in Shakespeare's play, Cassio]; and he wondered how he might remove the latter from her sight. Not only did he turn his mind to this, but the love which he had felt for the Lady now changed to the bitterest hate, and he gave himself up to studying how to bring it about that, once the Corporal were killed, if he himself could not enjoy the Lady, then the Moor should not have her either. Turning over in his mind divers schemes, all wicked and treacherous, in the end he determined to accuse her of adultery, and to make her husband believe that the Corporal was the adulterer.[143]

143. Bullough, *Sources*, 7:243–44.

It is important to recognise here that in Cinthio's story, the Ensign's resentment is focused entirely on Disdemona and not at all (as it will be in *Othello*) upon the Moor. In Cinthio, the Ensign's motivation is simply that of curdled, unrequited desire.

When Arrigo Boito adapted *Othello* into a libretto, he preserved much of the groundwork and the language of Shakespeare's play, but equally he was not afraid boldly to re-shape it. For instance, he dispensed with the whole of act I, opening his opera with Othello's landing in Cyprus. He also simplified the character of Jago. At the beginning of act II, scene ii, he gave Jago a chilling aria:

Credo in un Dio crudel che m'ha creato
simile a sè e che nell'ira io nomo.
Dalla viltà d'un germe o d'un atomo
vile son nato.
Son scellerato
perchè son uomo;
e sento il fango originario in me.
Si! questa è la mia fe!
Credo con ferm cuor,
siccome crede la vedovella al tempio,
che il mal ch'io penso e che da me procede,
per il mio destino adempio.
Credo che il giusto è un istrion beffardo,
e nel viso e nel cuor,
che tutto è in lui bugiardo:
lagrima, bacio, sguardo,
sacrificio ed onor.
E credo l'uom
giuoco d'iniqua sorte
dal germe della culla
al verme dell'avel.
Vien dopo tanta irrision la Morte.
E poi? E poi?
La morte è il nulla.
È vecchia vola il Ciel.[144]

144. 'I believe in a cruel God who has created me / in his image and whom, in hatred, I call upon. / From some vile germ or base atom / I was born. / I am evil / because I am a man; / and

It is a terrible creed, but it also makes Boito's Jago a much more comprehensible character than Shakespeare's Iago. At no point in *Othello* does Iago expound his character and philosophy for the benefit of the audience with the clarity of self-understanding shown in this aria by Boito's nihilistic, but uncomplicated, Jago.

The strangeness of the character created by Shakespeare can be appreciated if we review the multiple motives to which Iago at different moments attributes his resentment of Othello. In act I, scene i, in conversation with Roderigo, Iago dwells on what he sees as the unearned promotion of Cassio, while he, Iago, 'of whom his eyes had seen the proof / At Rhodes, at Cyprus, and on others' grounds', is passed over for the lieutenancy and becomes instead 'his moorship's ensign.'[145] For this failure on Othello's part to understand and respond appropriately to 'ocular proof', Iago will exact a revenge of terrible, precise appositeness and fashion Othello's downfall from his inability to draw sound inferences from visual evidence.[146]

But in act I, scene iii, in soliloquy, Iago traces his hatred of Othello to a different source:

> I hate the Moor,
> And it is thought abroad that twixt my sheets
> He's done my office.[147]

This motivation of a cuckold is repeated later in the play by Emilia, when she inveighs against the 'squire' who 'turned your [Iago's] wit the seamy-side without, / And made you to suspect me with the Moor.'[148] This motivation is repeated, but also varied, by Iago himself at the end of act II, scene i, when, again in soliloquy, he adds to it an echo of the motivation of Cinthio's Ensign, namely, desire for Desdemona:

I feel the original taint within me. / Yes! this is my faith! / I believe with a firm heart, / just like the young widow in church / that the evil which I think, and which from me proceeds / was decreed for me by fate. / I believe that the just man is a buffoonish clown, / and that in both face and heart / he is all false: / tears, kisses, glances, / sacrifice and honour. / And I believe that man / is the plaything of an unjust fate / from the germ of the cradle / to the worm of the grave. / Death comes to end this derision. / And then? And then? / Death is extinction. / Heaven is an old wives' tale.'

145. *Othello*, I.i.26–31.

146. *Othello*, III.iii.357.

147. *Othello*, I.iii.364–66.

148. *Othello*, IV.ii.144–46.

The Moor, howbeit that I endure him not,
Is of a constant, loving, noble nature,
And I dare think he'll prove to Desdemona
A most dear husband. Now do I love her, too,
Not out of absolute lust—though, peradventure,
I stand accountant for as great a sin—
But partly led to diet my revenge,
For that I do suspect the lusty Moor
Hath leaped into my seat, the thought whereof
Doth like a poisonous mineral gnaw my inwards,
And nothing can, or shall, content my soul
Till I am evened with him, wife for wife.[149]

What should we make of this confusion of motives? One possible response would be to follow Coleridge, who in a note on Iago's character spoke of 'the motive-hunting of motiveless Malignity—how awful!'[150] That is to say, Iago's malice towards Othello is simply the expression of his essentially evil nature and is thus an end in itself, not something pursued in an instrumental spirit to satisfy some deeper motive or arrive at any further objective. This, it seems to me, is close to the character we find in Verdi's opera. But it is not the character we encounter in Shakespeare's play. Such a reading of his character could explain why Iago offered a variety of motives to different people, but it does little to explain why he proposes such a range of motives in soliloquy *to himself*, when he evidently has no reason not to speak honestly.

A more fruitful approach might be to recognise that Iago is, on the contrary, perplexed and also preoccupied by his reasons for embarking on a course of action towards which he feels irresistibly impelled but for which he cannot offer any satisfactory account, even to himself. This would have important implications for our understanding of the kind of character Iago is.

It is tempting to see Iago as a version of the Machiavel or of the Vice: types of characters commonly encountered on the Elizabethan stage and types upon which Shakespeare had himself previously constructed a series of brilliant variations, in characters such as Richard III, Falstaff, the Bastard in *King John*, and Edmund in *King Lear*. The Machiavel and the Vice have a genealogy reaching back into classical drama, where we discover their forebears in the trickster,

149. *Othello*, II.i.271–82.
150. Coleridge, *Lectures*, 2:315.

or the clever servant of Terentian comedy. Often out of malice, sometimes out of a more innocent desire to create mischief, these characters set in motion and direct what we can think of as small plays set within the larger plays of which they are a part, in order to bring about certain well-defined outcomes. When we compare Iago with these models, however, we notice that he diverges from them, not only in respect of his equivocal and shifting motivation but also in respect of his control of events. A Machiavel such as Shakespeare's Richard III or Marlowe's Barabbas typically exerts an almost prescient control over events, up to the moment when their plots unravel and a reassuring morality is asserted (with whatever degree of conviction or persuasiveness) by the playwright. The other characters in the play are reduced to being little more than their puppets, while they themselves become almost playwrights within the play.

But Iago is never able to achieve this degree of control. From the outset, he has only a cloudy understanding of both his methods and his course of action. Time and again, he has to improvise and exploit unforeseen opportunities, such as the accident of Roderigo's anger in act IV, scene ii, or (even more strikingly) the fact that in act IV, scene i, Bianca should arrive onstage and throw the handkerchief at Cassio. It is at moments such as these that we understand how precarious is Iago's control over the action. As he says at the end of act V, scene i, musing momentarily on the insecure state of his designs, 'This is the night / That either makes me or fordoes me quite'.[151] Indeed, so fragile is Iago's control over what happens in the play that one is led to wonder whether it takes us very far to think of him as the instigator and administrator of a plot entirely of his own devising. We might do better to see him as increasingly more on a level with Othello himself. That is to say, as the play moves towards its catastrophe, Iago increasingly is reduced to the status of being a party in a process of which he has only a faltering and imperfect understanding.

This cloudiness of motivation is a development crystallised at the end of act III, scene iii. Persuaded that Cassio is the lover of Desdemona, Othello takes a dreadful vow and is joined by Iago:

OTHELLO. Never, Iago! Like to the Pontic Sea,
Whose icy current and compulsive course
Ne'er keeps retiring ebb, but keeps due on
To the Propontic and the Hellespont,

151. *Othello*, V.i.127–28.

Even so my bloody thoughts, with violent pace,
Shall ne'er look back, ne'er ebb to humble love
Till that a capable and wide revenge
Swallow them up. Now, by yond marble heaven,
In the due reverence of a sacred vow
I here engage my words.

IAGO. Do not rise yet.
[IAGO *kneels.*]
Witness, you ever-burning lights above,
You elements that clip us round about,
Witness that here Iago doth give up
The execution of his wit, hands, heart,
To wronged Othello's service. Let him command,
And to obey shall be in me remorse,
What bloody business ever.

OTHELLO. I greet thy love
Not with vain thanks but with acceptance bounteous,
And will upon the instant put thee to't.
Within these three days let me hear thee say
That Cassio's not alive.

IAGO. My friend is dead.
'Tis done at your request. But let her live.

OTHELLO. Damn her, lewd minx! O, damn her! Damn her!
Come, go with me apart. I will withdraw
To furnish me with some swift means of death
For the fair devil. Now art thou my lieutenant.

IAGO. I am your own for ever.[152]

At that point, the scene ends, and Othello and Iago leave the stage together. This pattern of action is not what the audience has been led to expect. Earlier in the play, Iago is repeatedly left alone onstage at the end of a scene, to deliver a soliloquy direct to the audience in which he gives them access to his inner thoughts. Examples occur at the end of act I, scene iii, act II, scene i, and act II, scene iii. But after that point, Iago is never again given such a speech, even though opportunities for it exist (such as pre-eminently here at the end of act III, scene iii) or might easily be created.

152. *Othello*, III.iii.447–73.

This is a development in Iago's dramatic profile which unfolds its implications in two directions. On the one hand, his character becomes progressively more hidden from the audience, who are reduced to trying to construe behaviour in the light of information once privileged but now steadily scantier and more obsolescent. On the other, Iago's affinity with the models of the Machiavel and the Vice is steadily weakened, because in the case of both those models such speeches of gleeful self-disclosure served almost as a dramatic signature.

If we now return to the end of act III, scene iii, we can understand how enigmatic it is. When Iago swears to Othello, 'I am your own for ever', it would be only a determinedly shallow reading which saw in this profession a simple lie. So to read the line would imply a continued interpretation of Iago as a Machiavel or Vice. But these are both models of character from which, as we have seen, Shakespeare's handling of his character is gradually separating Iago. The truly disturbing aspect of *Othello* is not that Iago hates the Moor but rather that, in a manner which goes far deeper than can be understood in terms of conscious intention or the motives of rational calculating agents, he is genuinely and terribly devoted to him. And the interaction of the two men in the play shows us the familiar comic stage property of a fool being deceived by a trickster undergoing a transformation into the growth of a strange intimacy.

Iago and Othello do nothing less in this play than create a world together. It is a dreadful world, in which what is pure is desecrated and what is good destroyed. But as they create it, so the individuality of each of them is qualified and merged. It is a process in which they are both caught up in a way which exceeds conscious intent and in which they are both eventually broken. Othello's speeches in act IV, scene i, in which the true world of which he has direct experience and the world he has created with Iago out of signs and inferences collide, present us with the spectacle of mental dismemberment acted out in their dispersal between two opposed vocabularies: Desdemona is 'A fine woman! A fair woman! A sweet woman!' who yet must 'rot and perish, and be damned tonight', of 'so gentle a condition' yet who must be chopped 'into messes'.[153] This is the Dionysiac *sparagmos*, performed in language, acted out with painful slowness before our eyes, and stripped of any redemptive or consoling force.

After this, Othello's physical death is the merest formality. Yet even here we find *sparagmos*, or dismemberment. Othello's last speech shows him trying to

153. *Othello*, IV.i.167–68, 170, 181–82, 188.

recapture the man he was before all this began. In T. S. Eliot's measuredly casual phrase, it shows Othello trying to 'cheer himself up':

> Soft you, a word or two before you go.
> I have done the state some service, and they know't—
> No more of that. I pray you, in your letters,
> When you shall these unlucky deeds relate,
> Speak of me as I am; nothing extenuate,
> Nor set down aught in malice. Then must you speak
> Of one that loved not wisely, but too well;
> Of one not easily jealous but, being wrought,
> Perplexed in the extreme; of one whose hand,
> Like the base Judean, threw a pearl away
> Richer than all his tribe; of one whose subdued eyes,
> Albeit unusèd to the melting mood,
> Drop tears as fast as the Arabian trees
> Their medicinable gum. Set you down this,
> And say, besides, that in Aleppo once,
> Where a malignant and a turbaned Turk
> Beat a Venetian and traduced the state,
> I took by th'throat the circumcisèd dog
> And smote him thus.
> [*He stabs himself.*][154]

But there is no cheer to be found in these words. Notwithstanding their vivid reminiscences of a time when Othello and the Venetian state (though as we have seen, never truly identical) were nevertheless close, they point to no way back to the earlier, simpler, more sharply-defined and individual Othello who had existed before the play began. For with the blow that takes his life, Othello does not simply become again the untroubled, loyal servant of the state. He also becomes the antagonist of that lost Othello, namely, the malignant Turk who traduced the state. For Othello, there is now no route back to the lost condition of simple individuality.

And Iago? It is sometimes thought that his last line in the play, 'From this time forth I never will speak word', shows an inhuman fortitude in the face of

154. T. S. Eliot, 'Shakespeare and the Stoicism of Seneca', in Eliot, *Selected Essays*, p. 130; *Othello*, V.ii.331–49.

torture.[155] But what could he say? What, in the end, does he know? When asked by Othello for a reason for what has happened, he can say only, 'What you know, you know.'[156] Of course, he could pass on details of what we might call the mechanics of what has happened. But whereas Cinthio's Ensign could say, 'I did this out of frustrated love for Disdemona', or Boito's Jago could say, 'I did this to vindicate my belief that all human life is absurd', Shakespeare's Iago has at that level no alternative to silence.

In retrospect, that it would be so was intimated almost from the outset. Iago's first soliloquy, at the end of act I, scene iii, ends with a metaphor of pregnancy which is itself pregnant with implication:

> I have't! It is engendered. Hell and night
> Must bring this monstrous birth to the world's light.[157]

A mother carrying a child is part of something over which she has imperfect control. The birth will happen when the birth will happen. Iago is just as much a carrier as an agent.

Male pregnancies are rare events, but Greek mythology tells us of one. Zeus carried Dionysos in his thigh. Could Iago's 'monstrous birth' be the birth of the tragic god himself? Boito, for one, sensed the presence of Dionysos in the story of Othello. In the tavern scene, Cassio sings of the 'true bounty of the vine', and Jago invites him to taste 'the draught of Bacchus', *del ditirambo*.[158] Dionysos is abroad in the margins of *Othello*, and his rite is something in which Iago is but an instrument, not a ministrant or even an instigator. But here are none of the consolations so rapturously greeted by Nietzsche in *The Birth of Tragedy*. Here we have only the bleak terrors of the Dionysiac, from which Iago and Othello return in the final scene only to die.

It is for this reason that in *Othello*, Shakespeare can take such extraordinary risks with the dignity of his hero. He based his tragedy on that comic stand-by, the older man with a younger wife. He extended his source materials by adding the character of Roderigo, a fool who nevertheless is more astute than Othello in that he eventually manages to see through Iago's deceptions without assistance. And he has Emilia reproach Othello himself in the final scene as 'O gull! O dolt, / As ignorant as dirt'—language it is difficult to dispute and, moreover,

155. *Othello*, V.ii.297.

156. *Othello*, V.ii.296.

157. *Othello*, I.iii.381–82.

158. Arrigo Boito, *Otello*, act I, scene i.

one would have thought, language which is fatal to Othello's tragic dignity.[159] Shakespeare can take these risks because in the play's central scenes, he addressed so directly the anxieties surrounding individuality and its extinction, anxieties which from the very outset in ancient Greece have been the tap-root of tragedy.

———

I want now to extend what I have just set out concerning the exploration of identity in *Othello* by going back to the comedies Shakespeare had written beforehand. The precursors of much that would later be reworked into *Othello* can be found in those earlier plays, albeit in altered, sometimes simpler, forms. For instance, in *Two Gentlemen of Verona* or *Much Ado About Nothing* or *Love's Labour's Lost*, we are shown that, for heterosexual bonds to be formed, men have to leave the realm of exclusively male friendship in which they have been bred. In *Othello*, that movement is reversed, as an intense male bond supervenes upon and destroys a heterosexual union. In a similar way, the figuring of marriage as 'one flesh' that we see in, for instance, *The Comedy of Errors* is transformed from a relationship between man and wife to one between a general and his ensign.[160]

Much Ado About Nothing seems to have been a particularly rich source of material for *Othello*. At the centre of both plays lies the defamation of an innocent woman. But, beyond that shared fragment of plot, there are other tantalising proximities. *Much Ado* is set in a period of peaceful vacancy after war, when, in the absence of opportunities for fighting, men's thoughts turn instead to love, as Claudio explains to Don Pedro:

When you went onward on this ended action,
I looked upon her with a soldier's eye
That liked, but had a rougher task in hand
Than to drive liking to the name of love.
But now I am returned and that war thoughts
Have left their places vacant—in their rooms
Come thronging soft and delicate desires,

159. *Othello*, V.ii.158–59.

160. *Comedy of Errors*, II.ii.111–47. Cf. Genesis 2:23–24 and Ephesians 5:28–33. Cf. also *Julius Caesar*, II.i.272–73: 'that great vow / Which did incorporate and make us one'.

All prompting me how fair young Hero is,
Saying, I liked her ere I went to wars—[161]

In *Othello* the dispersal of the Turkish fleet transforms Cyprus from a scene of warfare to a post-military society in which it is easy to suggest to Othello that Michael Cassio's mind has, in a Claudio-like way, also been filled with 'soft and delicate desires'. Don John's malice against Claudio has its roots in resentment of this 'most exquisite' younger man, a 'young start-up' that 'hath all the glory of my overthrow'.[162] One element in Iago's hatred of Othello, as he tells Roderigo, is what he sees as the undeserved promotion of Cassio:

Three great ones of the city,
In personal suit to make me his lieutenant,
Off-capped to him—and, by the faith of man,
I know my price: I am worth no worse a place—
But he, as loving his own pride and purposes,
Evades them with a bombast circumstance
Horribly stuffed with epithets of war;
Nonsuits my mediators. For, 'Certes,' says he,
'I have already chose my officer.'
And what was he?
Forsooth, a great arithmetician:
One Michael Cassio, a Florentine,
A fellow almost damned in a fair wife,
That never set a squadron in the field,
Nor the division of a battle knows
More than a spinster—unless the bookish theoric,
Wherein the tonguèd consuls can propose
As masterly as he! Mere prattle without practice
Is all his soldiership.[163]

Not coincidentally, perhaps, both Cassio and Claudio are Florentines.[164] And in *Much Ado About Nothing*, too, we find a sceptical interrogation of identity. For instance, do the plots of Beatrice's and Benedick's friends *release* an

161. *Much Ado*, I.i.253–61. The same pattern, of love succeeding to warfare, is of course to be found in *A Midsummer Night's Dream*: see I.i.1–19.

162. *Much Ado*, I.iii.40 and 54–55.

163. *Othello*, I.i.7–25.

164. *Much Ado*, I.i.9; *Othello*, I.i.18.

attraction to each other that was always there, or rather do they *insert* such an attraction? Mimetic behaviour—that is, when we behave in accordance with how others behave towards us—has been a recurrent source of comic action for Shakespeare, from the deception of Christopher Sly in *The Taming of the Shrew* to the courting of Bottom by Titania in *A Midsummer Night's Dream* and the gulling of Malvolio in *Twelfth Night*. Is identity in *Much Ado* therefore a seed (which already contains its potentialities) or a shell (which needs to be filled from outside)? This dilemma between identity as potential and as vacancy will be repeated and expanded in *Othello*.

Nevertheless, comedy, although frequently preoccupied with questions of identity, tends to conceive of it differently from tragedy. In *Othello* Shakespeare echoed and also inverted his own earlier comic investigations of identity. As we have seen, it was in the strange, dazed, hypnotic dialogue between Othello and Iago in act IV, scene i, that Shakespeare used the exchange of repeated language between the two men to suggest an incipient porosity of identity. As the tragic process begins to take hold, and as the two men pass words to and fro between each other, the carapace of personality that keeps us distinct from one another in ordinary life starts to crack. The aesthetic and dramatic matrix for that moment, however, was formed by the experiments Shakespeare had already made with the unusual effects that can be produced by iterance or verbal repetition in some of the comedies. There, however, repetition had been used to very different effect.

Repetition is a feature of classical literary language that has received careful scholarly attention. The styles of both Homer and Lucretius are marked by repetition, although arguably for different reasons: orality in the case of the former; as a way of underlining particularly important concepts in the case of the latter.[165] However, the repetitions of whole lines and even sequences of lines in the *Aeneid* are particularly striking and helped to establish such repetition as a feature—often, a parodied feature—of epic style.[166] Milton was evidently

165. For commentary, see Gregory Nagy, 'Poetics of Repetition in Homer', in *Greek Ritual Poetics*, ed. D. Yatromanolakis and P. Roilos, Hellenic Studies, vol. 3 (Cambridge, MA: Harvard University Press, 2004), pp. 139–48; and Wayne B. Ingalls, 'Repetition in Lucretius', *Phoenix* 25, no. 3 (1971): 227–36.

166. Instances of extended repetition are relatively plentiful in the *Aeneid*, e.g., I.53–33 = III.163–66; II.792–94 = VI.700–2; III.192–95 = V.8–11; III.390–93 = VIII.43–46; IV.285–86 = VIII.20–21; IV.584–85 = IX.450–60; IX.104–6 = X.113–15; X.745–46 = XII.309–10. For commentary, see Walter

impressed by this element in the stylistic armoury of his epic predecessors, and he used it sparingly, but to wonderful and intelligent effect, in *Paradise Lost.* At the end of Book X, Adam offers comfort to Eve and urges contrition:

What better can we do, than to the place
Repairing where he judg'd us, prostrate fall
Before him reverent, and there confess
Humbly our faults, and pardon beg, with tears
Watering the ground, and with our sighs the Air
Frequenting, sent from hearts contrite, in sign
Of sorrow unfeign'd, and humiliation meek.
Undoubtedly he will relent and turn
From his displeasure; in whose look serene,
When angry most he seem'd and most severe,
What else but favour, grace, and mercy shone?
        So spake our Father penitent, nor *Eve*
Felt less remorse: they forthwith to the place
Repairing where he judg'd them prostrate fell
Before him reverent, and both confess'd
Humbly thir faults, and pardon beg'd, with tears
Watering the ground, and with thir sighs the Air
Frequenting, sent from hearts contrite, in sign
Of sorrow unfeign'd, and humiliation meek.[167]

Milton here takes a prominent but enigmatic feature of the epic style he has inherited from classical literature and aligns it with the Christian doctrine of his own poem. The near-identical repetition of some six and a half lines dramatizes the moral transformation that penitence has brought about in the identities of Adam and Eve. Their actions show that now they are, in a very literal sense, as good as their word. And the effect is deepened for the attentive reader when they recall that this instance of repetition itself echoes an earlier instance of repetition, in Book IV. Eve is explaining to Adam her devotion both to him and to God:

Moskalew, *Formular Language and Poetic Design in the Aeneid* (Leiden: Brill, 1982). For literary parodies of epic formulae, see, e.g., Henry Fielding, *Tom Jones*, bk. II, ch. 4, and bk. IV, ch. 8.

167. Milson, *Paradise Lost*, X.1086–1104.

My Author and Disposer, what thou bid'st
Unargu'd I obey; so God ordains,
God is thy Law, thou mine: to know no more
Is womans happiest knowledge and her praise.
With thee conversing I forget all time,
All seasons and thir change, all please alike.
Sweet is the breath of morn, her rising sweet,
With charm of earliest Birds; pleasant the Sun
When first on this delightful Land he spreads
His orient Beams, on herb, tree, fruit, and flour,
Glistring with dew; fragrant the fertil earth
After soft showers; and sweet the coming on
Of grateful Evening milde, then silent Night
With this her solemn Bird and this fair Moon,
And these the Gemms of Heav'n, her starrie train:
But neither breath of Morn when she ascends
With charm of earliest Birds, nor rising Sun
On this delightful land, nor herb, fruit, floure,
Glistring with dew, nor fragrance after showers,
Nor grateful Evening mild, nor silent Night
With this her solemn Bird, nor walk by Moon,
Or glittering Starr-light without thee is sweet.[168]

If the example of repetition in Book X is an instance in which word and deed perfectly correspond, the fact that that passage itself stands in a relationship of stylistic repetition to these lines from Book IV deepens and complicates its impact. For in the earlier book, Milton has used repetition to mark the reverse of being true to your word, since Eve will incur mortal sin precisely out of a desire to 'know . . . more'; and despite what she says concerning her need for and delight in Adam's company, she will smooth the path towards her fall by demanding that she be allowed to wander in the garden alone.[169]

Repetition is thus not inevitably the sign of authenticity; it may equally be a tool of deception and self-deception. But that Milton frames these two instances of repetition to suggest that repetition is a feature of style that may be redeemed for authenticity of identity is a small hint that those lines of Adam's

168. Milton, *Paradise Lost*, IV.635–56.

169. See Milton, *Paradise Lost*, IX.205–384.

that conspicuously are *not* repeated are not the expression of an entirely empty hope:

Undoubtedly he will relent and turn
From his displeasure; in whose look serene,
When angry most he seem'd and most severe,
What else but favour, grace, and mercy shone?

Redemption is possible for man, and the intimation of such redemption and a return to authenticity of character is made through the redemption of a feature of style.

Something similar to what we see in *Paradise Lost* occurs in act II, scene vii of *As You Like It*. Orlando, desperate to find food to sustain the expiring Adam, bursts in with drawn sword on Duke Senior and the banished lords in their forest lair and demands their food. Duke Senior replies mildly, 'Sit down and feed, and welcome to our table'. Orlando is amazed:

Speak you so gently? Pardon me, I pray you.
I thought that all things had been savage here,
And therefore put I on the countenance
Of stern commandment. But whate'er you are
That in this desert inaccessible
Under the shade of melancholy boughs,
Lose and neglect the creeping hours of time:
If ever you have looked on better days,
If ever been where bells have knolled to church,
If ever sat at any good man's feast,
If ever from your eyelids wiped a tear,
And know what 'tis to pity and be pitied,
Let gentleness my strong enforcement be,
In the which hope I blush and hide my sword.

To which Duke Senior replies with renewed courtesy, albeit intriguingly-phrased courtesy:

True it is that we have seen better days,
And have with holy bell been knolled to church.
And sat at good men's feasts and wiped our eyes
Of drops that sacred pity hath engendered;
And therefore, sit you down in gentleness

And take upon command what help we have
That to your wanting may be ministered.[170]

What is so striking here is the way Duke Senior repeats so much of Orlando's speech. It is not a case of perfect repetition—'looked on better days' becomes 'seen better days', 'bells have knolled to church' becomes 'with holy bell been knolled to', 'any good man's feast' becomes 'good men's feasts'. These slight adjustments can carry significance. When Duke Senior encourages Orlando to 'take upon command what help we have' (i.e., take what you will of what we have), he echoes and corrects Orlando's earlier description of himself as bearing the countenance 'Of stern commandment' (i.e., of physical compulsion). Duke Senior deftly converts Orlando's aggression into his own un-coerced hospitality through the medium of nearly perfect repetition.

But more generally, Duke Senior's modified tracing of the terms and sequences of Orlando's speech makes a different point, namely, that despite their clothing (the stage direction at the beginning of the scene says Duke Senior and the lords enter 'like outlaws'), Orlando has discerned who Duke Senior and his companions truly are. He has recognised their identities, and the courteous return to him of his own language is a reciprocating act of recognition on the part of Duke Senior. So here the repetition of language indicates not the merging of identities but a polite acknowledgement of their separateness and also of their durability through time. Despite the savage adversity into which Duke Senior has fallen, he is still recognisably a civilised man capable of piety, sociability, and sympathy.

Repetition as wary recognition is something we will find again in the late Hardy poem 'He Never Expected Much'. This poem adapts the form of the echo-poem and makes of it a dialogue between the world and the speaker, marked by refrains at the beginning of each of the three stanzas:

Well, World, you have kept faith with me,
        Kept faith with me; . . .
. . . .
'Twas then you said, and since have said,
        Times since have said, . . .
'I do not promise overmuch

170. *As You Like It*, II.vii.106–26.

Child; overmuch; . . .[171]

Here the mode of wistful repetition, shared by both world and speaker, marks the unillusioned yet compassionate understanding by each party of the other's mediocrity.

An instance of an uncanny repetition of language apparently closer to that in *Othello,* and again bearing on the question of identity, occurs in *The Comedy of Errors.* When Antipholus of Syracuse arrives in Ephesus, he comments on his position as a man on a hopeless quest:

I to the world am like a drop of water
That in the ocean seeks another drop,
Who, falling there to find his fellow forth,
Unseen, inquisitive, confounds himself.
So I, to find a mother and a brother,
In quest of them, unhappy, lose myself.[172]

It is a speech full of dramatic irony. This melancholy poet of isolation and self-estrangement is about to be laden with offers of money, hospitality, and sex by perfect strangers. As he will put it wonderingly later in the play, reflecting on his dream-like experience in Ephesus (which of course is the inverse of the nightmare experience his twin brother is having),

There's not a man I meet but doth salute me
As if I were their well-acquainted friend,
And everyone doth call me by my name.
Some tender money to me, some invite me,
Some other give me thanks for kindnesses.
Some offer me commodities to buy.
Even now a tailor called me in his shop,
And showed me silks that he had bought for me,
And therewithal took measure of my body.[173]

Antipholus's sense of bewilderment, however, should only have been intensified when Adriana, mistaking him for her husband, Antipholus of Ephesus, and pleading for him to come home and to leave off his coolness towards her,

171. Thomas Hardy, *Complete Poems,* ed. James Gibson (London: Macmillan, 1976), p. 886.

172. *Comedy of Errors,* I.ii.35–40.

173. *Comedy of Errors,* IV.iii.1–9.

uses the very same metaphor that Antipholus has used to evoke the impossibility of his quest to find his mother and brother:

> How comes it now, my husband, oh, how comes it,
> That thou art then estrangèd from thyself?
> Thy 'self' I call it, being strange to me
> That, undividable, incorporate,
> Am better than thy dear self's better part.
> Ah, do not tear thyself away from me;
> For know, my love, as easy mayst thou fall
> A drop of water in the breaking gulf
> And take unmingled thence that drop again
> Without addition or diminishing,
> As take from me thyself and not me too.[174]

As it is repeated, the metaphor of the drop of water is inflected to capture different aspects of the problem of identity that lie close to the centre of this play. For Antipholus, the image of the single drop of water in the ocean is intended to convey the impossibility of his quest—that is, how to find another single drop that is genuinely 'his fellow' when surrounded by a multitude of indistinguishable possibilities. For Adriana, the metaphor carries different connotations, namely, of the mingling of identities that occurs between husband and wife in a good marriage.

Antipholus seems not to notice—at least, does not respond to—this uncanny iteration of his language by a stranger. But for the attentive audience, it raises the provoking question of precisely how separate and individual the characters are who have been set in motion before us. As the complications of the plot and its manifold instances of mistaken identity mount up, a powerful illusion of the fragility of identity is created, voiced most pithily by Dromio of Syracuse: 'Do you know me, sir? Am I Dromio? Am I your man? Am I myself?'[175] Yet this is, precisely, an illusion.

So Shakespeare's early comedies take a complicated stance on the matter of identity. On the one hand, they offer astringent solvents of the social markers on which we are accustomed to plume ourselves and on which we rest our sense of being separate from those who surround us (*The Taming of the Shrew* is a particularly vivid example of this, as is *A Midsummer Night's Dream*). In

174. *Comedy of Errors*, II.ii.120–30.
175. *Comedy of Errors*, III.ii.73–74.

that respect, these plays affirm a common humanity that is camouflaged, but not destroyed, by accidents of birth or wealth.

However, although they view social difference with scepticism, these plays finally affirm the reality and stability of individual identity. As the confusions of *The Comedy of Errors* are cleared away in the *dénouement*, the characters speak in new, more confident accents:

> I will attend my husband, be his nurse,
> Diet his sickness, for it is my office,
> And I will have no attorney but myself,
> And therefore let me have him home with me.[176]

The apparent confusions of identity through which Adriana has recently lived have had the paradoxical effect of restoring her to a stronger sense of her own identity and self-sufficiency. Now she requires no 'attorney', or proxy. This early comic playing with identity is the seed-bed of the much more radical and sceptical searching of the concept of identity that we encounter in *Othello*.

176. *Comedy of Errors*, V.i.98–101.

2

Barbarism and Civilisation

HAMLET

When King Pyrrhus passed over into Italy, after he had reconnoitred the formation of the army that the Romans were sending to meet him, he said: 'I do not know what Barbarians these are' (for so the Greeks called all foreign nations), 'but the formation of this army that I see is not at all barbarous.'[1]

—MONTAIGNE

IN THE OPENING PARAGRAPHS of his *Politics*, Aristotle disguised a prejudice as a deduction:

> Therefore the impulse to form a partnership of this kind [civil society] is present in all men by nature; but the man who first united people in such a partnership was the greatest of benefactors. For as man is the best of the animals when perfected, so he is the worst of all when sundered from law and justice. For unrighteousness is most pernicious when possessed of weapons, and man is born possessing weapons for the use of wisdom and virtue, which it is possible to employ entirely for the opposite ends. Hence when devoid of virtue man is the most unscrupulous and savage of animals, and the worst in regard to sexual indulgence and gluttony. Justice on the

1. 'Quand le Roy Pyrrhus passa en Italie, après qu'il eut reconnu l'ordonnance de l'armée que les Romains luy envoyoient au devant: "Je ne sçay, dit-il, quels barbares sont ceux-ci (car les Grecs appelloyent ainsi toutes les nations estrangieres), mais la disposition de cette armée qu je voy n'est aucunement barbare"' (Montaigne, 'Des Cannibales', in Montaigne, *Œuvres*, p. 200).

other hand is an element of the state; for judicial procedure, which means the decision of what is just, is the regulation of the political partnership.[2]

Aristotle's apparently uncontroversial statement, that civil society is a perfection of a pre-existing state of barbarism, would enjoy lengthy currency in the West. Although it did not go unchallenged, particularly when the historical nature of barbarism came to be more fully understood in the eighteenth century, it broadly held the field until the late nineteenth century, when the profound implications of the Foucauldian shift whereby man moved from being the ground of investigation to being himself the object of investigation had begun to make themselves felt.[3]

It is within this context of the Western understanding of civilisation and its relationship to what lies outside it that I intend to discuss *Hamlet* and a group of other Shakespearean plays which also have this problematic issue at their core. But before we engage with those dramas, we need to set the intellectual scene.

The Sammlung Schack in Munich contains a large canvas by Joseph von Führich (1800–1876) entitled *Die Einführung des Christentums in die deutschen Urwälder* (1864)—'The Introduction of Christianity to the Primeval German Forest' (figure 1). It is not a very distinguished painting, but it has that common and useful characteristic of second-rate art, namely, the clear display of a single, simple idea, untroubled by interference arising from the operation of too much intelligence.

One reads the painting from left to right. At the extreme upper left, a half-clothed German forest-dweller is hunting what looks to be an auroch, the now extinct giant cattle that lived in the ancient German woods. In the left

2. Aristotle, *Politics*, 1253a.

3. 'Man is neither the oldest nor the most constant problem that has been posed for human knowledge. Taking a relatively short chronological sample within a restricted geographical area—European culture since the sixteenth century—one can be certain that man is a recent invention within it. It is not around him and his secrets that knowledge prowled for so long in the darkness. . . . Man is an invention of recent date' (Michel Foucault, *The Order of Things* [London: Tavistock Publications, 1970], pp. 386–87). Foucault dates the invention of man as an object of knowledge to the early nineteenth century (i.e., 'a century and a half ago' from 1966).

FIGURE 1: Joseph von Führich (1800–1876), *Die Einführung des Christentums in die deutschen Urwälder*, 1864.

foreground, the carcass of a wild boar is hanging from a tree, while a woman with an infant strapped to her back is stirring a cooking pot with a stick, and a naked boy brings wood for the fire. Beside them, a man—presumably the partner of the woman and the father of the boy—is asleep on an animal skin. Near him is a drinking horn and a bird that he has shot with a bow and arrow.

These forest-dwellers seem to have no habitation, with only the bare earth for a floor and the leaves of the trees for shelter. They are recognisably the ancient Germans as described by Tacitus in the *Germania*:

> When they are not entering on war, they spend much time in hunting, but more in idleness—creatures who eat and sleep, the best and bravest warriors doing nothing, having handed over the charge of their home, hearth, and estate to the women and old men and the weakest members of the family: for themselves they lounge about, by that curious incongruity of temperament which makes of the same men such lovers of laziness and such haters of quiet.[4]

4. Tacitus, *Germania*, XV.1–2.

However, this immemorial life is about to be disrupted. Two male figures mark the transition into the central section of the painting. One of them is looking fixedly towards the statue of the Madonna and Child placed in the centre of the image, while his wilder-looking older companion, wearing a horned helmet and grasping a spear, raises a warning or dissuading hand. The representative of an older generation, more steeped in paganism, mounts resistance to the new religion with its strange and paradoxical teachings that the last shall be first and the weak take precedence over the strong. Before the statue of the Madonna a knight kneels in prayer. This is, as it were, the hinge of the painting. It shows Christianity's transformation of German manhood away from the violence, sloth, and carnality on the left-hand side of the canvas and towards the idealism, chivalry, co-operation, and pious reverence we find on the right-hand side.

Moving further rightwards, we first see a monk who is teaching a group of children the doctrine of the Atonement. He is pointing to a crucifix, and a young boy in the foreground wipes away a tear. Behind the monk stands an older girl who also listens and who holds a distaff. The forced employment of children in menial tasks has given place to education, and Christian education has begun to soften and refine the emotional life of the child. Contrast the sullenness in the expression of the boy on the left of the picture, carrying wood, with the visible emotion of his counterparts on the right. The distaff, as well as connoting a distinctly female and creative sphere which is no longer characterised by mere drudgery, hints at the development of material refinement and the transition from hunting to pastoralism (in the far distance we see a flock of sheep, from which the girl has presumably taken her wool). It is striking that the right-hand side of the canvas contains no adult male figure who is not a monk.

Behind this group involved in Bible study we see monks cutting down trees, clearing the forest that the ancient Germans had been happy to leave wild and dense, the better to encourage the wild game on which they fed. Stumps of felled trees dot the ridge behind them. Another monk drives a plough drawn by a cow with full udders: the beast of prey on the left-hand side of the picture has been converted into man's assistant in the establishment of agriculture. That hint concerning a change of diet, away from meat and towards dairy and cereals, is reinforced by what seems to be a watermill in the upper right background of the picture: The innocent products of the field are turned into the staff of life. In the right foreground, a monk stretches to rescue a baby exposed and cast adrift on a shield: Christian charity and humaneness has replaced the cruelty and indifference of ancient paganism. Finally, in the upper right corner of the painting we see a walled, fortified town, with a church prominently at its centre. The advent of Christianity has remodelled the German personality, changed the character of human life, and re-shaped the landscape. It has introduced civilised security, compassion, and the further material and intellectual benefits which those advances make possible. Steady, purposive, collaborative application has supplanted a purposeless, static alternation of furious activity and abject lethargy. Mild, civilised sociability has replaced savage, arboreal isolation. Time itself has been transformed from a cycle of repetition to a line of progress.

Führich was celebrated for his pious canvasses, and to that extent this painting is typical of his output. However, it is not so much the historical role that Führich attributes to Christianity that interests me here as a deeper premise or assumption which is articulated through the insistent, point-by-point parallelism organising the details on either side of the painting. That premise is that the arrival of civilisation involves a thorough perfecting of the primitive life which preceded it, and furthermore that civilisation alone is what permits human beings to lead happy, healthy, productive lives.

This assumption concerning the nature and historical role played by civilisation—what Freud would describe as 'the enthusiastic prejudice [das enthusiastiche Vorurteil] which holds that our civilisation is the most precious thing that we possess or could acquire and that its path will necessarily lead to heights of unimagined perfection'—is common to the point almost of being inescapable.[5] But in fact it is neither quite immemorial nor perfectly ubiquitous. It has a history, and to trace that history we need to go back to ancient Greece.

Herodotus begins his account of the interactions between the Hellenes and the other ancient peoples who inhabited the eastern Mediterranean by stating it as his even-handed intention 'that great and marvellous deeds done by Greeks and foreigners and especially the reason why they warred against each other may not lack renown.'[6] The Greek word here translated as 'foreigners' is βαρβάροισι, 'barbarians'. Herodotus uses the term simply to refer to all those who are not Hellenes and who thus do not speak Greek.[7] Therefore, at the moment when the opposition between barbarism and civilisation entered the Western intellectual tradition, there was no simple or necessary hierarchy of

5. Freud, *Civilization*, p. 339.

6. Herodotus, I.1.

7. For a similarly non-censorious use of the word βαρβαρων to mean simply 'foreigners', see Plato, *The Republic*, bk. VI, 494d.

value between its two poles. It referred simply to a difference in linguistic ethnography, albeit a difference which drew in its wake further important differences of politics and culture.

Aeschylus's *The Persians* is akin to Herodotus in its extension of a measure of sympathy towards the barbaric. Indeed, Aeschylus's recognition that the barbaric might furnish material for tragedy is in itself a gesture of respectful acknowledgement to the opponents against whom he had fought at Marathon.[8] In the *Oresteia*, Aeschylus composed a drama of the emergence of civilisation (comprising the rule of law, a commitment to due process, and the abandonment of primitive notions of retribution, blood-guilt, and indelible pollution). But in that trilogy, civilisation arose not in opposition to the barbaric but rather from within the Hellenic world itself. There are no barbarians in the *Oresteia*.[9]

So for Aeschylus, as for Herodotus, the barbarian was not the primitive opposite of the civilised Greek. On the contrary. Given that the barbarian was Oriental, he was very possibly more advanced than his Hellenic antagonist, at least in material terms. But in becoming advanced, the Oriental barbarian had also become corrupted by luxury and consequently had lost or forgotten much of the virtue he had originally possessed. For Herodotus, it followed, it was the Hellene who was virtuously primitive, not the barbarian. Furthermore, Herodotus's Hellene recognises that his original, pristine, rustic virtues are the safeguard of his liberty, and consequently he cherishes them.[10] Hence Aristotle's political definition of the barbarian as a slave by nature, who does not live in a free city but is ruled by god-kings living apart from their subjects in palaces

8. For a well-balanced summary of the presence in this play of both 'the linked oppositions of tyranny and democracy, barbarian and Athenian' and 'the lauding of Athens and the values that led to triumph, and the extensive *mourning* for the enemy victims of that triumph', see Simon Goldhill, 'Battle Narrative and Politics in Aeschylus' *Persae*', in Harrison, *Greeks*, pp. 50–61.

9. There are, however, 'barbaric' Greeks: Hall, *Barbarian*, pp. 204–9. For an overview from a variety of standpoints of the whole topic of the relation between the Hellenic and the barbaric, see Harrison, *Greeks*. Harrison's later article 'Reinventing the Barbarian', *Classical Philology* 115 (2020): 139–63, offers a shrewd analysis of the development of the scholarly conversation on the question of the Hellenic and the barbaric over the preceding two decades.

10. Cf. Pausanias's witticism after the Greek victory at Plataea, when he has a meal prepared according to the Persian fashion and another according to the Spartan and invites his commanders to compare them, saying, 'Gentlemen, I asked you here in order to show you the folly of the Persians, who, living in this style, came to Greece to rob us of our poverty' (Herodotus, IX.82).

and who is governed as if he were a slave, even if his king does not in fact own him as he might a chattel or a serf.[11]

The surprising degree of parity within difference between Hellenes and Oriental barbarians we find in Aeschylus and Herodotus returns in a slightly altered form between Romans and northern barbarians in Tacitus's *Germania*, the most valuable ethnographic text that has come down to us from antiquity. In the *Germania*, those who lie outside the pale of Roman civilisation are now the northern, rather than the Oriental, barbarians. However, the *Germania* is an account of the German tribes coloured by imperial anxiety, and as such it is far from dispassionate. Tacitus is quite aware that the Germans are materially and technologically backward. They have not learned how to use stone or tiles in their buildings, they have hardly any iron, and the most elementary aspects of commercial life are unknown to them: 'To exploit capital and to increase it by interest is unknown; and the principle is therefore better observed than if it had been actually forbidden.'[12] How, then, could such a primitive people pose a potentially mortal threat to the empire?

Tacitus's implicit answer to this question is twofold. On the one hand, he contrasts the moral purity of the Germans with the decadence that has overtaken imperial Rome. Amongst the Germans, 'the marriage tie is strict: you will find nothing in their character to praise more highly. They are almost the only barbarians who are content with a wife apiece.'[13] The imperviousness of the Germans to moral corruption made them formidable on the battlefield. But it also placed them outside history. In the *Germania*, the barbarians experience time only as duration: as a repetitious cycle of unchanging activities, never as development, still less as purposive change. Tacitus depicts the ancient Germans locked in an eternal present of lethargy, gluttony, drunkenness, and violence:

> On waking from sleep, which they generally prolong into the day, they wash, usually in warm water, since winter bulks so large in their lives: after washing they take a meal, seated apart, each at his own table: then, arms in hand, they proceed to business, or, just as often, to revelry. To make day and night run into one in drinking is a reproach to no man: brawls are frequent,

11. Aristotle, *Politics*, I, 1252a–b.

12. Tacitus, *Germania*, XVI.3 (ignorance of the uses of stone), VI.1 (lack of iron), XXVI.1 (quotation).

13. Tacitus, *Germania*, XVIII.1.

> naturally, among heavy drinkers: they are seldom settled with abuse, more often with wounds and bloodshed.[14]

It was their ignorance of letters and money that had bound the primitive Germans to this hamster-wheel of sleeping, eating, drinking, and fighting. This is the way of life depicted by Führich on the left-hand side of *Die Einführung des Christentums in die deutschen Urwälder*.

The politics of the barbarian have also changed in the *Germania*. The slavish despotism of the Oriental barbarian has been replaced by the boisterous liberty of the northern barbarian, and as a result, barbarism has been transformed from the embodiment of empire to its freedom-loving antagonist. The opposition between Hellenic virtue and barbaric corruption has mutated in Tacitus into one between Roman corruption and barbaric virtue. At the same time, the separation of the barbaric from the imperial—characteristics we found conjoined in Herodotus and Aeschylus—had, as its necessary corollary, formed a new association between the barbaric and the pre-civilised, which would prove to be extremely durable.

The advent of Christianity added further complications. Even if in Herodotus there was no necessary hierarchy of development in the distinction between barbaric and civilised, his history was nevertheless narrated from within an Helleno-centric perspective, for to the Hellenes, the Oriental barbarians were different, remote, and strange—at once intimidating, impressive, and contemptible. However, the third Gothic sack of Rome in 410 AD generated one of the most vivid images of late antiquity and one that marked an important inflection of the relationship between the civilised and the barbaric. The Gothic leader Alaric, hearing that one of his soldiers had found and seized the sacred plate of St. Peter, immediately commanded that the treasure be returned to the basilica of the Apostle. The Spanish historian Paulus Orosius described the scene that followed:

> Consequently the gold and silver vessels were distributed, each to a different person; they were carried high above the head in plain sight, to the wonder of all beholders. The pious procession was guarded by a double line of drawn swords; Romans and barbarians in concert raised a hymn to God in public. In the sacking of the City the trumpet of salvation sounded far and wide and smote the ears of all with its invitation, even those lying in hiding. From every quarter the vessels of Christ mingled with the vessels

14. Tacitus, *Germania*, XXII.1–2.

of Peter, and many pagans even joined the Christians in making profession, though not in true faith. In this way they escaped, but only for a time, that their confusion might afterward be the greater. The more densely the Roman refugees flocked together, the more eagerly their barbarian protectors surrounded them. O sacred and inscrutable discernment of the divine judgment![15]

The image of the fierce barbarians refraining from pillaging the sacred vessels and giving safe conduct to the Christians of Rome (for the Goths too by this time are the co-religionists of the population of the city they have sacked, albeit in an heretical Arian form: hence Orosius's 'etsi non fide', not in *true* faith) not only underlines the confluence of Christian barbarism and Christian civilisation. It also shows the barbarian leaving behind him the seemingly eternal state of alternating idleness and blind activity described by Tacitus and painted by Führich. The barbarian enters history by means of his interactions with civilisation, church, and empire.

By the fifth century AD, imperial and barbarian interactions had increased to the point where the barbarians were to some extent the partners of the Romans in both empire and religion, a development crystallised in Orosius's image of 'a double line of drawn swords' and the detail of the Romans and barbarians in concert publicly raising a hymn to God. Barbarians had long served in the imperial armies. Barbarians had even become emperors. As recently as 409 AD, Attalus, the praefect of the city, had been created emperor by the joint action of Goths and Romans; and Alaric himself has been called almost an 'Elder Statesman' of Rome.[16] The barbarians were no longer, as they had been for Tacitus, those who lived beyond the frontiers (*limes*) of empire. With the collapse of Roman authority in the West in 476 AD and the claiming of the ancient title of *patrician* by the Ostrogothic king Odoacer, the distinction between the northern barbarians and Roman civilisation to the south had become almost a distinction without a difference.

This assimilation of the northern barbarians within the pale of civilisation would be strengthened many centuries later by the Crusades. Those expeditions undertaken by Western Christendom to recover the Holy Places were

15. Orosius, *Adversus paganos historiarum libri septem*, VII.39. For a later account, see Gibbon, *Decline*, 2:202–5.

16. Peter Brown, *Augustine of Hippo: A Biography* (Berkeley: University of California Press, 2000), p. 286. Cf. also W. Goffart, *Barbarians and Romans AD 418–584: The Techniques of Accommodation* (Princeton, NJ: Princeton University Press, 1980).

often represented as a struggle between civilised 'Europeans' (a term which, as deployed by Pius II and others in the fifteenth century, now gained currency) and Islamic barbarians, particularly after the fall of Constantinople in 1453. So once again the barbaric opposite of civilisation had shifted. It had returned to the Middle East, where we found its roots in the fifth century BC. But it had acquired, at least for a while, a new religious connotation, as the suddenly common phrase 'barbari infideles' suggests: 'It became common practice to refer to all Muslim peoples as barbarians, regardless of their particular cultural characteristics.'[17]

However, the term 'barbari' was still available to be used to refer to northern, Germanic peoples, particularly on the lips of Italians. The final chapter of Machiavelli's *The Prince* (published 1532; substantially composed before 1513) is entitled '*An exhortation to deliver* Italy *from the Barbarians*'. It is a plea to Lorenzo de' Medici to build on the example of Cesare Borgia and restore Italy to its former glory:

> And poor *Italy* left half dead, expecting who would be her *Samaritan* to bind up her wounds, put an end to the Sackings and devastations in *Lombardy*, the Taxes and Expilations in the Kingdom of *Naples*, and *Tuscany*, and cure her sores, which length of time had fester'd and imposthumated. . . . There is not, there is not any body but abhors, and nauseates this barbarous domination.[18]

Uppermost in Machiavelli's mind are the recent military reversals suffered by the Italians at the hands of foreigners.[19] But behind these recent disasters

17. See Noel Malcolm, *Useful Enemies: Islam and the Ottoman Empire in Western Political Thought, 1450–1750* (Oxford: Oxford University Press, 2019), pp. 7–19 (quotation on p. 19). Malcolm draws particularly on the work of Benjamin Weber, *Lutter contre les Turcs: Les formes nouvelles de la croisade pontificale au XVe siècle* (Rome: École française de Rome, 2013).

18. Machiavelli, *The Prince*, ch. 26, in Machiavelli, *Works*, pp. 234–35. Later English Machiavellians, such as James Harrington, would also disparage the 'ill features of Government' introduced into the western provinces of the former Roman Empire by the northern barbarians: a contamination for which the responsibility lay at the door of those, such as Julius Caesar, who had transformed the Roman government from a republic to an empire and had thereby paved the way for its eventual collapse (Norbrook, *Republic*, p. 37).

19. Specifically, the defeat at Fornovo in 1495, the conquest of Alessandria in 1499, the sack of Capua by the French in 1501, the suppression of the Genoan revolt against the French in 1507, the battle of Agnadello in 1509, the capture of Bologna by the French in 1511, and the destruction of Mestre and the routing of the Venetians by the Spanish in 1513.

loomed the much larger calamity of the Roman loss of empire in the West. That was the primal, ancient catastrophe which Machiavelli longed to reverse. *The Prince* was a call for the work of Italian regeneration to begin, while the *Discourses* (published 1531; composed ca. 1517) expounded the principles, derived from Livy, that might keep the restored state in good health.

Was such a rewinding of history really feasible? After a thousand years and thirty generations, were not the Italians themselves now more the descendants of barbarians than they were of those ancient Romans who had conquered most of the known world? Elsewhere in Europe during the sixteenth century, the fact of barbarian descent might prompt not dismay but satisfaction. In France, legal thinkers in particular had realised that they were the beneficiaries of a 'massive but partial replacement of Roman by barbaric culture'; and so they were naturally moved to inquire 'what the latter was and how it had displaced the former.'[20] It was in pursuing the concept of barbarism and by tracing the interactions of those who were called barbarians with civilisation that early modern intellectual culture acquired a discriminating sense of its own past and of its own complicated genealogy.

For, as legal scholars such as François Hotman in texts such as *Franco-Gallia* (1573) explored the ramifications of what they, without exception, characterised as a great catastrophe, they were in the same breath obliged to acknowledge the barbarian as their forebear. In antiquity—for Herodotus and Tacitus, say—the barbarian had been contemporary yet remote in space, dwelling either eastward of the Hellespont or beyond the northern borders of the *imperium*. In the early modern period, those characteristics were reversed. Now, the barbarian was remote in time and yet also in another sense closer to us, because he was our own ancestor. As a result of the passage of time, threads of barbarism were somewhere woven within the more civilised identity of the early modern man. The barbarian was no longer a geographical other who required to be fought and resisted here and now but rather a more equivocal figure from the past who could not easily be disentangled from the latter-day scholars who studied him. The barbarian was now temporally distant but genetically present. As Hume would note in 'Of the Standard of Taste', 'We are

20. Pocock, *Barbarism*, 3:262. On the preservation of elements of barbaric culture in legal systems and on the Renaissance recovery of those vestiges of barbarism by means of philological scholarship, see D. R. Kelley, *The Foundations of Modern Historical Scholarship* (Princeton, NJ: Princeton University Press, 1970); and also the same author's *The Human Measure: Social Thought in the Western Legal Tradition* (Cambridge, MA: Harvard University Press, 1990).

apt to call *barbarous* whatever departs widely from our own taste and apprehension: But soon find the epithet of reproach retorted on us.'[21] The result was a moment of puzzled introspection, in the manner of Rimbaud's famous realisation of self-estrangement in his letter of 13 May 1871 to Georges Izambard: 'Je est un autre.'[22]

What this introspection eventually provoked was a history and a theory of barbarism and its relation to eighteenth-century European civilisation, to be fully developed only in the later Enlightenment. It was a history in which the barbarian played a complex role. On the one hand, he had driven out and replaced the exhausted culture of ancient empire. On the other, he had contributed his own originally barbaric energy (an attachment to a form of negative liberty more turbulent than the positive *libertas* of the ancient republics because less related to the practice of *virtus* and the condition of being a citizen) to a subsequent process of civilisation which had eventually given birth certainly not to empires on the plan of antiquity but rather to what Gibbon, following Hume, would describe as the republic of Christian and commercial monarchies which made up modern Europe.[23]

However, during the later Enlightenment, there arose a growing interest in the possibility of the recrudescence of a new kind of barbarism from within the matrix of civilisation, albeit barbarism in an altered, outwardly more suave and more cultivated, but therefore possibly more insidious, form. In 1757, Antoine-Yves Goguet in his *De l'Origine des loix, des arts, et des sciences* had refurbished a biblical historical template and had presented barbarism, not as an original condition but rather as the social state into which the descendants of Noah had fallen after they had been dispersed over the earth following the destruction of the Tower of Babel. Barbarism was therefore subsequent, rather than prior, to civilisation: 'Ces transmigrations dûrent altérer considérablement ce qu'on avoit pû conserver des connoissances primitives. Les sociétés se trouvant rompues par la diversité du langage, & les familles demeurant isolées, la plûpart tomberent bien-tôt dans une profonde ignorance. . . . Il a été un tems où presque toute la terre fut plongée dans une barbarie extrême.'[24]

21. Hume, *Essays*, p. 227.

22. Arthur Rimbaud, *Œuvres complètes*, 'Éditions de la Pléiade' (Paris: Gallimard, 1972), p. 249.

23. Gibbon, *Decline*, 2:512–13. Cf. David Hume, 'Of the Rise and Progress of the Arts and Sciences', in Hume, *Essays*, pp. 118–21.

24. Goguet, *Origine*, 1:3.

Earlier writers had also toyed with the idea of barbarism as degeneration rather than primitivism. In part 4 of *Gulliver's Travels,* Swift had at first been tempted to suggest that the Yahoos were not the aboriginal inhabitants of the land of the Houyhnhnms but rather were the degenerate descendants of two English people who had arrived there many centuries beforehand, when he makes Gulliver refer to the report of 'the two Yahoos, said to have been seen many Ages ago on a Mountain in Houyhnhnmland, from whence the Opinion is, that the Race of those Brutes hath descended; and these, for any thing I know, may have been English, which indeed I was apt to suspect from the Lineaments of their Posterity's Countenances, although very much defaced.'[25] The idea of barbarism as degeneration would endure into the following century. In *Götterdämmerung,* Hagen, the offspring of the dwarf Alberich and Queen Grimhild, summons the Gibichungs to celebrate the twin marriages of Gunther to Brunnhilde and Gutrune to Siegfried and promises them an unmistakably barbaric feast of game and drunkenness.[26] Hagen is a barbarian, but he is not at all primitive, as his mastery of the advanced skills of deception and scheming demonstrates. We have travelled far from the comatose figure on the left of Führich's picture.

Valmont and Mme de Merteuil, in Laclos's *Les Liaisons dangereuses* (1782), would be further examples of this new type of the human personality, in which the civilised and the barbaric were so disconcertingly fused. On the one hand, Laclos's protagonists are extremely sophisticated products of a highly-developed civilisation. But, on the other, they are feral predators whose appetites have been complicated (but neither softened nor rendered socially beneficial) by the laborious trek made by the societies of western Europe from the left-hand to the right-hand side of Führich's canvas. This camouflaging of an unreformed inward ethical savagery within the trappings of outward refinement conferred upon barbarism a new and alarming power to devastate afresh the fragile achievements of civilisation.

For some, especially in England, the French Revolution seemed to be just such an outbreak of a new barbarism, more pernicious than the old because it had equipped moral blindness with an efficiency born of an amoral intellectual refinement. This new barbarism deployed the *techne,* but was a stranger to the humanitarian ethics, of the Enlightenment. From the very outset of the

25. Swift, *Gulliver,* p. 718. This was the text of this passage in part 4, chapter 12, that was published in all the pre-1735 editions of *Gulliver's Travels.*

26. Wagner, *Götterdämmerung,* II.iii.1111–29.

revolution—from before the Terror of 1793 and 1794, from before the execution of Louis XVI in 1793, from before even the September Massacres of 1792—Burke had painted the revolution in the colours of barbarism. The revolutionaries had forged a 'barbarous philosophy, which is the offspring of cold hearts and muddy understandings.'[27] Their reckless political and moral experiments promised to retrace the progressive course of centuries and to create 'a nation of gross, stupid, ferocious, and at the same time, poor and sordid barbarians, destitute of religion, honour, or manly pride, possessing nothing at present, and hoping for nothing hereafter'—a new race of barbarians, that is to say, even worse than those who had overrun the Roman Empire, because devoid of the characteristic barbaric virtues of religion, honour, and manliness (although similarly lacking in a sensitivity towards the rights of property and thus unmotivated towards progress).[28] In their policy of systematic expropriations, the revolutionaries of France had again outstripped the barbarians of the Dark Ages, for 'few barbarous conquerors have ever made so terrible a revolution in property.'[29] In the *Second Letter on a Regicide Peace* (1796), Burke would quote approvingly from the joint manifesto of the Emperor and the King of Prussia which had been published in 1792, and in which they had expressed the fear that the Revolution threatened the whole of Europe with 'the return of barbarism.'[30]

This late-Enlightenment anxiety concerning the return of the barbarian in a new and disturbing guise was accompanied by another shift of emphasis within the broad discursive field of barbarism and civilisation. As we have seen, from antiquity onwards, thinkers had tended to posit civilisation as the *telos* of the historical process. When civilisation is conceived as the goal towards which history is moving, it is easy for it to seem unnecessary to ask the question of what precisely civilisation is. However, in the late

27. Edmund Burke, *Reflections on the Revolution in France*, in Burke, *Writings*, 4:128. Cf. also p. 263, where Burke expresses his distaste for the 'barbarous metaphysics' of the revolutionaries.

28. Burke, *Writings*, 4:131. Burke is sometimes portrayed as an enemy of Enlightenment, so it is worth pointing out here how indebted he is for his sociology of barbarism and his understanding of the causes of social progress to unquestionable Enlightenment thinkers such as Hume and Adam Smith. Burke did not see the revolution as a natural, still less an inescapable, product of Enlightenment, no matter what role had been played by the *philosophes* in bringing it about. It was rather a mischievous perversion of Enlightenment.

29. Burke, *Writings*, 4:165.

30. Edmund Burke, *Second Letter on a Regicide Peace*, in Burke, *Writings*, 9:266.

Enlightenment we discover a new self-consciousness about civilisation itself, and this is marked by a development in the use of the word, at least in English. 'Civilisation' entered the English language in the mid-seventeenth century, but for the first century of its life it is used to refer solely to the action or process of becoming civilised.[31] In the 1760s, the meaning of the word was extended in two significant directions. In the first place, it began to be used to denote the state or condition of being civilised, as opposed to being primitive or barbarous.[32] And then, at almost the same moment, 'civilisation' began to be used without that implicit comparison with an alternative, inferior condition. The word could now denote simply the culture, society, and general way of life characteristic of *any* community (including communities that would normally have been classified as barbaric).[33] It may have been this complication in the meaning of the word that led Matthew Arnold, a writer always alert to nuance, to write in 1868 a book entitled *Culture and Anarchy*, rather than one entitled *Civilisation and Anarchy*.

The meaning of words is stretched in order to satisfy a felt, but currently unmet, expressive need.[34] That is to say, words change their meanings because people sense that they wish to use them in different ways and to address new and unfamiliar objects. For as long as the early modern teleology of barbarism and civilisation remained apparently unproblematic, 'civilisation' referred to nothing more than the process of movement from barbarism to something better. Indeed, the word seems to have been coined to refer precisely to this process. But once the implications of the Enlightenment's insights concerning barbarism and civilisation had been pondered—insights which had their roots in the findings of the humanist legal scholarship of the French Renaissance, which had discovered that western European civilisation was in large measure a creation of and by barbarism and which warned furthermore that variants of barbarism might revive within the matrix of an outwardly refined and civilised society—language was forced by those who used it to adapt to these new

31. *OED*, 1: first recorded usage, 1656.

32. *OED*, 3a: first recorded usage, 1760.

33. *OED*, 3b and c: first recorded usages, 1767 and 1811, respectively.

34. Cf. Montesquieu, *Esprit des lois* (1748), 'Author's Foreword' (first published in the 1757 edition): 'J'ai eu des idées nouvelles; il a bien fallu trouver de nouveaux mots, ou donner aux anciens de nouvelles acceptions'; 'I have had new ideas; new words have had to be found or new meanings given to old ones' (Montesquieu, *Esprit des lois*, 3 vols. [London, 1757], 1:lxxxiii–lxxxiv).

conditions of need, and the semantics of 'civilisation' were accordingly complicated.

On the one hand, the semantic innovation which suddenly surrounded the word 'civilisation' was summoned into existence by optimism and confidence, as Vincenzo Ferrone has noted:

> No less meaningful was the simultaneous appearance of the term 'civilisation' (*civilisation, Zivilisation, civiltà*) in Enlightenment circles in France, Britain, Germany and Italy at the end of the 1750s. This neologism . . . summarized the very essence of the new style of thought of the Enlightenment. It encapsulated its claim to universality and its view of the philosophy of history. The latter was seen at one and the same time as an evolutionary process ordered by stages that ran from the natural society of savages, through the violent society of barbarians, before reaching modern civil society, and also as a project for the future cultural transformation of man and society away from their *Ancien Régime* models.[35]

This was the normative use of the word 'civilisation', which as we have seen arrived in English in 1760 and in which the word refers to a moral and political ideal: in Ferrone's words, 'a society without slaves, that was cosmopolitan, egalitarian, and founded on justice, the rule of law, and the rights of man.'[36]

But, as we have also seen, that new and implicitly optimistic meaning was closely followed into the world by a less well-favoured semantic sibling, in which 'civilisation' no longer referred narrowly to an ideal but rather pointed more broadly and neutrally towards a social or cultural configuration of whatever kind or quality, either good or bad. That further meaning had been summoned into existence by the way in which the late Enlightenment had confused the categories of barbarousness and civilisation to the point where the distinction between them was no longer clear. A good example of this instability occurs when Herder discussed the barbarian invasions of the Roman Empire:

> We may rejoice, that people of such a strong, handsome, and noble form, chaste manners, generosity, and probity, as the germans, possessed the roman world, instead perhaps of huns or bulgarians: but on this account to

35. Vincenzo Ferrone, *The Enlightenment: History of an Idea* (Oxford: Oxford University Press, 2015), p. 111.

36. Ferrone, *Enlightenment*, p. 111.

esteem them God's chosen people in Europe, to whom the World belongs in right of their innate nobility, to whom other nations were destined to be subservient in consequence of this preeminence, would be to display the base pride of a barbarian. The barbarian lords it over those whom he has vanquished: the polished conqueror civilizes those whom he subdues.[37]

Were the ancient Germans barbarians or civilisers? If they were both, as Herder seems to suggest, what were the implications of that ambiguity for the distinction between barbarism and civilisation? By 1850, the issue of the cultural superiority of the Germans over the peoples living to the east of them could be raised by Wagner in a much starker form and without Herder's saving sense of moderation. In act I of *Lohengrin*, King Heinrich warns the men of Brabant that they too must contribute to defend 'das Deutsche Reich' from the danger posed by the Hungarians:

With wild threats the foe prepares for war.
Now the time has come to guard the kingdom's honour;
East and West—all of us share the task!
Let all who are German be prepared to fight,
Then none will ever again affront German soil![38]

Nevertheless, and notwithstanding that later coarsening of the matter, once Herder's question had been raised the way lay clear for the arrival of the more expansive, non-hierarchical meaning of 'civilisation' which was suddenly necessary. At the same time, analytic attention was focused away from barbarism and towards the newly-problematic and elusive category of civilisation itself.

What, after all, was civilisation? The question was posed explicitly by the author of *An Essay on Civilisation*, published in 1841 but allegedly composed 'thirty years ago':

The end to which all legislators have proposed to lead their respective nations is civilisation, yet strange as it may seem, no body of legislators whatever has attempted to define what civilisation means. There has, therefore, been no standard by which it could be determined, whether their public acts, or individual conduct, promoted or impeded their object; nor any rule by which it could be ascertained, whether they were nearer to it at one

37. J. G. von Herder, *Outlines of a Philosophy of the History of Man*, trans. T. Churchill (London, 1800), p. 489. Idiosyncratic capitalisation as in this translation.

38. Wagner, *Lohengrin*, I.i.

> period than another. . . . The natural consequence of this ignorance and levity in legislators is, that they have gone on, from generation to generation, producing anarchy instead of government; and it might have been expected, that according to the unnatural systems by which they have been ruled, the majority of all countries should have continued in a state of demi-barbarism.[39]

The strange medicine of radical levelling, utilitarianism, and birth control advocated as a remedy for 'demi-barbarism' by the author of this short pamphlet is, for our purposes, less interesting than the evidence it supplies for the new and perplexing salience of the concept of civilisation. As the nineteenth century progressed, it was increasingly civilisation rather than its barbarous antagonist that needed to be examined and understood. To what end or ends did civilisation tend? How secure were its achievements? Was it a natural state towards which humanity necessarily gravitated? Or was it rather something profoundly unnatural imposed on a human nature which, beneath its recently-acquired veneer of decorum and order, remained incorrigibly primitive?

Five years before this anonymous essay was published, John Stuart Mill, stimulated by his reading of the first volumes of Tocqueville's *De la Démocratie en Amérique* (1835), had been moved to contribute an essay entitled 'Civilization' to the *London and Westminster Review*, where it was published as the lead article in the issue for April 1836. Mill, too, chose as the keynote for his essay the ambivalence of civilisation, which he called a 'word of double meaning': 'It sometimes stands for human improvement in general, and sometimes for certain kinds of improvement in particular.'[40] This range of meaning in the word corresponded with an ambivalence of value in the thing itself, which had led to doubt arising as to the value of civilisation: 'the question has been seriously propounded, whether civilization is on the whole a good or an evil?'[41] Withstanding that sceptical tendency, Mill held that civilisation is a good, but he also noted that there were some kinds of good 'which civilization . . . does not provide for, some which it has a tendency . . . to impede.'[42] For Mill it is a sure sign of advancing civilisation that 'power passes more and more from individuals, and small knots of individuals, to masses: that the importance of the

39. Anonymous, *An Essay on Civilisation* (1841), title page and p. 4.
40. Mill, 'Civilization', p. 119.
41. Mill, 'Civilization', p. 119.
42. Mill, 'Civilization', p. 119.

masses becomes constantly greater, that of individuals less.'[43] The effects of civilised cooperation Mill acknowledges to be real and considerable. But he also detected in that principle of civilisation a tendency that suppressed the energies of the individual mind and character. The result was an historical moment of particular peril, for just as the 'spirit of combination . . . has grown up among the working classes', so this has been accompanied by a 'very marked decrease of vigour and energy' amongst the higher classes.[44] The advance of civilisation produces a dwindling of the heroic: 'there is in the opulent classes of modern civilized communities much more of the amiable and humane, and much less of the heroic.' The result is a 'moral effeminacy'.[45] To avert the catastrophe towards which this enfeeblement of the higher classes and this energising of the lower classes pointed, Mill placed his faith in the salvific powers of education. But, following on from his diagnosis, this could not help but seem an inadequate remedy. The threat was more pressing than the offered cure was encouraging.

In the nineteenth century, the possibility of a recurrence of barbarism became an aspect of the larger question of degeneration, a concern which is traceable in earlier nineteenth-century diagnoses of the psycho-pathologies of the crowd and the city and which would be given additional impetus by the advent of evolutionary theory. The publication in 1859 of Darwin's *The Origin of Species* released into society ideas and phrases—of natural selection, of 'the survival of the fittest' (a phrase in fact coined by Herbert Spencer), of the struggle for existence, of the war of nature, of the threat of extinction, and of the production of apparently distinct species by a lengthy process of minute incremental variation—which had the power to influence men's thoughts in areas far beyond zoology and botany.[46] In particular, Darwin's key ideas were quickly applied to questions of human society—so-called social Darwinism.[47]

In chapter 16 of *The Origin of Species*, Darwin had been at pains to bring his book to rest on a consoling prospect of endless progress:

43. Mill, 'Civilization', p. 121.

44. Mill, 'Civilization', pp. 125–26.

45. Mill, 'Civilization', p. 131.

46. Gillian Beer, *Darwin's Plots: Evolutionary Narrative in Darwin, George Eliot and Nineteenth-Century Fiction* (London: Routledge and Kegan Paul, 1983).

47. J. W. Burrow, *The Crisis of Reason: European Thought, 1848–1914* (New Haven, CT: Yale University Press, 2000), pp. 92–108.

> As all the living forms of life are the lineal descendants of those which lived long before the Silurian epoch, we may feel certain that the ordinary succession by generation has never once been broken, and that no cataclysm has desolated the whole world. Hence we may look with some confidence to a secure future of equally inappreciable length. And as natural selection works solely by and for the good of each being, all corporeal and mental endowments will tend to progress towards perfection.[48]

However, interpreters of Darwin were quick to see another implication of evolution, namely, that it might both explain the mechanism, and hint at the likelihood, of regression or degeneration.[49]

Two years before Darwin had published *The Origin of Species*, B. A. Morel had published in Paris his *Traité des Dégénérescences physiques, intellectuelles et morales de l'Espèce humaine et des Causes qui produisent ces Variétés maladives* (1857), a work which would profoundly influence Max Nordau's later and more notorious *Degeneration* (1892). Morel's definition of degeneration is, in its promiscuous mingling of the language of inheritance with that of disease ('germs'), certainly confused:

> The clearest notion we can form of degeneracy is to regard it as *a morbid deviation from an original type*. This deviation, even if, at the outset, it was ever so slight, contained transmissible elements of such a nature that anyone bearing in him the germs becomes more and more incapable of fulfilling his functions in the world; and mental progress, already checked in his own person, finds itself menaced also in his descendants.[50]

So anxiety about the prospect of degeneration was already in the intellectual air before the publication of *The Origin of Species* (we might equally find it in Gobineau's *Essai sur l'inégalité des races humaines*, published between 1853 and 1855). However, Darwin's theory supplied that anxiety with additional fuel and stiffened it with scientific credibility.

48. Charles Darwin, *The Origin of Species*, ed. Gillian Beer (Oxford: Oxford University Press, 1996), p. 395. Although note the more pessimistic comments in the later *The Descent of Man*: 'We must remember that progress is no invariable rule'; and 'Natural selection acts only in a tentative manner' (Charles Darwin, *The Descent of Man* [London: John Murray, 1871], pp. 177 and 178).

49. Daniel Pick, *Faces of Degeneration: A European Disorder, c. 1848–c. 1918* (Cambridge: Cambridge University Press, 1989).

50. Quoted in Max Nordau, *Degeneration* (Lincoln: University of Nebraska Press, 1993), p. 16.

What was the relation between the different kinds of degenerate produced by the pathologies of hyper-civilisation and barbarism? Were these civilised degenerates new types of barbarian, a vicious inflection of the sociological form? Sometimes they might seem to be so. Cesare Lombroso's account of the moment when he had his key insight into criminal anatomy suggests that remembered characteristics of barbarism had shaped his interpretation of what he believed he was merely observing:

> At the sight of that skull, I seemed to see all of a sudden, lighted up as a vast plain under a flaming sky, the problem of the nature of the criminal—an atavistic being who reproduces in his person the ferocious instincts of primitive humanity and the inferior animals. Thus were explained anatomically the enormous jaws, high cheek bones, prominent superciliary arches, solitary lines in the palms, extreme size of the orbits, handle-shaped ears found in criminals, savages and apes, insensibility to pain, extremely acute sight, tattooing, excessive idleness, love of orgies, and the irresponsible craving of evil for its own sake, the desire not only to extinguish life in the victim, but to mutilate the corpse, tear its flesh and drink its blood.[51]

Or was the barbarian rather the *cure* for hyper-civilised degeneration? Might not the pristine energies and virtues hidden beneath the unkempt exterior of the barbarian rescue a civilisation which had become spavined by its own refinement, as similar energies and virtues had already in the fifth century ravaged and eventually renewed the over-ripe civilisation of the Roman Empire?

The urban malaise of alcoholism was a regular locus for this anxiety. In 1895 Legrain would identify alcoholism as one of the social pathologies which were bringing about 'the slow but fatal brutalisation of the individual; intellectual and physical sterilisation of the race with its social consequences: the lowering of the intellectual level and depopulation, indubitable causes of the decline of civilised nations.'[52] Zola's *L'Assommoir* (1877) is the classic nineteenth-century novel of alcoholism, and of course it has a place in a whole series of novels—the 'Rougon-Macquart' series—that take as their fictional axioms the inescapable reality of heredity and regression.

But, as so often, it is a lesser work which reveals the contours of an underlying issue with the greatest clarity. Marie Corelli's *Wormwood* (1890) is on the

51. Quoted in Pick, *Faces of Degeneration*, p. 122.
52. Quoted in Pick, *Faces of Degeneration*, p. 51.

surface an indictment of absinthe-drinking as a social practice which threatens to drag down European civilisation. But Corelli also puts these alternative but arresting sentiments into the mouth of the absinthe-addicted artist Gressonex:

> My friend, I do not judge ill of its [absinthe's] effects!—there you quite mistake me! I say it will help us to recover our brute natures,—and that is precisely what I most desire! Civilization is a curse,—Morality an enormous hindrance to freedom. Man was born a savage, and he is still happiest in a state of savagery. He has been civilized over and over again, believe me, through innumerable cycles of time,—but the savage cannot be gotten out of him, and if allowed to do so, he returns to his pristine condition of lawless liberty with the most astonishing ease! Civilized, we are shackled and bound in a thousand ways when we wish to give the rein to our natural impulses; we should be much more contented in our original state of brutishness and nudity. And contentment is what we want,—and what in our present modes of constrained culture we never get.[53]

Corelli's novel is ostensibly alarmed by the thought that late nineteenth-century European society is 'only half a step away from absolute barbarism!'[54] But, like other late nineteenth-century works of fiction, such as Flaubert's *Salammbô* (1862) or Rider Haggard's *King Solomon's Mines* (1885) or collections of poems such as Leconte de Lisle's *Poèmes barbares* (1862)[55]—works which revel in the garish vivacities and terrifying violences of barbarism—*Wormwood* cannot entirely refuse itself to the possibility that barbarism may offer solace for the intolerable constraints imposed by an etiolated civilisation.

By the end of the nineteenth century, barbarism, which in the eighteenth century Goguet had presented as a degeneration from a state of civilisation,[56] had become the source of terrible natural energies which have the power to destroy an urban culture whose refinement is itself frequently figured as degeneration, as in J. K. Huysmans's *À Rebours* (1884) or Wilde's *The Picture of Dorian Gray* (1890). As early as 1846, Michelet had hailed the rise of the

53. Corelli, *Wormwood*, pp. 255–56.

54. Corelli, *Wormwood*, p. 274.

55. On which see Alison Fairlie, *Leconte de Lisle's Poems on the Barbarian Races* (Cambridge: Cambridge University Press, 1947).

56. See above, p. 93.

working classes as a barbarian invasion with the power to renew an ailing culture: '*Barbares*! Oui, c'est-à-dire pleins d'une sève nouvelle, vivante et rajeunissante. *Barbares*, c'est-à-dire voyageurs en marche vers la Rome de l'avenir.'[57] Sometimes, it is true, this later nineteenth-century vogue for the barbaric could become deeply confused. Giosuè Carducci's *Ode Barbari* (1877, 1882, 1889) celebrate not so much the genuinely barbaric as a pre-Christian classicism. Barbarism here appears to mean nothing more specific than 'pre-modern' and (bizarrely, given the actual religious history of the northern barbarians) 'un-Christian'. Even the well-known poem 'In una chiesa gotica' is less an exploration of 'barbarici tumulti' than an indulgence of invective against the hated 'semetico nume'.[58]

The *fin-de-siècle* was thus a point of balance between fear and craving. But over time the craving came to predominate over the fear. The proximity and imminence of the barbaric came increasingly to be seen as necessary, as invigorating, even perhaps as redeeming. The fiction of Thomas Mann—one thinks of *Buddenbrooks* (1901) or of *The Magic Mountain* (1924)—repeatedly places before us images of the crushing weight of *Kultur* from which his characters long to escape, even if escape means death, as it surely must for Hans Castorp, whom at the end of *The Magic Mountain* we see singing while also charging across an infernal First World War battlefield, too befuddled by explosions to think, fearful and homesick, and yet at the same time exhilarated and animated by joy at his escape from the suffocating ministrations of the sanatorium into which the nineteenth century had transformed civilisation.[59] In *Death in Venice*

57. Jules Michelet, 'À M. Edgar Quinet' (1846), quoted in Anne Green, *Flaubert and the Historical Novel: Salammbô Reassessed* (Cambridge: Cambridge University Press, 1982), pp. 60–61. I owe this reference to the kindness of my Oxford colleague Ritchie Robertson.

58. G. L. Bickersteth, *Carducci: A Selection of His Poems, with Verse Translations, Notes, and Three Introductory Essays* (London: Longmans, 1913), pp. 208 and 210.

59. Thomas Mann, *The Magic Mountain*, trans. John E. Woods (London: Everyman's Library, 2005), pp. 852–53. This moment had been foreshadowed, although without the sobering awareness of Germanic *débâcle*, in Mann's notorious essay of 1914, *Thoughts in Wartime*: 'We were familiar with this world of peace and frivolous manners. . . . A ghastly world that no longer exists—or will not exist once the storm has passed! Wasn't it swarming with vermin of the spirit like maggots? Didn't it seethe and stink of civilization's decay? . . . How could the artist—the soldier in the artist—not have thanked God for the collapse of this peaceful world he was fed up with, just fed up?' 'Wir kannten sie ja, diese Welt des Friedens und der cancanierenden Gesittung . . . Gräßliche Welt, die nun nicht mehr ist—oder doch nicht mehr sein wird, wenn das große Wetter vorüberzog! Wimmelte sie nicht von dem Ungeziefer des Geistes wie von Maden? Gor und stank sie nicht von den Zersetzungsstoffen der Zivilisation? . . . Wie hatte der Künstler,

(1912), the embodiment of European high culture, Von Aschenbach, has a terrible nightmare that is both the enactment of his deepest longings and a shameless challenge to the values he claims to uphold and by reference to which he ostensibly orders his existence.[60] The scenario is evidently Bacchic, but also barbaric; and Mann's novella explores the equal and opposite madnesses both of resisting and of succumbing to those perennial antagonists of the disciplined life of the *polis* and its stifling ethic of *souci de soi.*

The most direct challenge to the Aristotelian prejudice that civilisation is a perfection of what precedes or opposes it was launched in 1929 by Sigmund Freud, in his *Civilization and Its Discontents* (although he had covered similar ground in his work of 1927, *The Future of an Illusion*). In *Civilization and Its Discontents,* Freud explicitly and repeatedly dissociated himself from the axiom that civilisation should be viewed as the perfection of a pre-existing barbarism: 'We have been careful not to fall in with the prejudice that civilization is synonymous with perfecting, that it is the road to perfection preordained for men.'[61] For Freud, civilisation was radically ambiguous. It entailed both the realisation (after a fashion) of fantasies and also the curbing of instincts. It was this doubleness in civilisation, its simultaneous character of fulfilment and frustration, which, according to Freud, made men uneasy within it:

> These things that, by his science and technology, man has brought about on this earth, on which he first appeared as a feeble animal organism and on which each individual of his species must once more make its entry ('oh inch of nature!') as a helpless suckling—these things do not only sound like a fairy tale, they are an actual fulfilment of every—or of almost every—fairy-tale wish. All these assets he may lay claim to as his cultural acquisition. Long ago he formed an ideal conception of omnipotence and omniscience which he embodied in his gods. To these gods he attributed

---

der Soldat im Künstler nicht Gott loben sollen für des Zusammenbruch einer Friedenswelt, die er so satt, so überaus satt hatte!' (Mann, *Reflections*, p. 496).

60. Thomas Mann, *Der Tod in Venedig*, ed. T. J. Reed (Munich: Carl Hanser Verlag, 1983), ch. 5, pp. 73–75.

61. 'Dabei have wir uns gehütet, dem Vorurteil beizustimmen, Kultur sei gleichbedeutend mit Vervollkommnung, sei der Weg zur Vollkommenheit, die dem Menschen vorgezeichnet ist' (Freud, *Civilization*, p. 285). Freud's initial brusque equation of culture and civilisation is no doubt an implicit *riposte* to Mann's hierarchical separation of the two concepts in the opening paragraphs of *Thoughts in Wartime* (Mann, *Reflections*, pp. 493–94).

everything that seemed unattainable to his wishes, or that was forbidden to him. One may say, therefore, that these gods were cultural ideals. To-day he has come very close to the attainment of this ideal, he has almost become a god himself. Only, it is true, in the fashion in which ideals are usually attained according to the general judgement of humanity. Not completely; in some respects not at all, in others only half way. Man has, as it were, become a kind of prosthetic God. When he puts on all his auxiliary organs he is truly magnificent; but those organs have not grown on to him and they still give him much trouble at times. Nevertheless, he is entitled to console himself with the thought that development will not come to an end precisely with the year 1930 A.D. Future ages will bring with them new and probably unimaginably great advances in this field of civilization and will increase man's likeness to God still more. But in the interests of our investigations, we will not forget that present-day man does not feel happy [nicht glücklich fühlt] in his Godlike character.[62]

Civilisation provides shabby, *ersatz* substitutes for the full gratification of fantasy. We long to fly, and civilisation gives us economy-class jet travel. We dream of annihilating space, and civilisation gives us television and Skype. We nurse a desire for eternal life, and civilisation gives us palliative care.[63]

But if Freud finds the benefits of civilisation disappointing and over-sold, the same cannot be said of its discipline, which is direct and uncompromising. In particular, civilisation requires a vigilant policing of physicality. Dirt is abhorred: 'Dirtiness [Unsauberkeit] of any kind seems to us incompatible with civilization. We extend our demand for cleanliness to the human body too. . . . Indeed, we are not surprised by the idea of setting up the use of soap as an actual yardstick of civilization.'[64] As a corollary of this civilised suspicion of physicality, intellectual idealism is installed as the pinnacle of human activity: 'No feature, however, seems better to characterize civilization than its esteem and encouragement of man's higher mental activities [höhere psychischen

62. Freud, *Civilization*, pp. 279 80.

63. 'The dream has been fulfilled. As the dreams of men usually are. The whirring plane has made it [the dream of flight] a disillusioning reality. Flying is a neutral, mechanical experience; you read the paper as you soar godlike in the air' (Thomas Mann, 'Goethe's Faust', in Mann, *Essays*, p. 15).

64. Freud, *Civilization*, pp. 281–82.

Tätigkeiten]—his intellectual, scientific and artistic achievements—and the leading role it assigns to ideas in human life.'[65]

Civilisation demands that human instincts are ruthlessly suppressed: 'it is impossible to overlook the extent to which civilization is built up upon a renunciation of instinct [Triebverzicht], how much it presupposes precisely the non-satisfaction (by suppression, repression or some other means?) of powerful instincts.'[66] The instinct of revenge must yield to the institutions of law:

> The first requisite of civilization, therefore, is that of justice [Gerechtigkeit]—that is, the assurance that a law once made will not be broken in favour of an individual. This implies nothing as to the ethical value of such a law. The further course of cultural development seems to tend towards making the law no longer an expression of the will of a small community—a caste or stratum of the population or a racial group—which, in its turn, behaves like a violent individual towards other, and perhaps more numerous, collections of people. The final outcome should be a rule of law to which all—except those who are not capable of entering a community—have contributed by a sacrifice of their instincts, and which leaves no one—again with the same exception—at the mercy of brute force.[67]

Most importantly of all, under conditions of civilisation the sexual instinct is subjected to the most severe restrictions concerning both its permitted objects and its permitted modes of gratification:

> As regards the sexually mature individual, the choice of an object is restricted [in a state of civilisation] to the opposite sex, and most extra-genital satisfactions are forbidden as perversions. The requirement, demonstrated in these prohibitions, that there shall be a single kind of sexual life for everyone, disregards the dissimilarities, whether innate or acquired, in the sexual constitution of human beings; it cuts off a fair number of them from sexual enjoyment, and so becomes the source of serious injustice. The result of such restrictive measures might be that in people who are normal—who are not prevented by their constitution—the whole of their sexual interests would flow without loss into the channels that are left open. But heterosexual genital love, which has remained exempt from outlawry, is itself

65. Freud, *Civilization*, p. 283.
66. Freud, *Civilization*, p. 286.
67. Freud, *Civilization*, p. 284.

> restricted by further limitations, in the shape of insistence upon legitimacy and monogamy. Present-day civilization makes it plain that it will only permit sexual relationships on the basis of a solitary, indissoluble bond [einer einmaligen, unauflösbaren Bindung] between one man and one woman, and that it does not like sexuality as a source of pleasure in its own right and is only prepared to tolerate it because there is so far no substitute for it as a means of propagating the human race.[68]

Given the bad bargain that civilisation seems to offer, at least in Freud's account of it, why would men and women forsake the pleasures and relaxations of their pre-civilised condition to burden themselves with such an onerous way of life? Why would they ever move away from the condition of animal contentment depicted on the left-hand side of Führich's *Die Einführung des Christentums in die deutschen Urwälder*?

At this point in his argument Freud shifts into thinking about barbarism and civilisation less as historical stages or patterns of human social existence and more as phases in the psychological lives of individuals (and it is a legitimate critique of *Civilization and Its Discontents* that this difficult but silent transition in the argument is never explicitly acknowledged and the problems it entails are never openly addressed, let alone solved). The sense of conscience on which the structures of civilisation depend arises 'through the suppression of an aggressive impulse, and . . . it is subsequently reinforced by fresh suppressions of the same kind.'[69] Not just any aggressive impulse, however, but a very specific one—the desire of the son to kill the father:

> Now, I think, we can at last grasp two things perfectly clearly: the part played by love in the origin of conscience and the fatal inevitability of the sense of guilt. Whether one has killed one's father or has abstained from doing so is not really the decisive thing. One is bound to feel guilty in either case, for the sense of guilt is an expression of the conflict due to ambivalence, of the eternal struggle between Eros and the instinct of destruction or death. This conflict is set going as soon as men are faced with the task of living together. So long as the community assumes no other form than that of the family, the conflict is bound to express itself in the Oedipal complex, to establish the conscience and to create the first sense of guilt. When an

68. Freud, *Civilization*, p. 294.
69. Freud, *Civilization*, p. 322.

> attempt is made to widen the community, the same conflict is continued in forms which are dependent on the past; and it is strengthened and results in a further intensification of the sense of guilt. Since civilization obeys an internal erotic impulsion which causes human beings to unite in a closely-knit group, it can only achieve this aim through an ever-increasing reinforcement of the sense of guilt. What began in relation to the father is completed in relation to the group. If civilization is a necessary course of development from the family to humanity as a whole, then—as a result of the inborn conflict arising from ambivalence, of the eternal struggle between the trends of love and death—there is inextricably bound up with it an increase of the sense of guilt, which will perhaps reach heights that the individual finds hard to tolerate.[70]

I have discussed Freud's dystopian account of civilisation in some detail because I find his formulations apposite to what I will go on to say about *Hamlet*. But before finally we turn to Shakespeare, we should briefly review the fortunes of the concepts of civilisation and barbarism after 1930.

At Nuremberg the French prosecutor Menthon posed a vital but unanswerable question: 'How can we explain how Germany could have come to this astonishing return to primitive barbarism?'[71] In one sense the rise and eventual fall of Nazism seemed like a return of the kind of barbarism detected by counter-revolutionaries such as Burke and de Maistre in the French Revolution: a barbarism, that is to say, engendered within civilisation and uniting moral degradation to a technical expertise which bestowed upon it a hideous strength and reach.

However, the mass displacement of peoples which war had brought in its wake also revealed a new facet of barbarism. These nomadic refugees—stateless, without political identity, and thus liable to be dismissed as not possessing rights—might become barbaric simply in virtue of their banishment beyond the palisades of civilisation. Hannah Arendt pondered the dark possibilities created by the aftermath of the war in *The Origins of Totalitarianism* (1951): 'The danger is that a global, universal interrelated civilisation may produce barbarians from its own midst by forcing people into conditions which,

70. Freud, *Civilization*, pp. 325–26.

71. Quoted in Lawrence Douglas, *The Memory of Judgment: Making Law and History in the Trials of the Holocaust* (New Haven, CT: Yale University Press, 2001), p. 85.

despite all appearances, are the condition of savages.'[72] In *Waiting for the Barbarians* (1980), J. M. Coetzee pursued Arendt's line of thought and applied the category of the barbaric to the condition of those whom a dominant civilisation—in the case of his novel, the anonymous 'Empire'—oppresses. Coetzee's title echoes Cavafy's poem of the same title, composed in 1904, in which a great display of civic might and power is laid on in preparation for the arrival of barbarians who, however, do not appear. The result of the non-arrival of the barbarians is not relief or joy amongst the civilised but rather disarray and disappointment:

> Why this sudden restlessness, this confusion?
> (How serious people's faces have become.)
> Why are the streets and squares emptying so rapidly,
> everyone going home so lost in thought?
>
> Because night has fallen and the barbarians have not come.
> And some who have just returned from the border say
> there are no barbarians any longer.
>
> And now, what's going to happen to us without barbarians?
> They were, those people, a kind of solution.[73]

Cavafy's dry insight, that barbarism is a concept created by civilisation because it is useful to those who hold power within the social structures the barbarian is supposed to threaten, is expanded by Coetzee into the story of a magistrate in a remote outpost of empire whose loyalty to the *régime* he serves is unsettled when it undertakes reprisals against the 'barbarians' who live to the north.

At first the magistrate's disaffection takes the comparatively mild form of a wish for the empire to be 'corrected' or educated by the barbarians:

> Shall I tell you what I sometimes wish? I wish that these barbarians would rise up and teach us a lesson, so that we would learn to respect them. We think of the country here as ours, part of our Empire—our outpost, our settlement, our market centre. But these people, these barbarians don't think of it like that at all. . . . They will outlast us.[74]

72. Hannah Arendt, *The Origins of Totalitarianism* (New York: Schocken Books, 2004), p. 384.

73. *Voices of Modern Greece: Selected Poems*, ed. Edmund Keeley and Philip Sherrard (Princeton NJ: Princeton University Press, 1981), pp. 7–8.

74. Coetzee, *Barbarians*, p. 55.

Soon that disaffection strengthens into complete rupture, with its accompanying realisation that the empire is the true barbarism: 'I am aware of the source of my elation: my alliance with the guardians of the Empire is over, I have set myself in opposition, the bond is broken, I am a free man. Who would not smile? But what a dangerous joy! . . . The new barbarians usurping my desk and pawing my papers.'[75] Eventually he denounces the empire to the face of the military officers who have been sent to the outpost to pursue the war against the barbarians: '*You* are the enemy Colonel! . . . *You* are the enemy, *you* have made the war, and *you* have given them all the martyrs they need—starting not now but a year ago when you committed your first filthy barbarities here! History will bear me out!'[76]

But that final appeal to history as a court of judgement is replete with irony, as the magistrate finally realises that imperial civilisation is not just a political structure. The empire is nothing less fundamental than a distinctive modelling of time, a dimension of human existence which civilisation has colonised and forced into a particular shape:

> What has made it impossible for us to live in time like fish in water, like birds in air, like children? It is the fault of Empire! Empire has created the time of history. Empire has located its existence not in the smooth recurrent spinning time of the cycle of the seasons but in the jagged time of rise and fall, of beginning and end, of catastrophe. Empire dooms itself to live in history and plot against history. One thought alone preoccupies the submerged mind of Empire: how not to end, how not to die, how to prolong its era. By day it pursues its enemies. It is cunning and ruthless, it sends its bloodhounds everywhere. By night it feeds on images of disaster: the sack of cities, the rape of populations, pyramids of bones, acres of desolation. A mad vision yet a virulent one.[77]

The elusive barbarians beyond the frontiers of the empire are thus both its victims and also the representatives of a lost freedom: 'I wanted to live outside the history that Empire imposes on its subjects, even its lost subjects. I never wished it for the barbarians that they should have the history of Empire laid upon them.'[78] The barbarians are once more objects of civilised yearning, but

75. Coetzee, *Barbarians*, p. 85.
76. Coetzee, *Barbarians*, p. 125.
77. Coetzee, *Barbarians*, p. 146.
78. Coetzee, *Barbarians*, p. 169.

not because their energies might renew civilisation. Rather, they now hold out the promise of escape from the oppressive cruelties of empire and civilisation.

What emerges from this compressed survey? In the first place, it is clear that the antinomy between civilisation and barbarism is a foundational opposition in the history of the West. It is both ubiquitous and perennial. Secondly, it is also clear that the opposition between barbarism and civilisation has been unstable and protean over the past two and a half millennia—so unstable and protean, indeed, that civilisation is not even always invoked as the opposite and antagonist of barbarism. Thirdly and finally, because of that instability, the concepts of barbarism and civilisation have over the centuries performed a variety of functions. Barbarism is both the matrix of civilisation and what threatens it. It is both elsewhere and here. It lies in wait for us in the future, even as it has shaped our past.

The first audiences of *Hamlet* must have felt in its opening moments that they knew what kind of play this was going to be. The action opens with an emphasis on international relations in the Baltic, a keynote established by Marcellus's questioning of his fellow sentries:

> Good now, sit down, and tell me he that knows,
> Why this same strict and most observant watch
> So nightly toils the subject of the land,
> And why such daily cast of brazen cannon
> And foreign mart of implements of war,
> Why such impress of shipwrights, whose sore task
> Does not divide the Sunday from the week.
> What might be toward that this sweaty haste
> Doth make the night joint-labourer with the day,
> Who is't that can inform me?[79]

Just a few years before, Sidney's *A Defence of Poetry* had praised 'the high and excellent Tragedy, that openeth the greatest wounds, and showeth forth the ulcers that are covered with tissue; that maketh kings fear to be tyrants, and tyrants manifest their tyrannical humours; that, with stirring the affects of

79. *Hamlet*, I.i.69–78.

admiration and commiseration, teacheth the uncertainty of this world, and upon how weak foundations gilden roofs are builded'.[80] In the play's opening minutes, it seems as if *Hamlet* will conform to this high-political model of tragedy.

In fact, *Hamlet* does contain an example of this kind of Sidneian tragedy: 'The Mousetrap' is a perfect instance of it. But this form of tragedy is quoted or sampled within Shakespeare's play rather than itself defining it. International politics, so important in a precursor play such as Thomas Kyd's *The Spanish Tragedy*, are in *Hamlet* pushed into the wings to make way for a different kind of tragedy, one that, as it were, erupts from within this, for the play's first audiences, more customary or familiar form.[81]

The opening scenes of *Hamlet* thus initiate a movement of generic eruption which is duplicated and amplified in details of plot and language. The appearance of the ghost of Old Hamlet is feared by Horatio to bode 'some strange eruption to our state'.[82] Crime, we are told by Hamlet, does not lie quiet but returns disruptively into the very present from which the criminal had hoped to banish it:

> Foul deeds will rise,
> Though all the earth o'erwhelm them, to men's eyes.[83]

Hamlet figures the intrusion of Old Hamlet's ghost explicitly as an eruption, as a violent bursting upward of the subterranean:

> Oh, answer me!
> Let me not burst in ignorance, but tell
> Why thy canonized bones, hearsed in death,
> Have burst their cerements, why the sepulcher,
> Wherein we saw thee quietly interred,
> Hath oped his ponderous and marble jaws
> To cast thee up again.[84]

80. Sir Philip Sidney, *A Defence of Poetry*, in *Miscellaneous Prose of Sir Philip Sidney*, ed. Katherine Duncan-Jones and Jan van Dorsten (Oxford: Clarendon Press, 1973), p. 96.

81. Thomas Kyd, *The Works of Thomas Kyd*, ed. F. S. Boas (Oxford: Clarendon Press, 1901), pp. xxix–xxxi.

82. *Hamlet*, I.i.68.

83. *Hamlet*, I.ii.256–57.

84. *Hamlet*, I.iv.45–51.

The repetition of 'burst', at first glance a failure of verbal variation, in fact suggests how the eruption enacted by the father threatens to provoke a further eruption in the son. The echoing of language foreshadows an echoing of experience.

The poisoned body of Old Hamlet displays the ravages of somatic eruption in the most lurid way:

> sleeping within my orchard—
> My custom always of the afternoon—
> Upon my secure hour thy uncle stole
> With juice of cursed hebona in a vial
> And in the porches of my ears did pour
> The leprous distilment, whose effect
> Holds such an enmity with blood of man
> That swift as quicksilver it courses through
> The natural gates and alleys of the body,
> And with a sudden vigor it doth possess
> And curd, like eager droppings into milk,
> The thin and wholesome blood. So did it mine,
> And a most instant tetter barked about,
> Most lazar-like, with vile and loathsome crust,
> All my smooth body.[85]

Finally, we should recall Hamlet's own first soliloquy, which erupts out of its dramatic context.[86] At the beginning of this scene, in dialogue with Claudius and Gertrude before the other courtiers, Hamlet has been clipped, oblique, and laconic.[87] But as soon as he is left alone onstage, a torrent of language pours from his mouth, as he can no longer contain his indignation at the intolerableness of the situation in which he finds himself.

Why do the early scenes of *Hamlet* dramatise and thematise eruption so insistently and so variously? They do so, I believe, because the fact of

85. *Hamlet*, I.v.59–73.

86. *Hamlet*, I.ii.129–59.

87. The compression in Hamlet's speech is clear if we note that the final couplet of his reply to his mother, 'But I have that within which passes show—/ These but the trappings and the suits of woe' (*Hamlet*, I.ii.85–86) is a distillation of no fewer than four lines from *Richard II*: ''Tis very true, my grief lies all within; / And these external manner of laments / Are merely shadows to the unseen grief / That swells with silence in the tortured soul' (*Richard II*, IV.i.288–91).

catastrophic change, in respect of both individuals and whole societies, lies at the heart of the play's mystery.[88] In respect of individuals, that catastrophic change is the transition to a heightened but diseased ethical awareness. In respect of societies, it is the movement from a form which was in certain respects pre-civilised to one which exhibits the prosthetic character that Freud found typical of civilisation or *Kultur*.

It is this latter point that I wish first to address by means of a significant intertext within *Hamlet*, namely, the presence within the play of Trojan materials and memories. The siege of Troy and its aftermath were understood by the writers of antiquity as a significant point of inflection in human history. For Virgil in *The Aeneid*, the fall of Troy had led to the foundation of Rome and a lasting *imperium* in the West. For Aeschylus in *The Oresteia*, it had led to something even more fundamental, namely, the creation of civilisation itself, understood not as material improvement but rather as an escape from the conditions of atavistic vendetta that hitherto had tethered human societies in a destructive, backward orientation of endless attrition.

It is worth just briefly noting how variously, and in ways both great and small, *Hamlet* engages with Greek and Trojan material, for (as Victor Hugo would later put it) 'Hamlet does at Elsinore what Orestes did in Argos.'[89] The speech that Hamlet has the First Player rehearse is an ekphrastic account of the death of Priam at the hands of Pyrrhus during the sack of Troy.[90] Long before the action of the play has begun, Polonius has christened his son Laertes—not a very Danish name, one might think, but (as it happens) the name of the father of Odysseus. And the basic plot of *Hamlet*—a martial king murdered by the future husband of his widow, whose son is then obliged to seek revenge—closely parallels the fortunes of the Greek commander Agamemnon, who on his return from Troy is murdered by Aegisthus, the lover of his wife, Clytemnestra, and whose son Orestes then pursues revenge. It was these episodes that had provided the groundwork for Aeschylus's trilogy *The Oresteia*.

In one sense *The Oresteia* is a dramatisation of the movement from barbarism to civilisation, construed as the rule of law, which entails the transferral of the responsibility for retribution and punishment from the injured individual to society as a whole. Aeschylus places onstage the movement from a

88. Cf. *Hamlet*, III.ii.339.

89. 'Et Hamlet fait dans Elseneur ce qu'Oreste a fait dans Argos' (Victor Hugo, *Ninety-Three*, pt. III, bk. 2, ch. 11 [Paris: Lévy Frères, 1874], 2:263).

90. *Hamlet*, II.ii.358–419.

primitive honour system to a more sophisticated system of law and due process, in which, however, there is residual respect for the principle of retribution, which is recognised and incorporated into the institutions of justice.

Obedient to the imperative of revenge, Orestes kills his mother in retribution for the murder of his father, Agamemnon, and then is pursued by the Furies, supernatural beings whose duty it is to exact punishment for the shedding of blood. Orestes seeks sanctuary in Athens at the temple of Pallas Athene. The goddess listens to the pleas of both Orestes and the Furies. Aeschylus puts powerful words into the mouths of the Furies, explaining the terrible consequences which will follow if the principles of wild justice and pure revenge which they represent are simply dismissed by Athene and if Orestes is allowed to go scot-free:

You, you younger gods!—you have ridden down
    the ancient laws, wrenched them from my grasp—
and I, robbed of my birthright, suffering, great with wrath,
    I loose my poison over the soil, aieee!—
poison to match my grief comes pouring out my heart,
            cursing the land to burn it sterile and now
rising up from its roots a cancer blasting leaf and child,
    now for Justice, Justice!—cross the face of the earth
the bloody tide comes hurling, all mankind destroyed.
. . . Moaning, only moaning? What will I do?
    The mockery of it, Oh unbearable,
mortified by Athens,
we the daughters of the Night,
our power stripped, cast down.[91]

Athene acquits Orestes on a casting vote, but the Furies—now re-named the Eumenides, or 'kindly ones'—are incorporated into Athens when Athene offers them an honourable position in the city:

This is the life I offer, it is yours to take.
Do great things, feel greatness, greatly honoured.
Share this country cherished by the gods.[92]

91. Fagles, *Oresteia*; *The Eumenides*, ll. 792–805.

92. Fagles, *Oresteia*; *The Eumenides*, ll. 876–78.

Returning now to *Hamlet,* we can see that it does not precisely follow the Aeschylean and later Aristotelian paradigm, in which civilisation arrives to resolve, perfect, and heal a pre-existing state of barbarism.

One of the most significant and consequential changes Shakespeare introduced into his version of *Hamlet* (at least, so far as we know, this was Shakespeare's innovation: it could of course also have been incorporated in the lost *Ur-Hamlet* play which had been performed before English audiences by 1589) was to transpose the action from a heathen to a Christian setting.[93] In both Saxo Grammaticus's Danish history and François de Belleforest's *Histoires Tragiques* (1570), by contrast, the action is located in a pre-Christian society.

It is interesting, however, to note that in *Hamlet,* the advent of Christianity has not brought about the moral improvements that would be celebrated on canvas by Joseph von Führich nearly three hundred years later. In *Hamlet,* material improvement has not been accompanied by any parallel moral refinement. If anything, the reverse is true. Old Hamlet was no doubt a Christian of a sort. But much of the little that we hear about Old Hamlet's behaviour as king is expressive of a more ancient culture that had subscribed to fiercer values remote from the imperatives of forgiveness and peace that characterise the new religion:

> Such was the very armor he had on
> When he the ambitious Norway combated;
> So frowned he once, when in an angry parle
> He smote the sledded Polacks on the ice.
>
> . . . Our last king,
> Whose image even but now appeared to us,
> Was, as you know, by Fortinbras of Norway,
> Thereto pricked on by a most emulate pride,
> Dared to the combat, in which our valiant Hamlet—
> For so this side of our known world esteemed him—
> Did slay this Fortinbras, . . .[94]

93. For an account of some of the implications of this change of setting, see Stephen Greenblatt, *Hamlet in Purgatory* (Princeton, NJ: Princeton University Press, 2001).

94. *Hamlet,* I.i.59–62 and 79–85.

Old Hamlet is a warrior-chieftain, who breaks up a summit meeting with the Poles to brawl and who kills Old Fortinbras in single combat.[95] Even his habit of sleeping in his orchard during the afternoon recalls the addiction of the northern barbarians to lethargy noted by Tacitus and depicted by von Führich.[96] Claudius, by contrast, is an administrator and a diplomat, not a warrior. He sends *communiqués* to young Fortinbras and throughout the play uses proxies, instruments, and intermediaries to achieve his ends.[97] Indeed, Elsinore is a place in which it seems that everyone—not just Claudius, not just Polonius, but also Hamlet himself (witness the commissioning of 'The Mousetrap' and the ruse whereby Rosencrantz and Guildenstern are despatched)—is committed to the use of 'windlasses and . . . assays of bias' and is persuaded that 'indirections' are the best way 'to find directions out'.[98] Elsinore under the rule of Claudius shows us Freud's prosthetic civilisation suddenly in full strength.

Accordingly, the world in which *Hamlet* is set exhibits features of both advancement and degradation. Denmark has passed—almost in an instant, it seems—beyond the barbaric feudal directness that characterised the reign of Old Hamlet and has moved into the domain of Claudian indirection which, according to Freud, characterises civilisation. But whereas for Freud the condition of civilisation was accompanied by an oppressive ethical rigour and austerity, in *Hamlet* the Danish court—at least, in the persons of the king and queen—exhibits moral coarseness and laxity. It is only in the character of Hamlet himself that we find the urgent ethical inquiry, and resulting restless anxiety, that Freud associated with civilisation. And in Hamlet's case, it is noteworthy that ethical introspection is figured as disease and experienced as torment. Thought is a sickness, rather than a cure, and reflection is an ailment that leads to nausea: 'thus the native hue of resolution / Is sicklied o'er with the pale cast of thought'.[99] Hamlet's soliloquies are also eruptions in that they often take the form of vomits of moral disgust directed at both himself and those

95. It is a detail obliquely recollected in *Antony and Cleopatra*, when Antony challenges Octavian to single combat and is mockingly rejected. There too we find a transition from a former, heroic and personal style of leadership to a more instrumental, indirect, and (in Freud's word) prosthetic successor.

96. *Hamlet*, I.v.59–60. Cf. above, pp. 84 and 88–89.

97. For instance, consider Claudius's instrumental exploitation of Rosencrantz and Guildenstern, and later of Laertes.

98. *Hamlet*, II.i.62–63.

99. *Hamlet*, III.i.83–84.

who surround him.[100] But in their passionately ethical and ratiocinative quality, Hamlet's soliloquies are also very unusual as soliloquies. For instance, in Kyd's *The Spanish Tragedy*—a play which we know influenced *Hamlet*—Hieronimo's soliloquies are anguished, yet formally-patterned, depictions of the exquisite torment of his inner state.[101] What we do not sense in Hieronimo's soliloquies is what we surely see in those of Hamlet, namely, a mind working through and experiencing the implications of what is happening to and around him. Sometimes in *Hamlet* this happens at a level of generality that loosens or veils the connection between a particular speech and the specific predicament of the person uttering it. Hamlet's most famous soliloquy, 'To be or not to be', as has often been noted, is remarkable for not containing any first-person pronouns. It is pitched entirely at the level of generality.

What should we make of this pathologising of thought and ethical introspection in *Hamlet*? Just as the scabs on Old Hamlet's body are the metabolite of poison, so young Hamlet's soliloquies, with their intense ethical quality, are the imaginative metabolite of crime, for it is the fact of outrageous crime that has provoked young Hamlet into a state of ethical awareness. So young Hamlet stands in a figurative relation to Old Hamlet as well as a biological one. This is the thrilling but unintended point of Ophelia's description of young Hamlet as, weirdly but appropriately, also Old Hamlet:

> Lord Hamlet . . .
> As if he had been loosèd out of hell
> To speak of horrors, he comes before me.[102]

As has often been remarked, both Hamlets have been poisoned through the ear (Old Hamlet literally, young Hamlet metaphorically); and as a result both Hamlets have been propelled into an at once ecstatic and blasted realm of terrible and forbidden knowledge.

In the case of Old Hamlet, that knowledge is his familiarity with the terrors of purgatory:

> But that I am forbid
> To tell the secrets of my prison house,
> I could a tale unfold whose lightest word

100. Examples include *Hamlet*, I.ii.129–59, II.ii.468–524, and IV.i.31–65.
101. E.g., Thomas Kyd, *The Spanish Tragedy*, II.v.1–33.
102. *Hamlet*, II.i.75–81.

> Would harrow up thy soul, freeze thy young blood,
> Make thy two eyes like stars start from their spheres,
> Thy knotted and combinèd locks to part,
> And each particular hair to stand on end
> Like quills upon the fearful porcupine.
> But this eternal blazon must not be
> To ears of flesh and blood.[103]

For young Hamlet, more figuratively, that knowledge is a sudden and catastrophic awareness of ethics, here dramatised as a kind of knowledge that is both refining and distressing (here the parallelism with the terrible processes of purgatory is clear).

Hamlet places before us two opposed images of human life. On the one hand, there is a perspective of intellectual idealism: 'What a piece of work is man—how noble in reason, how infinite in faculties, in form and moving how express and admirable, in action how like an angel, in apprehension how like a god, the beauty of the world, the paragon of animals—and yet to me what is this quintessence of dust?'[104] However, as Hamlet's abrupt veering from this idealism to the materialism of 'dust' suggests, his mind is also host to an opposed view of human life, in which idealism has very little purchase. This is the note we hear when Claudius is questioning Hamlet about the whereabouts of Polonius's corpse:

> KING. Now, Hamlet, where's Polonius?
> HAMLET. At supper.
> KING. At supper? Where?
> HAMLET. Not where he eats, but where 'a is eaten: a certain convocation of politic worms are e'en at him. Your worm is your only emperor for diet. We fat all creatures else to fat us, and we fat ourselves for maggots. Your fat king and your lean beggar is but variable service, two dishes but to one table. That's the end.
> KING. Alas, alas.
> HAMLET. A man may fish with the worm that hath ate of a king, and eat of the fish that hath fed of that worm.
> KING. What dost thou mean by this?

103. *Hamlet*, I.v.13–22.
104. *Hamlet*, II.ii.264–69.

HAMLET. Nothing but to show you how a king may go a progress through the guts of a beggar.[105]

We hear that materialist note once more in the graveyard when Hamlet is meditating on the transformations of death with Horatio:

> Alexander died, Alexander was buried, Alexander returneth to dust, the dust is earth, of earth we make loam, and why of that loam whereto he was converted might they not stop a beer-barrel?
>
> Imperious Caesar, dead and turned to clay,
> Might stop a hole to keep the wind away.
> Oh, that that earth which kept the world in awe
> Should patch a wall t'expel the winter's flaw.[106]

In this materialist perspective, the ethical questions which trouble Hamlet are too trifling to register. Why worry about your uncle having sex with your mother, why even be troubled by the murder of your father, when to focus on the whirligig of matter and the process whereby, over time, matter is exchanged and circulated through a variety of bodies, with so wild a disregard for the rankings of society and so complete an indifference to the fates of the sentient beings who act as its temporary hosts, brings to light so profound an extent and thoroughness of material miscegenation?

Such materialism creates an ethical landscape in which the issues which trouble Hamlet are barely worth discussing. And in that landscape, Hamlet's ethical preoccupations, far from representing the pinnacle of human nature,

105. *Hamlet*, III.vi.16–30.

106. *Hamlet*, V.i.188–95. These lines read like a concentrated and bitter re-working of Richard II's maudlin 'sad stories of the death of kings', a catalogue of 'graves, of worms, and epitaphs' which exhibits a number of detailed points of contact with events in *Hamlet*: 'How some have been deposed, some slain in war, / Some haunted by the ghosts they have deposed, / Some poisoned by their wives, some sleeping killed—/ All murdered. For within the hollow crown / That rounds the mortal temples of a king / Keeps Death his court, and there the antic sits, / Scoffing his state and grinning at his pomp, / Allowing him a breath, a little scene / To monarchize, be feared, and kill with looks, / Infusing him with self and vain conceit, / As if this flesh which walls about our life / Were brass impregnable; and humored thus, / Comes at the last and with a little pin / Bores through his castle walls—and farewell, king' (*Richard II*, III.ii.140 and 151–65). Cf. also Prince Henry's response to the death of King John: 'What surety of the world, what hope, what stay, / When this was now a king and now is clay?' (*King John*, V.vii.68–69).

are rather a morbid development. Ethical thought has ceased to be the cure it had seemed to be for Aeschylus and instead has become a disease, that of being 'thought-sick'.[107] How should we understand that change in status? It is here that Freud's *Civilization and Its Discontents* is so helpful. It invites us to see Hamlet as the embodiment of Freud's civilised man, catastrophically launched into ethical knowledge by the death of his father and obliged to inhabit an element which frustrates and re-directs his natural, animal life. Hamlet's recurrent expressions of dis-ease are signs and tokens of this uncomfortable displacement:

> I have of late, but wherefore I know not, lost all my mirth, forgone all custom of exercises, and indeed it goes so heavily with my disposition that this goodly frame, the earth, seems to me a sterile promontory; this most excellent canopy, the air, look you, this brave o'erhanging firmament, this majestical roof fretted with golden fire—why, it appeareth nothing to me but a foul and pestilent congregation of vapors.
>
> . . . My wit's diseased.
>
> . . . Thou wouldst not think how ill all's here about my heart[108]

Hamlet's agonistic relationship to civilisation (both its embodiment and its antagonist) was surely in Thomas Mann's mind when, thinking about the First World War and figuring it as a clash between German culture and French civilisation, he was drawn to represent Germany as like Hamlet, 'not actually born to action, but . . . unavoidably called to it.'[109]

Another such token, on a larger scale, is a soliloquy such as 'O, what a rogue and peasant slave am I!'[110] Provoked by the verbal and emotional facility of the First Player to a sharpened sense of his own contrasting and puzzling reluctance to exact revenge, Hamlet expostulates against his inability to abandon a world of words for a world of deeds:

> This is most brave,
> That I, the son of a dear murdered,
> Prompted to my revenge by heaven and hell,

107. *Hamlet*, III.iv.51.

108. *Hamlet*, II.ii.257–64; III.ii.297; V.ii.183–84.

109. 'Zur Tat nicht eigentlich geboren, aber unausweichbar berufen war' (Mann, *Reflections*, p. 121).

110. *Hamlet*, II.ii.469–524.

Must like a whore unpack my heart with words
And fall a-cursing like a very drab,
A stallion! Fie upon't, foh![111]

For Hamlet, there is no way back to the primary world of direct action once inhabited and still exemplified by his dead, barbarically heroic, father.[112] He is trapped within the civilised Claudian world of indirection: a world of symbols, instruments, and words. So there is both pathos and irony in the fact that, at the end of this soliloquy of enraged frustration at his translation into the realm of civilised insight, the expedient Hamlet comes up with is 'The Mousetrap'—perhaps the most ingenious instance of prosthetic indirection in the play.

It is in the 'Closet Scene' (act III, scene iv) that Hamlet's uncomfortable location within the heightened and anxious ethical awareness characteristic of civilisation is dramatized most vividly. Often in the theatre this scene is staged as the moment when Hamlet's Oedipal longing for his mother finds most vivid expression. For instance, during this scene in the Kenneth Branagh production at Stratford in 1992 the audience witnessed a virtual rape onstage. But is this scene really about sexual intercourse? Or is it rather about ethical intercourse?[113] If we look closely at the language of the speeches, what we see is Hamlet doing to his mother what the ghost of his father has done to him, namely, uttering the words and imparting the knowledge that will usher her into an uncomfortable and dis-eased (but nevertheless sophisticated and therefore civilised) state of ethical awareness and experience, in which the curbing of natural instinct is laid upon us as an indefeasible obligation. Hamlet's simultaneous command and threat to Gertrude is the appropriate keynote to the tutorial in uncomfortable self-awareness that he is about to conduct:

Come, come and sit you down, you shall not budge;
You go not till I set you up a glass
Where you may see the inmost part of you.[114]

111. *Hamlet*, II.ii.501–6.

112. Hamlet's longing for that lost world is expressed also in his comparison to Gertrude of Old Hamlet with Claudius: *Hamlet*, III.iv.53–76.

113. T. S. Eliot sensed that the Oedipal explanation was inadequate: 'Hamlet (the man) is dominated by an emotion which is inexpressible, because it is in *excess* of the facts as they appear. . . . Hamlet is up against the difficulty that his disgust is occasioned by his mother, but that his mother is not an adequate equivalent for it; his disgust envelops and exceeds her' ('Hamlet and His Problems', reprinted as 'Hamlet', in Eliot, *Essays*, p. 145).

114. *Hamlet*, III.iv.18–20.

The result of Hamlet's passionate reproaches is a transformation in Gertrude's understanding of her moral condition:

> O Hamlet, speak no more!
> Thou turn'st my very eyes into my soul,
> And there I see such black and grievèd spots
> As will leave there their tinct.[115]

The topic of reproach that has produced this complete introversion of ethical awareness is Hamlet's hyper-civilised (in Freud's terms) revulsion at Gertrude's unregulated genital sexuality:

> Nay, but to live
> In the rank sweat of an enseamèd bed,
> Stewed in corruption, honeying and making love
> Over the nasty sty—
> But go not to my uncle's bed—
> Assume a virtue if you have it not. . . .
> Not this, by no means that I bid you do:
> Let the bloat King tempt you again to bed,
> Pinch wanton on your cheek, call you his mouse,
> And let him for a pair of reechy kisses,
> Or paddling in your neck with his damned fingers,
> Make you to ravel all this matter out . . .[116]

And the result of this deepening and sharpening of moral insight within Gertrude is a loss of wholeness and a lapse into a Hamlet-like condition of fractured self-awareness: 'O Hamlet, thou hast cleft my heart in twain.'[117] Thereafter, Gertrude, like Hamlet, has the 'sick soul' characteristic of the estrangement from instinctual nature that civilisation brings in its wake.[118]

As we saw, Freud speculated that the emotional burdens imposed by the renunciation of instinct demanded by civilisation might become too great:

> If civilization is a necessary course of development from the family to humanity as a whole, then—as a result of the inborn conflict arising from

115. *Hamlet*, III.iv.88–91.

116. *Hamlet*, III.iv.91–94, 160–61, and 182–87.

117. *Hamlet*, III.iv.157.

118. *Hamlet*, Folio text, IV.v.17.

> ambivalence, of the eternal struggle between the trends of love and death—there is inextricably bound up with it an increase of the sense of guilt, which will perhaps reach heights that the individual finds hard to tolerate.[119]

Accordingly, we sense in Hamlet towards the end of the play a depletion of intellectual energy, an exhausted retreat from the pitch of ethical scruple that civilisation demands. Elsinore under the technocrat Claudius is a world which, in virtue of its administrative and instrumental pressures, has already destroyed Ophelia, maddening her and driving her back towards—as the innuendoes in her language suggest—a more primal state of sexual promiscuity and availability. Something parallel occurs in Hamlet himself. The casual arrangement of the executions of Rosencrantz and Guildenstern, the acquiescence evident in Hamlet's invocation of providence,[120] and above all the absence of soliloquies after act IV, scene ii, which thereafter closes off Hamlet's interiority from the audience, suggests also a dwindling of intellectual self-questioning within him and so marks his re-absorption into the more common run of the play's humanity. All these features of Hamlet's dramatic profile in act V announce his retreat from the unsustainable ethical stretch he is obliged to undergo and attempts to maintain in acts II, III, and IV.

The final phases of the action of *Hamlet* are puzzling for the audience. Retribution occurs but as neither revenge nor justice: rather, as retaliatory spasm. The closing scenes of the play are suspended between states. There is no way back to the world of barbaric heroism, the world of Old Fortinbras and Old Hamlet; and the arrival of Young Fortinbras offers nothing by way of resolution to the issues that the play has set in motion. But equally the play can show us no way of being at ease, of avoiding (to use Freud's word) 'discontents', 'Unbehagen', in the new, 'civilised' world. For civilisation springs a trap on the human personality. It creates a world of indirection, proxies, instrumentality, and moral evasiveness which nevertheless obliges its most sensitive and intelligent inhabitants to adhere to an impossibly elevated moral standard.

Hamlet is a dramatic meditation on civilisation understood as anxiety, ailment, dis-ease, and disquiet. It was written in the middle of a series of plays in which

119. Freud, *Civilization*, p. 326.

120. *Hamlet*, V.ii.191–94.

Shakespeare explored situations in which the civilised and the barbaric (or pre-civilised) are placed in conjunction or competition. Typically, conflicted or isolated individuals find themselves in unstable societies in transition. Hamlet has acquired a civilised personality in a society which is still vestigially pre-civilised. The warrior-feudalism of Old Hamlet has as yet not been fully extinguished by the bureaucratic monarchy of Claudius. The feudal world still exists within Denmark as an object of nostalgic longing, while to the north in Norway, and in the person of Young Fortinbras, who intends to recover his lost lands 'by strong hand', it exists in full and literal force.[121] Young Fortinbras dwells in an untroubled, pre-civilised condition 'in the skirts of Norway'—that is to say, he is a resident of the margins of the world, where barbarians can live undisturbed by the burdensome imperatives of civilisation.[122] (And the Baltic geography of the play is not random. The Danes are under pressure from the north [Norway] and the east [Poland]. These are the customary directions from which the barbarians have in the past invaded western Europe.) The desire of Young Fortinbras's followers is to locate an enterprise that 'hath a stomach in't'—that is to say, an adventure that is exciting, concrete, courageous, and intrepid but not overly troubled by any tedious abstract scruples about right and wrong or justice.[123]

The unsettling proximities between the civilised and the barbaric we find in *Hamlet* are first pre-figured and then subsequently echoed in Shakespeare's Roman plays, which emerge as both departure and destination for this particular Shakespearean preoccupation. In *Titus Andronicus,* the line between the civilised and the barbaric is thoroughly smudged when the military hero who has defended Rome from the Goths is also the instrument whereby, in the play's first scene, the Goths are introduced within the palisades of civilisation. In *Julius Caesar,* Brutus is a hyper-civilised man in a society which is regressing from civilisation to something more chaotic. In *Coriolanus,* Marcus is a warrior chief whose virtues are problematic in the political society which his victories have created, as Rome begins to move along the path which will take it from being a pre-civilised village of warriors to becoming a metropolitan empire of aristocrats and politicians. In *Antony and Cleopatra,* Antony, with magnificent recklessness, immerses himself in Oriental barbarism while the Roman world

121. *Hamlet,* I.i.101.

122. *Hamlet,* I.i.96. Cf. Claudius's noting Young Fortinbras's rejection of 'all bands of law' (ibid., I.ii.24).

123. *Hamlet,* I.i.99.

into which he was born is mutating into a higher phase of civilised organisation, in which the charismatic individual will be hard to accommodate. Shakespeare sets Antony and Caesar (who is the embodiment of this new world) on strongly repulsive paths, as Caesar himself recognises when he learns of Antony's suicide: 'We could not stall together / In the whole world.'[124] Two later plays, neither of them Roman, sustain the theme but reverse the perspective. *Timon of Athens* shows us a man cleaving to a barbaric conception of the gift in the midst of a post-barbaric civilisation and being destroyed as a result. Finally, in *The Tempest*, an initial act of sophisticated barbarism is the prelude to a play which richly interleaves the barbaric and the noble or civilised. The civilised prevails—but only at the cost of forgetting and forgiving the moral barbarism camouflaged in its midst.

When drawing a connection with Aeschylus's *The Oresteia* we have already noted the prominence of the matter of Troy in *Hamlet*. What must now be added is the acknowledgement that, given the role of the fall of Troy in the Virgilian founding myth of Rome, the presence of Trojan material drew in its wake also Roman material. Some of the links between *Hamlet* and Shakespeare's Roman plays are slight or circumstantial. *Hamlet* was probably written shortly after *Julius Caesar*, and both plays have at their centre a man maimed and eventually broken by his determination to abide by the stern moral requirements of civilisation. We are told that Polonius had acted in a play on the subject of Julius Caesar when he was a student:

> I did enact Julius Caesar. I was kill'd i'th' Capitol—
> Brutus killed me.[125]

Horatio, eager to drain the poisoned cup ahead of Hamlet, proclaims, 'I am more an antique Roman than a Dane.'[126] When Hamlet is taken prisoner by pirates on his journey from Denmark to England, an element of Caesarean biography has been transplanted north of the Alps, without any warrant from Shakespeare's sources.[127] When Hamlet wants to illustrate the mortifying indifference of brute matter to human greatness, it is to Caesar that his thoughts turn:

124. *Antony and Cleopatra*, V.i.39–40.

125. *Hamlet*, III.ii.94–95.

126. *Hamlet*, V.ii.318.

127. *Hamlet*, IV.iii.14–27. Cf. Suetonius, 'Divus Iulius', IV. Saxo Grammaticus does not report that Amleth was captured by pirates on his way to Britain (Bullough, *Sources*, 7:66–67).

Imperious Caesar, dead and turned to clay,
Might stop a hole to keep the wind away.
O, that that earth which kept the world in awe
Should patch a wall t'expel the winter's flaw.[128]

However, less obvious affiliations between *Hamlet* and the Roman plays run deeper and raise more interesting questions.

In *Julius Caesar*, Shakespeare had put into the mouth of Casca an explanation of why ghosts walk the earth. According to Casca, they do so in response to moral outrage by men:

Either there is a civil strife in heaven,
Or else the world, too saucy with the gods,
Incenses them to send destruction.[129]

Strangely, no one in Denmark seems to have quite this theory of why ghosts walk (although Horatio remembers the manifestations which preceded the death of Caesar).[130]

The parallel of course is not exact. The manifestations in Rome *preceded* the death of Caesar; those in Denmark *follow* the death of Old Hamlet. Even so, the discrepancy in interpretative practice is remarkable. Hamlet's view is in one sense the complete inverse of Casca's:

I doubt some foul play. . . .
Foul deeds will rise,
Though all the earth o'erwhelm them, to men's eyes.[131]

Hamlet understands the presence of the ghost as a response to past crime, rather than as a sign of disturbances which lie in the future: that is to say, not as an omen but as a trace. Whereas most characters see the ghost of Old Hamlet through the lens of a superstitious fear of what is to come—that is to say, as a *portent*—Hamlet reads his father's ghost as the spore of past wickedness—that is to say, as a *symptom*. For him, it is a diagnostic remnant, not a forerunner of crime or outrage. His freedom from superstition—the fact that he reads the

128. *Hamlet*, V.i.192–95.
129. *Julius Caesar*, I.iii.11–13.
130. *Hamlet*, I.i.111–24.
131. *Hamlet*, I.ii.255–57.

ghost of his father as trace rather than as omen—is an indication of his position towards the civilised end of the spectrum; and this is why he alone is unafraid of his father's ghost.[132] Brutus, another maimed paragon of civilisation whose Stoicism has instilled a ruthless disciplining of instinct and nature, shows a similar Hamlet-like firmness when confronted by Caesar's ghost on the evening before Philippi and Stoically ignores the reflexive somatic responses to which he, like other men, is liable ('thou . . . mak'st my blood cold and my hair to stare'):

BRUTUS. How ill this taper burns. Ha! Who comes here?
I think it is the weakness of mine eyes
That shapes this monstrous apparition.
It comes upon me.—Art thou any thing?
Art thou some god, some angel, or some devil,
That mak'st my blood cold and my hair to stare?
Speak to me what thou art.
GHOST OF CAESAR. Thy evil spirit, Brutus.
BRUTUS. Why com'st thou?
GHOST OF CAESAR. To tell thee thou shalt see me at Philippi.
BRUTUS. Well, then I shall see thee again?
GHOST OF CAESAR. Ay, at Philippi.
BRUTUS. Why, I will see thee at Philippi, then.[133]

Both Hamlet and Brutus carry the wound that civilisation inflicts on human nature, and in both these characters, successively imagined as they were, Shakespeare embarked on a sustained exploration of the unease of the civilised condition.

The congruence between *Hamlet* and the Roman plays is grounded on their shared preoccupation with the impact exerted by civilisation on the personalities of those who embrace it most fully. It is a shaping preoccupation already evident in Shakespeare's first Roman play. *Titus Andronicus* begins with the triumphant return of the hero from victorious campaigns against the Goths on the northern frontier of the empire. His brother, Marcus, praises him in significant terms:

132. Cf. *Hamlet*, V.ii.191: 'We defy augury.'

133. *Julius Caesar*, IV.iii.279–90.

A nobler man, a braver warrior,
Lives not this day within the city walls.
He by the Senate is accited home
From weary wars against the barbarous Goths, . . .[134]

Within the space of a few lines Marcus presents his audience with a significant juxtaposition, that between the 'city walls' and the 'barbarous Goths'. In this first scene, we have dramatised before us the fragility of the city in the face of the barbarians. We see that the hubristic triumphs of civilisation may introduce the seeds of barbarism within its pale and, moreover—in the persons of Tamora and Aaron—place subtle barbarians at its political apex: barbarians who are, at least to begin with, able easily to manipulate and out-manoeuvre the civilised men and women they encounter, whose moral honesty becomes a vulnerability. The porousness of civilisation before barbarism, and the fact that the very rites of civilisation expose it to the pathogens of revenge, lust, and atrocity that barbarism carries within itself, are made dramatically and visually vivid in this scene, when Tamora appears on the balcony as empress.

It is a matter of historical fact that Roman triumphs frequently included the ritual killing of captives, so Titus has a point when he remarks that his living sons 'religiously' demand the death of Alarbus.[135] Furthermore, the description offered by his sons of the sacrifice of Alarbus is not inaccurate. These were indeed 'Roman rites', and such killings had a cultic significance:

See, lord and father, how we have performed
Our Roman rites. Alarbus' limbs are lopped
And entrails feed the sacrificing fire,
Whose smoke like incense doth perfume the sky.[136]

However much we may sympathise with Chiron's expostulation at these 'Roman rites'—'Was never Scythia half so barbarous!'—Chiron's point, though apparently plausible, is in fact misleading.[137] It is not that civilisation and barbarism are indistinguishable, still less that the play argues for some flat

134. *Titus Andronicus*, I.i.25–28.

135. *Titus Andronicus*, I.i.127. On the place of such ritual killings in the Roman triumph, see Mary Beard, *The Roman Triumph* (Cambridge, MA: Belknap Press of Harvard University Press, 2007), pp. 14, 94, and 128–32.

136. *Titus Andronicus*, I.i.145–48.

137. *Titus Andronicus*, I.i.134.

equation between the two. Rather, it is that in *Titus Andronicus* barbarism and civilisation become mutually permeable.

Moreover, we see that these two concepts are thoroughly positional and comparative. For the Goths, the Scythians on their northern and eastern frontiers are the barbarians. Absolute barbarism is never to be found, as there is always a further shore of degraded difference upon which to fix the pejorative label 'barbarian'. So when Marcus urges Titus to allow the body of Mutius to be buried in the monument of the Andronici by saying, 'Thou art a Roman; be not barbarous', the injunction is not meaningless (as it would be were there no essential difference between the civilised and the barbaric). Rather, on close inspection it emerges as an injunction obscure and difficult to comply with.[138]

When Tamora is enticing her lover, Aaron, while Andronicus and his sons are out hunting, she refers to the Virgilian founding myth of Rome, which linked the origin of the city to the fall of Troy and the flight westward of the Trojan prince Aeneas:

> Let us sit down and mark their [the hounds'] yellowing noise.
> And after conflict such as was supposed
> The wandering prince and Dido once enjoyed,
> When with a happy storm they were surprised
> And curtained with a counsel-keeping cave,
> We may, each wreathèd in the other's arms,
> Our pastimes done, possess a golden slumber, . . .[139]

The same primal myth is invoked by the anonymous Roman Lord when he invites Lucius to relate the story of his expulsion from Rome and his eventual victorious return:

> Speak, Rome's dear friend, as erst our ancestor,
> When with his solemn tongue he did discourse
> To lovesick Dido's sad-attending ear
> The story of that baleful burning night
> When subtle Greeks surprised King Priam's Troy.
> Tell us what Sinon hath bewitched our ears,
> Or who hath brought the fatal engine in
> That gives our Troy, our Rome, the civil wound.[140]

138. *Titus Andronicus,* I.i.381.
139. *Titus Andronicus,* II.iii.20–26.
140. *Titus Andronicus,* V.iii.79–86.

The availability of this myth for deployment both by a spokesman for Rome and by Rome's most deadly enemy might seem to enforce the sceptical view that, in this play at least, the distinction between the barbaric and the civilised is empty. But that would be to push the play's vision of the interactions of these two social formations too far. Lucius will reconquer Rome with the help of Gothic soldiers, it is true, but he presents his exploit as that of a scapegoat:

> I am the turned-forth, be it known to you,
> That have preserved her [Rome's] welfare in my blood,
> And from her bosom took the enemy's point,
> Sheathing the steel in my advent'rous body.[141]

Lucius has taken the guilt and impurity of the whole community on himself in order to restore and safeguard its purity. Thus the play ends with an emphatic discrimination of the genuinely Roman from the irremediably barbaric when Lucius, now acclaimed as Rome's emperor, gives orders for the disposal of the corpses that fill the stage:

> Some loving friends convey the Emperor hence,
> And give him burial in his father's grave.
> My father and Lavinia shall forthwith
> Be closèd in our household's monument.
> As for that ravenous tiger, Tamora,
> No funeral rite, nor man in mourning weed,
> No mournful bell shall ring her burial,
> But throw her forth to beasts and birds to prey:
> Her life was beastly and devoid of pity,
> And, being dead, let birds on her take pity.[142]

This decisive expulsion of the barbaric is a necessary act of cultural hygiene, which reverses and remedies the pollution represented by the introduction of the Goths at the beginning of the play.

In *Titus Andronicus*, the civilised is conceived as a social formation: that is to say, as a collection of cultural and religious practices and norms shared by a self-defined group. In *Julius Caesar*, Shakespeare took the further step (so important for the composition of *Hamlet*) of conceiving of the civilised as a kind of human character rather than as a kind of community: that is to say, as

141. *Titus Andronicus*, V.iii.108–11.

142. *Titus Andronicus*, V.iii.190–99.

a form of the human personality endowed with a distinctive psychological life. Brutus, who displays a super-human ethical probity, is a case-study of the problems arising from the civilised personality. Shakespeare recognises both the double-think and the hypocrisy such commitments can entail, as well as the broader social chaos they can bring in their wake. (Stoicism can serve as a proxy for civilisation more generally given Freud's analysis of the ruthless self-discipline that civilisation, or 'Kultur', demands of its adherents.) Antony, by contrast, is (at least in *Julius Caesar*) a study of the imperfectly civilised personality, in which ethical flexibility and sensual indulgence are fused. This imperfect civilisation proves to be more effective in the real world than Brutus's rigid Stoicism.

At the end of the play Antony's words over Brutus's corpse are both a eulogy and an indictment:

> This was the noblest Roman of them all.
> All the conspirators save only he
> Did that they did in envy of great Caesar;
> He only in a general honest thought
> And common good to all made one of them.[143]

It is with the phrase 'general honest thought' (echoing Brutus's own earlier claim that he is motivated by 'the general good')[144] that Antony puts his finger on the flaw in Brutus's character. Brutus's determination to view and engage with the world, in his own significant word, 'indifferently', without any preference for his own merely personal advantage and comfort, is a strenuously and wilfully maintained stance: 'I love / The name of honor more than I fear death'.[145]

143. *Julius Caesar*, V.v.68–72.

144. *Julius Caesar*, I.ii.85.

145. *Julius Caesar*, I.ii.87–89. It is interesting that *Julius Caesar* should contain a number of local points of contact with the poetry of *Macbeth*, another play which also has at its centre a man who is determined to drive himself onward by, if necessary, 'hard use' (*Macbeth*, III.iv.145) and who is exiled from the common refreshment of sleep (cf. *Julius Caesar*, II.i.229–33; and *Macbeth*, II.ii.38–46). Points of verbal contact include 'for we are at the stake' (*Julius Caesar*, IV.i.48) and 'They have tied me to a stake' (*Macbeth*, V.vii.1); 'Now I have taken heart, thou vanishest' (*Julius Caesar*, IV.iii.291) and 'Why, so. Being gone, / I am a man again' (*Macbeth*, III.iv.109–10); 'Why now, blow wind, swell billow, and swim bark' (*Julius Caesar*, V.i.66) and 'Blow, wind, come, wrack! / At least we'll die with harness on our back' (*Macbeth*, V.v.51–52).

In Brutus's own understanding, his posture towards the world is a pitch of rectitude, as he states to Cassius in the republican camp before the battle of Philippi:

> There is no terror, Cassius, in your threats,
> For I am armed so strong in honesty
> That they pass by me as the idle wind,
> Which I respect not.[146]

This is the apogee of hubristic Stoicism. But it is brittle, and the audience will very soon have the staginess which underlies it dramatised before them in the double announcement of Portia's death.

Shakespeare so organises his play that the audience has good reason not to take Brutus at his own self-evaluation. For instance, the audience knows that—whatever Brutus may say about the disinterestedness of his reasons for joining the conspiracy against Caesar—he has in fact been 'played' by the other conspirators, as Cassius explains to Casca:

> Three parts of him
> Is ours already, and the man entire
> Upon the next encounter yields him ours.[147]

Furthermore, the present of the supernatural (omens, ghosts, strange apparitions) in the play (another important point of contact with *Hamlet*) creates a backdrop to human assertions of will, control, and shaping power which tends to ironise those acts of the will. The worlds of both *Hamlet* and *Julius Caesar* are organised around episodes of supernatural involvement in human affairs too powerful to be controlled by the schemes of mere men. Such an environment is particularly damaging to those, such as Brutus, whose sense of their own identity is connected so strongly to exertions of the will. Decius, speaking of Caesar, mockingly notes that 'he loves to hear / That unicorns may be betrayed with trees'—a reference to the mythical practice of catching unicorns by tempting them to impale their horn into a tree.[148] The rarest and most precious part of the unicorn is also the site of its vulnerability. Brutus too is a kind of unicorn. He is a creature of legend, the mark of whose fabulousness (his rigid virtue) is also his undoing.

146. *Julius Caesar*, IV.iii.66–69.
147. *Julius Caesar*, I.iii.154–56.
148. *Julius Caesar*, II.i.203–4.

The curious textual feature of the double announcement of Portia's death in act IV, scene iii is the clearest example of the inauthenticity of Brutus's Stoicism, of its staged and performed character. Having quarrelled, Brutus and Cassius are reconciled over a bowl of wine:

CASSIUS. I did not think you could have been so angry.
BRUTUS. O Cassius, I am sick of many griefs.
CASSIUS. Of your philosophy you make no use
If you give place to accidental evils.
BRUTUS. No man bears sorrow better. Portia is dead.
CASSIUS. Ha? Portia?
BRUTUS. She is dead.[149]

It is significant that Cassius should make mention of Brutus's Stoical 'philosophy', since this scene is about to become an exposure of its assumed nature. After Brutus and Cassius have buried 'all unkindness' in wine, Titinius and Messala enter.[150] Cassius is still dazed by the news of Portia's death. 'Portia, art thou gone?' he muses, at which point Brutus interjects, breaking into the line, 'No more, I pray you.'[151] Brutus proceeds to cross-examine Messala about the military movements of the Caesarean party. Then Messala changes the subject:

MESSALA. Had you your letters from your wife, my lord?
BRUTUS. No, Messala.
MESSALA. Nor nothing in your letters writ of her?
BRUTUS. Nothing, Messala.
MESSALA. That methinks is strange.
BRUTUS. Why ask you? Hear you aught of her in yours?
MESSALA. No, my lord.
BRUTUS. Now, as you are a Roman, tell me true.
MESSALA. Then like a Roman bear the truth I tell,
For certain she is dead, and by strange manner.
BRUTUS. Why, farewell, Portia. We must die, Messala.
With meditating that she must die once,
I have the patience to endure it now.
MESSALA. Even so great men great losses should endure.

149. *Julius Caesar*, IV.iii.142–48.
150. *Julius Caesar*, IV.iii.158.
151. *Julius Caesar*, IV.iii.164–65.

CASSIUS. I have as much of this in art as you,
But yet my nature could not bear it so.[152]

The previous discussion of the death of Portia between Brutus and Cassius requires us to see Brutus's textbook Stoicism before Messala as a performance, not as genuine ingrained virtue (Brutus even refers to one of the Stoical exercises designed to produce the desired state of αταραξια—'With meditating that she must die once, / I have the patience to endure it now'). Brutus's surreptitious manipulation of a situation naïvely accepted as unscripted by his interlocutors (although Cassius must realise its falsity, a circumstance which lends interest to his reference to Stoicism as a philosophy to be acquired and strengthened through 'art') is one further way in which his character reveals Shakespeare experimenting with forms of action he would develop in more surprising directions in *Hamlet*.

Like Hamlet, Brutus suffers from an unspecified malaise—'I am not well in health', he tells Portia.[153] Like Hamlet, Brutus is inwardly disturbed when on the threshold of a momentous action:

Between the acting of a dreadful thing
And the first motion, all the interim is
Like a phantasma or a hideous dream:
The genius and the mortal instruments
Are then in council, and the state of man,
Like to a little kingdom, suffers then
The nature of an insurrection.[154]

And, again as with Hamlet, the creation of the character of Brutus entailed on Shakespeare an exploration of the finally unendurable pressures that can be created within the human personality by a commitment to the pitiless disciplines of civilisation.

In *Julius Caesar*, the quick-spirited Antony[155] is introduced to us as a participant in an ancient Roman fertility ritual, the Lupercalia, in which two celebrants, anointed with the blood of a sacrificed goat and dog, ran naked through and round the city, touching bystanders with goatskin thongs. Caesar

152. *Julius Caesar*, IV.iii.180–94.
153. *Julius Caesar*, II.i.257. Cf. *Hamlet*, V.iii.183–85.
154. *Julius Caesar*, II.i.63–69. Cf. *Hamlet*, II.ii.469–24.
155. *Julius Caesar*, I.ii.29.

commands Antony to be sure to strike Calphurnia, 'for our elders say / The barren touchèd in this holy chase / Shake off their sterile curse.'[156]

Shakespeare derived the circumstance of the Lupercalia from his source, Plutarch, but also changed its application, as we can see from the relevant passage of Plutarch's *Life of Caesar*:

> There was added to these causes of offence his [Caesar's] insult to the tribunes. It was, namely, the festival of the Lupercalia, of which many write that it was anciently celebrated by shepherds, and has also some connection with the Arcadian Lycaea. At this time many of the noble youths and of the magistrates run up and down through the city naked, for sport and laughter striking those they meet with shaggy thongs. And many women of rank also purposely get in their way, and like children at school present their hands to be struck, believing that the pregnant will thus be helped to an easy delivery, and the barren to pregnancy. These ceremonies Caesar was witnessing, seated upon the rostra on a golden throne, arrayed in triumphal attire. And Antony was one of the runners in the sacred race; for he was consul.[157]

Plutarch describes this ancient ritual, which he traces back to a pastoral, and so pre-urban, possibly even pre-Roman period. But he does not suggest that Caesar had any personal interest in it as a remedy for his wife's sterility. For Plutarch the Lupercalia was merely the backdrop to Caesar's display of reluctance to assume the diadem and to his later ejection of the tribunes from their offices. However, Shakespeare's imagination quickened at the possibility of linking Caesar's personal situation to the magical function of the Lupercalia. When he did so, he also made this fertility ritual an element in the characterisation of Antony, who as a result is associated from the outset of the play with atavistic natural magic and fecundity.[158]

That association between Antony and the pre-civilised is reinforced later in the play when he and Brutus deliver their funeral orations for Caesar. The brilliance of Antony's speech has been long and widely recognised, and the unspoken corollary seems to be that Brutus is, by contrast, an incompetent

156. *Julius Caesar*, I.ii.7–9.

157. Plutarch, *Life of Caesar*, LXI.1–3.

158. Plutarch reports that the Lupercalia was 'anciently' (παλαιὸν) celebrated by shepherds; Shakespeare makes this more concrete when he has Caesar attributes the function of the ritual to the oral tradition of what 'our elders say' (*Julius Caesar*, I.ii.7).

speaker. In fact, what Shakespeare presents is something more nuanced and profound than simply a contrast between good and bad public speaking.

As a conspirator, Brutus knows that he will have a chance to speak to the people after Caesar's assassination, whereas Antony asks to speak only once Caesar is dead.[159] So it is unsurprising that Brutus's speech smacks of premeditation and preparation.[160] It is saturated with rhetorical figures and structured around a series of parallelisms and oppositions. (It is, strangely enough, a speech that has a certain kinship with the ludicrously inappropriate rhetoric of Polonius, which draws from Gertrude the dry but stinging command, 'More matter with less art.')[161] Brutus's oration is a textbook, if not unflawed, example of forensic, civilised rhetoric.[162]

And, notwithstanding—indeed, perhaps because of—its insistent formal patterning, Brutus's speech is far from ineffective. Before he begins, the plebeians are in a mood of calm and rational evaluation:

First Plebeian. I will hear Brutus speak.
Second Plebeian. I will hear Cassius and compare their reasons
When severally we hear them renderèd.[163]

When Brutus has finished, the plebeians approve enthusiastically but also temperately:

All. Live, Brutus, live, live.
First Plebeian. Bring him with triumph home unto his house.
Second Plebeian. Give him a statue with his ancestors.
Third Plebeian. Let him be Caesar.
Fourth Plebeian. Caesar's better parts
Shall be crowned in Brutus.
First Plebeian. We'll bring him to his house with shouts and clamors.[164]

159. *Julius Caesar*, III.i.229–32.

160. *Julius Caesar*, III.ii.12–43.

161. *Hamlet*, II.ii.95. For Polonius's speeches, see ibid., II.ii.85–168. For commentary, see Skinner, *Forensic*, pp. 148–54, 187–90, and 243–44.

162. For the speech's merits and demerits, in terms of the rhetorical theories of antiquity, see Skinner, *Forensic*, pp. 108–11.

163. *Julius Caesar*, III.ii.8–10.

164. *Julius Caesar*, III.ii.44–48.

The proposed expressions of the plebeians' approval of Brutus's actions remain within civic bounds and take customary metropolitan forms: a triumph, a statue, and a peaceful, if noisy, celebratory procession.

Antony's oration, as we have recently been convincingly shown, also follows the rhetorical theory of antiquity very closely.[165] Yet it wears on its surface a very different relation to rhetorical precept. Towards the end of his speech, when he is already aware that he has won over the plebeians to his point of view, Antony (in a great stroke of artifice, exemplifying the principle *ars est celare artem*) disavows all rhetorical skill:

> I come not, friends, to steal away your hearts.
> I am no orator, as Brutus is,
> But, as you know me all, a plain blunt man
> That love my friend, and that they know full well
> That gave me leave to speak of him.
> For I have neither wit, nor words, nor worth,
> Action, nor utterance, nor the power of speech
> To stir men's blood. I only speak right on.
> I tell you that which you yourselves do know,
> Show you sweet Caesar's wounds, poor poor dumb mouths,
> And bid them speak for me.[166]

Brutus's careful following of rhetorical theory is manifest in the ostensible patterning of its language, whereas Antony's speech conceals its devotion to rhetorical precepts. When Antony says, 'I am no orator, as Brutus is', it is tempting to read his words as a disavowal of all rhetorical skill; and Antony surely intends it to be received as such by his audience. But a more accurate, albeit latent, meaning is that Antony is not the same *kind* of orator as Brutus.

Antony differs from Brutus not simply in the disingenuousness of his relationship with rhetorical theory but also in the objects of his oratory. Brutus's commitment to the forms and paradigms of civilisation is clear (if perhaps naive). Speaking to the plebeians, Brutus had employed the civic art of oratory to the civil ends of persuasion and the quest for a new political settlement in

165. Skinner, *Forensic*, pp. 111–17, 183–85, and 217–19.
166. *Julius Caesar*, III.ii.214–24. Note how 'dumb mouths' echoes III.i.262.

the wake of Caesar's assassination. In the same way, he had insisted on styling the assassination of Caesar as a rite rather than as an atrocity:

Let's be sacrificers, but not butchers, Caius. . . .
Let's kill him boldly, but not wrathfully;
Let's carve him as a dish fit for the gods,
Not hew him as a carcass fit for hounds.[167]

Antony, however—who 'revels long a-nights' and who is given to 'sports, to wildness'—has pronounced affinities with whatever lies outside the severe disciplines of civilisation.[168] And his funeral speech, unlike that of Brutus, aims not at outcomes which lie within the pale of civil society but rather at a levelling of the boundaries, norms, and distinctions upon which civil society depends. We know that such will be Antony's intention even before he speaks to the crowd:

Over thy [Caesar's] wounds now do I prophesy,
Which like dumb mouths do ope their ruby lips
To beg the voice and utterance of my tongue,
A curse shall light upon the limbs of men;
Domestic fury and fierce civil strife
Shall cumber all the parts of Italy;
Blood and destruction shall be so in use
And dreadful objects so familiar
That mothers shall but smile when they behold
Their infants quartered with the hands of war,
All pity choked with custom of fell deeds;
And Caesar's spirit, ranging for revenge,
With Ate by his side come hot from hell,
Shall in these confines with a monarch's voice
Cry havoc and let slip the dogs of war,
That this foul deed shall smell above the earth
With carrion men groaning for burial.[169]

'Havoc' was the cry in medieval warfare which signalled the temporary abandonment of martial discipline and which thus gave a general permission for

167. *Julius Caesar*, II.i.166, 172–74.
168. *Julius Caesar*, II.iv.116 and II.i.189.
169. *Julius Caesar*, III.i.261–77.

an indiscriminate pillaging and massacre.[170] These words hover between prophecy and enactment, for Antony's speech to the plebeians will impel Rome towards just such an unravelling of civilisation as he here both foresees and invokes.

When addressing the plebeians three times, Antony ostentatiously denies that his speech is intended to inspire them to 'mutiny' or even that he would be able to inspire such insurrection.[171] Yet an overthrow of the boundaries on which civil society depends is the objective to which his speech tends. Moreover, it is also what he achieves. Obedient to Antony's prompting, the enraged plebeians adopt his language. They declare 'We'll mutiny', and threaten the destruction of the city's fabric:

ALL. Revenge! About! Seek! Burn! Fire! Kill! Slay! Let not
a traitor live! . . .
FIRST PLEBEIAN. Come, away, away!
We'll burn his body in the holy place
And with the brands fire the traitors' houses.
Take up the body.
SECOND PLEBEIAN. Go fetch fire
THIRD PLEBEIAN. Pluck down benches.
FOURTH PLEBEIAN. Pluck down forms, windows, anything.[172]

Although 'forms' here is a near-synonym for 'benches', the undiscriminating omnivorousness of the plebeians' appetite for disorder makes it easy for 'forms' also to draw within the ambit of their violence all orderly arrangement and regularity, which is another of the word's available meanings.[173]

Shakespeare would revisit the association he had forged in *Julius Caesar* between the character of Antony and an antagonism with civilisation when, about seven or eight years later, he wrote *Antony and Cleopatra*. In the meantime, however, he would write a series of plays in which the claims of nature

170. *OED*, 'havoc', *n.*, 1. The word is another small point of contact between the linguistic and moral worlds of *Hamlet* and *Julius Caesar*. When Fortinbras enters Elsinore at the end of the play, the sight of the royal and noble corpses draws from him the remark 'This quarry cries on havoc' (*Hamlet*, V.ii.342).

171. *Julius Caesar*, III.ii.120, 209, and 228.

172. *Julius Caesar*, III.ii.202–3 and 251–57.

173. *OED*, 'form', *n.*, II.17, 'a long seat without a back, a bench'; I.8, 'Due shape, proper figure; orderly arrangement of parts, regularity, good order'. A few years before Shakespeare wrote *Julius Caesar*, he had used 'form' in this wider sense: cf. *King John*, III.iv.101.

against restraint or being overtaxed are sympathetically explored. In *Twelfth Night,* the riotous Sir Toby Belch rebukes the hypocritical Puritan Malvolio: 'Dost thou think because thou art virtuous, there shall be no more cakes and ale?'[174] In *Macbeth,* the hero pursues his violent, unnatural, and criminal ends relentlessly—

My strange and self-abuse
Is the initiate fear that wants hard use[175]

—until the inhumane discipline of that 'hard use' creates the numbed man we see in act V, from whom all the natural comforts of life have been stripped away:

I have lived long enough. My way of life
Is fall'n into the sere, the yellow leaf,
And that which should accompany old age,
As honor, love, obedience, troops of friends,
I must not look to have, . . .[176]

In *Measure for Measure,* Shakespeare imagined a Vienna (by a wonderful accident, later to be the city of Freud) in which the representatives of legal, spiritual, and political authority are unmasked as in various ways hypocritical. In the nearly-contemporary *King Lear,* the maddened old king rages against the bad faith embodied in figures of authority:

a dog's obeyed in office.
—Thou rascal beadle, hold thy bloody hand.
Why dost thou lash that whore? Strip thine own back;
Thy blood hotly lusts to use her in that kind
For which thou whipp'st her.[177]

In *Measure for Measure,* the authoritarian regent Angelo, a 'man of stricture' whose blood seems to Lucio to be 'very snow-broth',[178] attempts to trade justice for sexual favours, just as the returned Duke himself will attempt to do, albeit more subtly, in the play's resolution. Isabella, the noviciate nun, desires from

174. *Twelfth Night,* II.iii.106–7.

175. *Macbeth,* III.iv.144–45.

176. *Macbeth,* V.iii.22–26.

177. *King Lear,* IV.vi.152–56 (quarto text). I will discuss the parallelisms and oppositions between *King Lear* and *Measure for Measure* at greater length in chapter 4.

178. *Measure for Measure,* I.iii.12 and I.iv.59.

her convent a more stringent regime of mortification, 'a more strict restraint',[179] although the language in which she expresses her hyper-civilised disciplining of natural appetite reveals (as has often been observed) an undertow of erotic relish. Her words reveal a thorough confusion of the desires civilisation must hold in check with the technology of that enforcement—the beadle's whip that Lear would cite as the metonymic instrument of a perverted desire:

were I under the terms of death,
Th'impression of keen whips I'd wear as rubies,
And strip myself to death as to a bed
That longing have been sick for, ere I'd yield
My body up to shame.[180]

Over against these maimed embodiments of civilisation's rigid order, the play offers us an array of criminals and the inhabitants of the fringes of regulated, 'respectable', society. (It is significant that, in Shakespeare's Vienna as in the historical London of his own day, the sex industry that exists metaphorically on the margins of society, yet serves its needs, has been gradually moved into a literal and physically marginal position, outside the city walls and into the suburbs.)[181] These are the seedy yet unignorable spokesmen of natural impulse against external restraint: Froth, Mistress Overdone, Pompey, and Barnardine—above all, the 'fantastic' Lucio, who reminds the disguised Duke that Angelo's attempts to revive and enforce Vienna's severe laws regulating sexual behaviour are doomed to fail: 'Yes, in good sooth, the vice [lechery] is of a great kindred, it is well allied; but it is impossible to extirp it quite, Friar, till eating and drinking be put down.'[182] Early in the play, the Duke reminds Friar Thomas that Vienna has 'strict statutes and most biting laws, / The needful bits and curbs to headstrong jades.'[183] His words recall Plato's famous image

179. *Measure for Measure*, I.iv.4.

180. *Measure for Measure*, II.iv.97–101.

181. For the location of Vienna's brothels, see *Measure for Measure*, I.ii.87–92 and II.i.61. For a broader discussion of the peripheral suburban areas or 'Liberties' that surrounded the early modern city proper, see Steven Mullaney, *The Place of the Stage: License, Play, and Power in Renaissance England* (Ann Arbor: University of Michigan Press, 1988), *passim* and especially: 'London's Liberties were places of exile, yet the banishment enacted in them was of a more ambivalent order. What was lodged outside the city was excluded, yet retained; denied a place within the community, yet not merely exiled' (p. 22).

182. *Measure for Measure*, III.i.347–49.

183. *Measure for Measure*, I.iii.19–20.

of reason the charioteer controlling and restraining the passions.[184] But by the end of the play, the representatives of civilisation's regulatory impulse have been obliged to reach an uneasy accommodation with those who are, by contrast, happy to feed their natural appetites. These reprobates can be rebuked, shamed, and punished, but also (as Lucio has understood) cannot and should not be 'extirp[ed] quite'. In Lucio's own case, he is to be both penalised and drawn into civilised patterns of behaviour by means of marriage to the whore he has made pregnant—Christian marriage, that instrument of civilisation which the Prayer Book of 1559 tells us was ordained 'for a remedy agaynste synne and to avoide fornication'.[185]

To trace in many of the plays Shakespeare composed between 1599 and 1607 this thread of sympathetic engagement with the natural and instinctive resistance to the disciplines imposed by civilisation is also to begin to understand how the character of Antony was inflected between *Julius Caesar* and *Antony and Cleopatra*. In the earlier play Antony is riotous and given to revelry, but he is also politically shrewd and ruthless, as his calm and prudent behaviour in the chilling 'proscription' scene sufficiently shows.[186] In the later play, however, the well-attested infatuation of the historical Antony with the Oriental barbarism of Egypt (a barbarism not harshly primitive but rather the outcome of a lush degeneration) is used by Shakespeare to bring into focussed connection a range of extravagant tendencies and dispositions in Antony which are schematically opposed to the political and rational values associated with Rome and which also point towards satisfactions and attainments unachievable within the boundaries of civilisation.

In *Antony and Cleopatra*, the earlier association between Antony and the orgiastic or Dionysiac is deepened, while the cold political acuity demonstrated by the Antony of *Julius Caesar* is absent. Despite Pompey's praise of Antony's soldiership as 'twice the other twain', the Antony of *Antony and Cleopatra* makes a series of terrible political and military errors.[187] He alienates Caesar by his behaviour towards Octavia, and he chooses to ignore good advice and to fight by sea rather than on land.[188] Nor does he merely show poor

184. Plato, *Phaedrus*, 246a 254e.

185. *The Book of Common Prayer: The Texts of 1549, 1559, and 1662*, ed. Brian Cummings (Oxford: Oxford University Press, 2011), p. 157.

186. *Julius Caesar*, IV.i.

187. *Antony and Cleopatra*, II.i.36.

188. *Antony and Cleopatra*, III.vii.

generalship. The bungled suicide reveals the more fundamentally degrading reality of a soldier unable to use his sword.[189] Antony's order that Caesar's emissary Thidias should be whipped is petty and vindictive: the very reverse of magnanimous.[190]

Disgrace and degradation have been associated with Antony from the very first words of the play, when Philo inveighs against 'this dotage of our general's' which has transformed the 'triple pillar of the world' into 'a strumpet's fool'. These are sentiments which fall also from the lips of many Romans in the play (including the lips of Antony himself).[191] However, this severe Roman judgement on the transformation that has overtaken Antony does not go unchallenged, and neither are the instrumental political values that motivate and guide that Roman perspective hegemonic within the world of the play. Thidias may refer to Caesar as the 'universal landlord', and this is accurate enough as far as it goes. But as the play moves towards its close it gives ever more patient reception to values to which Rome is blind.[192]

The crucial character here is Enobarbus.[193] In Plutarch's *Life of Antony*, Domitius Ænobarbus is mentioned no more than twice, and then only glancingly: first, as the officer to whom Antony on one occasion gave the task of addressing the troops before an encounter with the Parthians; and, second, as the future husband of one of the daughters of Octavia and Antony.[194] Shakespeare expands this unimportant figure in his source into a major character, whose despairing (and quite unhistorical) suicide in act IV is decisive in guiding the audience's response to the emotional dynamics of the play's final phases.

Enobarbus's 'plainness', both of speaking and of sentiment, is clearly established in the play's early scenes.[195] On hearing the news of Fulvia's death, he

189. *Antony and Cleopatra*, IV.xiv.101–19.

190. *Antony and Cleopatra*, III.xiii.97–102.

191. *Antony and Cleopatra*, I.i.1 and 12–13. For echoes, see ibid., I.ii.115–16 (Antony himself); I.iv.1–9, 16–33 (Caesar); II.i.20–27 (Pompey); III.vii.10–14 (Enobarbus); III.xi.7–24 (Antony himself); III.xiii.111–16 (Antony himself).

192. *Antony and Cleopatra*, III.xiii.72.

193. As has long been recognised: see M. W. MacCallum, *Shakespeare's Roman Plays and Their Background* (London: Macmillan, 1910), pp. 349 ff.; and Howard Erskine-Hill, *The Augustan Idea in English Literature* (London: Edward Arnold, 1983), pp. 139–40.

194. Plutarch, *Life of Antony*, XL.5 and LXXXVII.3–4. Cf. Bullough, *Sources*, 5:317. Bullough's selection from North's translation of Plutarch omits the first reference to Ahenobarbus.

195. *Antony and Cleopatra*, II.vi.79 (said approvingly by Pompey).

says drily, 'the tears live in an onion that should water this sorrow.'[196] Later in the play, on the eve of the last battle with Caesar, Enobarbus will reach for that customary cynical vocabulary again; yet he will transform it from a figure of emotional hardness into an expression of unfeigned feeling. When Antony asks his officers to 'wait on me tonight . . . two hours', Enobarbus replies,

What mean you, sir,
To give them this discomfort? Look, they weep,
And I, an ass, am onion-eyed. For shame!
Transform us not to women.[197]

It is appropriate that Shakespeare should here place 'shame' alongside 'transform', since the play's last scenes draw those two things powerfully together.

For Antony's military and political decline (so unredeemably shameful in a Roman perspective) leads, within the world of the play, not to annihilation but to enlargement, in its double sense of both expansion and emancipation. The drawn-out catastrophe of his fortunes is studded with images of bodily rebellion and disintegration:

Oh,
I followed that I blush to look upon.
My very hairs do mutiny, for the white
Reprove the brown for rashness, and they them
For fear and doting.
My good knave Eros, now thy captain is
Even such a body: here I am Antony,
Yet cannot hold this visible shape, my knave.[198]

The disarming which precedes Antony's suicide is in one sense the shameful prelude to an action which, in its bungledness, compounds and amplifies the 'baseness' for which Antony intends it as a cure.[199] But the poetry in which the disarming is described finds other, more positive, attributes within it:

Off, pluck off!
The sevenfold shield of Ajax cannot keep

196. *Antony and Cleopatra*, I.ii.164–65.
197. *Antony and Cleopatra*, IV.ii.20, 32, 33–36.
198. *Antony and Cleopatra*, III.xi.11–5, IV.xiv.12–14.
199. *Antony and Cleopatra*, IV.xiv.57 and 78.

The battery from my heart. Oh, cleave my sides!
Heart, once be stronger than thy continent—
Crack thy frail case. Apace, Eros, apace!
No more a soldier.—Bruisèd pieces, go!
You have been nobly borne.[200]

The rich confusion of these lines, their mingling of shame ('no more a soldier') and pride ('you have been nobly borne') suggests how Antony's disintegration, spread so painfully through so many scenes, is as much release as annihilation. The separation of breast- and back-plate, which Antony figures as the cracking of the body beneath ('Oh, cleave, my sides!') is a welcome enfranchisement from the chafing and outworn.

One word in particular, to which Shakespeare was repeatedly drawn in this play in various forms, crystallises this paradoxical conjunction of decay, fulfilment, and enlargement: 'blow'. Cleopatra tells Proculeius she would prefer 'a ditch in Egypt' where the water-flies would 'blow me into abhorring' than to become Caesar's prisoner.[201] After the asp has bitten Dolabella, she notices that 'on her breast / There is a vent of blood and something blown'.[202] When Enobarbus learns that Antony has sent his treasure after him, 'blows' is the word around which his speech of bitter self-reproach is organised:

I am alone the villain of the earth
And feel I am so most. O Antony,
Thou mine of bounty, how wouldst thou have paid
My better service when my turpitude
Thou dost so crown with gold! This blows my heart.
If swift thought break it not, a swifter mean
Shall outstrike thought; but thought will do't, I feel.
I fight against thee? No, I will go seek
Some ditch wherein to die. The foul'st best fits
My latter part of life.[203]

Antony's magnanimity 'blows' Enobarbus's heart in many senses: It afflicts, inspires, and enlarges. Although Enobarbus sees himself as overcome with

200. *Antony and Cleopatra*, IV.xiv.37–43.
201. *Antony and Cleopatra*, V.ii.56 and 59.
202. *Antony and Cleopatra*, V.ii.344–45.
203. *Antony and Cleopatra*, IV.vi.31–40.

'turpitude', for the audience, this former cynic is never more noble than in his belated understanding of the fruitful greatness that accompanies Antony's decline.

At one point in the play, Antony, enraged with Cleopatra, compares himself with Hercules, to whom he was, we are told, particularly devoted:

> The shirt of Nessus is upon me. Teach me,
> Alcides, thou mine ancestor, thy rage.[204]

Antony refers to Hercules's agonizing and protracted death, caused by the shirt poisoned with the blood of the centaur Nessus eating into his flesh. In *The Women of Trachis,* Sophocles had, in a rare departure from normal Athenian practice concerning the obscene, put this lingering death onstage in full view of the audience.[205] Hyllus ends the play by telling the audience that, although they have seen terrible and unprecedented suffering, nevertheless 'all of these things are Zeus', that is, divine.[206]

Antony's death, like his ancestor's, also entangles pain and degradation with a mysterious sense of transcendence, expressed in its shadowing of myth and caught most memorably in the extraordinary poetry in which Cleopatra celebrates the rarity of her husband in a sequence of outlandish comparisons which culminates, paradoxically, in an invocation of one of the most common objects imaginable, 'plates':

> An Antony it was,
> That grew the more by reaping. His delights
> Were dolphin-like; they showed his back above
> The element they lived in. In his livery
> Walked crowns and crownets. Realms and islands were
> As plates dropped from his pocket.[207]

In this strange, mesmerising, final image of Antony—abstracted, inattentive to the immense bounty that falls from him and of the power ('crowns and

204. *Antony and Cleopatra,* IV.xii.43–44. For Antony's devotion to Hercules, see ibid., IV.iii.21–22.

205. The initial ecphrasis by Heracles's son, Hyllus, is followed by the arrival of the tormented Heracles onstage: Sophocles, *The Women of Trachis,* ll. 749–812 (Hyllus's narration), ll. 972–1278 (the death-agony of Heracles).

206. 'μεγάλους μὲν ἰδοῦσα νέους θανάτους, / πολλὰ δὲ πήματα <καὶ> καινοπαθῆ, / κοὐδὲν τούτων ὅ τι μὴ Ζεύς' (Sophocles, *The Women of Trachis,* ll. 1276–78).

207. *Antony and Cleopatra,* V.ii.86–91. 'Plates' here may mean coins.

crownets') that is in thrall to him ('in his livery')—we are given an idea of the richness that lies within barbarism but which the prudent calculations of civilisation refuse to acknowledge and for which civilisation can find no place.

If, as seems likely, Shakespeare wrote *Coriolanus* either immediately or very soon after writing *Antony and Cleopatra,* this would exemplify well his tendency to seek out contrast and inversion (something we will see again in chapter 4 in respect of those close contemporaries, *King Lear* and *Measure for Measure*). From the hyper-developed world of *Antony and Cleopatra,* where Rome is the centre of a Mediterranean empire, with *Coriolanus* we move far back in time, to a Rome which is little more than a village. Luxury is replaced by harsh austerity. Antony, although he may not always understand his own experience, is nevertheless eloquent in discussing it, and he also moves others to eloquence. Caius Martius, by contrast, virtually shuns soliloquy[208] and baffles the comprehension of those who encounter him. Not for nothing does his mother evoke her son in terms of a death-dealing vacancy:

> These are the ushers of Martius: before him
> He carries noise, and behind him he leaves tears.
> Death, that dark spirit, in's nervy arm doth lie,
> Which, being advanced, declines, and then men die.[209]

Caius Martius, as much a thing as a person, occupies the lethal and ineffable space that exists between alarm and grief.[210]

Yet beneath these obvious ruptures with Shakespeare's recent dramatic output, we find also continuities. In *Coriolanus,* Shakespeare would return to and re-explore a dramatic element present also in his first Roman play, *Titus Andronicus*: namely, the victorious return of a Roman outcast. The opposition between the male world of fighting and the softer, social imperatives of sexuality, so prominent in the comedies and also in *Othello,* will resurface in *Coriolanus.*[211] There is also a continuity of source material: like *Antony and Cleopatra,* the story of *Coriolanus* is drawn from Plutarch. And, again as in *Antony and*

208. Caius Martius is given two speeches *solus*: *Coriolanus,* II.iii.105–18 and IV.iv.12–26. However, neither of them reveals interiority in the way one expects of soliloquy.

209. *Coriolanus,* II.i.147–50.

210. On many occasions Caius Martius is referred to as a 'thing': see *Coriolanus,* II.ii.106, IV.v.115, IV.vi.90, IV.vii.42, V.iv.13, V.iv.20.

211. Comedies in which that opposition is structural include *Much Ado About Nothing* and *All's Well That Ends Well.* For examples of the confusion between fighting and sexuality in *Coriolanus,* see, e.g., I.iii.2–5, I.iii.37–39, I.vi.29–32, II.ii.79–119, IV.v.112–25, and IV.v.195–96.

Cleopatra and also in *Julius Caesar*, civilisation and the peremptory demands it places on the human personality lie at the heart of the play.

What is the origin of political power? One answer offered by the thinkers of antiquity was that it was founded in military success. For these thinkers suspected that civil society itself had begun in the personal loyalty felt by soldiers towards a successful commander.[212] Yet they also knew that, for a city to endure, the duty of obligation, although it may have originated in the personal ascendancy enjoyed by a charismatic *imperator* as a result of his immediate contact with the *manus* he led, had to be institutionalised and transferred to the *urbs*: hence the strong component of city-worship in classical paganism. Were that transference ever to falter, the threat to the state would be grave. Yet such an eventuality was always to be feared. For the qualities of a good general, the Roman thinkers of the later empire well knew, were also naturally imperial qualities.[213] *Coriolanus*, like *Macbeth*, is at one level a play about how military prowess does—or, rather, in this case, does not—translate into political authority.[214]

The awkwardness of Caius Martius before the plebeians, and his stubborn refusal to ingratiate himself with them when petitioning for the consulship, in a way that other patricians seem perfectly willing to do, has of course attracted much critical attention.[215] Less common, however, has been any desire to juxtapose that painful dramatisation of a failure of connection between the orator and his audience with an earlier moment when Caius Martius rouses the previously fearful common soldiers to renew the attack on Corioles:

> If any such be here—
> As it were sin to doubt—that love this painting
> Wherein you see me smeared; if any fear

212. Polybius, VI.4–6.

213. 'Ducis boni imperatoriam virtutem esse' (Tacitus, *Agricola*, XXXIX.2); 'the strengths required of a good leader are those required also of a general'. The Latin word *imperator* initially denoted a military commander but later was attached to the political office of emperor.

214. That Macbeth and Caius Martius were linked in Shakespeare's imagination is suggested by a striking coincidence of language, when Macbeth's words to Macduff, 'Of all men else I have avoided thee' (*Macbeth*, V.vii.4), are echoed by Caius Martius to Aufidius, 'of all the men i'th'world / I would have 'voided thee' (*Coriolanus*, IV.v.80–81).

215. Menenius and Cominius both show a willingness to be flexible. Cominius's words when executing a strategic withdrawal from the walls of Corioles are significant: 'We are come off / Like Romans, neither foolish in our stands / Nor cowardly in retire' (*Coriolanus*, I.vi.1–3). Caius Martius is no typical representative of the patrician class.

Lesser his person than an ill report;
If any think brave death outweighs bad life
And that his country's dearer than himself,
Let him alone, or so many so minded,
Wave thus [*waving his sword*] to express his disposition,
And follow Martius.

They all shout and wave their swords, take him up in their arms, and cast up their caps.

Oh, me alone! Make you a sword of me?
If these shows be not outward, which of you
But is four Volsces? None of you but is
Able to bear against the great Aufidius
A shield as hard as his.[216]

In *Coriolanus*, Caius Martius's effectiveness with the plebeians in battle is very sharply contrasted with his incompetence in persuasion in a time of peace. And Shakespeare seems deliberately to have heightened this contrast, by suppressing everything that Plutarch says about Caius Martius's success and stature in Roman public life prior to his failed bid for the consulship.[217] Moreover, Shakespeare also invented the dialogue between Volumnia and Caius Martius in which she challenges him over why it is that he will employ ruses in war but not in peacetime:

VOLUMNIA. I have heard you say
Honor and policy, like unsevered friends,
I'th'war do grow together. Grant that, and tell me
In peace what each of them by th'other lose
That they combine not there?
CORIOLANUS. Tush, tush.
MENENIUS. A good demand.

216. *Coriolanus*, I.vi.67–80. Cominius has just disparaged the plebeians for their feebleness in battle: 'The mouse ne'er shunned the cat as they did budge / From rascals worse than they' (ibid., I.vi.43–44). The conjectural emendation adopted in Philip Brockbank's 1976 Arden edition, and derived apparently from Style and Tucker Brooke, in which l. 76 is given to the common soldiers, accentuates further Caius Martius's closeness to the plebeians as a group in this scene and sharpens the contrast with the solicitation of the consulship in act II, scene iii.

217. See, e.g., Plutarch, *Life of Caius Marcius Coriolanus*, V.1, X.4, XIII.3.

VOLUMNIA. If it be honor in your wars to seem
The same you are not, which for your best ends
You adopt your policy, how is it less or worse
That it shall hold companionship in peace
With honor as in war, since that to both
It stands in like request?
CORIOLANUS. Why force you this?
VOLUMNIA. Because that now it lies you on to speak
To th'people, not by your own instruction,
Nor by th'matter which your heart prompts you,
But with such words that are but roted in
Your tongue, though but bastards and syllables
Of no allowance to your bosom's truth.
Now, this no more dishonors you at all
Than to take in a town with gentle words,
Which else would put you to your fortune and
The hazard of much blood.
I would dissemble with my nature where
My fortunes and my friends at stake required
I should do so in honor.[218]

Shakespeare's Caius Martius is, therefore, not quite the same character we find in Plutarch.

In *Coriolanus*, Shakespeare set his play in a Rome which is just beginning to negotiate a perilous transition, moving from a state of affairs in which military and political authority are very close to one in which they are becoming more disengaged and in which, as a consequence, the sphere of the political is acquiring a measure of autonomy.[219] The creation at the very beginning of the

218. *Coriolanus*, III.ii.41–64. Plutarch states that, after his rebuff from the plebeians, Caius Marcius was on the contrary encouraged to persist in his stiff-necked attitude by the patrician youth who flocked to his house (Plutarch, *Life of Caius Marcius Coriolanus*, XV.5; Bullough, *Sources*, 5:519).

219. Plutarch himself hints that Rome is on threshold between one social formation and another in the opening chapter of his life of Caius Marcius: 'Verily, among all the benefits which men derive from the favour of the Muses, none other is so great as that softening of the nature which is produced by culture and discipline, the nature being induced by culture to take on moderation and cast off excess. It is perfectly true, however, that in those days Rome held in highest honour that phase of virtue which concerns itself with warlike and military

play of the office of the tribunes—a purely political office without a military character—is a sign of this movement of the *urbs* from a permanent war footing to a more advanced, to some eyes more corrupt, but certainly more political and administrative or managerial state.[220] 'This is strange', says Menenius of the creation of the tribunes, using 'strange' in the sense of 'unfamiliar'.[221] It is indeed an innovation, but one that leads towards the later greatness of Rome that Menenius himself has just dimly foreseen when he extolled to the plebs 'the Roman state, whose course will on / The way it takes'.[222]

Within the world of the play, the course Rome takes at first is towards a peaceful state of commercial thriving, briefly evoked for us in the opening of act IV, scene vi. Sicinius the tribune describes, with understandable satisfaction,

> the present peace
> And quietness of the people, which before
> Were in wild hurry. Here do we make his friends
> Blush that the world goes well, who rather had,
> Though they themselves did suffer by't, behold
> Dissentious numbers pest'ring streets than see
> Our tradesmen singing in their shops and going
> About their functions friendly.[223]

But this 'happier and more comely time' is vulnerable and transient and is mortally threatened by the destructive descent of Caius Martius and the Volsces.[224]

Caius Martius embodies, in a way which must draw from the audience both admiration and censure, a nostalgia for the simple forcefulness in which

---

achievements, and evidence of this may be found in the only Latin word for virtue, which signifies really manly valour; they made valour, a specific form of virtue, stand for virtue in general' (Plutarch, *Life of Caius Marcius Coriolanus*, I.4).

220. Caius Martius observes the moment when the office of tribune is created and reports it to Menenius (*Coriolanus*, I.i.206–12).

221. *Coriolanus*, I.i.212.

222. *Coriolanus*, I.i.62–63.

223. *Coriolanus*, IV.vi.2–9.

224. *Coriolanus*, IV.vi.39–43. It is worth noting that the plebeians in *Coriolanus* are not as self-contradictory and ridiculous as the plebeians in *Julius Caesar*. In the later play, Shakespeare is prepared to accord them more dignity, and the result is a more even-handed depiction of aristocrats and commoners.

civilisation has its roots and an aversion to those civilised complexities, and, above all, the sometimes shabby compromises, that society is forced to embrace as it moves forward. 'Here remain with your uncertainty!' rebukes Caius Martius as he leaves the city, packing up into that word 'uncertainty' all the horse-trading endemic to civil peace but absent from war, where only one as 'absolute' as Caius Martius can really thrive.[225] Accordingly, he is able to conceive of the new political assertiveness of the plebeians as nothing more than degeneration:

> I would they [the plebeians] were barbarians, as they are,
> Though in Rome littered; not Romans, as they are not,
> Though calved i'th'porch o'th'Capitol.[226]

He is, he understands, not well-adapted to the new, and more complicatedly political, condition into which Rome is moving:

> I had rather be their servant in my way
> Than sway with them in theirs.[227]

Caius Martius is thus both aligned with and opposed to civilisation, and his character exposes a complication in the settled state, as it moves from an early to a mature phase. He embodies the warrior virtues on which civilisation initially depends; but he is unable to exist in the transformed political world that those very virtues make possible. It is in this perspective that the speeches of the Volscian servingmen, dispraising peace and praising war, are deepened beyond the mere rhetorical exercise (the paradoxical encomium) which provides their form:

> SECOND SERVINGMAN. Why, then, we shall have a stirring world again. This peace is nothing but to rust iron, increase tailors, and breed ballad-makers.
>
> FIRST SERVINGMAN. Let me have war, say I. It exceeds peace as far as day does night. It's sprightly walking, audible, and full of vent. Peace is a very apoplexy, lethargy, mulled, deaf, sleepy,

225. *Coriolanus*, IV.i.121 and III.ii.39 (Volumnia's epithet for her son).

226. *Coriolanus*, III.i.231–33. Cf. ibid., III.i.87–109, for Caius Martius's dire diagnosis of the significance of the creation of the tribunes.

227. *Coriolanus*, II.i.191–92.

insensible, a getter of more bastard children than war's a destroyer of men.

SECOND SERVINGMAN. 'Tis so, and as wars in some sort may be said to be a ravisher, so it cannot be denied but peace is a great maker of cuckolds.

FIRST SERVINGMAN. Ay, and it makes men hate one another.

THIRD SERVINGMAN. Reason: because they then less need one another. The wars for my money. I hope to see Romans as cheap as Volscians.[228]

That transition had been also touched on in *Hamlet,* in the movement from the warrior reign of Old Hamlet to the bureaucratic, prosthetic regime of Claudius. Caius Martius embodies, and through his death pays, the high price of civilisation—the sacrifice of the fundamental strengths upon which it at first depended but which it must disavow in order to survive. The state, as Menenius suddenly sees with horror, must devour its own children if it is to progress and thrive:

Now the good gods forbid
That our renownèd Rome, whose gratitude
Towards her deservèd children is enrolled
In Jove's own book, like an unnatural dam
Should now eat up her own![229]

Coriolanus is a rueful meditation on the sacrifice that civilisation requires of those who wish to live within its convenience and security: both the sacrifices they must make in terms of what they must personally renounce and also the propitiatory sacrifices they must make of others. Caius Martius's words to Volumnia after she has prevailed on him to spare Rome express a mysterious sense of fate and futurity:

O my mother, mother! O!
You have won a happy victory to Rome;
But for your son—believe it, oh, believe it—
Most dangerously you have with him prevailed,
If not most mortal to him. But let it come.[230]

228. *Coriolanus,* IV.v.218–32.
229. *Coriolanus,* III.i.281–85.
230. *Coriolanus,* 185–89.

That echo of Hamlet's words of resignation to providence—'If it be, 'tis not to come; it be not to come, it will be now; if it be not now, yet it will come; the readiness is all'[231]—heralds *Coriolanus*'s final movement towards a moment of both murder and sacrifice, as Aufidius and the Volscian conspirators assassinate Caius Martius. Once the deed is done, Aufidius is left dazedly contemplating a paradox:

My rage is gone,
And I am struck with sorrow.—Take him up.
Help, three o'th'chiefest soldiers; I'll be one.
Beat thou the drum that it speak mournfully;
Trail your steel pikes. Though in this city he
Hath widowed and unchilded many a one,
Which to this hour bewail the injury,
Yet he shall have a noble memory. Assist.[232]

Caius Martius is both the scourge of Corioles and its palladium; indeed, he is able to be the city's palladium perhaps precisely *because* he was previously its scourge. It is remarkable that Aufidius's expression of the saddened numbness he feels after the assassination—

My rage is gone,
And I am struck with sorrow.

—uses the very same word ('struck') that Cominius has previously used to evoke the terrific violence of Caius Martius's assault on Corioles:

Alone he entered
The mortal gate of th'city, which he painted
With shunless destiny; aidless came off,
And with a sudden reinforcement struck
Corioles like a planet.[233]

In like manner, civilisation both enshrines and yet also must dispense with, and either renounce or severely control, the original, military virtues upon which the foundations of civil society rest.

231. *Hamlet*, V.ii.192–94.
232. *Coriolanus*, V.vi.145–52.
233. *Coriolanus*, II.ii.107–11.

When the approach of the vengeful Caius Martius is announced, the citizens of Rome immediately begin to dissociate themselves from responsibility for the imminent catastrophe:

> ALL CITIZENS. Faith, we hear fearful news
> FIRST CITIZEN. For mine own part,
> When I said banish him, I said 'twas pity.
> SECOND CITIZEN. And so did I.
> THIRD CITIZEN. And so did I, and to say the truth, so did very many of us. That we did, we did for the best, and though we willingly consented to his banishment, yet it was against our will.[234]

The obvious contradiction—'though we willingly consented to his banishment, yet it was against our will'—makes a satirical point about the comical absurdity of the lower orders that would have been familiar to Shakespeare's audiences from, for example, *Julius Caesar* and *2 Henry VI*.

However, what we are shown in *Coriolanus* is slightly different from what those earlier plays suggested was an essential and perennial feature of the lower fractions of society, namely, their unfitness for serious responsibility. For in *Coriolanus*, Shakespeare sketches a social and political genealogy for the fickleness of the citizens. This confusion of mind and mutability on the part of the citizens contrast with the sturdy truculence they show to Menenius in act I, scene i; with their willingness to be inspired to valour in act I scene vi; with their patience and good humour (at least initially) in act II, scene iii; and with their prosperity and gratitude towards the tribunes earlier in act IV, scene vi. It is as if this degeneration in their moral character has arrived with the advent of a more advanced stage of civil society and the creation of the office of the tribunes—the tribunes, who have introduced into Rome an element of calculated deception and self-interested malfeasance that is clearly distinguishable from the prudence and statecraft shown by Menenius and Cominius.[235]

Evidence for my next claim is difficult to come by. But nevertheless, it does seem as if Shakespeare had made a careful study of the works of Jean-Jacques Rousseau and Adam Smith before writing his later classical plays, *Coriolanus*

234. *Coriolanus*, IV.vi.139–45.

235. For the duplicity of the tribunes, see *Coriolanus*, II.i.193–258 and II.ii.152–57.

and *Timon of Athens*, as well as *The Tempest*.[236] *Coriolanus* is in part a Rousseauvian drama of the corruption which accompanies refinement, while *Timon* dramatizes a Rousseauvian fantasy of retreat from sophistication to the wilderness, as well as a Rousseauvian satire on the artificiality of refined society. *The Tempest*, on the other hand, is a Smithian play in which a return to civilisation from a desert island is made possible by Prospero's virtuoso manipulation of surveillance, of precisely that 'living in the eyes of others' that Rousseau would indict as the source of all our civilised discontents, but which Adam Smith would install at the centre of a natural and healthy moral nature.

It would be Rousseau, in the *Discours sur l'origine et les fondemens de l'inegalité parmi les hommes* (Amsterdam, 1755) who would, some one hundred and fifty years after Shakespeare wrote *Coriolanus*, propose a conjectural but mesmerising account which inverted the relationship between civil society and what preceded it that had been described by Aristotle and with which we began this chapter. Aristotle had said that civil society was the remedy for the ills of the state of nature (a line of argument in which he would be followed, with variations of detail, by Thomas Hobbes and John Locke). For Hobbes, civil society provides peace and settled order in place of a war of all against all. For Locke, it provides the security for property and the apparatus of justice that are absent from the state of nature (notwithstanding the moral sense that Locke, in distinction to Hobbes, finds there). But for Rousseau, civil society had itself created the evils for which it claimed to provide the remedies.

236. It is easier, however, to corroborate the comparatively banal claim that Rousseau was very interested in Shakespeare's *Timon*, to the point in 1776 of encouraging Jean-François Ducis to adapt it for the French stage. See John Golder, in 'Jean-Jacques Rousseau, Jean-François Ducis et une version perdue de "Timon d'Athènes"', *Revue de Littérature Comparée* 47, no. 1 (1973): 124–30, who concludes: 'Ce sujet [that of *Timon*] semble aussi bien se prêter à l'illustration de certains aspects de la philosophie de Rousseau que *Le Roi Léar, Macbeth,* ou *Othello*' (p. 230). Voltaire, irritated by Rousseau's allegations that he had betrayed the *philosophe* cause, sensed the affinity and attacked Rousseau as 'a new Timon, a miserable and hypocritical misanthrope' (Judith Shklar, 'Missed Opportunities', *London Review of Books* 5, no. 14 [4 August 1983]). See also David Mazella, *The Making of Modern Cynicism* (Charlottesville: University of Virginia Press, 2007). On the relation between Rousseau and Smith, see most recently Pierre Force, 'Rousseau and Smith: On Sympathy as a First Principle', in *Thinking with Rousseau: From Machiavelli to Schmitt*, ed. Helena Rosenblatt and Paul Schweigert (Cambridge: Cambridge University Press, 2017), pp. 115–31.

Furthermore, for Rousseau it was in civil society rather than in the state of nature that (*contre* Hobbes) man was subjected to the 'plus horrible état de guerre.'[237]

In Rousseau's prize-winning *Discours* of 1750, written on the theme of 'Si le rétablissement des Sciences & des Arts a contribué à épurer les Mœurs', he had already challenged the prevailing orthodoxy that the growth of arts and sciences had promoted human happiness. For Rousseau, the function of arts, letters, and sciences had (on the contrary) been to reconcile us to our social 'esclavage' and our organisation into 'Peuples policés', inducing us to forget our 'liberté originelle.'[238] The result was that 'nos ames se sont corrompues à mesure que nos Sciences & nos Arts se sont avancés à la perfection.'[239] And the source of this corruption was an artificiality of manners that the progress of society had introduced into the human character and that had its roots in the moment when 'l'Art eut façonné nos maniéres [*sic*], & appris à nos passions à parler un langage apprêté.'[240] The effect of living in civil society had not in fact been to improve human nature but rather to create a new and synthetic kind of reassurance adapted to comfort what would become an unprecedented, and degenerate, form of the human personality: 'La nature humaine, au fond, n'étoit pas meilleure; mais les hommes trouvoient leur sécurité dans la facilité de se pénétrer réciproquement.'[241]

It was this thrilling but explosive insight about the synthetic and reciprocal psychology created by civil society that Rousseau would explore at much greater length a few years later in the *Discours sur l'inegalité*. At the outset of that later work, Rousseau posits the plasticity of human nature and draws attention to 'tous les changemens que la succession des temps & des choses a dû produire dans sa constitution originelle.'[242] He refracts the state of nature into three distinct phases:

1. An original phase, of innocent contented isolation;
2. A later phase, where man is social but not yet unhappy; and

237. Rousseau, *Inegalité*, p. 131.
238. Rousseau, *Discours*, p. 9.
239. Rousseau, *Discours*, p. 16.
240. Rousseau, *Discours*, p. 12.
241. Rousseau, *Discours*, p. 12.
242. Rousseau, *Inegalité*, p. liv.

3. A third phase, in which language, property, specialization of function, and the reciprocal gaze characteristic of civil society is beginning to inflict harm on men.[243]

It is in this third phase that man comes to live exclusively in the eyes of others: 'A force de se voir, on ne peut plus se passer de se voir encore.'[244] This was, in Rousseau's conjectural re-description of the early life of man, the real fall from innocence:

> Chacun commença à regarder les autres & à vouloir être regardé soi-même, & l'estime publique eut un prix. . . . & ce fut-là le premier pas vers l'inégalité, & vers le vice en même-temps: De ces premieres préférences naquirent d'un côté la vanité & le mepris, de l'autre la honte & l'envie; & la fermentation causée par ces nouveaux levains produisit enfin des composés funestes au bonheur & à l'innocence.[245]

Rousseau neatly avoids the possibility of any empirical correction by insisting that all the savages existing in the world in the eighteenth century have already passed into this third, degenerate phase and have been contaminated by exposure to 'les lumieres funestes de l'homme civil'.[246] His postulated state of nature is neither confirmable nor confutable by any contemporary observations.

One consequence of this catastrophic change ('quelque funeste hazard' is Rousseau's phrase)[247] was the introduction of a ruinous distinction between

243. Rousseau, *Inegalité*, pp. 105–14.

244. Rousseau, *Inegalité*, p. 111. The notions of 'living in the sight of others', and of the perniciousness of so doing, Rousseau may very possibly have derived from earlier French moralists. In 'De la vanité', Montaigne had deplored 'Qui que ce soit, ou art ou nature, qui nous imprime cette condition de vivre par la relation à autruy, nous faict beaucoup plus de mal que de bien. Nous nous defraudons de nos propres utilitez pour former les apparences à l'opinion commune. Il ne nous chaut pas tant quel soit nostre estre en nous et en effaict, comme quel il soit en la cognoissance publique. Les biens mesmes de l'esprit et la sagesse nous semble sans fruict, si elle n'est jouie que de nous, si elle ne se produict à la veuë et approbation estrangere' (Montaigne, *Œuvres*, p. 932). Blaise Pascal, in his *Pensées*, had noted that 'Nous ne nous contentons pas de la vie que nous avons en nous et en notre propre être: nous voulons vivre dans l'idée des autres d'une vie imaginaire, et nous nous efforçons pour cela de paraître. Nous travaillons incessament à embellir et conserver notre être imaginaire, et négligeons le véritable' (Blaise Pascal, *Oeuvres Complètes*, ed. Jacques Chevalier, Bibliothèque de la Pléiade [Paris: Gallimard, 1954], pensée 145, pp. 1127–28).

245. Rousseau, *Inegalité*, p. 112.

246. Rousseau, *Inegalité*, p. 114.

247. Rousseau, *Inegalité*, p. 116.

being and seeming. The introduction of this distinction acted as a stimulus for the development of a whole series of vicious, deceptive human characteristics:

> Ces qualités [beauty, strength, address, merit, talents] étant les seules qui pouvoient attirer de la considération, il fallut bientôt les avoir ou les affecter; Il fallut pour son avantage se montrer autre que ce qu'on étoit en effect. Etre & paroître devinrent deux choses tout à fait différentes; & de cette distinction sortirent le faste imposant, la ruse trompeuse, & tous les vices qui en sont le cortége.[248]

In civil society 'l'homme sociable toujours hors de lui ne sait vivre que dans l'opinion des autres', and this creates a new form of the human personality: 'une sorte d'hommes qui comptent pour quelque chose les regards du reste de l'univers; qui savent être heureux & contens d'eux-mêmes sur le témoignage d'autrui plutôt que sur le leur propre.'[249] It is this artificial, 'political' society that Shakespeare shows coming into existence in *Coriolanus*; and the devious tribunes Sicinius and Brutus are examples of the kind of degenerate, 'political' human personality (in Rousseau's terms, 'foible, craintif, rampant') that, in the future, will find in such a society the ethical and psychological habitat in which they can most easily thrive.[250]

If in *Coriolanus* Shakespeare sketched the emergence of Rousseauvian civil society, it would, however, be in another play (although, interestingly enough, also a play derived in large measure from a Plutarchan source) that Shakespeare would anatomise, with the most acute satiric severity and on a larger scale, the workings of this Rousseauvian civil society. The order of composition of *Coriolanus* and *Timon of Athens* is uncertain. The former was probably composed in 1608, the latter at some point between 1606 and 1608.[251] Yet what is nevertheless very clear is the overlap between the material of the two plays. Both plays dramatise a collision between martial and civil imperatives. In *Timon of Athens*, the character of Caius Martius is divided between Timon and Alcibiades, Timon taking Caius Martius's rage, Alcibiades echoing Caius Martius's re-direction of the sentence of banishment and later duplicating before

248. Rousseau, *Inegalité*, p. 127.

249. Rousseau, *Inegalité*, p. 181.

250. Rousseau, *Inegalité*, p. 25.

251. Geoffrey Bullough speculates that 'Shakespeare abandoned *Timon* to write *Coriolanus*' (Bullough, *Sources*, 6:239).

the gates of Athens the pattern of vengeance, at first pursued and then discarded, that Caius Martius follows outside the gates of Rome.[252]

However, despite that substantial duplication of theme and material, and notwithstanding the broad contemporaneity of the historical material on which both plays are based, the Athens of *Timon* is a very different society from the Rome of *Coriolanus*.[253] Menenius's vision of the greatness of the 'Roman state' lies far in the future.[254] The nascent city in which *Coriolanus* is set is fragile and precarious, its institutions contested, in places improvised, and still emergent: 'Confusion's near', as Menenius realises, and that in two respects—'near' in the recent past, as much as in the ominous future.[255] The Athens of *Timon*, by contrast, is a sophisticated and commercially-advanced society. Luxury trades—painting, jewellery, the literary arts—flourish, exhibiting clear specialization of function (identified by Rousseau as a key stage in the formation of civil society).[256] The citizens of Athens also display theoretical self-awareness, as the opening dialogue between the Poet, the Painter, the Jeweller, and the Merchant shows.[257]

The mutual self-congratulation of the various artists illustrates Rousseau's formulation of what follows from the 'commerce des Muses', namely, 'le désir de se plaire les uns aux autres par des ouvrages dignes de leur approbation mutuelle.'[258] The later, bitter, exchange between Timon and Alcibiades is apposite here, in Timon's unflinching Rousseauvian redescription of praise as harm:

ALCIBIADES. I never did thee harm.
TIMON. Yes, thou spok'st well of me.
ALCIBIADES. Call'st thou that harm?
TIMON. Men daily find it. Get thee away,
And take thy beagles with thee.[259]

252. 'Banish me? / Banish your dotage, banish usury / That makes the Senate ugly' (*Timon*, III.vi.96–98; cf. *Coriolanus*, III.iii.120).

253. Timon is reported to have been born in the fifth century BC; Livy dates the events that Shakespeare dramatised in *Coriolanus* to the early fifth century BC, for instance placing the taking of Corioli in 493 BC.

254. *Coriolanus*, I.i.62.

255. *Coriolanus*, III.i.184.

256. Rousseau, *Inegalité*, pp. 117–18 and 122–23.

257. *Timon*, I.i.1–95.

258. Rousseau, *Discours*, p. 8.

259. *Timon*, IV.iii.172–74.

Moreover, the gathering at Timon's mansion accurately foreshadows Rousseau's account of the social mode of a sophisticated society, as 'un assemblage d'hommes artificiels & de passions factices', who meet in a milieu in which the arts and sciences have been continuously refined: 'Ce concours tumultueux d'hommes de tout âge & de tout état, qui semblent empressés depuis le lever de l'Aurore jusqu'au coucher du Soleil à s'obliger réciproquement.'[260] After the entry of Timon at l. 96, the opening scene of the play takes the form of a series of episodes which are superficially differentiated but structurally identical: the paying of Ventidius's debt, the provision of a marriage portion for Lucilius, the purchase of various luxury goods (a painting, a jewel), and finally the equal welcomes extended by Timon to both Alcibiades and the aggressively cynical Apemantus.

What unites all these ostensibly different actions is the exuberant performance, on Timon's part, of a certain theatrical generosity of character (in the double sense of both nobility and open-handedness). As Timon says when settling Ventidius's debt, 'I am not of that feather to shake off / My friend when he must need me.'[261] The various transactions, financial and personal, that Timon undertakes in act I, scene i, are all intended to display and vindicate precisely what 'feather' he is of. Athens, at least in Timon's mansion, is a Rousseauvian society where worth lies in the esteem of others rather than being self-poised, as Timon reveals in his words to the First Lord: 'I have told more of you to myself than you can with modesty speak in your own behalf, and thus far I confirm you.'[262] When he is besieged by his creditors, Timon's anger resolves into a concern for his 'honor', for how things look:

> How goes the world that I am thus encountered
> With clamorous demands of debt, broken bonds,
> And the detention of long-since-due debts
> Against my honor?[263]

At the end of the play, the Poet hopes to curry favour with Timon by giving him 'a personating of himself—a satire against the softness of prosperity, with a discovery of the infinite flatteries that follow youth and opulency.'[264]

260. Rousseau, *Discours*, pp. 179 and 15.

261. *Timon*, I.i.102–3.

262. *Timon*, I.ii.89–91. Cf. Timon's eventual understanding that the function of gold is to create 'admired reverence' (ibid., V.i.49).

263. *Timon*, II.ii.36–39.

264. *Timon*, V.i.32–34.

Two quotations from Rousseau are particularly relevant to this scene. The first concerns the display of opulence as a symptom of sickness and fragility and the opposite of health and resilience (or, in Rousseau's words, what is 'sain & robuste'): 'La richesse de la parure peut annoncer un homme opulent, & son élégance un homme de goût; l'homme sain & robuste se reconnoît à d'autres marques: c'est sous l'habit rustique d'un Laboureur, & non sous la dorure d'un Courtisan, qu'on trouvera la force & la vigueur du corps.'[265] The second quotation concerns a tell-tale use of language, which marks for Rousseau the arrival of the calamitous moment when man has moved from a natural to an artificial mode of living: namely, the moment when 'l'Art eut façonné nos maniéres [*sic*], & appris à nos passions à parler un langage apprêté.'[266] The difficult, compacted poetry of act I, scene i, is evidently 'un langage apprêté', a Mandarin idiom exchanged between the inhabitants of a sophisticated society in the manner of a shibboleth. And the same is true of the harsh cynical language used by Apemantus. (As Timon later realises, 'All's obliquy'.)[267] The contrast between his cynical language and the Parnassian idiom in which the scene opens is very marked, but it would be an error to construe that contrast as one between the sophisticated and the natural. Apemantus's language (a language which Timon himself will adopt and intensify later in the play) is unadorned and aggressive, rather than decorated and courtly. But it is not therefore any the less artificial than the discourse of the Painter and the Poet. They are both diseased and contagious forms of discourse, as Timon will finally understand: 'There is no leprosy but what thou speak'st.'[268] It is appropriate that Timon's last speech in the play craves a cessation of language itself: 'Lips, let four words go by and language end'.[269]

Apemantus is no more Rousseau's natural man than is Timon in his misanthropic phase. For in the violence of their eventually shared revulsion from society, both men are recognisable Rousseauvian types, their cynicism necessarily posterior to (because provoked by an experience of) civil society. When Timon embraces cynicism, of course what he cannot shake off is his knowledge of his earlier life. Indeed, it is clear that he cannot stop thinking about that earlier life. It is easier to renounce Athens than thoroughly to rid yourself

265. Rousseau, *Discours*, p. 11.

266. Rousseau, *Discours*, p. 12.

267. *Timon*, IV.iii.18.

268. *Timon*, IV.iii.357.

269. *Timon*, V.ii.105.

of all trace of its poisonous sophistication. The loyalty and gentleness shown towards Timon by his Steward in act IV, scene iii, draws from Timon the response that it 'almost turns my dangerous nature wild.'[270] To become genuinely wild, genuinely free of any trace of civil society, would be to be cured. Timon's misanthropy is, despite its rejection of civilisation—indeed, precisely because of that rejection—a state that could arise only within civilisation. Genuinely to become wild, for Timon, would be to become untormented, settled, at peace with himself, once more natural.

So both Timon and Apemantus exemplify, at all points of both affluence and destitution, that 'rafinement d'intempérance' that Rousseau would indict as the true essence of apparent but corrupt sophistication. Both men are, throughout the play, trapped in that 'fureur de se distinguer' that Rousseau would identify as the essential characteristic of the inhabitant of civil society.[271] As we will find frequently in this play, what at first glance seems to announce itself as an opposition very quickly resolves itself into an identity.[272]

It is a striking confirmation of the Rousseauvian character of act I, scene ii, that, with the single exception of the jewel Timon gives to the First Lord, Timon's generosity is expressed in the form of promises and not by the physical transfer of actual, concrete objects.[273] Apemantus sees the derivative character of Timon's largesse clearly: 'I fear me thou will give away thyself *in paper* shortly.'[274] Towards the end of the play the Painter will unmask Athenian society as a tissue of promises that only the unsophisticated would ever try to cash out:

> Promising is the very air o'th'time. It opens the eyes of expectation. Performance is ever the duller for his act, and but in the plainer and simpler kind of people, the deed of saying is quite out of use. To promise is most courtly and fashionable; performance is a kind of will or testament which argues a great sickness in his judgement that makes it.[275]

270. *Timon,* IV.iii.484.

271. Rousseau, *Discours,* p. 14.

272. It is worth recalling that in Plutarch's *Life of Antony,* Timon is *already* misanthropic, 'a vyper, and malicious man unto mankind', when still wealthy (Bullough, *Sources,* 6:251).

273. *Timon,* I.ii.165–67.

274. *Timon,* I.ii.239–40; emphasis added.

275. *Timon,* V.i.22–28. Cf. J. K. Huysmans, *À Rebours,* ch. 11, in which the central character, the decadent Des Esseintes, is on the point of making a trip to England but experiences his destination vicariously and imaginatively in advance and then goes home, realising that actually

As the Steward's use of the terms of literariness and the verbal discloses when reflecting on his master's exorbitancy, Timon's lavishness is a lavishness of financial instruments, not of concrete material substances:

> His *promises* fly so beyond his state
> That what he *speaks* is all in debt. He owes
> For every *word*. He is so kind that he now
> Pays interest for't. His land's put to their *books*.[276]

The translation of land into books, the reduction of gifts to words: these devaluing metamorphoses that preoccupy Timon's Steward also draw attention to the entanglement of the origin of language with the progress of civil society. For, as the Steward also realises, in Athens, language is the common denominator of all things, and hence all things may be reduced to words:

> STEWARD. O my good lord, the world is but a word.
> Were it all yours to give it in a breath,
> How quickly were it gone.
> TIMON. You tell me true.[277]

In the Athens of *Timon*, worth is but praise, praise is but breath, and breath is proverbially evanescent, as the Steward instructs his master a few lines later:

> How many prodigal bits have slaves and peasants
> This night englutted? Who is not Timon's?
> What heart, head, sword, force, means, but is Lord Timon's?
> Great Timon, noble, worthy, royal Timon!
> Ah, but when the means are gone that buy this praise,
> The breath is gone whereof this praise is made.[278]

As Timon will say when he learns of the refusal of his friends to meet his needs, 'They have e'en put my breath from me, the slaves'.[279] This emphasis on

---

to make the trip would be both banal and to court disappointment: 'En somme, j'ai éprouvé et j'ai vu ce que je voulais éprouver et voir. Je suis saturé de vie anglaise depuis mon départ; il faudrait être fou pour aller perdre, par un maladroit déplacement, d'impérissables sensations' (J. K. Huysmans, *À Rebours*, ed. Daniel Grojnowski [Paris: Flammarion, 2004], p. 171).

276. *Timon*, I.ii.194–97: emphases added.

277. *Timon*, II.ii.147–49.

278. *Timon*, II.ii.160–65.

279. *Timon*, III.v.1.

language rather than on the objects to which language refers confirms the Rousseauvian character of *Timon.*

For Rousseau's civil society could not exist without language. His natural man, by contrast, lives without language, without possessions, without property, without needs, and without desires.[280] Rousseau is clear that language is not transparently or neutrally referential but rather stimulates and expands the activities of which it was initially only a representation. The priority here is crucial: 'à l'Art d'écrire se joignit l'Art de penser.'[281] A few years later he would state the conundrum about priority more explicitly in the *Discours de l'inegalité* when posing 'ce difficile Problême, Lequel a été le plus nécessaire, de la Société déja liée, à l'institution des Langues; ou des Langues déja inventées, à l'établissement de la Société.'[282] Language, exclusive property, and that catastrophic 'premier regard qu'il porta sur lui-même, [qui] y produisit le premier mouvement d'orgueil': Rousseau sees these separate yet powerfully interactive developments lying entangled in the foundations of civil society, where their mutual and repeated reactions upon each other produce an artificial form of the human personality, addicted to the tribute of the regard of others, for 'a force de se voir, on ne peut plus se passer de se voir encore':

> Chacun commença à regarder les autres & à vouloir être regardé soi-même, & l'estime publique eut un prix. . . . & ce fut-là le premier pas vers l'inégalité, & vers le vice en même-temps: De ces premieres préférences naquirent d'un côté la vanité & le mepris, de l'autre la honte & l'envie; & la

280. Rousseau, *Inegalité*, pp. 84–86. It seems entirely possible that Rousseau's portrait of the savage life in terms of what it happily lacks ('sans industrie, sans parole, sans domicile, sans guerre, & sans liaison, sans nul besoin de ses semblables, comme sans nul désir de leur nuire, peut-être même sans jamais en reconnoître aucun individuellement') derives from a famous passage in Montaigne's 'Des Cannibales' extolling savage life, which is similarly evoked in terms of what is absent: 'C'est une nation, diroy je à Platon, en laquelle il n'y a aucune espece de trafique; nul cognoissance de lettres; nulle science de nombres; nul nom de magistrat, ny de superiorité politique; nul usage de service, de richesse ou de pauvreté; nuls contrats; nulles successions; nuls partages; nulles occupations qu'oysives; nul respect de parenté que commun; nuls vestmens; nulle agriculture; nul metal; nul usage de vin ou de bled. Les paroles mesmes qui signifient la mensonge, la trahison, la dissimulation, l'avarice, l'envie, la detraction, le pardon, inouïes' (Montaigne, *Œuvres*, p. 204). The equivalent passage in Florio's translation of 1613 would also leave an impression on *The Tempest* (see below, p. 191 and n. 366).

281. Rousseau, *Discours*, p. 8.

282. Rousseau, *Inegalité*, p. 60.

fermentation causée par ces nouveaux levain produisit enfin des composés funestes au bonheur & à l'innocence.[283]

Timon's reckless generosity in the first act of the play has encouraged scholars to contextualise his behaviour within the anthropological, philosophical, and historical framework of 'the Gift', drawing on the seminal early twentieth-century work of Marcel Mauss and its later elaborations by Jacques Derrida, Maurice Godelier, and Natalie Zemon Davis.[284] It gradually becomes clear that Timon's understanding of gifts and giving is contradictory. On the one hand, and in defence of the asymmetry of his extravagance, Timon (at this point a Derridean *avant la lettre*) asserts that 'there's none / Can truly say he gives if he receives.'[285] But a little later he also consoles himself with the thought that he is part of a network of friends, all prepared to practice a mutual interchange of support: 'Oh, what a precious comfort 'tis to have so many like brothers commanding one another's fortunes!'[286] And once his eyes have been opened to the parlousness of his situation, Timon is confident that his past lavishness will have created in his 'friends' a reservoir of wealth that he can now apply to his own emergencies:

283. Rousseau, *Inegalité*, pp. 100, 111, and 112.

284. Mauss, *The Gift*; Jacques Derrida, *Donner le temps* (Paris: Éditions Galilée, 1991); Maurice Godelier, *L'Énigme du don* (Paris: Fayard, 1996); Natalie Zemon Davis, *The Gift in Sixteenth-Century France* (Oxford: Oxford University Press, 2000).

285. *Timon*, I.ii.10–11. Or perhaps it would be more accurate to say that here Timon anticipates Cicero, who in *De Amicitia* makes Laelius say that the virtuous man is disinterested in friendship: 'it seems to me that friendship springs rather from nature than from need, and from an inclination of the soul joined with a feeling of love rather than from calculation of how much profit the friendship is likely to afford' (VIII.27). Cf. Derrida's characteristically hyperbolical statement of the 'conditions of possibility of the gift': 'For there to be a gift, there must be no reciprocity, return, exchange, countergift, or debt. If the other *gives* me *back* or *owes* me or has to give me back what I give to him or her, there will not have been a gift, whether this restitution is immediate or whether it is programmed by a complex calculation of long-term deferral or differance' (Jacques Derrida, *Given Time*, trans. Peggy Kamuf [Chicago: University of Chicago Press, 1992], p. 12. But, as has been observed in connection with Derrida's arguments for the irrecoverability of authorial intentions, 'the sceptic [i.e., Derrida] is insisting on too stringent an account of what it means to have reasons for our beliefs. Haunted as Derrida appears to be by the ghost of Descartes, he has concentrated on attacking a position that no theorist of intentionality need defend' (Skinner, *Visions*, 1:122). *Mutatis mutandis*, the same *caveat* applies to Derrida's understanding of gifts.

286. *Timon*, I.ii.99–100.

TIMON. Come, sermon me no further.
No villainous bounty yet hath passed my heart.
Unwisely, not ignobly, have I given.
Why dost thou weep? Canst thou the conscience lack
To think I shall lack friends? Secure thy heart.
If I would broach the vessels of my love
And try the argument of hearts by borrowing,
Men and men's fortunes could I frankly use
As I can bid thee speak.
STEWARD. Assurance bless your thoughts.
TIMON. And in some sort these wants of mine are crowned
That I account them blessings. For by these
Shall I try friends. You shall perceive how you
Mistake my fortunes: I am wealthy in my friends.[287]

So there is clearly a clash of rival conceptions of giving and receiving present within Timon. On the one hand, in his pomp he subscribes to what we might call the high, abstract, and difficult conception of the gift as a pure 'acte gratuit'. On the other hand, in extremity he also clings to an alternative conception of the gift as a way of binding and obliging the recipient. Marcel Mauss described the prevalence of this second conception of the gift in the tribes of the Pacific Northwest, and he gave it the Chinook name of 'potlatch':

> These very rich tribes . . . spend their winter in endless celebration: banquets, fairs, and markets, which represent at the same time the solemn assembly of the tribe. . . . But this prestation takes on, through the chief, a very marked agonistic demeanor. It is essentially usurious and extravagant, and one is participating in something that is, first and foremost, a struggle between nobles to establish a hierarchy amongst themselves from which eventually their clan will profit.[288]

Therefore this apparent recklessness is not uninstrumental, and in these tribal societies the penalties for any failure to reciprocate are devastating:

287. *Timon*, II.ii.167–79. Cf. ibid., II.ii.224–25: 'Never speak or think / That Timon's fortunes 'mong his friends can sink.'

288. Mauss, *Gift*, pp. 62–63.

> The potlatch should always be repaid with interest. The rates generally vary from 30 to 100 percent per year. . . . The obligation to reciprocate worthily is imperative. One loses "face" forever if one does not reciprocate or if one does not destroy equivalent values. . . . The individual who has failed to return the loan or the potlatch loses his rank and even his status as a free man.[289]

However, Timon alone among the Athenians subscribes to this tribal, pre-civil, notion of the gift.[290] The Senator who enters at the beginning of act II is not unsympathetic to Timon's predicament ('Still in motion / Of raging waste? It cannot hold, it will not').[291] But nevertheless he understands that, prudentially, he cannot extend further credit to Timon:

> My uses cry to me. I must serve my turn
> Out of mine own. His days and times are past,
> And my reliances on his fracted dates
> Have smit my credit. I love and honor him
> But must not break my back to heal his finger.
> Immediate are my needs, and my relief
> Must not be tossed and turned to me in words
> But find supply immediate.[292]

Timon will later revile the recipients of his generosity as 'detested parasites, / Courteous destroyers, affable wolves, meek bears'.[293] But a more sympathetic response to the cautious behaviour of Timon's fellow Athenians is surely possible. As Adam Smith famously observes close to the beginning of *The Wealth of Nations,* it is 'not from the benevolence of the butcher, the brewer, or the baker, that we expect our dinner, but from their regard to their own interest.'[294] Smith's account of the gradual and natural development of civil society lays its emphasis on a network of interconnecting and overlapping contracts, all entered into by both parties out of a perception of self-interest, which supports

289. Mauss, *Gift,* p. 128.

290. As an anthropologist, Mauss naturally wishes to resist any attachment of the labels 'primitive' or 'backward' to the societies which engage in the potlatch (Mauss, *The Gift,* p. 60). Historians need not follow him in such fastidiousness, however.

291. *Timon,* II.i.3–4. Note Timon's later use of the same phrase when he reproaches the guests at his mock-banquet: 'What, all in motion?' (ibid., III.vii.97).

292. *Timon,* II.i.20–27.

293. *Timon,* III.vii.89–90.

294. Smith, *Wealth,* 1:26–27.

and shapes human interactions in the manner of a web. We see this Smithian model of civil society also in *Timon*, alongside its Rousseauvian obverse. Smith had already analysed the character of the prudent man in *The Theory of Moral Sentiments* (1759). In certain respects the prudent man is wholly admirable:

> In the steadiness of his industry and frugality, in his steadily sacrificing the ease and enjoyment of the present moment for the probable expectation of the still greater ease and enjoyment of a more distant but more lasting period of time, the prudent man is always both supported and rewarded by the entire approbation of the impartial spectator, and of the representative of the impartial spectator, the man within the breast.

Financially, his prudence expresses itself in the disciplined, rational stewardship of his assets with a view to long-term, but reasonable, growth:

> The man who lives within his income, is naturally contented with his situation, which, by continual, though small accumulations, is growing better and better every day. He is enabled gradually to relax, both in the rigour of his parsimony and in the severity of its application; and he feels with double satisfaction this gradual increase of ease and enjoyment, from having felt before the hardship which attended the want of them. He has no anxiety to change so comfortable a situation, and does not go in quest of new enterprises and adventures, which might endanger, but could not well increase, the secure tranquillity which he actually enjoys. If he enters into any new projects or enterprises, they are likely to be well concerted and well prepared. He can never be hurried or drove into them by any necessity, but has always time and leisure to deliberate soberly and coolly concerning what are likely to be their consequences.

However, the prudent man is more the object of others' temperate approval than of any stronger emotion:

> Prudence, in short, when directed merely to the care of health, of the fortune, and of the rank and reputation of the individual, though it is regarded as a most respectable and even, in some degree, as an amiable and agreeable quality, yet it never is considered as one, either of the most endearing, or of the most ennobling of the virtues. It commands a certain cold esteem, but seems not entitled to any very ardent love or admiration.[295]

295. Smith, *Sentiments*, VI.i.11–14, pp. 215–16.

The other Athenians we observe conform for the most part to Smith's model of prudence, and Athens as a society displays the paradox of civilisation that lies at the centre of Smith's vision of civil society: namely, impersonal calculations of self-interest take the place of the sense of personal obligation and, when grossed up across a whole society, produce what look like the same effects of mutuality and apparent benevolence.

Nevertheless, the emotional and ethical *habitus* of this civilised world is very different, as the First Stranger observes:

> Men must learn now with pity to dispense,
> For policy sits above conscience.[296]

It is an insight elaborated in the following scene by the Servant when reflecting on Sempronius:

> Excellent. Your lordship's a goodly villain. The devil knew not what he did when he made man politic. He crossed himself by't, and I cannot think but in the end the villainies of men will set him clear. How fairly this lord strives to appear foul, takes virtuous copies to be wicked. Like those that under hot ardent zeal would set whole realms on fire, of such a nature is his politic love.[297]

The ascendancy of the political above the personal in Athens is dramatised in act III, scene vi, the strangely unattached scene in which Alcibiades pleads for the life of one of his soldiers who has killed a man. At the level of plot, the function of this scene is to explain Alcibiades's banishment from Athens. However, Shakespeare elaborates this transaction, which might have been presented more economically or even simply reported, into an *agon* between competing ideas of justice which draws in its wake important ideas about human development.

The Senators repeatedly take their stand on strict law:

> My lord, you have my voice to't. The fault's bloody;
> 'Tis necessary he should die.
> Nothing emboldens sin so much as mercy.
>
> We are for law. He dies. Urge it no more
> On height of our displeasure. Friend or brother,
> He forfeits his own blood that spills another.[298]

296. *Timon*, III.ii.81–82.
297. *Timon*, III.iii.27–33.
298. *Timon*, III.vi.1–3 and 85–87.

It is not difficult to recognise in this insistence on law the accent of civilisation. Against it, Alcibiades mounts a series of would-be extenuations. In the first place, he points out that the accused soldier attacked his victim 'with a noble fury and fair spirit', to which the First Senator explains that this excuse might have had some force in an earlier stage of human development:

> Your words have took such pains as if they labored
> To bring manslaughter into form and set quarreling
> Upon the head of valor, which indeed
> Is valor misbegot and came into the world
> When sects and factions were newly born.

Civil society has driven out that ethical and political immaturity and the imperative of revenge which thrived within it. Such primitivism has been replaced with new, patient, and ultimately prudentially-calculating forms of virtue:

> He's truly valiant that can wisely suffer
> The worst that man can breathe, and make his wrongs his outsides,
> To wear them like his raiment, carelessly,
> And ne'er prefer his injuries to his heart,
> To bring it in to danger.
> If wrong be evils and enforce us kill,
> What folly 'tis to hazard life for ill.[299]

As the Senator summarises, encapsulating the Aeschylean transition from justice as revenge to justice as law, 'To revenge is no valor, but to bear.'[300] Alcibiades replies with two observations (and here the scene begins to cover the same ethico-political ground as is covered in *Coriolanus*). Firstly, if patience is virtue, then why do men defend themselves against aggression? And secondly, his soldier killed in passion, not cold blood:

> Who cannot condemn rashness in cold blood?
> To kill, I grant, is sin's extremest gust,
> But in defense, by mercy, 'tis most just.
> To be in anger is impiety,
> But who is man that is not angry?
> Weigh but the crime with this.[301]

299. *Timon*, III.vi.17, 25–29, and 30–36.
300. *Timon*, III.vi.48.
301. *Timon*, III.vi.52–57.

When these arguments also fail, Alcibiades mentions his soldier's creditable military service, when his gift for violence was a benefit to the state:

> Why, I say, my lords, he's done fair service
> And slain in fight many of your enemies.
> How full of valor did he bear himself
> In the last conflict and made plenteous wounds![302]

However, the Second Senator then seizes on the words 'plenteous' and 'valor', and twists Alcibiades's defence into the pretext for an attack on the soldier's rowdiness:

> He has made too much plenty with him.
> He's a sworn rioter; he has a sin
> That often drowns him and takes his valor prisoner.
> . . . 'Tis inferred to us
> His days are foul and his drink dangerous.[303]

Finally, Alcibiades rests his plea for mercy to be shown towards his soldier on his own merit and desert (the quality of personal worth the Romans called *dignitas*): 'My lords, I do beseech you know me. . . . Call me to your remembrances. . . . My wounds ache at you.'[304] The foundation of this appeal—namely, that individuals may enjoy a different relationship with justice in the light of their past meritorious behaviour—strikes at the heart of the civilised, law-based, regime of justice with which the Senators have associated themselves, and so it is unsurprising that it should provoke Alcibiades's banishment and the immediate execution of his soldier.

However, Alcibiades's bitter response to this imperious treatment opens up a new side-light on the civilised, law-based world of Athens, which reveals that it is not as austerely impersonal as it proclaims itself to be:

> I'm worse than mad; I have kept back their foes
> While they have told their money and let out
> Their coin upon large interest, I myself

302. *Timon*, III.vi.62–65.

303. *Timon*, III.vi.66–68 and 72–73. Cf. Rudyard Kipling, 'Tommy', ll. 37–38: 'For it's Tommy this, an' Tommy that, an' "Chuck him out, the brute!" / But it's "Saviour of 'is country" when the guns begin to shoot'.

304. *Timon*, III.vi.88, 89, and 94. Cf. the importance of Coriolanus's wounds (*Coriolanus*, II.iii.47, 70–71, and 121).

> Rich only in large hurts. All those, for this?
> Is this the balsam that the usuring Senate
> Pours into captains' wounds? Banishment![305]

The heat of anger crystallises Alcibiades's insight that the facade of civilised rectitude the Senators have erected in Athens masks a system of surreptitious private profit to the benefit of 'the usuring Senate', while its soldiers bleed and die. The insight reflects back sharply on the earlier part of the scene and on Alcibiades's failed pleas for mercy. Alcibiades had hoped that there might be some atoning equivalence for spilled blood that fell short of strict retribution. The Senators took their stand on the high moral ground that there could be no equivalence for blood except blood itself: 'He forfeits his own blood that spills another.'[306] Yet their own pursuit of private, usurious profit secured by the valiant actions of the Athenian soldiery is in effect just such a trade of blood for cash, just as prostitution (the only industry we see at work in Athens, apart from the purveyors of luxury goods in act I) is a trade of flesh for cash. The scene as a whole, in its dramatisation of a collision between the military and the civic, *dignitas* and *iustitia*, and the immemorial and the recent, recalls Carlyle on the way that, in the early nineteenth century, the ascendancy of cash was changing human relations and perceptions of value:

> *Cash Payment* had not then grown to be the universal sole nexus of man to man; it was something other than money that the high then expected from the low. Not as buyer and seller alone, of land or what else it might be, but in many senses still as soldier and captain, as clansman and head, as loyal subject and guiding king, was the low related to the high. With the supreme triumph of Cash, a changed time has entered; there must a changed Aristocracy enter.[307]

This scene both displays in action and finally offers a devastating critique of the self-contradictory pretensions of Athens to be a civilised state and of the virtue of the 'changed Aristocracy' of Senators that governs it.

305. *Timon*, III.vi.104–9.

306. *Timon*, III.vi.87.

307. Carlyle, *Chartism*, p. 36. Cf. also 'epochs when Cash Payment has become the sole nexus of man to man!' (ibid., p. 38); 'In these complicated times, with Cash Payment as the sole nexus between man and man' (ibid., p. 40); 'Cash Payment the sole nexus; and there are so many things which cash will not pay! Cash is a great miracle; yet it has not all power in Heaven, nor even on Earth' (ibid., p. 41).

So it is perhaps unsurprising, given this fundamental contradiction in their ethico-political mode of being, that the Athenian senators, for all their display of inflexible rectitude and Smithian prudence, are easily corrupted when brought into contact with the reckless extravagance shown by Timon. For it is this encounter that elicits the various kinds of moral deformity we see anatomised in Lucius, Lucullus, Ventidius, and Sempronius in act III. In the same way, we might say that Timon's imprudence creates and provokes the cynicism of Apemantus. Apemantus, no less than Timon's flattering friends, is Timon's creature.

Timon's exorbitant generosity thus leads to an unexpected 'zero-sum' situation, in which it stimulates not (on the model of the potlatch) an inflation of heedless generosity in those who first receive and then reciprocate it but rather a guileful and pre-meditated strategy of subtle fleecing and a deep perversion of the idea of the gift into that of a reliably profitable venture. The words of the Senator show how Timon's largesse acts as a corrupting temptation to the prudent man and as an economically-distorting influence in a society largely made up of prudent men:

> If I want gold, steal but a beggar's dog
> And give it Timon, why, the dog coins gold!
> If I would sell my horse and buy twenty more
> Better than he, why, give my horse to Timon.
> Ask nothing, give it him; it foals me straight
> And able horses.[308]

The apparent ingratitude of Lucius, Lucullus, Ventidius, and Sempronius is not the obverse of Timon's blind open-handedness. Rather, it is its offspring. The Athenian nobles display the corruption that Smithian prudence naturally undergoes when it meets Rousseauvian 'orgueil' in the form of Timon's ostentatious largesse. Underneath the apparent discontinuity of flattery succeeded by desertion there is a constancy of contempt, as Apemantus notes: 'The middle of humanity thou never knewest, but the extremity of both ends. When thou wast in thy gilt and thy perfume, they mocked thee for too much curiosity; in thy rags thou know'st none, but art despised for the contrary.'[309]

308. *Timon*, II.i.5–10. Timon will later seem to detect just such a prudent, calculating generosity in his Steward: 'Is not thy kindness subtle, covetous, / If not a usuring kindness, and, as rich men deal gifts, / Expecting in return twenty for one?' (ibid., IV.iii.500–503).

309. *Timon*, IV.iii.301–5.

In this perspective, Timon remains a victim. But, in the final analysis, he is a victim of himself and of the changes his exorbitancy produces in those around him, rather than being simply a victim of the malice or ingratitude of others. 'The malice of mankind' is what motivates Timon in act IV, as the first bandit realises. But Timon's extravagant largesse in act I was also, in its tendency at least, if not in conscious intention, malicious, because of the way it corrupted the characters of his flatterers. Again, we find a paradoxical equivalence—and it is this sense of equivalence that prevents *Timon* from being in the fullest sense tragic. Over the course of the play Timon does not really undergo a fall, just a translation into ostensibly very different, but on closer inspection curiously similar, conditions of life.

I earlier mentioned the surprising observation that, in a Rousseauvian perspective, Apemantus and Timon in act I, although apparently opposites, are in fact images of each other; and I want now to explore a little further the insight that, in this play, opposites become identities by considering the extraordinary act IV, scene iii, and the prelude to it in act III, scene vii, Timon's mock-banquet.[310] Timon's friends attend the banquet expecting 'the old man still' but instead are treated to only hot water, prefaced by a mock-grace and followed by blows and insults from Timon.[311] The friends see this as a shocking reversal of behaviour:

> He gave me a jewel th'other day, and now he has beat it out of my hat.
> One day he gives us diamonds, next day stones.[312]

But in fact there are clear continuities between Timon generous and Timon mad, for his generosity was insane and his madness is exorbitant. And Apemantus sees this, too:

> Thou hast cast away thyself being like thyself,
> A madman so long, now a fool.[313]

Timon's open-handedness towards his fellow-Athenians tended, as we have seen, to corrupt them. As such, although it was more acceptable to them, it

310. The mock-banquet is not present in any of Shakespeare's sources for *Timon*. Viewed in terms of Shakespeare's own past dramatic practice, it is in part a *rifacimento* of the mock-banquet in *Titus Andronicus* (which is present in the sources for that play and is itself a duplicate of the banquet served by Atreus to Thyestes in Greek mythology).

311. *Timon*, III.vii.58.

312. *Timon*, III.vii.105–6 and 110.

313. *Timon*, IV.iii.221–22.

was no more in their true interest than the beating and abuse he bestows on them in the mock-banquet; it gave effect in advance to the misanthropy Timon will express so extravagantly later in the play. Moreover, there was mockery also in the first banquet, which was paid for out of mortgages, and so in a sense was in the final analysis the equivalent of the 'Smoke and lukewarm water' Timon serves in act III, scene vii.[314] A recurrent motif in the play is the notion that people can ingest one another's substance.[315] But if the food at Timon's first banquet is in fact paid for with money borrowed from the guests, then this becomes a disguised kind of auto-cannibalism, as the guests consume their own substance in a ritual, not of genuine hospitality but rather of pollution, which thus recalls some of the atrocious meals recorded in Greek mythology.[316] When analysed, the apparently generous hospitality of act I resolves itself into something even more abusive, albeit surreptitiously so, than the mock-banquet of act III.

So by the time we reach act IV, scene iii, we are already familiar with the characteristic dramatic and poetic style of this play, in which apparent oppositions, on closer inspection, dissolve into identities. Towards the end of the scene, Timon's Steward exclaims, at a sight he construes as a vision of dreadful alteration, 'Is yond despised and ruinous man my lord? / Full of decay and failing?'[317] But was not Timon also despised and ruinous (albeit secretly so) at the beginning of the play? And was he not, also in fact, full of decay and failing then, too? The Steward's words are a declaration of alteration which in fact is an unwitting proclamation of continuity; and as such it summarises the scene, and indeed the play, of which it forms a part. In act IV, scene iii itself, the fact of continuity is conveyed through scenic form. It comprises six sections: (1) Timon *solus*; (2) Timon, Alcibiades, and the whores; (3) Timon *solus*; (4) Timon and Apemantus; (5) Timon and the bandits; and (6) Timon and the Steward. This structure echoes that of act I, scenes i and ii, which are also

314. *Timon*, III.vii.84.

315. E.g., Flaminius's reproach of Lucullus: 'This slave / Unto this hour has my lord's meat in him. / Why should it thrive and turn to nutriment, / When he is turned to poison?' (*Timon*, III.i.50–53). I will return shortly to the parodic echoes of Christian communion or mass in the play.

316. Such as, for instance, Cronus's yearly consumption of the children born to him by Rhea or Atreus's feeding Thyestes with the flesh of his own children.

317. *Timon*, IV.iii.452–53.

arranged as a series of self-contained encounters between Timon and the various guests at his house.[318]

This pattern of the collapsing of opposites into identities is found once more in the play's final scene, where Rousseauvian Athens is re-created. The end of the play thus returns us to its beginning. Coming back to Athens with his soldiers, Alcibiades, like Caius Martius, is adamant to the Senators on the city walls that the state will now be purged and reformed. Alcibiades, is, like Coriolanus, talked out of his revenge. But whereas Volumnia's appeal to Caius Martius touches on the deepest issues, the Senators talk Alcibiades out of his revenge with laughable, almost trivial, ease.

Alcibiades announces his arrival under the walls of Athens with a promise to destroy the bad faith with which the Senators have administered law, that cornerstone of civil society: 'making your wills / The scope of justice'.[319] In response, the Senators say that they have tried to make amends to both Alcibiades and Timon, that the truly guilty have died, that it would be unjust to kill those who remain. But the next phase of the dialogue is fascinating:

SECOND SENATOR. What thou wilt,
Thou rather shalt enforce it with thy smile
Than hew to't with thy sword.
FIRST SENATOR. Set but thy foot
Against our rampired gates, and they shall ope,
So thou wilt send thy gentle heart before
To say thou'lt enter friendly.[320]

The mention of 'smile' and 'gentle heart' suggests that Alcibiades's abandonment of violence will only initiate a revival of that 'living in the eyes of others', that judging of our own actions by the responses they provoke in others, that lay at the root of Timon's devastating experience.

So this is no convincing purging of Athens but just a resumption of the old ways. And that suggestion of a return to 'living in the eyes of others' is reinforced and amplified by the mention of 'thy glove / Or any token of thine honor' and the reassurance that Alcibiades's agreement to what is proposed is

318. Shakespeare has earlier used this scenic form in, e.g., *King Lear*, I.ii; and *Richard III*, I.i.
319. *Timon*, V.v.4–5.
320. *Timon*, V.v.44–49.

'most nobly spoken', since reputation and language were, as we have seen, two of the hinges on which the old Athens turned.[321]

Moreover, Alcibiades's assurance that his soldiers will be subject to strict law marks an extraordinary capitulation on his part, since it was precisely over the rigorous imposition of strict law that he put himself into exile from Athens in act III, scene vi:

> not a man
> Shall pass his quarter or offend the stream
> Of regular justice in your city's bounds
> But shall be remedied to your public laws
> At heaviest answer.[322]

Civil society (law, living in the eyes of others) has smoothly reimposed itself after the transient rupture made by Timon. This is therefore an enigmatic ending, which does nothing to solve the problem that the play has posed. Yet how could it? That problem—stemming from a profound clash of differing social formations and the attitudes and values they respectively promote—lies beyond resolution. In this view, the occasional anachronistic allusions to the Last Supper and to the rites of communion and the mass which flow from it are sardonically misplaced. In this play, the consuming of the substance of others delivers no atonement, no eternal life, not even temporary release from sorrow or need. It eventuates only in aggravated repetitions of the original offence.[323]

Rousseau's two *Discours* had an immediate impact throughout literary Europe. From Adam Smith, then professor of moral philosophy at Glasgow, the *Discours sur l'inegalité* (1755) had drawn both admiration and acute critique. In a letter to the fledgling *Edinburgh Review* encouraging the editors to widen the scope of their journal to include works of literature published in continental Europe, Smith had highlighted the importance of recent French philosophy by reviewing the *Discours sur l'inegalité*, which had been published earlier that year.[324] Smith had evidently read the *Discours* very quickly, but nevertheless with great penetration:

321. *Timon*, V.v.49–50 and V.v.63.

322. *Timon*, V.v.59–63.

323. E.g., *Timon*, III.ii.60–61.

324. Smith's letter to the *Edinburgh Review* is undated, but it appears to have been written in July 1755 and was published in the second issue of the *Review* in 1756. Rousseau's *Discours* was printed in April 1755, and it was on sale in June of that year. For further details relating to its

> Whoever reads this last work [the *Discours*] with attention, will observe, that the second volume of the Fable of the Bees has given occasion to the system of Mr. Rousseau, in whom however the principles of the English author are softened, improved, and embellished, and stript of all that tendency to corruption and licentiousness which has disgraced them in their original author. Dr. Mandeville represents the primitive state of mankind as the most wretched and miserable that can be imagined: Mr. Rousseau, on the contrary, paints it as the happiest and most suitable to his nature. Both of them however suppose, that there is in man no powerful instinct which necessarily determines him to seek society for its own sake: but according to the one, the misery of his original state compelled him to have recourse to this otherwise disagreeable remedy; according to the other, some unfortunate accidents having given birth to the unnatural passions of ambition and the vain desire of superiority, to which he had before been a stranger, produced the same fatal effect.[325]

In so framing his response to Rousseau, Smith drew on material he was then engaged in writing up and which would shortly be published as *The Theory of Moral Sentiments* (1759).[326] In that work, Smith would offer an account of the origin of civilisation and refinement different from both Mandeville's *pis-aller* and Rousseau's catastrophe; and he would do so by identifying in human nature the element that he had noticed was lacking in Mandeville's and Rousseau's accounts, namely, a 'powerful instinct which necessarily determines him [man] to seek society for its own sake'.[327]

Like other sentimentalist thinkers—Shaftesbury, Hutcheson, Hume—Smith believed that, to begin with at least, the moral experience of men and women was more a question of feeling than of thinking. The principle he placed in the foundation of his moral system is sympathy, that imaginative faculty by which we participate in the experiences (both good and bad, and for better or worse) of strangers. The repeated moral feelings stimulated by sympathy we eventually formalise into moral rules. But although our moral

publication, see *Diskurs über di Ungleichheit*, ed. Heinrich Meier (Paderborn: F. Schöningh, 1984), p. 6. The text of Smith's letter is reprinted in Smith, *Essays*, pp. 242–56.

325. Smith, *Essays*, p. 250.

326. *The Theory of Moral Sentiments* is an elaboration and systematisation of lectures on moral philosophy that Smith had been giving in Glasgow since 1752 (Smith, *Sentiments*, 'Introduction', pp. 2–3).

327. Smith, *Essays*, p. 250.

feelings thereby attain propositional clarity and may even be rationally debated, such authority as they exert over our actions remains more affective than intellectual, more a matter of passion than of judgement.

Smith argues that our moral characters are shaped by the endlessly iterated process of experiencing moral sentiments, upon which we subsequently reflect. The result is a modulation of our raw human nature, in which the sociableness embedded within us as sympathy leads us to find our well-being in the imagined approbation of others: 'We desire both to be respectable and to be respected. We dread both to be contemptible and to be contemned.'[328] Over time, this custom of imagining the assessments of our actions that would be made by impartial spectators bestows a kind of theatricality upon our moral sense:

> We become anxious to know how far we deserve their [other people's] censure or applause, and whether to them we must necessarily appear those agreeable or disagreeable creatures which they represent us. We begin, upon this account, to examine our own passions and conduct, and to consider how these must appear to them, by considering how they would appear to us if in their situation. We suppose ourselves the spectators of our own behaviour, and endeavour to imagine what effect it would, in this light, produce upon us. This is the only looking-glass by which we can, in some measure, with the eyes of other people, scrutinize the propriety of our own conduct.[329]

In Smith's moral paragon, the 'man of real constancy and firmness', this complicated process of sympathetic imagination and self-reflection becomes second nature:

> He has never dared to forget for one moment the judgment which the impartial spectator would pass upon his sentiments and conduct. He has never dared to suffer the man within the breast to be absent one moment from his attention. With the eyes of this great inmate he has always been accustomed to regard whatever relates to himself. . . . He does not merely

328. Smith, *Sentiments*, I.iii.3.2, p. 62. Cf. the theatrical metaphor Smith selects to express the satisfaction felt by the virtuous man: 'He enjoys his own complete self-approbation, and the applause of every candid and impartial spectator' (ibid., III.iii.28, p. 148; cf. also 'the applause of his own breast', ibid., III.v.13, p. 170).

329. Smith, *Sentiments*, III.i.5, p. 112.

> affect the sentiments of the impartial spectator. He really adopts them. He almost identifies himself with, he almost becomes himself that impartial spectator, and scarce even feels but as that great arbiter of his conduct directs him to feel.[330]

Hence it is that, by an entirely natural process, our sense of our own well-being and happiness is tangled around our imagined estimates of the opinions of strangers: 'in order to attain this satisfaction [of being genuinely admirable], we must become the impartial spectators of our own character and conduct. We must endeavour to view them with the eyes of other people, or as other people are likely to view them.'[331]

Smith thus agrees with Rousseau that modern man lives out his life 'in the eyes of others'. But whereas Rousseau had stigmatised this as a source of inauthenticity and self-estrangement, Smith instead makes our natural sensitivity to the opinions of others the foundation of our rectitude and sense of self-worth: 'Our sensibility to the feelings of others, so far from being inconsistent with the manhood of self-command, is the very principle upon which that manhood is founded.'[332] For nature has endowed the virtuous man 'not only with a desire of being approved of, but with a desire of being what ought to be approved of; or of being what he himself approves of in other men.'[333]

If *Timon of Athens* is Shakespeare's Rousseauvian satire on the poisonous inauthenticity of civilisation, then *The Tempest* is his Smithian *riposte* to that earlier play. Smith supposed that, were we to live 'in the eyes of others' without reservation, the result would be morally salutary: 'If we saw ourselves in the light in which others see us, or in which they would see us if they knew all, a reformation would generally be unavoidable. We could not otherwise endure the sight'.[334] In *The Tempest,* Prospero's design, which takes effect in large measure by controlling what is seen and what unseen by the other characters, puts onstage and culminates in just the kind of moral reformation (at least in the case of Alonso) that Smith here imagines.

330. Smith, *Sentiments,* III.iii.25, pp. 146–47.
331. Smith, *Sentiments,* III.ii.2, p. 114.
332. Smith, *Sentiments,* III.iii.34, p. 152.
333. Smith, *Sentiments,* III.ii.7, p. 117.
334. Smith, *Sentiments,* III.iv.6, pp. 158–59.

'No tongue, all eyes!' commands Prospero before the 'most majestic vision' of the masque of Juno begins.[335] Prospero's four words are in many ways the keynote of *The Tempest*. The visual richness of this play (evident, for instance, in the masque of Juno itself, in the mock-banquet, and in Ariel's shape-shifting) has received much comment and has usually been associated with the wider and more ambitious possibilities of staging that were open to Shakespeare once his company, the King's Men, had in 1608 acquired the lease of the Blackfriars theatre. This enclosed playing space was smaller than the Globe but was equipped with more advanced stage machinery and offered greater possibilities for musical embellishment than were available in the public theatres for which Shakespeare had previously written.

However, the recurrent emphases on eyes, on sight, and on the act of beholding that we find throughout *The Tempest* are not merely a reflection of its visually-enhanced dramaturgy and the superior technical resources of the playing spaces for which it was written. In *The Tempest*, the eyes are a moral organ (as they had previously been, but more distressingly, in *King Lear*: 'Look there. Look there!').[336] When Miranda and Ferdinand have met and fallen in love, Prospero expresses what has happened in language which is surely unexpected yet entirely appropriate to this play: 'At the first sight / They have changed *eyes*.'[337] Juliet had expressed a more conventional idea of how love takes effect on the body: 'God joined my *heart* and Romeo's', she tells Friar Laurence.[338] In *A Midsummer Night's Dream*, Helena had spurned the thought that the eyes have any role to play in love: 'Love looks not with the eyes but with the mind.'[339] In *The Merchant of Venice*, the song that Portia has performed while Bassanio is making his choice of casket seemed to make the eyes sovereign in love:

Tell me where is fancy bred:
Or in the heart or in the head;
How begot, how nourishèd?
Reply, reply!
It is engend'red in the eye,

335. *The Tempest*, IV.i.59 and 118.

336. *King Lear*, V.iii.287.

337. *The Tempest*, I.ii.439–40; emphasis added.

338. *Romeo and Juliet*, IV.i.55; emphasis added.

339. *A Midsummer Night's Dream*, I.i.234.

With gazing fed; and fancy dies
In the cradle where it lies.[340]

But this is a backdrop to a moment of decision in which Bassanio will need to discount what his eyes tell him, if he is going to win Portia by choosing the leaden casket. Accordingly, he responds to the song intelligently by recalling how easily the eyes may be deceived: 'There is no vice so simple but assumes / Some mark of virtue on his outward parts.'[341]

But Prospero would disagree. When he brings Miranda and Ferdinand together, he does so by marshalling and directing Miranda's eyes, not her mind:

The fringèd curtains of thine *eye* advance
And say what thou *seest* yond.[342]

And when Miranda is smitten by Ferdinand, it is surely significant that she responds initially to what she notices about the conspicuously active quality of his seeing: 'Lord, how it *looks* about.'[343] She then reassures Prospero about the strength of her feelings by once more invoking the sense of sight: 'I have no ambition / To *see* a goodlier man.'[344]

Turning to Ferdinand, it is a certain possibility of future vision that consoles him for all the manifold losses he believes he has suffered in the shipwreck:

My father's loss, the weakness which I feel,
The wreck of all my friends, nor this man's threats
To whom I am subdued, are but light to me,
Might I but through my prison once a day
Behold this maid.[345]

And later in the play, he will assure Miranda that his love for her began in a moment of seeing:

340. *The Merchant of Venice*, III.ii.63–69.

341. *The Merchant of Venice*, III.ii.81–82. Sonnets 46 and 47 also show Shakespeare debating the merits of heart and eye as the organ of love.

342. *The Tempest*, I.ii.407–8; emphases added.

343. *The Tempest*, I.ii.409; emphasis added.

344. *The Tempest*, I.ii.481–82; emphasis added.

345. *The Tempest*, I.ii.486–90; emphasis added.

The very instant that I *saw* you did
My heart fly to your service, there resides
To make me slave to it, and for your sake
Am I this patient log-man.[346]

For in *The Tempest*, the eyes are not the embodiment of superficiality and ease of deception, as the device of the juice of 'love-in-idleness' figures them to be in *A Midsummer Night's Dream*.[347] Rather, as Prospero's explanation to Miranda of the shipwreck she has just witnessed implies, the eyes are the organs that, in morally-healthy individuals, mobilise, guide, and feed the moral sense:

Wipe thou thine *eyes*; have comfort.
The direful *spectacle* of the wreck, which touched
The very virtue of compassion in thee,
I have, . . . [348]

Similarly, when Prospero has narrated the circumstance of their expulsion from Milan, Miranda's awakened but imagined distress finds expression through the eyes:

Alack, for pity!
I, not remembering how I cried out then,
Will cry it o'er again; it is a hint
That wrings mine *eyes* to't.[349]

Therefore, in this play, it is entirely right that, in Ariel's fiction of the drowned Alonso, his bones are enriched into coral, but his eyes undergo a 'sea-change' into something yet more rare and precious: 'Those are pearls that were his eyes'.[350]

346. *The Tempest*, III.i.64–67; emphasis added.

347. *A Midsummer Night's Dream*, II.i.155–74.

348. *The Tempest*, I.ii.25–28; emphases added.

349. *The Tempest*, I.ii.132–34; emphasis added.

350. *The Tempest*, I.ii.399 and 397. T. S. Eliot's use of this line in *The Waste Land* ('II. A Game of Chess', l. 125) transposes it parodically into a setting of moral and emotional sterility. Ariel's song seems to have exerted a strong grip over Eliot's moral and literary imagination. When, in 'Shakespeare and the Stoicism of Seneca', he wanted to evoke his understanding of what a poet does when writing, it was to another line of this song that he turned for the necessary words: 'Shakespeare, too, was occupied with the struggle—which alone constitutes life for a poet—to transmute his personal and private agonies into something rich and strange, something universal and impersonal' (Eliot, *Essays*, p. 137). Ariel's song is a compressed version of lines that

So in *The Tempest*, the language of seeing is associated closely with the emotions of love and compassion. That feature of the play's language, as we have suggested by comparison with *Romeo and Juliet* and *A Midsummer Night's Dream*, was not an automatic or inevitable association for Shakespeare but rather seems to have been deliberately chosen and closely adapted to the needs of this later play. That connotation, however, is given further depth by the fact that Prospero's artful management of the action on the island is intended to bring about a moral reformation. Smith would insist that

> There is no commonly honest man . . . who does not inwardly feel the truth of that great stoical maxim, that for one man to deprive another unjustly of any thing, or unjustly to promote his own advantage by the loss or disadvantage of another, is more contrary to nature, than death, than poverty, than pain, than all the misfortunes which can affect him, either in his body, or in his external circumstances.[351]

It is to such 'common honesty' that Prospero wishes to awaken Alonso, Antonio, and Sebastian. And Prospero seeks to attain this Smithian object by Smithian ends—by means, that is, of a stringent control of the visible, as his commands to Ariel reveal:

> Go make thyself like a nymph o'th'sea. Be subject
> To no sight by thine and mine, invisible
> To every eyeball else. Go, take this shape
> And hither come in't.
>
> This was well done, my bird.
> Thy shape invisible retain thou still.[352]

Prospero's art allows him to foresee danger, while his management operates by controlling what his playthings see—negatively by corralling them into separate parts of the island, positively through Ariel's visions and illusions.[353] 'Behold' commands Prospero, as his drama of manifold anagnorisis begins in

---

Shakespeare had many years earlier, in *Richard III*, put into the mouth of Clarence, when relating his dream of drowning to his jailer Brakenbury. Clarence refers to this dream (surely significantly) as 'the tempest to my soul' (*Richard III*, I.iv.23–31 and 41).

351. Smith, *Sentiments*, III.iii.6, p. 138.

352. *The Tempest*, I.ii.301–4 and IV.i.184–85.

353. *The Tempest*, II.i.290.

act V, scene i.[354] The play culminates in a coerced rendezvous ('enforce them to this place') which involves not just the physical recognition of those thought lost but the moral recognition of past crimes believed to have been buried beyond recovery, as Alonso acknowledges: 'Thy dukedom I resign and do entreat / Thou pardon me my wrongs.'[355]

Adam Smith, as we have seen, insists on the visual character of our moral sense. Prospero's artificial control of what the shipwrecked survivors see turns the island into a moral laboratory. By keeping Antonio and Sebastian awake while sending Alonso, Gonzalo, Francisco, and Adrian to sleep in act II, scene i, Prospero creates a moment of 'occasion' for Antonio and Sebastian: an opportunity to repeat Antonio's treasonable usurpation of the dukedom of Milan and allow Sebastian to seize the throne of Naples.[356] It is the circumstance of being unobserved that permits Antonio's and Sebastian's vicious natures to ripen into action. Of course, Smith would argue that, even when the virtuous man is literally unobserved, his moral sense will remain active because of his imagination of the judgement of an impartial spectator, 'the man within the breast'.[357] But Antonio, in an eerie anticipation of Smith's moral language, denies the existence of any such being in his case. When Sebastian asks, 'But for your conscience?', Antonio replies:

> Ay, sir, where lies that? If 'twere a kibe,
> 'Twould put me to my slipper; but I feel not
> This deity in my bosom. Twenty consciences
> That stand twixt me and Milan, candied be they,
> And melt ere they molest.[358]

354. *The Tempest*, V.i.106.

355. *The Tempest*, V.i.100 and 118–19.

356. *The Tempest*, II.i.200 and 283–87.

357. Smith, *Sentiments*, III.ii.33, p. 132.

358. *The Tempest*, II.i.268–73. In another point of contact with *Richard III* (see above, p. 186, n. 350), Antonio's scornful rejection of conscience reworks the Second Executioner's denunciation of conscience as 'a blushing shamefast spirit that mutinies in man's bosom' and a 'dangerous thing' that every man who 'means to live well' should 'live without', and also echoes Richard's own final rejection of conscience as 'but a word that cowards use / Devised at first to keep the strong in awe' (*Richard III*, I.iv.126–32 and V.iii.307–8). In *King John*, Shakespeare makes King Philip appeal to 'that supernal judge that stirs good thoughts / In any breast of strong authority, / To look into the blots and stains of right' (*King John*, II.i.112–14).

Compare Smith's characterisation of our moral sense as 'the great inmate, the great demi-god within the breast', and his idea of moral principles as 'the commands and laws of the Deity, promulgated by those vicegerents which he has thus set up within us'.[359]

If Antonio and Sebastian are images of Smithian vice, then Miranda and Ferdinand are images of Smithian rectitude. We have seen how Miranda's response to the shipwreck demonstrates that she possesses a healthy sense of sympathy. Act III, scene i, dramatises a competition of Smithian virtue, as both Ferdinand and Miranda strive to appear ever more lovable in the eyes of the other.[360] When Ferdinand, *solus* for the moment, takes moral consolation from the compassion he sees awakened in Miranda by her beholding of his labours, it is a richly Smithian moment of moral and sympathetic living in the eyes of others:

> My sweet mistress
> Weeps when she sees me work and says such baseness
> Had never like executor. I forget;
> But these sweet thoughts do even refresh my labors,
> Most busil'est, when I do it.[361]

If Miranda and Ferdinand are images of Smithian virtue, then Alonso, Antonio, and Sebastian are images of Smithian moral failing. The spectacle of the banquet which Ariel disrupts in the guise of a harpy has, as Prospero intended, reduced his enemies to 'fits' and 'knit' them up in 'their distractions' of remembered guilt.[362] Gonzalo understands well the inward moral drama that is being acted out:

> All three of them are desperate: their great guilt,
> Like poison given to work a great time after,
> Now gins to bite the spirits.[363]

When Smith describes the effect of remorse, his account, though generalised, nevertheless describes very precisely the effect of Prospero's design on Alonso,

359. Smith, *Sentiments*, VI.iii.18, p. 245, and III.v.6, p. 165.

360. It is a virtuous wrestling match that is parodied in the various contests of vice staged in the comic scenes featuring Stefano and Trinculo (act II, scene ii, and act III, scene ii).

361. *The Tempest*, III.i.11–15.

362. *The Tempest*, III.iii.90–92.

363. *The Tempest*, III.iii.105–7.

who repents, and in part on Antonio and Sebastian, whose sullenness suggests an inward mortification that however cannot rise to an outward expression of regret. The entire passage is worth quoting, because at so many points it seems to comment pertinently upon the action of *The Tempest*:

> The violator of the more sacred laws of justice can never reflect on the sentiments which mankind must entertain with regard to him, without feeling all the agonies of shame, and horror, and consternation. When his passion is gratified, and he begins coolly to reflect on his past conduct, he can enter into none of the motives which influenced it. They appear now as detestable to him as they did always to other people. By sympathizing with the hatred and abhorrence which other men must entertain for him, he becomes in some measure the object of his own hatred and abhorrence. The situation of the person, who suffered by his injustice, now calls upon his pity. He is grieved at the thought of it; regrets the unhappy effects of his own conduct, and feels at the same time that they have rendered him the proper object of the resentment and indignation of mankind, and of what is the natural consequence of resentment, vengeance and punishment. The thought of this perpetually haunts him, and fills him with terror and amazement. He dares no longer look society in the face, but imagines himself as it were rejected, and thrown out from the affections of all mankind. He cannot hope for the consolation of sympathy in this his greatest and most dreadful distress. The remembrance of his crimes has shut out all fellow-feeling with him from the hearts of his fellow-creatures. The sentiments which they entertain with regard to him, are the very thing which he is most afraid of. Every thing seems hostile, and he would be glad to fly to some inhospitable desert, where he might never more behold the face of a human creature, nor read in the countenance of mankind the condemnation of his own crimes. But solitude is still more dreadful than society. His own thoughts can present him with nothing but what is black, unfortunate, and disastrous, the melancholy forebodings of incomprehensible misery and ruin. The horror of solitude drives him back into society, and he comes again into the presence of mankind, astonished to appear before them, loaded with shame and distracted with fear, in order to supplicate some little protection from the countenance of those very judges, who he knows have already all unanimously condemned him. Such is the nature of that sentiment, which is properly called remorse; of all the sentiments which can enter the human breast the most dreadful. It is made up of shame from the sense of the

impropriety of past conduct; of grief for the effects of it; of pity for those who suffer by it; and of the dread and terror of punishment from the consciousness of the justly provoked resentment of all rational creatures.[364]

The overwhelmingly Smithian character of *The Tempest* is further confirmed by its sole Rousseauvian element, namely, Gonzalo's playful account of what he would do had he the 'plantation of this isle':

I'th'commonwealth I would by contraries
Execute all things. For no kind of traffic
Would I admit; no name of magistrate;
Letters should not be known; riches, poverty,
And use of service, none; contract, succession,
Bourn, bound of land, tilth, vineyard, none;
No use of metal, corn, or wine, or oil;
No occupation, all men idle, all;
And women too, but innocent and pure;
No sovereignty . . .
All things in common nature should produce
Without sweat or endeavor. Treason, felony,
Sword, pike, knife, gun, or need of any engine
Would I not have; but nature should bring forth
Of it own kind, all foison, all abundance,
To feed my innocent people.[365]

It has long been known that in these lines Shakespeare was recalling a passage from John Florio's translation of Montaigne's 'Les Cannibales'.[366] Less often remarked, however, is a further detail in the *nachleben* of this essay. For it would be precisely this same passage from Montaigne that would seem to have guided Rousseau's pen when he was trying to evoke what human society was

364. Smith, *Sentiments*, II.ii.3, pp. 84–85.

365. *The Tempest*, II.i.142–51 and 154–59.

366. 'It is a nation . . . that hath no kinde of traffike, no knowledge of Letters, no intelligence of numbers, no name of magistrate, nor of politike superioritie; no vse of service, of riches or of povertie; no contracts, no successions, no partitions, no occupation but idle, no respect of kinred, but common, no apparell but naturall, no manuring of lands, no vse of wine, corne, or mettle. The very words that import lying, falshood, treason, dissimulations, covetousnes, envie, detraction, and pardon, were never heard of amongst them' (Montaigne, *Essayes Written In French by Michael Lord of Montaigne*, trans. John Florio [1613], sig. K3^{v}, p. 102).

like before the calamitous advent of refinement and inequality.[367] Yet Gonzalo is not offering this image of a commonwealth as a serious suggestion. It is merely 'merry fooling', or as we might say a thought experiment, offered in a gentle and kindly attempt to distract Alonso from his sorrow after the insensitive rebukes he has just received from Antonio and Sebastian.[368] Caliban serves as a standing and vivid reminder in *The Tempest* of what human savagery is really like.

Yet to Caliban Shakespeare nevertheless gave lines that, albeit perhaps unconsciously, respond powerfully and precisely to the place of *The Tempest* in Shakespeare's work and to its relationship with its predecessors:

> Be not afeard: the isle is full of noises,
> Sounds and sweet airs that give delight and hurt not.[369]

Just as the island resonates with artful sounds, so *The Tempest* resonates with memories and revisions of earlier Shakespearean drama. Prospero, like Vincentio in *Measure for Measure*, has neglected the duties of rule to pursue private study.[370] The dialogue between Antonio and Sebastian, in which the former tempts the latter, is a reworking of several Shakespearean predecessors: of the guarded tempting of Brutus by Cassius, of Macbeth first by the witches and then by Lady Macbeth, and finally of Young Pompey by Menas.[371]

But it is with *Hamlet* that *The Tempest* is most extensively and intensively engaged. The two plays share so many elements. The pre-histories of both plays turn on the resentments felt by younger brothers for their older and more entitled siblings. Like Old Hamlet, Prospero gives an opportunity to those who would take his life because ''tis a custom with him / I'th'afternoon to sleep.'[372] Gonzalo is a benevolent re-imagining of Polonius, and Antonio and Sebastian's disparaging commentary on his attempts to console Alonso are a transcription of the audience response to Polonius that, as Quentin Skinner

367. See above, p. 167, n. 280.

368. *The Tempest*, II.i.171.

369. *The Tempest*, III.ii.128–29.

370. *Measure for Measure*, I.iii.19–31 and 34–54; *The Tempest*, I.ii.66–77.

371. *Julius Caesar*, I.ii.25–300; *Macbeth*, I.iii.39–79 and I.vii.29–82; *Antony and Cleopatra*, II.vii.56–85.

372. *The Tempest*, III.ii.81–82. Cf. *Hamlet*, I.v.59–60.

has shown, Shakespeare seems deliberately to have fostered by manipulating the principles of forensic oratory.[373]

That these two plays should be dramatic isomers of each other is perhaps not surprising, since together they mark the full span of Shakespeare's engagement with questions of civilisation and the alternatives to it: *Hamlet*, a dyspeptic Freudian exploration of civilisation's discontents; *The Tempest*, an affectionate Smithian tribute to its consolations.

373. Skinner, *Forensic*, principally pp. 150–54 and 187–90.

3

Throne and Altar

MACBETH

> This is by no means the only difficulty in the dominion of Law. The brute force for its execution must be purchased; and the mass of its subjects must be persuaded to respect the authority which employs this force. But how is such respect to be implanted in them if they are unable to comprehend the thought of the lawgiver? Clearly, only by associating the legislative power with such displays of splendor and majesty as will impress their senses and awe their imaginations. The god turned lawgiver, in short, must be crowned Pontiff and King. Since he cannot be known to the common folk as their superior in wisdom, he must be known to them as their superior in riches, as the dweller in castles, the wearer of gold and purple, the eater of mighty feasts, the commander of armies, and the wielder of powers of life and death, of salvation and damnation after death.
>
> —GEORGE BERNARD SHAW[1]

IN *BISHOP BURNET'S HISTORY OF HIS OWN TIME*, Burnet pauses in his narrative of the events leading up to the Exclusion Crisis of 1681 to give a summary account of the various arguments deployed, on the one hand, by those who had advocated the exclusion of the Roman Catholic Duke of York (later James II) from the succession to the throne and, on the other, by those who had opposed it. Many of these arguments had involved technical questions of English

1. Shaw, *Wagnerite*, p. 12.

law and precedent. But each side had also staked out their ground on more general and universal principles. Those who supported the exclusion of the Duke of York, so Burnet tells us, relied upon a particular view of the ends that government had been created to serve: 'Government was appointed for those that were to be governed, and not for the sake of Governors themselves: Therefore all things relating to it were to be measured by the publick interest, and the safety of the people.' In resisting such arguments as these, the opponents of exclusion had relied upon a quite different idea of the origin and purpose of government. They had contended that government had been received by men but had not been fashioned, still less created, by them: 'Monarchy was said to be by divine right: So the Law could not alter what God had settled.'[2]

It is tempting for us to see in this clash of arguments and assumptions a frontier between modernity (utilitarian in its understanding about the purposes of political institutions;[3] sceptical about claims that those institutions either could possess, or even stood in need of, any divine sanction) and pre-modernity (drawn to the belief that government had been handed down to men by a god or gods; tending to see political institutions as autotelic, rather than as primarily serving any utilitarian purpose, at least in this

2. Gilbert Burnet, *Bishop Burnet's History of His Own Time*, 2 vols. (1724–1734), 1:457–58. Cf. Figgis, *Divine Right*, p. 147. Burnet's wording perhaps distantly recalls Locke's 'First Treatise,' § 140: 'if the right of the Heir be the Ordinance of God, a Divine Right, no Man, Father, or not Father, can alter it' (Locke, *Two Treatises*, p. 243). Cf. Paul Monod: 'The Exclusion Crisis was a contest over the language of kingship. For the Whigs the monarch was a common person in whom all Protestants might be represented. He was the sign of a rational state that was based on human law and sectarian individualism. . . . For Tories, by contrast, the king was a sign of Anglican confessional unity. They saw the state as founded on a collective religious identity and governed by a divinely appointed sovereignty' (Monod, *Power of Kings*, p. 233). 'No doubt in some societies, at some stages of their development, the whole or at least a part of the code of laws habitually observed, or at least recognized as binding, has been believed to be of divine or semi-divine institution; or perhaps from mere antiquity to possess a sanctity superior to that of any living authority; so that such laws are of right unalterable' (Sidgwick, *Ethics*, p. 266).

3. 'Utilitarianism seems to be commonly accepted in Politics to a much greater extent than it is in the sphere of private conduct: many who recognize absolute rules of private duty, to be obeyed without regard to consequences, still hold that it is a question of expediency what actions and abstinences morally right or allowable should be made compulsory under legal penalties; and similarly that the right form of government for any society is to be determined on grounds of expediency only' (Sidgwick, *Ethics*, p. 18).

world; attracted by the notion that the proper discharge of political life was in itself a kind of service of deference or obedience to the divine). The temptation, in other words, is to see this moment as a staging post in Max Weber's characterisation of modernity as a progressive disenchantment of the world.[4]

Yet to succumb to that temptation would be an error. *Pace* Weber, it is probably a safer assumption that there is always a constant (perhaps—so the events of the global pandemic of 2020–2022 suggest—even an increasing) amount of credulity circulating in human society and that this credulity is always hungry to find a home. All that changes over time are the objects to which that mass of credulity attaches itself, as it is laboriously driven out by reasoned argument from its present location and then goes in search of a new habitat. This is a quest in which (so far at least in human history) credulity has always been successful.

At any rate, and to return to our proper subject, in the realm of human politics, considerations of secular public utility and persuasions of divine or mystical endorsement have been connected since the earliest antiquity. And those connections endure today, albeit in altered or disguised forms, as various proxy superstitions and creeds have encroached upon the domain previously monopolised by formal religion. It may be true that over the course of the eighteenth century in Europe, 'the ideological dependence of the rational state on confessionalism would steadily diminish. Despite many attempts to halt that process over the past two hundred years, it has never been reversed.'[5] Nevertheless, as we will see, at the same time that confessionalism went into retreat, the state found new ways to engage not so much with religion itself as with the emotions and psychological needs that formal religion in the past had stimulated and directed. At the same time, the state and the political actors who operated within it found ways still to avail themselves of the various kinds of authority that religion (or religiosity) had commanded. No matter how enlightened and reasonable a society may consider itself to be, it seems nevertheless uniformly to be the case that its political arrangements cannot support themselves by reliance on appeals to rational utility alone. Supplements, whether of religion or symbolism, or sentiment, or ideology, or opinion, seem always to be required to achieve and maintain the level of social cohesion and

4. 'Entzauberung der Welt' (Max Weber, *Wissenschaft als Beruf* [delivered 1917; published, Munich: Duncker und Humblot, 1919], p. 36).

5. Monod, *Power of Kings*, p. 299.

stability necessary for the attainment of the very goals prescribed by rational utility itself.[6]

The debate on the Exclusion Crisis, it follows, was not a dividing line between one conceptual dispensation or *episteme* and another. Instead, it was a vivid instance of the unending dance in human politics between (as Augustine might have put it) *aeternitas* and *saeculum*: between what we believe to be the *civitas Dei* (whether or not that takes the form of traditional religion) and what we experience as the *civitas terrena.*

The reinforcement of civil authority by religion is a feature of the earliest societies, as Herodotus's relation of the origin of monarchy amongst the Medes suggests.[7] The Medes had managed to throw off their enslavement at the hands of the Assyrians and so had regained their freedom. However, one of their number, an astute man named Deioces, to whom the Medes habitually turned for judgement in their disputes, aspired to sovereignty. By suddenly refusing to act as an arbitrator, Deioces induced the Medes to invite him to be their king. Deioces unsurprisingly accepted the invitation he had subtly solicited, but his conditions were heavy. The Medes had to provide him with a bodyguard and build him a series of fortified palaces, the most elaborate of which was the seven-walled fortress at Agbatana. The intention was not just security but also to insinuate something about the nature of the monarch, namely, that he was different from other men:

> Deioces built these walls for himself and around his own palace; the people were to dwell without the wall. And when all was built, it was Deioces first who established the rule that no one should come into the presence of the king, but all should be dealt with by the means of messengers; that the king should be seen by no man; and moreover that it should be in particular a disgrace for any to laugh or to spit in his presence. He was careful to hedge himself with all this state in order that the men of his own age (who had been bred up with him and were as nobly born as he and his equals in manly

6. For a stimulating recent account of the necessity of religion or a religion-substitute for humans, see Robin Dunbar, *How Religion Evolved* (London: Pelican, 2022).

7. 'In some form the sanctity of kingship has been held from very early times' (Figgis, *Divine Right*, p. 17).

> excellence), instead of seeing him and being thereby vexed and haply moved to plot against him, might by reason of not seeing him deem him to be changed from what he had been.[8]

'ἀλλ' ἑτεροῖός σφι δοκέοι εἶναι μὴ ὁρῶσι', 'changed from what he had been': In other words, the purpose of Deioces's estrangement of himself from his fellow-Medes, and his introduction of court ceremonial, was to suggest that in becoming a king he had at the same time become a kind of god: invisible, aloof, but also authoritative and all-powerful. Under these theocratic conditions, political life tended to assume the form of a ritual of service and devotion, ultimately to a deity but proximately to his remote yet ruling representative here on earth.

The ancient Greeks viewed the political culture of their eastern neighbours with suspicion and contempt. To Aristotle, for example, the political culture of the Persians exemplified the natural slavishness of the peoples of Asia.[9] The Greeks' own political culture was very different. Instead of being ruled by a god-king living apart from his subjects in an impregnable palace-fortress, the Greek citizens participated in their government, and their magistrates mingled with them in the *agora*. The gods still played a role in the civic life of the Greek city-states. Sacrifices were offered, and individual gods might be revered as tutelary or palladial presences (for instance, Athena in Athens). But the gods of Olympus, though immortal and immensely powerful, were neither omniscient nor necessarily benevolent. Their 'justice' might look alarmingly like spite or vindictiveness, and their favouritism for certain men and cities was brazen and flaunted. They were not all equally mighty, and their status as gods was not utterly secure (the pantheon could accommodate both promotions and demotions).[10] They were a prey to human passions and human errors in amplified forms, and as such they might be mocked, reviled, and even punished by men. The result was that, in the Greek city-states, worship and derision could combine to confusing effect. The Dionysia of Athens were religious festivals celebrated in honour of the god Dionysus. Nevertheless, in *The Frogs*,

8. Herodotus, *Persian Wars*, I.99.

9. 'τὰ δὲ περὶ τὴν Ἀσίαν διανοητικὰ μὲν καὶ τεχνικὰ τὴν ψυχήν, ἄθυμα δέ, διόπερ ἀρχόμενα καὶ δουλεύοντα διατελεῖ'; 'The peoples of Asia on the other hand are intelligent and skilful in temperament, but lack spirit, so that they are in continuous subjection and slavery' (Aristotle, *Politics*, VII.vi.1).

10. Demotions: e.g., the ejection of the Titans by the Olympian gods. Promotions: e.g., Heracles.

a play put on during one of these festivals, Aristophanes has Dionysus, absurdly disguised as Heracles, begin the drama with a ludicrous and undignified dialogue with the slave Xanthias about bad jokes and needing to shit.[11] The Greek gods, it is clear, were not always dignified and did not always need to be approached with reverence. Nor were the Greeks unable to co-exist with those of different religious persuasions. In the Bosporan kingdom, where Iranians were Hellenized and Greeks in their turn became acculturated to the Iranians alongside whom they lived, an ambivalent political state came into existence, of which the ruler was, for the Greeks, an elected magistrate and, for the Iranians, a divine-right monarch.[12]

So the political life of the Greek city-states was neither conceived of nor pursued as a practice of devotion to the gods. The Greek philosophers were very clear that the purpose of government was the well-being of the governed, not the adoration of either the governor or the deities supposed to exist above him. In *The Republic*, Plato repeatedly captured this understanding of the purpose of government in a metaphor which would enjoy a long afterlife in the political theory of the West, a metaphor of shepherds caring for their flocks.[13] Plato made Socrates explicitly state on several occasions in *The Republic* what this metaphor means:

> Shepherding is surely directed only toward how to provide the best for its charges. . . . I thought just now that agreement among us was inevitable that every form of government, seen purely as government, considers what is best solely for those who are governed and under its care in both the public and private domain.
>
> No art or rule provides its own benefit, but, as we said long ago, it provides and dictates for the benefit of those who are governed by looking to the advantage of the weaker, and not that of the stronger. . . . Whoever intends to exercise his art well never acts to his own best advantage, nor gives orders to that end . . . but acts in the interests of his subject; . . . .
>
> Our guardians must abandon the practice of all other pursuits and in a very strict sense be workers for the freedom of our state and practice nothing else unless it has a relevance to the state.[14]

11. Aristophanes, *The Frogs*, ll. 1–164.

12. As noted by Rostovtzeff: see Nicholas V. Riasanovsky and Mark D. Steinberg, *A History of Russia*, 7th ed. (Oxford: Oxford University Press, 2005), p. 14.

13. E.g., *The Republic*, 343b, 416a, 440d, 451c.

14. Plato, *The Republic*, 345d, 346e–347a.

In his *Politics* Aristotle took issue with many aspects of the political vision of *The Republic* (for instance, Plato's advocacy of the community of goods and women).[15] But he nevertheless agreed with Plato that the purpose of political society was to promote the general public good, not the advantage of one or a few: 'it is the business of the good lawgiver to study how a state, a race of men or any other community is to partake of the good life and the happiness possible for them.'[16] The objective of political society is 'lasting prosperity' and the attainment of the good life for its citizens.[17]

For Aristotle, *all* constitutional forms—democracies, aristocracies, and monarchies—had the potential to serve the true political end of the common good.[18] This fundamental indifference concerning nice details of constitutional design is of a piece with Aristotle's concentration on the practical, human outcomes in this world that political association is intended to serve. The dominant conception in Western antiquity, that politics is a human contrivance intended to further the well-being of the governed, was also implicit in the example of the great legislators of the ancient past: Lycurgus, Solon, and Numa. These men were all reformers of existing states rather than creators of new ones, and their wisdom was exercised in re-casting inherited political institutions that over time had become sclerotic.[19] The solutions they prescribed for, respectively, Sparta, Athens, and Rome diverged widely. Common to them all, however, was the assumption that politics and its refinement was a human art, rather than a divine gift. As Machiavelli would observe in *The Discourses*, they may have availed themselves of a pretence of religion: 'And certainly never any man brought in new Laws, or set up any Doctrine extraordinary, but with pretence of Religion; because otherwise they would never have been admitted; for a man may be wise, and know many things are good, and yet want reasons and argument to convince other people; wherefore to remove that difficulty, prudent men do make that always their pretence, and *Solon*, *Lycurgus*, and several others who had the same design, practised the

15. Aristotle, *Politics*, II.i.2–10.

16. Aristotle, *Politics*, VII.ii.10.

17. Aristotle, *Politics*, VI.iii.4 and I.i.8.

18. Aristotle, *Politics*, III.v.2–4.

19. Cf. Machiavelli: 'All which things considered, that Prince certainly which aims at glory, and reputation in the world should desire a Government where the manners of his Subjects are corrupted and depraved, not to subvert and destroy it like *Cæsar*, but to rectifie and restore it like *Romulus*, than which the Heavens cannot confer, nor man propose to himself greater honour' (*Discourses*, in Machiavelli, *Works*, p. 282).

same.'[20] Nevertheless, religion seems to have supplied neither their motivation nor their goals.

The Roman republic shared the emphasis found in the Greek city-states on the common good, albeit with a change of accent. Virgil, putting words into the mouth of Anchises, expressed the Roman consciousness of an imperial destiny this way:

> Others, I doubt not, shall with softer mould beat out the breathing bronze, coax from the marble features to the life, plead cases with greater eloquence and with a pointer trace heaven's motions and predict the risings of the stars: you, Roman, be sure to rule the world (be these your arts), to crown peace with justice, to spare the vanquished and to crush the proud.[21]

This consciousness intensified the element of city-worship (what Ernst Kantorowicz would call 'the solemn Roman cult of gods and public functions') that had also been present, in a more muted form, in the political culture of the Greek city-states.[22] It was for this reason that Polybius attributed the flourishing of the Roman republic to its deep-rooted religious culture, which he viewed as a tool for the management of the common people.[23] Nevertheless, the Romans of the republic could be just as brusquely disrespectful as the Greeks when it came to the numinous. The Roman practice of divination from either the behaviour or the condition of the internal organs of animals was elaborate and for the most part practised with solemnity (although, of course, the sincerity of the *haruspices* themselves might be doubtful). Even so, when the sacred chickens refused to provide an auspicious sign by eating the corn that was scattered before them, Publius Claudius Pulcher, the Roman commander at the sea-battle of Drepana against the Carthaginians, had them thrown into the sea, exclaiming in irreverent exasperation, 'if they do not wish to eat, let them drink!'[24]

20. Machiavelli, *Discourses*, in Machiavelli, *Works*, p. 283.

21. Virgil, *Aeneid*, VI.847–53.

22. Kantorowicz, *Two Bodies*, p. 189.

23. Polybius, VI.lvi.6–11. 'ὃ καὶ δόξειεν ἂν πολλοῖς εἶναι θαυμάσιον'; 'My own opinion at least is that they have adopted this course for the sake of the common people' (Polybius, VI.lvi.9).

24. 'Iussit, ut biberent quoniam esse nollent' (Cicero, *De Natura Deorum*, II.7). The Romans did, however, lose the battle. Machiavelli was aware of the pure instrumentality of Roman religion: 'these *Auguries* were invented for no other end, but that the Soldiers might go to the fight with more confidence and alacrity' (Machiavelli, *Discourses*, in Machiavelli, *Works*, p. 287).

Even after the Roman republic had been transformed into an absolute monarchy under Augustus, it took more than two centuries for at least the appearances of a republic devoted to the common good to be seriously compromised. Augustus himself, although in practice he wielded an absolute power over the subjects of the empire, was careful to observe the outward proprieties and the ceremonial *formulae* of the republican political culture he had usurped. He shunned the poisoned titles of 'rex' or 'dominus' (which would have suggested the authority of a master over his slaves, rather than that of a prince over his subjects), preferring instead to be known as the 'princeps'; and he offered at least ostensible support to the institutions and offices of the republic.

Augustus's successors were not so prudent. Although the practice had arisen of deifying good emperors after their deaths (an honour conferred on both Julius Caesar and Augustus), Caligula had himself declared a god during his reign. The insignia of royalty, particularly the diadem (nothing more than a simple white headband set with pearls) which Julius Caesar himself had hesitated to wear, were now recklessly assumed.[25] The unbounded power of the emperors, which Augustus had wisely dissembled, was now brazenly proclaimed. 'Remember,' Caligula is reported to have warned his chiding grandmother, 'I can do anything to anyone.'[26]

This encroachment upon the West of the political culture of the East, with its confusions of divinity and magistracy, which had been initially suspected and resisted by the Romans, was formalised in the early fourth century under the persecuting emperor Diocletian (that is—importantly—before Constantine had adopted Christianity as the religion of the empire). The historian Eutropius reported the innovation as a watershed in the political culture of the Romans:

> Diocletian was a cunning man, sagacious too, and very subtle-witted, . . . a very industrious and dextrous prince, who first brought into the Roman empire the manner of regal custom, rather than Roman liberty; and ordered

25. For Caesar's hesitation, see Plutarch, *Lives*, 'Caesar', LXI.3–5; and Cicero, *Philippic 5*, XXXVIII. For an instance of a later emperor flaunting the diadem, see *Historia Augusta*, 'Elagabalus', XXIII.5. Aurelius Victor says that Caligula was the first emperor to wear the diadem and order himself to be referred to as a god: 'Primus diademate capiti imposito, Dominus se jussit appellari' (*Epitome*, cap. III.8).

26. 'Monenti Antoniae aviae tamquam parum esset non oboedire: "Memento," ait, "omnia mihi et in omnis licere"' (Suetonius, *Gaius Caligula*, XXIX.1).

> himself to be adored, whereas all the Emperors before him were saluted only; he put ornaments of jewels in his clothes and shoes: for hitherto the badge of the Imperial dignity was only a purple robe.[27]

It was this new Asiatic court *régime*, ceremonial, and language which in a few years would be yet further developed and intensified by Constantine and which interacted in complicated ways with the great world-historical event of that reign, namely, the legal establishment of Christianity as at first *a* but within a century *the* religion of the empire.[28]

The character of the Christian god—eternal, omniscient, benevolent, and (at least until this was complicated by the formulation of the doctrine of the Trinity) a single entity—added new subtleties, fresh problems, and enticing opportunities to the already rich confusions of religion and politics present in antiquity.[29]

In the first place, it was clearly impossible for a Christian emperor to follow his pagan predecessors and claim to be divine. To do so would demonstrate a degree of madness far exceeding even that of Caligula.[30] Nevertheless, a Christian emperor might claim to rule by divine permission, even perhaps by divine appointment, and so the aura of divinity might surreptitiously be restored to the throne of an earthly monarch.

Secondly, the progress made by Christianity in the empire gave rise to a refinement and division of authority unknown to antiquity, namely, the

27. Eutropius, IX.26.

28. Constantine is reported by Lactantius to have converted to Christianity from paganism in 306 AD (*Divine Institutions*, I.59), but it seems that for many years after that conversion, Christianity and paganism would co-exist within the emperor's religious sentiments. It is surely significant that he was baptised only on his death-bed in 337 AD. The legal establishment of Christianity within the empire had been accomplished in 313 AD by the Edict of Milan, but no religious monopoly was thereby conferred on the new religion. The inhabitants of the empire were still free to practise paganism if they chose to do so, until the sacrifices which lay at the heart of that religion were prohibited and suppressed by Theodosius in 390 AD.

29. The doctrine of the Trinity, apparently an application of the language and forms of Platonic philosophy to the Christian god, was, it seems, discussed in Christian circles in the second century AD, before being crystallised in a trenchant form, designed to smite the Arians, at the Council of Nice in 325 AD.

30. 'The Christian version of sacred monarchy, unlike divine rulership in the ancient world, did not involve making the king into an actual god; he was always essentially human. The sense of the "abject", of human weakness underlying the sacred, was therefore never expunged from western European monarchy' (Monod, *Power of Kings*, p. 41).

distinction between church and state. In Greece and Rome, temples had officials who assumed priestly functions, such as performing sacrifices. But equally, the civil magistrate might officiate at a sacrifice, and at least in Rome, there was no obstacle to such a magistrate being simultaneously *pontifex maximus* and thus occupying the highest priestly office.[31] There seem to have been no separate religious corporations, corresponding to our notion of a 'church', in either Rome or the Greek city-states, nothing equivalent, that is, to the entities that came into existence with the Christian *ecclesia* (whatever that much-disputed term may have originally meant to the first Christians, as opposed to the powerful institution and priesthood it would soon become). Therefore, in pagan antiquity, the possibility of conflict between church and state could hardly arise.

At first, the political posture of the Christians towards the power of the Roman state was characterised by the passive obedience towards authority that had been shown by Christ himself when he had submitted to the will of the Father and suffered crucifixion. When persecuted, the early Christians stretched out their necks to receive the blow or greeted the wild beasts of the arena with hymns. When the persecutions had ceased and the emperors had themselves become Christian, their Christian subjects conformed themselves to the laws. But the seeds of later discord and resistance were already present.

The infection of an obscure Semitic sect with the disputatious philosophy of Greece would eventually equip Christianity with something originally absent from it except in the most rudimentary form, namely, a theology: and the arrival of theology drew in its wake the divisive notions of orthodoxy and heterodoxy, of true doctrine and heresy, and hence of true believers and heretics.[32] Furthermore, the power claimed by the Christian church of holding the keys to heaven had the potential to make the church a source of authority to rival, perhaps even to eclipse, that of the throne itself.[33] As Hobbes would later remark, surveying the wreckage arising from centuries of clerical ambition

31. As was the case, for instance, with Julius Caesar.

32. Hobbes would identify the infection of Christianity with Greek philosophy as one of the sources of darkness, which arose 'by mixing with the Scripture divers reliques of the Religion, and much of the vain and erroneous Philosophy of the Greeks, especially of Aristotle' (Hobbes, *Leviathan*, p. 418). This would become a mainstay of the later deistic attack on Christianity. The doctrine of purgatory was a particularly egregious theological fruit pollinated by 'contagion of the Daemonology of the Greeks' (Hobbes, *Leviathan*, p. 426).

33. Matthew 16:19.

across a whole continent, 'every man would stand in awe of the Pope and clergy, more than they would of the King'.[34] The church's pretended power to determine one's fate in the *next* world had been manipulated into the basis of an exorbitant power in *this* world: 'There is but one way to salvation; that is, extraordinary devotion and liberality to the Church, and readiness for the Church's sake, if it be required, to fight against their natural and lawful sovereigns.'[35] The consequence of this ecclesiastical usurpation was that mischievous religious opinions had proved to be a principal cause of rebellions: 'The most frequent praetext of Sedition, and Civill Warre, in Christian Common-wealths hath a long time proceeded from a difficulty, not yet sufficiently resolved, of obeying at once, both God, and Man, then when their Commandements are one contrary to the other.'[36] However, these seeds of resistance to the civil magistrate sown by Christianity had germinated long before the seventeenth century and far outside England. Only a few decades after the Edict of Milan had given legal standing to the Christian church, the obdurate resistance mounted by the archbishop of Alexandria, Athanasius, both to the anti-Trinitarian doctrine of Arius and to the Arian emperors, such as Constantius, who favoured that heresy, demonstrated how the Christian innovations of dogmatic theology and the birth of a separate ecclesiastical authority might combine to politically explosive effect.

A new and terrible possibility had come into existence, again one unknown to antiquity: the possibility of religious war.[37] And these religious wars might take a variety of forms: for instance, a civil war waged by a prince against those of his subjects whose religious opinions differed from his own; or a civil war waged by subjects against a prince they viewed as a heretic and his equally heretical adherents; or a war waged by a whole nation against a nation of a different religious confession; or a war waged by the church itself against a backsliding or otherwise heretical prince. Even Augustine, whose guarded and elusive political opinions, insofar as they can be sifted from *The City of God*,

34. Hobbes, *Behemoth*, p. 14. Hobbes would give extended consideration to this question in chapter 38 of *Leviathan* (Hobbes, *Leviathan*, pp. 306–20).

35. Hobbes, *Behemoth*, p. 43. The relevant biblical text is Matthew 16:19: 'And I will give unto thee the keys of the kingdom of heaven: and whatsoever thou shalt bind on earth shall be bound in heaven: and whatsoever thou shalt loose on earth shall be loosed in heaven.' Cf. Matthew 18:18.

36. Hobbes, *Leviathan*, p. 402.

37. Antiquity naturally saw frequent wars between peoples of different religious persuasions; however, religion seems never to have been a *casus belli* before the advent of Christianity.

seem to have tended towards seeing earthly states as embodiments of the ruinous human passions liberated by the Fall, does not absolutely banish the possibility that a state ruled by a godly prince might be 'happy' if the prince were to use his power 'to spread his [God's] worship to the greatest possible extent' and thereby assist the church in its 'labours against the ungodly'.[38] It is not difficult to see in such apparently casual remarks fuel for the religious persecutions that would disfigure later European history—including, of course, in Shakespeare's day in the neighbouring kingdoms of France and Scotland, as well as in England itself.

One further change that followed in the wake of Christianity should be mentioned. Paganism offered only shadowy and sometimes contradictory ideas of the afterlife. There was Elysium, where the dead were happy, and Hades, where they wandered disconsolately, although not necessarily in actual torment. Yet, for the pagans of antiquity, where one ended up after death was no necessary reflection on, or consequence of, how one had lived while on earth, for the simple reason that paganism recognised no single, infallible deity that could administer such faultless justice. In the 'Somnium Scipionis', Scipio's father tells him to cultivate justice and duty if he hopes to enjoy a happy afterlife; but the Cumaean Sibyl tells Aeneas that, in addition to the virtuous, also those whom Jupiter has loved (for whatever reason) might end up in heaven, 'ad aethera'.[39]

Christianity replaced this pagan vagueness with a strictly dichotomous afterlife of rewards and punishments, in a heaven of eternal bliss and a hell of eternal torment. This reconfiguration of men's ideas of the afterlife created new and dreadful possibilities in the realm of social action. For now the church might argue that it was for the ultimate benefit of heretics to be persecuted and compelled to repent in this life so that they might be rewarded in the next. Christ's parable of the banquet, and the master's instruction to his servants to 'compel them to come in', now revealed (or perhaps was made to reveal) its appalling dark side.[40] The principle of the purpose of political society that we

38. 'Felices'; 'si suam potestatem ad Dei cultum maxime dilatandum maiestati eius famulam faciunt'; 'adversus impios laboranti ecclesiae subvenire' (Augustine, *City of God*, V.24 and 26).

39. 'Iustitiam cole et pietatem' (Cicero, *De Republica*, VI.xvi); Virgil, *Aeneid*, VI.129–30.

40. Matthew 22:1–14; Luke 14:16–24. For later interpretations of this parable as a justification of religious intolerance and even violent persecution, see St. Augustine, Letter 39, to Donatus, para. 10; and Jean Calvin, *A Harmonie vpon the Three Euangelistes* (1610), pp. 386–91, especially pp. 389–90.

found in Plato and Aristotle—namely, that government existed for the good of the governed—might be adopted by the Christian church but with a drastically changed tendency. When the principle of seeking the good of the governed was interpreted in a Christian context, the tolerant Epicureanism of antiquity might yield to a different felicific calculation, in which persecution in this world could be justified (indeed, wildly overpaid) by the prospect of eternal happiness in the next. The Augustinian doctrine of the comparative unimportance of *tempus* as opposed to *aeternitas* would have tended also to downplay the importance of human happiness in this life (as opposed to in the next life) and hence may have discouraged men from thinking of earthly happiness as an important, let alone the *only* important, objective of politics.[41]

The language of 'public good' and the pursuit of the well-being of the governed might thus remain the same. The range and purpose of the disciplinary and punitive practices such language could legitimate had, however, been transformed and greatly enlarged by Christianity. The metaphor of shepherding for government that we noted in Plato's *Republic* was retained, and even strengthened, in Christendom. But the object of Christian shepherding was the good of the soul and not necessarily the good of the body. Indeed, Christian shepherding might require the mortification, even the painful death, of the body. When, in 'Lycidas', Milton reproached the time-serving and ignorant clergy of his own day, the bodily disease of the 'hungry Sheep' is unmistakably nothing more than a poetic figure for spiritual ailments:

> Blind mouthes! that scarce themselves know how to hold
> A Sheep-hook, or have learn'd ought els the least
> That to the faithfull Herdmans art belongs! . . .
> The hungry Sheep look up, and are not fed,
> But swoln with wind, and the rank mist they draw,
> Rot inwardly, and foul contagion spread.[42]

One of the most remarkable metamorphoses of the early Middle Ages was the mutation of the Roman church from what at the outset had been an informal entity concerned overwhelmingly with the spiritual welfare of its congregations to a corporation that annexed temporal dominion to its religious authority, asserted at first only in Rome but thereafter claimed with an

41. Kantorowicz, *Two Bodies*, p. 275.

42. Milton, 'Lycidas', ll. 119–21 and 125–27.

ever-broadening latitude. Reviewing the effects of this mutation in 1776, Adam Smith was moved to denounce the Roman Catholic Church as 'the most formidable combination that ever was formed against the authority and security of civil government, as well as against the liberty, reason, and happiness of mankind, which can flourish only where civil government is able to protect them.'[43] The clerical imposture of the supposed 'Donation of Constantine', whereby the first Christian emperor had invested Pope Sylvester and all subsequent bishops of Rome with a multitude of privileges, including the secular rule of that city, together with all the other cities of Italy and, for good measure, the entirety of the Western empire, was widely believed to be authentic, until the greater jurisprudential and philological knowledge of a later age would demonstrate its falsity. Legal scholars would argue that an emperor was unable to alienate a portion of the sovereignty of the empire, let alone the sovereignty of so significant and extensive a territory. Literary scholars, for their part, would be able to demonstrate that the language of the 'Donation' indicated a date of composition several centuries later than the early fourth century AD, when Constantine was alleged to have made this tremendous grant of power and privilege to Pope Sylvester I.[44]

Notwithstanding the exposure of the 'Donation' as a forgery, the papal invasion of the authority of secular rulers of which it was both a token and an attempted legitimation continued for long afterwards.[45] Popes claimed the right both to crown and to dethrone kings, to release from their oaths and duty of obedience the subjects of kings they had excommunicated, and to absolve from sin the regicidal subjects of monarchs deemed to be heretics (such as Elizabeth I).[46] The result, as Hobbes would note, was the division of sovereignty within the state and a chaos of competing loyalties within the subject:

43. Smith, *Wealth*, pp. 802–3, V.i.g.24.

44. Lorenzo Valla, *De falso credita et ementita Constantini donatione* (composed ca. 1440; first published 1517; English translation 1534?). For modern commentary, see most recently Johannes Fried, *'Donation of Constantine' and 'Constitutum Constantini': The Misinterpretation of a Fiction and Its Original Meaning* (Berlin: De Gruyter, 2012). The 'Donation' was forged probably in the eighth century AD. The principle of the inalienability of the *fisc* (state property attached to the Crown) was one ground on which lawyers began to challenge the Donation, reasoning that the emperor could not legally diminish the empire (Kantorowicz, *Two Bodies*, p. 177).

45. For instance, in the papal donations of the Americas to Spain and Portugal in 1493.

46. See *Regnans in Excelsis* (1570), cl. 5. Catholic anti-monarchical resistance theory (as composed by Doleman, Bellarmine, and Suarez) was manufactured to support papal claims over secular monarchs. No commitment to liberty lies behind it (Figgis, *Divine Right*, p. 104).

'This power of absolving subjects of their obedience, as also that other of being judge of manners and doctrine, is as absolute a sovereignty as is possible to be; and consequently there must be two kingdoms in one and the same nation, and no man be able to know which of his masters he must obey.'[47]

The resulting struggle for temporal ascendancy between the popes and, in the first place, the Holy Roman emperors, and thereafter the princes of western Europe, gave rise to momentous developments in political theory. The popes had claimed a divine right to supremacy over earthly monarchs. In retaliation, those monarchs claimed an equal but opposite right of their own:

> In the contest of the Popes with the Emperors was evolved a theory that was destined to play an important part in future anti-papal conflicts, and to perform during the period of the Reformation, the work that was too hard for it, when Pope John XXII. crushed Lewis of Bavaria. This theory was *the divine right of secular governments to be free from Papal control.* It took shape in the fourteenth century as the Divine Right of the Emperors. With various additions, of less importance than is commonly supposed, it was to re-form itself in the sixteenth and seventeenth centuries as the Divine Right of Kings.[48]

Thus, the doctrine of the divine right of kings, which seventeenth-century English writers of a Whiggish or republican tendency would condemn as an instrument of clerical ascendancy over civil authority, a slavish doctrine preached from the pulpit which allowed priests and prelates to ingratiate themselves with princes to their own ecclesiastical advantage, was in fact forged as a means of *resisting* clerical encroachment on the part of the pope (as we will see later in this chapter, Shakespeare seems to have been well aware of the origins of this doctrine in the defiance of over-reaching prelates by kings):

> In the Age of Jurisprudence the sovereign state achieved a hallowing of its essence independent of the Church, though parallel to it, and assumed the eternity of the Roman empire as the king became an 'emperor within his own realm.' But this hallowing of the *status regis et regni,* of state institutions and utilities, necessities and emergencies, would have remained incomplete had not that new state itself been equated with the Church also in its corporational aspects as a secular *corpus mysticum.*[49]

47. Hobbes, *Behemoth,* p. 8.
48. Figgis, *Divine Right,* pp. 44–45.
49. Kantorowicz, *Two Bodies,* p. 192.

This is why committed advocates of divine-right monarchical absolutism, such as William Barclay, tended at the same time to be resolute opponents of papal pretensions to authority over secular monarchs.[50] John Locke seems to have been unaware of the deep roots of the divine right of kings in the struggles of popes and emperors during the Middle Ages, but he was well able to see the, in his opinion, oppressive uses to which that doctrine had been put since the accession of the Stuarts ('this last age'):

> In this last age a generation of men has sprung up among us, who would flatter princes with an Opinion, that they have a Divine Right to absolute Power, let the Laws by which they are constituted, and are to govern, and the Conditions under which they enter upon their Authority, be what they will, and the Engagements to observe them never so well ratified by solemn Oaths and Promises.[51]

This re-purposing of divine-right theory, from being a bulwark against papal encroachment to being a conduit allowing ecclesiastical interests to flourish and thrive under secular monarchs, is one of the great ironies of the history of political thought.[52]

The fifteenth century saw developments that would disrupt this thorough Christianizing of Western political theory. The major philosophers of antiquity either had been assimilated to the new religion (as was the case with Aristotle)[53] or had otherwise contributed to it. It is arguable, for example, that

50. For Barclay's advocacy of divine-right absolutism, see his *De Regno et Regali Potestate* (1600); for his attacks on papal pretensions to temporal dominion, see his *De Potestate Papae* (1609), which elicited a response from Cardinal Bellarmine.

51. Locke, 'First Treatise', § 3 (Locke, *Two Treatises*, p. 142; cf. 'Second Treatise', § 112, p. 343). Locke was certainly in grievous error when he unguardedly claimed that 'I believe it will be hard for him [Filmer] to find any other Age or Country of the World, but this which has asserted Monarchy to be *Jure Divino*' (ibid., p. 143, § 4).

52. However, Alexander Pope (perhaps sensitized by his Roman Catholic faith and his Jacobite inclinations) seems to have noticed it: 'Force first made Conquest, and that conquest, Law; / 'Till Superstition taught the tyrant awe, / Then shar'd the Tyranny, then lent it aid, / And Gods of Conqu'rors, Slaves of Subjects made' (*An Essay on Man*, III.245–48). 'The supremacy of the Crown might be extolled to any extent by a Caroline divine. For it was known that, as a matter of fact, so long as it remained in the hands of the King, it would be used to promote the welfare of the Church' (Figgis, *Divine Right*, p. 204).

53. For Hobbes's attacks on the conscription of Aristotle to the purposes of Christian scholasticism, see Hobbes, *Leviathan*, pp. 14, 24, 25, 34–36, 58–59, and 81.

Plato came to exert a greater influence over the theological doctrines of Christianity than even Christ himself. But the discovery by Poggio Bracciolini in January 1417 of a manuscript of Lucretius's Epicurean philosophical poem *De Rerum Natura* suddenly gave the scholars and thinkers of western Europe access to a pristine ancient philosophy unmediated by Christian commentary or manipulation.[54]

De Rerum Natura had been composed at some point in the first century BC and hence was a document quite free from any trace of Christianity in both its thought and language.[55] Lucretius's poem was an act of extended intellectual homage to the ancient Greek philosopher Epicurus, hardly any of whose writings have come down to us in their entirety.[56] The doctrine of the poem was, like the philosophy of Epicurus itself, materialistic, and its vision of the world was one in which the gods took no active part. Space and time were both infinite, and human effort was most wisely directed to attaining pleasurable tranquillity (αταραξια) in this life rather than being wasted in the anxious appeasement of divinities. If the gods did exist, they were (according to Epicurus and Lucretius) remote and, in any case, so it seemed, perfectly uninterested in what happened on earth.[57]

In Book V of *De Rerum Natura* Lucretius sketched an Epicurean account of the origin of political societies. Just as Lucretius denies that the gods had

54. Stephen Greenblatt, *The Swerve: How the Renaissance Began* (London: Bodley Head, 2011), is an engaging, popular, and at points tendentious account of the cultural significance of the re-discovery of Lucretius's poem. See pp. 98–103 for an account of the mortal antipathy between Epicureanism and Christianity, which made that ancient philosophy (unlike Aristotelianism and Platonism) unassimilable to the new religion. However, Greenblatt says little about the impact Lucretius's poem had on political thought. On the avidity with which the pristine doctrine of Lucretius was received, see (still) Burckhardt: 'The century which escaped from the influence of the Middle Ages felt the need of something to mediate between itself and antiquity in many questions of morals and philosophy; . . . Much which appears to us as mere commonplace in their writings, was for them and their contemporaries a new and hardly-won view of things upon which mankind had been silent since the days of antiquity' (Burckhardt, *Renaissance*, p. 144).

55. Lucretius had been born ca. 99 BC and had died ca. 55 BC.

56. Epicurus (341–270 BC). Lucretius's poem remains our most complete guide to Epicurus's philosophy.

57. 'Epicurean' came to denote the pursuit of merely bodily pleasure through reckless overindulgence in food, drink, and sex (*OED*, A 2; first recorded use, ca. 1435 by Lydgate); but this is a caricature of the genuine doctrine of Epicurus.

created the world as an abode for men, so he denies that human political society has a divine origin.[58] Originally men had lived in the woods, without society or law, and had survived as hunter-gatherers.[59] However, over time they had become softened and socialised by family life. Compassion and language arrived together, and a little afterwards fire was discovered, which stimulated still higher levels of social organisation:

> More and more daily they were shown how to change their former life and living for new ways and for fire by those who were pre-eminent in genius and strong in mind. Kings began to found cities and to build a citadel for their own protection and refuge; and they divided cattle and lands, and gave them to each according to beauty and strength and genius; for beauty had great power, and strength had importance, in those days. Afterwards wealth was introduced and gold was discovered, which easily robbed both the strong and the handsome of their honour; for however strong and handsome in body, men for the most part follow the party of the richer.[60]

However, the accumulation of riches gradually stimulated ambition, and kings had been thereby led to become tyrants. Eventually the burdens of tyranny became insupportable. Kings were expelled, and men, exhausted by violence and insecurity, allowed the wisest amongst them to craft laws and political societies for the common good:

> Kings therefore were slain; the ancient majesty of thrones and proud sceptres lay over thrown in the dust; the illustrious badge of the topmost head, bloodstained beneath the feet of the mob, bewailed the loss of its high honour; for men are eager to tread underfoot what they have once too much feared. So things came to the uttermost dregs of confusion, when each man for himself sought dominion and exaltation. Then there were some who taught them to create magistrates, and established law, that they might be willing to obey statutes. For mankind, tired of living in violence, was fainting from its feuds, and so they were readier of their own will to submit to statutes and strict rules of law. For because each man in his wrath would

58. Gods did not create the earth: Lucretius, *De Rerum Natura,* V.156–65. Political society was created by men: ibid., V.1011–150.

59. Lucretius, *De Rerum Natura,* V.945–69.

60. Lucretius, *De Rerum Natura,* V.1105–16.

> make ready to avenge himself more severely than is permitted now by just laws, for this reason men were utterly weary of living in violence.[61]

In these more settled and peaceful societies agriculture and the arts were cultivated, and human life became sweet and pleasant. The only blemish was the growth of religion, which was grounded in human fears, imposed meaningless and burdensome ceremonies, and as a result became a principal cause of human suffering:

> O unhappy race of mankind, to ascribe such doings to the gods and to attribute to them bitter wrath as well! What groans did they then create for themselves, what wounds for us, what tears for generations to come! It is no piety to show oneself often with covered head, turning towards a stone and approaching every altar, none to fall prostrate upon the ground and to spread open the palms before shrines of the gods, none to sprinkle altars with the blood of beasts in showers and to link vow to vow; but rather to be able to survey all things with tranquil mind.[62]

It is easy to see why the Roman Catholic Church would be alarmed and angered by the re-discovery and dissemination of such opinions—opinions which, ironically enough, had re-emerged only because of a manuscript produced by monks and curated in a monastic scriptorium.[63]

Just as disruptive as the beguiling image of a world-view untouched by Christian dogma contained in *De Rerum Natura*, however, was the encouragement towards an ethical and historical de-centring of Christianity that this exhilaratingly pagan poem placed before its readers. For it was not only the philosophical content of the poem that challenged Christianity. Perhaps more disruptive even than that was its explosive implication that, notwithstanding

61. Lucretius, *De Rerum Natura*, V.1136–50.

62. Growth and spread of religion, Lucretius, *De Rerum Natura*, V.1161–1203. Quoted passage, ibid., V.1194–1203.

63. Cf. Machiavelli: 'The institution of the Christian Religion, whose first establishers did principally intend the cancelling and extirpation of all old Ethnick Customs, Ceremonies, and Theology: . . . For so diligent and zealous was Saint *Gregory*, and other Moderators of the Christian Religion, in abolishing the superstitions of the Gentiles, that they caused the works of all the Poets and Historians to be burn'd, which made any mention of them; they threw down their Images and Idols, and destroy'd all that might afford the least memory of Paganism; to which diligence of theirs, if a new language had been added, in a short time all would have been utterly forgotten' (Machiavelli, *Discourses*, in Machiavelli, *Works*, p. 340).

the pretensions of Christianity to, in some way, stand outside human time, the Christian church and the religion it claimed to embody had a history which might be framed in terms other than those preferred by, and hence favouring, its subject.

Machiavelli, we know, made a personal copy of the Lucretian manuscript, and it is easy to see how what he read within that document would have stimulated (or perhaps merely corroborated) his thinking. For instance, the account Machiavelli gives of the origins of government and civil society amongst men follows that of Lucretius very closely.[64] In particular, however, Lucretius's poem might also have encouraged Machiavelli towards heterodox opinions (which, of course, he may well have been on the way to forming already) about the harmful influence exerted by Christianity on human society.[65] For example, in the *Florentine History*, Machiavelli presented the secular government of the popes as a criminal squandering of the precious civic legacy of antiquity:

> But in my description of Occurrences betwixt those times and our own, I shall not inlarge upon the ruine of the Empire, which in truth, receiv'd but little assistance from the Popes, or any other Princes of *Italy*, till the dayes of *Charles* the 8*th*. but discourse rather how the Popes with their Censures, Comminations and Arms, mingled together with their indulgences, became formidable and reverenced, and how having made ill use both of the one and the other; they have lost the one intirely, and remain at the discretion of other people for the other.[66]

And in *The Discourses*, which drew on his Epicurean 'continued reading of the affairs of this World', Machiavelli would give several instances of how the Christian church had blighted the social and political life of his own country.[67] The temporal power of the popes was responsible for the fragmented political state of Italy:

> The *Church* therefore being neither so strong as to conquer all Italy, nor so weak as to suffer it to be over-run by any body else, has been the occasion that it never fell into the hands of one person, but has been cantonized into several Principalities, by which means it has been so weak and disunited,

64. Compare Machiavelli, *Discourses*, bk. I, ch. 2, para. 3, with Lucretius, *De Rerum Natura*, V.945 ff.

65. Greenblatt, *Swerve*, p. 221.

66. Machiavelli, *Florentine History*, in Machiavelli, *Works*, p. 7.

67. Machiavelli, *Discourses*, in Machiavelli, *Works*, p. 265.

> that it has been not only exposed as a prey to the power of the *Barbarians*, but to every one that thought good to invade it, which is an unhappiness we *Italians* owe only to the Church.[68]

More generally, the other-worldliness of Christian values had corrupted and undermined the moral strength of men:

> But it may (not unfitly) be admir'd in this place what should be the cause that the ancients should be more zealous for publick liberty than we in our days: if my opinion may pass, I think it is for the same reason, that in those times men were more robust, and stronger than now; which proceeded much from the diversity betwixt their Education, their Religion, and ours: for whereas our Religion gives us a just prospect and contemplation of things, and teaches us to despise the magnificence and pomp of the World; the Ethnicks valued them so highly, that believing them their chiefest happiness, it made them more fierce and busy to defend them.[69]

And this enfeeblement had led to a general abjection across the whole of Christendom:

> Moreover the Religion of the Gentiles did not place their beatitude any where but upon such as were full of worldly glory, and had done some great action for the benefit of their Country. In our Religion the meek and humble, and such as devote themselves to the contemplation of divine things, are esteemed more happy than the greatest Tyrant, and the greatest Conqueror upon earth; and the *summum bonum*, which the others placed in the greatness of the mind, the strength of the body, and what-ever else contributed to make men active, we have determined to consist in humility, abjection, and contempt of the World; and if our Religion requires any fortitude, it is rather to enable us to suffer than to act. So that it seems to me, this way of living, so contrary to the ancients, has rendred the Christians more weak and effeminate; and left them as a prey to those who are more wicked, and may order them as they please, the most part of them thinking more of Paradise than Preferment, and of enduring than revenging of injuries; as if Heaven was to be won rather by idleness than arms: but that explication of our Religion is erroneous, and they who made it were poor and pusillanimous, and more given to their ease than any thing that

68. Machiavelli, *Discourses*, in Machiavelli, *Works*, p. 285.
69. Machiavelli, *Discourses*, in Machiavelli, *Works*, p. 336.

> was great: for if the Christian Religion allows us to defend and exalt our Country, it allows us certainly to love it, and honour it, and prepare our selves so as we may be able to defend it. But that lazy and unactive way of education, and interpreting things falsly has been the cause that there are not so many Common-wealths as formerly in the World, nor so many Lovers and Champions for their liberty.[70]

The undermining and erosion of Europe's political culture (for Machiavelli makes a series of pointed comparisons with what he suggests is the contrasting strength of Ottoman political institutions and martial vigour) is, in this account, to be laid squarely at the door of the Catholic Church.[71]

Machiavelli's writings were clearly *élite* texts and in many quarters aroused great (in some respects, justified) suspicion, just as in others they were received with almost rapturous enthusiasm.[72] But vulgar Epicureanism leached out into the broader culture through more accessible texts that enjoyed wider currency; and Lucretius's poem excited the imaginations of poets (such as Milton and Dryden) who would not have swallowed its dangerous doctrines whole.[73] As an example of such diffuse Epicureanism, we might consider Traiano Boccalini's work of miscellaneous satire *I Ragguagli di Parnasso* (Venice, 1612–1615), which was twice translated into English in the century following its first publication as *Advertisements from Parnassus*[74] and which acquired a European reputation in the seventeenth century, in the process disseminating broadly Epicurean views on government across the continent.

Boccalini was no devoted follower of the 'mischievous' Machiavelli.[75] The eighty-ninth Advertisement of the first century relates an imaginary trial of the Florentine politician, as a result of which he is sentenced to be burnt for

70. Machiavelli, *Discourses*, in Machiavelli, *Works*, p. 336.

71. Comparisons with the Ottoman Empire: Machiavelli, *Discourses*, in Machiavelli, *Works*, pp. 292, 332, 355. Cf. also Machiavelli, *The Prince* (ibid., pp. 200, 227).

72. On the reception of Machiavelli in England, see (still) Felix Raab, *The English Face of Machiavelli: A Changing Interpretation 1500–1700* (London: Routledge and Kegan Paul, 1964).

73. Philip Hardie, 'The Presence of Lucretius in *Paradise Lost*', *Milton Quarterly* 29 (1995): 13–24; Paul Hammond, 'Dryden, Milton, and Lucretius', *The Seventeenth Century* 16 (2001): 158–76; Paul Hammond, 'The Integrity of Dryden's Lucretius', *Modern Language Review* 78 (1983): 1–23.

74. Trajano Boccalini (1556–1613), Italian author and satirist. Boccalini, *Parnasso*; Boccalini, *Advices from Parnassus*, trans. John Hughes (1706).

75. Boccalini, *Parnasso*, p. 38.

atheism and also for the crime of opening the eyes of the populace to dangerous political realities.[76] In Advertisement fifty-five, Machiavelli is reproached for his 'mad and desperate Policy'.[77] And, unlike Machiavelli, who unmistakably favoured the expansionist republic of Rome, Boccalini extolled the static republic of Venice as 'the perfectest Aristocracie that ever was'.[78] In corroboration of this anti-Machiavellian preference, in the twenty-third Advertisement of the first century, Boccalini made Tacitus explain to his modern editor Lipsius that the purpose of his writings had been to warn states against the temptation to become empires 'which know not how to perfix bounds to their insatiate desire of Reign.'[79]

Yet alongside this evident resistance to the doctrines of Machiavelli, we also find in Boccalini Epicurean points of contact with his fellow-Italian. Like Machiavelli, Boccalini found things to admire in the government of the Ottoman Empire, including its policy of mitigated religious toleration.[80] He wrote two Advertisements in praise of wine.[81] Apollo's resolutely secular teaching is that the three 'felicities' that make men happy are 'Peace, Justice, and Plenty'.[82] Boccalini insists on the duty of magistrates to seek the well-being (in this world) of their subjects, enforcing the point by means of a parable:

> This man presenting himself before *Apollo*, in the name of *Hannibal* the Carthaginian, gave him that Lyon, which his Majesty was very well pleased withal; who asked the African what Art he had used to tame so fierce, ravenous, jealous, and cruel a Beast? The *African* answered, By feeding him continually with his own hand. *Apollo* then turned towards the Princes, who, for the honour of that Audience, were there in great numbers, and said unto them; Learn, Lords, by the Miracle of this Lyon which you see is become

76. Boccalini, *Parnasso*, pp. 119–20.

77. Boccalini, *Parnasso*, p. 72. Cf. ibid., pp. 148 and 198.

78. Boccalini, *Parnasso*, p. 163. The sixth 'Advertisement' of the second century praises the German commonwealths for their peaceable abstention from conquest and expansion (ibid., pp. 138–46).

79. Boccalini, *Parnasso*, p. 26. Cf. ibid., p. 44, where the 'safe preserving of what was got' is identified as the height of political wisdom.

80. Boccalini, *Parnasso*, p. 81 (religious toleration), pp. 220–23 (civil religion), pp. 232–33 (artful policy). Note also, however, Boccalini's criticisms of the Ottomans for their hostility to learning (ibid., p. 105) and for the instability that their empire shares with all overgrown states (ibid., pp. 194–95).

81. Boccalini, *Parnasso*, pp. 26–27 and 178–79.

82. Boccalini, *Parnasso*, p. 220.

> so tame, that fair treatment doth domestichize even savage beasts; do you the like by your Subjects, and make them not come hardly by their food through your angersom Taxes upon things necessary for human life; for, by so doing, you shall not be beloved, served, and honoured by your own natural Subjects only, but even by the more Forraign and Barbarous Nations of the earth.[83]

Such good government was more often encountered in republics than in monarchies, for in 'well governed Commonwealths', the objective of government tends always to be 'the common Good, not private Interest, as it is often found to be in Principalities.'[84] As is usually the case with the political doctrines that Boccalini wished unreservedly to recommend, he placed this point of view in the mouth of Tacitus:

> *Tacitus* . . . had no other intention, than to let the Senators of Commonwealths see, into what deplorable calamities they run, when preferring the hatred of their private passions, and their own self-interests before the publick good, they suffer the precious Jewel of their Countries Liberty, which they ought so diligently to keep and preserve, to be stollen away from them by cruel Tyrants.[85]

The necessity for governors to seek the public good, rather than their own private benefit, was not for Boccalini entirely a matter of disinterested virtue, and he enforced the point using a familiar metaphor of which he was very fond. A wise ruler would look after and cherish his subjects, Apollo argues, since 'those Shepherds that dealt ill with their flocks, were chiefly cruel to themselves; for it was a certain truth, that wounds shamefully given to sheep, did usually kill the Shepherd.'[86]

A final Epicurean touch in the *Ragguagli di Parnasso* concerns religion. Boccalini was very circumspect on confessional issues, as perhaps was only to be expected in a man who numbered cardinals amongst his pupils and friends. Nevertheless, the short thirteenth Advertisement from the second century suggests something of his private thoughts on the relation between church and state. Theodoric, the Arian king of Italy, petitions to be admitted to Parnassus,

83. Boccalini, *Parnasso*, p. 41.

84. Boccalini, *Parnasso*, p. 145.

85. Boccalini, *Parnasso*, p. 166. Cf. also ibid., p. 224.

86. Boccalini, *Parnasso*, p. 119. For other examples of Boccalini's use of the pastoral metaphor for government, see ibid., pp. 34, 61–63, 84–85, 93, 118, 125, 168, 175, 195, 210, 220, and 274–75.

an honour that has been repeatedly denied him.[87] Apollo again refuses Theodoric's request and is gracious enough to explain why:

> For, to be plain, he did not think him worthy admittance into *Parnassus*; since the world ought to thank none but him [i.e., Theodoric] for the Horrible Atheism which was of late introduced into many Provinces of *Europe*; for, whereas the doubts about Religion, risen up amongst Divines, were after some dispute cleared, and their errors taken away by the Councils, which were made capable of declaring what was truth; and were all extirpated out of the world, by making bonefires of such as were obstinate: When he, as the Head thereof, took upon him the protection of the wicked Sect of the *Arians*, he did not only turn Heresies, which require whole Armies to root them out, into interest of State, but with unheard-of effrontedness; he made the whole world see, that he made use of Heresie to work division amongst people, to weaken Princes who were his enemies, to have adhearers in his Neigh[b]ours States, to make himself head of new Sects, and to steal away the Hearts of other mens Subjects; and that in this heart he had no other esteem of Holy Religion, but as of a powerful means and excellent way to obtain Government.[88]

Boccalini stops short of specifying precisely what form the relationship between church and state ought to take. But it is clear that making religious doctrine an instrument of political aggrandisement is wrong; and the passage teeters on the edge of perhaps concluding that church and state ought to be carefully separated, however much this would obstruct the worldly ambitions of the Roman Catholic Church.

The revival of Epicureanism was far from being the greatest challenge faced by the Roman Catholic Church in the early modern period. The heterodoxy which spread from Germany in the early sixteenth century, and which built upon the foundations laid by earlier critics of papal authority such as Wycliffe and Hus, ripened into full-blown schism. Initially the Reformed religion presented itself as the natural ally of the civil magistrate. Whereas the pope and the political theorists of Roman Catholicism had smiled on rebellion and even looked forgivingly on regicide, the Reformers insisted on passive obedience from their followers. Paul's admonition to the Romans, that Christians should 'be subject unto the higher powers. For there is no power but of God: and the

87. Theodoric the Great (454–526), Arian Ostrogothic king of Italy (493–526).

88. Boccalini, *Parnasso*, p. 152.

powers that be are ordained of God', was a text that dropped from many Protestant lips and was transcribed by many Protestant pens.[89]

Yet the principle of private (albeit conscientious) judgement that lay at the heart of Protestantism's stance of challenge towards the massive institutional authority of Roman Catholicism clearly had the potential ultimately to conflict with the political subordination that was repeatedly preached from reformed pulpits.[90] Soon Protestantism was equipped with resistance theories of its own, usually composed by the persecuted subjects of Roman Catholic princes.[91] Moreover, the Protestant detestation of idolatry (one of the principal failings that the Reformers had identified and deplored in Roman Catholicism) held implications for the cult of sacral kingship that had attached itself to the doctrine of the divine right of kings. The sacredness of the royal body was placed under critical pressure: 'By 1589 the sacred royal body was sick not just in France but throughout Europe. It was under severe assault from religious reformers, both Protestant and Catholic, who called for a stripping away of its mystical trappings and a return to a godly or purified governance more compatible with the piety of the Christian self.'[92] And these attacks on sacral kingship might be delivered with a particular force and spin from the quarter of reformed religion: 'Because Protestantism rejected physical holiness . . . it could easily clash with a kingship that made the body of the ruler sacred.'[93]

The Protestant erosion of what Claudius in *Hamlet* would refer to as the 'divinity' that 'doth hedge a king' no doubt contributed to the rash of civil conflicts across Europe in the mid-seventeenth century, which all (at least in the eyes of the rebellious) took the form of conflicts between erring monarchs and godly nations.[94] But these conflicts did not herald any deep separation of religion from politics but, rather, only a relocation of the point of contact

89. Romans 13:1.

90. In an English context, that vehemence can be most readily sampled in the homily 'Against disobedience and wilfull rebellion', published in the many-times-reprinted *Certain Sermons or Homilies appointed to be read in Chvrches* (1562).

91. E.g., John Ponet, *A Short Treatise of Politic Power* (1556); Christopher Goodman, *How Superior Powers Ought to Be Obeyed of Their Subjects* (1558); François Hotman, *Francogallia* (1573); Hubert Languet (?), *Vindiciae, Contra Tyrannos* (1579).

92. Monod, *Power of Kings*, p. 36.

93. Monod, *Power of Kings*, p. 47.

94. *Hamlet*, IV.ii.123.

between those two realms of human concern.[95] The altar was moved away from the throne and closer to the nation itself (or perhaps to the spiritual *élite* or godly 'elect' that made up a fraction of the nation).

The English Civil Wars in one sense ended with the execution of Charles I in January 1649, the military potency of the Royalist cause being finally extinguished two years later by the battle of Worcester in 1651. But at the level of political theory, the execution of the king was more a starting pistol than a chequered flag. Many of those who resisted Charles in the 1640s would also have claimed to be monarchists. Their grievance was not that Charles was a king but rather that, in some respects and in their eyes, he had fallen short of what a king should be. Consequently, it is surely an error to see Charles's execution as an expression of a resurgent republicanism. It is hard to find more than a handful of declared republicans in England before 1649, although historians have brought to light how English monarchy in the sixteenth and seventeenth centuries might nevertheless create sheltered habitats in which fragments of commonwealth thinking and practice could survive.[96] (Adam Smith would wonder at the short-sightedness of medieval kings, who by granting privileges and charters to towns, thereby 'voluntarily erected a sort of independent republicks in the heart of their own dominions.')[97] Charles's execution, however, announced in letters of blood that, for the time being at least, England would be no longer a monarchy. That powerful message was ratified in law on 17 March 1649, when Parliament passed an act abolishing the monarchy, declaring the office of king to be 'unnecessary, burdensome, and dangerous', and announcing a freedom of 'consciences, persons and estates'.

But if not a monarchy, what then *would* England be? [98] In the spring of 1649, there was not just an opportunity for inventive constitutional thinking; there

95. Cf. Blair Worden: 'It is easy, and it may be correct, to describe the shift, over a long term, from a God-centred conception of liberty in religion to a man-centred one as a process of secularization. Yet the story is one not of the retreat, or not only of the retreat, of Christianity, but of its adjustment and revision. It was from within Puritanism, not in reaction against it, that the civil wars produced demands for "civil and religious liberty"' (Worden, *Instruments*, p. 325).

96. Patrick Collinson, 'The Monarchical Republic of Queen Elizabeth I', *Bulletin of the John Rylands University Library of Manchester* 69 (1987): 394–424. For critique, discussion, and response, see John F. McDiarmid, ed., *The Monarchical Republic of Early Modern England: Essays in Response to Patrick Collinson* (London: Routledge, 2007).

97. Smith, *Wealth*, p. 401, III.iii.7.

98. This paragraph summarises the argument of Blair Worden, 'Civil and Religious Liberty', in Worden, *Instruments*, pp. 313–54.

was an unignorable need for it. The 'Puritan Revolution' of the mid-century had united two kinds of liberty, originally distinct: namely, civil liberty and religious liberty. Both of those types of freedom were in themselves complex. Religious liberty was a matter of godliness or of liberty in Christ, not of uncontrolled freedom of social action or disobedience to the magistrate, while ecclesiastical liberty referred to the immunity of the church from state control. Civil liberty, on the other hand, might (perhaps, usually did) encompass some very ungodly actions. But Parliament had resisted Charles I on grounds of both politics and religion, and in the victory of Parliament, those two, initially separable and always conceptually heterogeneous, causes had become in the minds of men very closely associated: 'Men who in the civil war fought and suffered for a cause that was both political and religious found a unifying bond in the conjunction of the two kinds of liberty'.[99] This convergence strengthened over the later 1640s and throughout the 1650s. By the late seventeenth century, it is common to find the survivors and descendants of the Parliamentarian cause arguing that men had a right to judge for themselves in matters of religion and a consequent right publicly to follow and exercise the form of religion that satisfied their consciences. Many came to agree with the political writer James Harrington that 'where there is no liberty of conscience, there can be no civil liberty; and where there is no civil liberty, there can be no security unto liberty of conscience.'[100] The yoking together of those two kinds of liberty became, in the minds of those who reflected on England's mid-seventeenth-century travails, a defining feature of the 'Good Old Cause'.

One man who was appalled by these developments was Thomas Hobbes. He was dismayed by the material carnage of the English Civil Wars. But arguably he was even more discouraged by what the origins and conduct of those wars had revealed about the state of human political understanding. In *Leviathan* (1651), Hobbes set out to correct men's political opinions in the light of his diagnosis of what had gone wrong in England during recent decades.

Hobbes discovered the causes of the English Civil Wars not in misgovernment or oppression on the part of Charles I but rather in the spread of mischievous opinions concerning religion and government amongst his subjects. Concerning religion, both Roman Catholic and Protestant priests had trespassed on the authority of the monarch: 'I may attribute all the changes of

99. Worden, *Instruments*, p. 331.
100. Harrington, *Works*, p. 703.

Religion in the world, to one and the same cause; and that is, unpleasing Priests; and those not onely amongst Catholiques, but even in that Church that hath presumed most of Reformation.'[101] Far from being the Antichrists of vulgar anti-Catholic polemic, in Hobbes's eyes, the popes had been nothing more than normal men who had either created or otherwise enjoyed unusually generous opportunities for the indulgence of their natural, if immoderate, worldly ambition.[102] Nonconformists and sectaries were also guilty on this count: 'For it is not the Romane Clergy onely, that pretends the Kingdome of God to be of this World, and thereby to have Power therein, distinct from that of the Civill State.'[103] Pretended private revelations were just as harmful to the commonwealth as were the ambition and rapacity of prelates.[104]

Hobbes, however, was adamant that no church of any stripe could rightly claim temporal authority.[105] His argument was ultimately based on Scripture. There had been no kingdom of God on earth after the ministry of Moses, and there would not be another such kingdom before the Second Coming: 'Which second coming not yet being, the Kingdome of God is not yet come, and wee are not now under any other Kings by Pact, but our Civill Soveraigns.'[106] Therefore, no minister or priest could legitimately claim civil authority on earth, and no earthly church might justly exercise temporal power: 'whatsoever Power Ecclesiastiques take upon themselves (in any place where they are subject to the State) in their own Right, though they call it Gods Right, is but Usurpation.'[107]

Hobbes saw this process of clerical trespass as a Europe-wide phenomenon. Its roots were detectable in some Levantine countries, such as Egypt, before the Christian era. But it had accelerated with great force after the

101. Hobbes, *Leviathan*, p. 86.

102. For Hobbes's denial that the pope is Antichrist, see Hobbes, *Leviathan*, p. 381. It is a point of some importance, because if the pope were indeed Antichrist, that would make him, as the Bible says, 'prince of this world' (John 12:31 and 16:11), and he therefore would enjoy a Scripturally-attested right to secular power, at least until the Second Coming. Hobbes's denial that any church enjoys such power entails a denial that any prelate is Antichrist.

103. Hobbes, *Leviathan*, p. 482.

104. See Hobbes, *Leviathan*, pp. 299–300.

105. This is the position Hobbes took up in his mature political philosophy. In earlier writings, such as the *Elements of Law* and *De Cive*, he had been prepared to allocate the power authoritatively to interpret Scripture to the church. See Tuck, *Hobbes*, pp. 84–86.

106. Hobbes, *Leviathan*, p. 419.

107. Hobbes, *Leviathan*, p. 474.

establishment of the Christian church and its spread throughout Europe.[108] The political consequences had been devastating: 'The most frequent praetext of Sedition, and Civill Warre, in Christian Common-wealths hath a long time proceeded from a difficulty, not yet sufficiently resolved, of obeying at once, both God, and Man, then when their Commandements are one contrary to the other.'[109] In England during the early years of the reign of Charles I, those consequences had been particularly malign: 'ministers, as they called themselves, of Christ; . . . pretending to have a right from God to govern every one his parish and their assembly the whole nation.'[110] These aspiring and overreaching clerics had spread opinions favourable to disobedience and resistance throughout the land, particularly among the common people, who, although they were normally resistant to the pseudo-doctrines of intellectuals, were nevertheless vulnerable in the quarter of religion.[111]

Concerning erroneous opinions about government, Hobbes discovered the source of mischief not in the churches but in the universities (although Hobbes presents the universities of his day as little more than ecclesiastical catspaws: founded for the most part by clerics; staffed almost exclusively by clerics; and eager to spread doctrines favourable to the pretensions of ecclesiastical corporations).[112] In the colleges of Oxford and Cambridge, the gentry had been made to read the republican political theory of ancient Greece and

108. Hobbes's *Historia Ecclesiastica, authore Thoma Hobbio* (1688), published in an English translation in 1722, offers a lively and pungent satirical narrative of this historical trend.

109. Hobbes, *Leviathan*, p. 402. Cf. the similar passage in *Behemoth*: 'This power of absolving subjects of their obedience, as also that other of being judge of manners and doctrine, is as absolute a sovereignty as is possible to be; and consequently there must be two kingdoms in one and the same nation, and no man be able to know which of his masters he must obey' (Hobbes, *Behemoth*, p. 8).

110. Hobbes, *Behemoth*, p. 2.

111. 'But they say again, that though the Principles [of absolute sovereignty] be right, yet Common people are not of capacity enough to be made to understand them. I should be glad, that the Rich, and Potent Subjects of a Kingdome, or those that are accounted the most Learned, were no lesse incapable than they. But all men know, that the obstructions to this kind of doctrine, proceed not so much from the difficulty of the matter, as from the interest of them that are to learn' (Hobbes, *Leviathan*, p. 233).

112. For expressions of this critique of universities, see Hobbes, *Behemoth*, pp. 16, 17, 40, 56, and 58. For the encouragement given by universities to clerical encroachment, see Hobbes, *Leviathan*, p. 237: 'till the later end of *Henry the eighth*, the Power of the Pope, was alwayes upheld against the Power of the Common-wealth, principally by the Universities; and . . . the doctrines maintained by so many Preachers, against the Soveraign Power of the King, and by so many

Rome, 'the democratical principles of Aristotle and Cicero'; and from them they had derived mistaken ideas of liberty and government.[113] The result was that a frequent cause of rebellion had been 'the Reading of the books of Policy, and Histories of the antient Greeks, and Romans':

> And by reading of these Greek, and Latine Authors, men from their childhood have gotten a habit (under a false shew of Liberty,) of favouring tumults, and of licentious controlling the actions of their Soveraigns; and again of controlling those controllers, with the effusion of so much blood; as I think I may truly say, there was never any thing so deerly bought, as these Western parts have bought the learning of the Greek and Latine tongues.[114]

By the mid-seventeenth century, the foundations of secular authority in England had been thoroughly sapped by this unholy alliance of classical republicans, ambitious prelates, and unruly sectarians.

At the end of the 1700s, Gotthold Lessing, taking the measure of the intellectual landscape of the earlier years of that century, would wearily deplore the standard of the Enlightenment debate on religion:

> It is not true that all the objections have already been stated. It is even less true that they have all been answered. A great many of them, at least, have been answered as deplorably as they were stated. To the superficiality and ridicule of the one side, the other has not infrequently replied with pride and disdain. Great offence has been taken if one side has equated religion with superstition; but the other side has not scrupled to denounce doubt as irreligion, and belief in the sufficiency of reason as infamy. The one party has disparaged every clergyman as a scheming priest, while the other has disparaged every philosopher as an atheist. Thus each side has turned its adversary into monster so that, if it cannot defeat him, it can pronounce him beyond the law.[115]

Lawyers, and others, that had their education there, is a sufficient argument, that though the Universities were not authors of those false doctrines, yet they knew not how to plant the true.'

113. Hobbes, *Behemoth*, p. 43. Cf. ibid., pp. 155 and 158.

114. Hobbes, *Leviathan*, pp. 225 and 150.

115. Gotthold Ephraim Lessing, *Philosophical and Theological Writings*, ed. and trans. Hugh Nisbet (Cambridge: Cambridge University Press, 2005), pp. 63–64. I am indebted for this quotation to Dr. Till Kinzel.

Hobbes was an early and important casualty in the 'teratological turn' which was liable (as Lessing explains) to overtake the participants in public debate on religious subjects during the long Enlightenment. Hobbes's anti-clericalism was immediately misread as monstrous atheism.[116] It is beyond question that Hobbes entertained an 'extraordinarily heterodox vision of the role of religion in human society'.[117] It is, however, not the case that this undeniably heterodox vision necessarily amounted, either then or now, to a denial of the existence of God.[118] As Hobbes himself maintained, 'not onely Christians, but all manner of men do . . . believe in God.'[119] Hobbes was of course aware of the Lucretian doctrine, that 'some of the old Poets said, that the Gods were at first created by humane Feare'; but this was true of only the many gods of the Gentiles, not of the 'one God Eternall, Infinite, and Omnipotent'.[120]

It is also true that (as Richard Tuck has said) 'in all his works, Hobbes firmly denied the relevance of a conventional concept of a benevolent God to any philosophical enquiry.'[121] But that, too, does not amount to saying that God does not exist. Hobbes's position (at least on the surface) was that we have good Scriptural grounds for believing both that God has intervened in human history in the past and furthermore that he has promised to do so again in the future.[122] In the interim, God, to be sure, governs the world, and *Leviathan* is at one level an exposition of the natural art whereby he does so.[123]

116. See the classic account: S. I. Mintz, *The Hunting of Leviathan* (Cambridge: Cambridge University Press, 1962). In the following century, as well-informed and intelligent a writer as David Hume could say of Hobbes, almost in passing and without substantiation, that Hobbes 'lay not under any restraint of religion, which might supply the defects of his philosophy' (Hume, *Enquiry*, p. 91). So commonplace had the attribution to Hobbes of atheism become.

117. Hobbes, *Leviathan*, p. ix.

118. Cf. J.G.A. Pocock: 'when we call him [Hobbes] an atheist—it is not certain that he was one' (J.G.A. Pocock, 'Atheist or Enthusiast?', *History of Political Thought* 11 [1990]: 742). See also J.G.A. Pocock, 'Time, History and Eschatology in the Thought of Thomas Hobbes', in *Politics, Language and Time: Essays on Political Thought and History* (London: Methuen, 1972), pp. 148–201.

119. Hobbes, *Leviathan*, p. 49.

120. Hobbes, *Leviathan*, p. 76.

121. Richard Tuck, 'Introduction', in Hobbes, *Leviathan*, p. xxiii.

122. For Hobbes's claim that his political theory enjoys 'Authority of Scripture', see Hobbes, *Leviathan*, p. 233.

123. Hobbes defines nature as 'the Art whereby God hath made and governes the World' (Hobbes, *Leviathan*, p. 9).

But God no longer intervenes directly in earthly events.[124] The age of miracles is past:

> Seeing therefore Miracles now cease, we have no sign left, whereby to acknowledge the pretended Revelations, or Inspirations of any private man; nor obligation to give ear to any Doctrine, farther than it is conformable to the Holy Scriptures, which since the time of our Saviour, supply the place, and sufficiently recompense the want of all other Prophecy; and from which, by wise and learned interpretation, and carefull ratiocination, all rules and precepts necessary to the knowledge of our duty both to God and man, without Enthusiasme, or supernaturall Inspiration, may easily be deduced.[125]

It follows that religious considerations (which tend to be more ecclesiological than theological) are of only uncertain relevance to questions of politics and human social organisation. Hobbes's apparent private belief in the reality and existence of God thus did not oblige him to recognise any need for a church either to represent God on earth or to act as a gatekeeper to Paradise.[126] Salvation was not in the gift of any ecclesiastical corporation: 'All that is NECESSARY *to Salvation*, is contained in two Vertues, *Faith in Christ*, and *Obedience to Laws*.'[127] Hence Hobbes's firm Erastian preference for a 'civil religion' is strictly speaking (and notwithstanding the denunciations of his pious contemporaries) without implication for the question of whether or not he was an atheist.

So we should pause before dismissing the presence of religious language in Hobbes's statements of the political arrangements he approves as nothing more than camouflage arranged over an underlying atheism in the hope of hoodwinking the orthodox (and if that had indeed been Hobbes's strategy, the outrage stimulated by *Leviathan* showed that it failed lamentably). Hobbes's

124. 'They therefore that believe there is a God that governeth the world, and hath given Praecepts, and propounded Rewards, and Punishments to Mankind, are Gods Subjects; all the rest, are to be understood as Enemies' (Hobbes, *Leviathan*, p. 246).

125. Hobbes, *Leviathan*, p. 259.

126. The practice of confession and the pope's control over damnation or salvation meant that 'every man would stand in awe of the Pope and clergy, more than they would of the King' (Hobbes, *Behemoth*, p. 14).

127. Hobbes, *Leviathan*, p. 403. Cf. ibid., p. 407: 'The (*Unum Necessarium*) Onely Article of Faith, which the Scripture maketh simply Necessary to Salvation, is this, that JESUS IS THE CHRIST.'

solution for the disorder released into mid-seventeenth-century England was a thorough-going absolutism. The argument Hobbes mounted to vindicate this very traditional stance concerning authority and obligation was, however, couched in unfamiliar terms.[128] It proceeded, in the manner of a demonstration in geometry, by means of a strict deduction from apparently innocuous definitions of key terms, in the course of which Hobbes gleefully produced extraordinary and counter-intuitive, but nevertheless necessarily-entailed, outcomes. Having assented innocently to the definitions, Hobbes's reader was ambushed by the shocking but inescapable conclusions.

This was always going to be a mode of argument that stunned rather than persuaded. Nevertheless, Hobbes did take trouble, if not precisely to make his argument genuinely seductive (one senses that Hobbes, like many bold thinkers, was no stranger to the pleasure of shocking), then at least to hint to his reader about the cost of rejecting the conclusions implicit within the argument by which they had been uncomfortably ambushed. It is partly for this reason that Hobbes was careful to incorporate familiar language, drawn from traditional topics in political theology, in the expression of his novel assertions. For instance, Hobbes maintained the hallowed view that kings are God's representatives on earth: 'And whereas some men have pretended for their disobedience to their Soveraign, a new Covenant, made, not with men, but with God; this also is unjust: for there is no Covenant with God, but by mediation of some body that representeth Gods Person; which none doth but Gods Lieutenant, who hath the Soveraignty under God.'[129] Hobbes also goes out of his way to suggest that his own preferred political remedies are compatible with divine-right theory:

> The Monarch, or the Soveraign Assembly only hath immediate Authority from God, to teach and instruct the people; and no man but the Soveraign, receiveth his power *Dei gratiâ* simply; that is to say, from the favour of none but God: All other, receive theirs from the favour and providence of God, and their Soveraigns; as in a Monarchy *Dei gratiâ & Regis*; or *Dei providentiâ & voluntate Regis*. . . .

128. Hobbes insisted that politics should be a deductive science, rather than a prudential art monopolised by a sect of adepts (Hobbes, *Leviathan*, pp. 145 and 458; cf. Hobbes, *Behemoth*, pp. 70, 144, and 160). As a consequence, he repudiated all reliance on historical example, which hitherto had been a principal support of arguments about politics, seeing no demonstrative force in '*Examples of former times*' (Hobbes, *Leviathan*, p. 204).

129. Hobbes, *Leviathan*, p. 122. Cf. ibid., p. 306.

> The King, and every other Soveraign, executeth his Office of Supreme Pastor, by immediate Authority from God, that is to say, *in Gods Right*, or *Iure Divino*. . . .
>
> But if a man may be said to have his Jurisdiction *de Jure Divino*, and yet not immediately; what lawfull Jurisdiction, thought but Civill, is there in a Christian Common-wealth, that is not also *de Jure Divino*? For Christian Kings have their Civill Power from God immediately; and the Magistrates under him exercise their severall charges in vertue of his Commission; wherein that which they doe, is no lesse *de Jure Divino mediato*, that that which the Bishops doe, in vertue of the Popes Ordination. All lawfull Power is of God, immediately in the Supreme Governour, and mediately in those that have Authority under him.[130]

Again, Hobbes cited approvingly the biblical text that compares kings to gods.[131]

Yet, as well as the rhetorical function of giving the reader pause for thought, these vestiges of religious language, common both to Hobbes's argument and to expressions of the familiar political positions he was determined to defeat, serve also to remind us that it would be a mistake to conclude that, for all his strident anti-clericalism, Hobbes was trying to do away with all and any connection between politics and religion. Rather, the survival into *Leviathan* of religious language suggests instead that Hobbes was intent on reshaping, not removing altogether, the joint between our religious and our political ideas. Hobbes's experience told him that, in England in the mid-seventeenth century, that vital joint had become malformed. In *Leviathan*, he attempted to reset it, but not by any crude amputation of the religious from the political. It is for that reason that, in the famous frontispiece to *Leviathan*, the sovereign grasps both a sword and a crozier. For if the civil magistrate were to ignore religion and grant thereby a sphere of autonomy to priests, by so doing he would open the way for priests to invade his own power. That is why Hobbes's ideal commonwealth is (again referring to the language of the frontispiece) both 'Ecclesiasticall and Civil'.[132]

Hobbes's great successor in England as a political theorist, John Locke, was also concerned to remodel the joint between politics and religion. The

130. Hobbes, *Leviathan*, pp. 167–68, 374, and 391.

131. Hobbes, *Leviathan*, p. 234. Cf., for James I's citation of the same biblical passage, see James I and VI, *Political Writings*, p. 181.

132. Hobbes, *Leviathan*, p. xciii.

relationship between the two thinkers, whose lives overlapped,[133] has recently become freshly controversial.[134] In broad terms, it would be true to say that Locke's earlier political thought was close to the doctrines Hobbes had put forward in *Leviathan*. Locke's earliest 'correspondence, reading, notes and sketches show that he was first concerned with the authority of the state in religion, then with the Natural Law which sanctioned that authority, and with the basis of Natural Law in experience.'[135] These topics are recognisably close to those of Hobbes (while also showing that the proper joining—or separation—of civil and religious authority was from the first a primary concern of Locke's). Moreover, the two men shared a vision of the ultimate purpose of government. Like Hobbes, for Locke the end of 'Humane Society' is to secure 'Peace and Tranquility'.[136] Like Hobbes, Locke believed that '*there cannot be done a greater Mischief to Prince and People, than the Propagating wrong Notions concerning Government*', although of course Locke would have differed from Hobbes about what precisely constituted '*wrong Notions*'.[137] Like Hobbes, Locke had little time for the theory of the ancient constitution, which had been invoked so frequently by both king and Parliament during the Civil Wars.[138]

133. Hobbes, *b.* 1588, *d.* 1679; Locke, *b.* 1632, *d.* 1704.

134. Peter Laslett, the editor of Locke's *Two Treatises of Government*, contended that, while Locke of course was aware of Hobbes and well-versed in his writings and indeed 'never escaped the shadow of *Leviathan*' (Locke, *Two Treatises*, p. 72), it is nevertheless a mistake to suggest that in the *Two Treatises*, Hobbes was a major target of Locke's analysis: 'If Locke wrote his book as a refutation of Sir Robert Filmer, then he cannot have written it as refutation of Thomas Hobbes. It is almost as mistaken to suppose that he was arguing deliberately against *Leviathan* as to believe that he wrote to rationalize the Revolution' (ibid., p. 67). More recently, the work of Felix Waldmann ('John Locke as Reader of Thomas Hobbes's *Leviathan*: A New Manuscript', *Journal of Modern History* 93 [2021]: 245–82; summarised in *The Guardian*, 24 June 2021) has revitalised the view that Locke saw Hobbes as a principal adversary, albeit not a declared target in the manner of Filmer. In truth, although Laslett and Waldmann present themselves in exaggerated terms as alternatives, there is much common ground between their positions, which reflect variations of judgement and emphasis rather than entirely incompatible theories.

135. Locke, *Two Treatises*, p. 19.

136. Locke, *Two Treatises*, p. 219.

137. Locke, *Two Treatises*, p. 138.

138. Cf. John Locke, 'First Treatise', § 58: 'When Fashion hath once Established, what Folly or craft began, Custom makes it Sacred, and 'twill be thought impudence or madness, to contradict or question it. He that will impartially survey the Nations of the World, will find so much of their Governments, Religions, and Manners brought in and continued amongst them by these means, that he will have but little Reverence for the Practices which are in use and credit

But in central areas, Locke's later political thought would invert the authoritarian emphasis of his own earlier writings and would open up a large interval between his ideas and those of Hobbes. The points of divergence between the mature thought of the two men are obvious and plentiful. For instance, the young Locke had, like Hobbes, been impressed by the biblical texts that compare kings to gods.[139] But in the *Two Treatises*, kings are not gods, and the people are not beasts. Hobbes defended absolute power; Locke attacked it, using 'absolute' and 'arbitrary' as synonyms.[140] The concept of the state of nature is important in the work of both men, but their understandings of the state of nature varied sharply.[141] Hobbes saw political theory as a deductive science and so dissociated himself from the prudential tradition of political thought in which historical examples were so important.[142] Locke, however, saw politics as a matter of prudence and sagacity, not demonstrable science.[143] Whereas for Hobbes law was a 'Command' and hence entailed a curtailment of freedom, for Locke '*the end of Law* is not to abolish or restrain, but *to preserve and enlarge Freedom*'.[144] And so on.

This relationship of both aversion and continuity between the political theories of the two men is evident too when we turn to the question of how

---

amongst Men, and will have Reason to think, that the Woods and Forests, where the irrational untaught Inhabitants keep right by following Nature, are fitter to give us Rules, than Cities and Palaces, where those that call themselves Civil and Rational, go out of their way, by the Authority of Example' (Locke, *Two Treatises*, p. 183). Cf. Hobbes's denial that 'Praescription of time' confers authority or legitimacy to an institution or other political arrangement (Hobbes, *Leviathan*, p. 186) and his dismissal of ancient constitutionalism as 'an useless digression' (Hobbes, *Behemoth*, pp. 76–78).

139. Locke, *Two Treatises*, p. 20, quoted by Laslett from Locke's MS essay on the 'Civil Magistrate'. For Hobbes's references to these biblical texts, see above, p. 229, n. 131.

140. Locke, *Two Treatises*, p. 284.

141. For Hobbes, the state of nature is a state of lawlessness and war, in which men are apt to 'invade, and destroy one another' (Hobbes, *Leviathan*, p. 89). For Locke, man in the state of nature is not bereft of moral guidance, for the '*State of Nature* has a Law of Nature to govern it, which obliges every one: And Reason, which is that Law, teaches all Mankind, who will but consult it, that being all equal and independent, no one ought to harm another in his Life, Health, Liberty, or Possessions' (Locke, *Two Treatises*, p. 271). Locke's observation that 'some Men have confounded' the state of nature and a state of war is clearly directed at Hobbes, although he does not specify as much (Locke, *Two Treatises*, p. 280).

142. Malcolm, *Reason of State*, pp. 119–23.

143. Not, however, that Locke believed men should be slavishly bound by precedent: cf. Locke, *Two Treatises*, p. 183.

144. Hobbes, *Leviathan*, p. 187; Locke, 'Second Treatise', § 58, in Locke, *Two Treatises*, p. 306.

politics and religion mesh. Locke's *Two Treatises* took aim at the patriarchal politics of Sir Robert Filmer. Filmer had died in 1653, and his *Patriarcha,* which had been composed in the years preceding the English Civil Wars and provided the fullest statement of his views, had been published only posthumously in 1680. However, the work had circulated in manuscript before that, and its teachings had been disseminated by the clergy. As Locke observed, '*the Pulpit, of late Years, publickly owned his* [Filmer's] *Doctrine, and made it the Currant Divinity of the Times.*'[145]

Locke levelled two principal charges against *Patriarcha.* The first was that its doctrines paved the way to '*Slavery and Ruine*' and made Filmer '*an Advocate for Slavery*'.[146] *Patriarcha* 'can serve for nothing but to unsettle and destroy all the Lawful Governments in the World, and to Establish in their room Disorder, Tyranny, and Usurpation.'[147] Locke's point is that Filmer's politics, for all that they seem to be so favourable to the pretensions of kings, in fact offer equal support to the *de facto* power of usurpers and tyrants and hence destroy the authority of legitimate rulers.

The second charge was that, although Filmer advertised the Scriptural basis of his views, he had in fact been a poor reader of the Bible and only 'pretends to build wholly on Scripture'.[148] Locke repeatedly castigates Filmer for want of '*Scripture-proofs*'.[149] For instance, Filmer abbreviates the fifth commandment, 'Honour thy Father and Mother', to 'Honour thy Father' and repeatedly 'warp[s] the Sacred Rule of the Word of God'.[150] In the end, Locke theatrically throws up his hands at Filmer's abuse of Scripture: 'If this be to argue from Scripture, I know not what may not be proved by it, and I can scarce see how much this differs from that *Fiction and Phansie,* or how much surer Foundation it will prove than the opinions of *Philosophers and Poets,* which our *A.* so much condemns in his Preface.'[151] By contrast, Locke is keen to display the power of his Scriptural scholarship: by, for instance, quoting Hebrew and deploying the interpretative technique of 'parallel places'.[152]

145. Locke, *Two Treatises,* p. 138.

146. Locke, *Two Treatises,* p. 137.

147. Locke, 'First Treatise', § 72, in Locke, *Two Treatises,* p. 194. Cf. ibid., pp. 148 and 233.

148. Locke, 'First Treatise', § 32, in Locke, *Two Treatises,* p. 163. Cf. ibid., p. 262.

149. Locke, *Two Treatises,* p. 138.

150. Locke, 'First Treatise', § 6, in Locke, *Two Treatises,* p. 145; 'First Treatise', § 60, ibid., p. 184. For other examples of Filmer's shortcomings as a reader of the Bible, see ibid., pp. 149, 164, 176, 184–85, and 223.

151. Locke, 'First Treatise', § 34, in Locke, *Two Treatises,* p. 165.

152. Locke, *Two Treatises,* pp. 158–60, 166, 169, and 184–85.

So it would be an error to present the dispute between Locke and Filmer as a struggle between a proto-utilitarian and a Scriptural politician, since they are both emphatically Scriptural politicians. Locke, just as much as Filmer—indeed, arguably more than Filmer or at least more adequately—intended to outline a political theory that was compatible with 'the Constitution and Order which God had settled in the World'.[153] Locke's own positive political vision, described and argued for in the 'Second Treatise,' is also Scripturally-grounded, even though Locke does not claim to find it exemplified in the historical books of the Old Testament. The central concept around which his distinctions between paternal, political, and despotic power pivot is that of property. Property is God-given, but for the purpose of improvement rather than mere inert possession, as important biblical texts make clear.[154] The purpose of civil society is to preserve property, and hence only those who possess property can take part in civil society. Locke's materials, language, and ideas were eventually made to contribute to the arguments of modern liberals. But he was certainly no modern liberal himself.

The matter over which Locke and Filmer quarrel is what precisely the political significance of Scripture is for the organisation of human society. Therefore, the dispute between them is at one level a dispute about how to read the Bible. According to Locke, Filmer had fashioned the necessary joint between religion and politics in a false way, on the basis of incomplete or inadequate readings of Scripture. Locke intended, not by any means to repudiate religion but rather (in this, like Hobbes) to break and re-set that joint in a way that was more closely aligned with a true reading of Scripture. Thus, all Locke's careful corrections of Filmer's errors of Scriptural interpretation and understanding should be read as signs that, for Locke, politics and Scripture must be co-ordinated, albeit correctly. If Locke had been unconcerned to co-ordinate politics and Scripture, he would not have bothered to correct Filmer's mistaken interpretations of the Bible. He would simply have asserted that political arguments drawn from the Bible were irrelevant. But clearly for Locke, biblically-grounded arguments continued to have force, which is why Scripture needed to be read and understood with the greatest care and scruple. Neither Filmer (of course) but nor Locke was reaching for a political dispensation or theory which is incompatible with, or even proceeds without regard to, Scripture. They disagree in their readings of Scripture and in their understanding of its political significance; that is to say, the lessons it instills or which

153. Locke, 'First Treatise', § 137, in Locke, *Two Treatises*, p. 242.

154. Cf. Genesis 1:26–31 and 8:21–9:7.

can be derived from it. However, the point is not that Filmer embraces Scripture and Locke repudiates it. Rather, it is that Locke regards Filmer's doctrine as a travesty of what, by careful reading, we can deduce about politics while at the same time relying on Scripture.

I have considered at some length the way Hobbes and Locke sustained (while reshaping) the relationship between religion and politics because the later seventeenth century has been identified as the period in which that connection began to unravel. In certain lights, that is surely correct, at least in an English context. The appeal of the divine right of kings to Englishmen between 1530 and 1688 was related to their perceptions of the precariousness of the Reformation, of the possibility of the nation's being absorbed once more within Roman Catholicism, and hence of falling once again under the power of the pope. Divine-right theory was necessary because it gave expression to the national desire to be free from papal interference and vindicated a secular power that was fully divine and independent in its own right. It was therefore at bottom a doctrine of liberty and asserted 'the freedom of political societies from subjection to an ecclesiastical organization.'[155] The revolution of 1688 achieved that liberty and that security, at least to a satisfactory extent; and hence, at that point, the need for divine-right theories of English kingship fell away.[156]

However, it is striking that the successors of William III still wished to grapple to the throne the fragments of sacral kingship that 1688 had cast to the ground.[157] Touching for scrofula was allowed to fall into disuse after the death

155. Figgis, *Divine Right*, p. 257.

156. 'It was the work of the supporters of the Divine Right of Kings to make this [the utilitarian and historical character of modern politics] possible. It was impossible for the state to develope [*sic*] its principles, so long as its very existence, as an independent power, was constantly threatened by clericalism. To set it free from ecclesiastical control it was needful to claim Divine institution for its head. But when this purpose was realized, and independence attained, the state, secure in its new-found freedom, may develope [*sic*] principles of politics without reference to theology' (Figgis, *Divine Right*, p. 162).

157. 'The theory of Divine Right had a great work to do in assisting Englishmen to free themselves from the Papal yoke. The proof that the work was done was not reached until, in their fear of Rome, men were ready to cast aside the very weapon which had hitherto aided them in the struggle', by, i.e., abandoning James II and adhering to William of Orange (Figgis, *Divine Right*, p. 212). And again: 'The theory of Divine Right did not lose its popularity because it was absurd, but because its work was done. There were just as good reasons for disbelieving in its validity in 1598 or 1660 as there were at the Revolution [i.e., 1688]. Certainly some writers were well acquainted with them even at the earlier date, a fact proved by such a treatise as that of Parsons.

of Queen Anne; but the Hanoverian dynasty still afforced its fundamentally Parliamentary title to the throne by claims of ruling by divine ordinance. The Hanoverian theory of kingship was not fully divine; but the power of divine language and of divine concepts of authority that had been employed by their predecessors were too valuable to be discarded altogether. The revolution of 1688 replaced divine-right kingship with a constitutional monarchy, hereditary in its mode of transmission but ultimately grounded on a Parliamentary title. Parliament itself now sat continuously, rather than being (as had been the earlier practice, even up to and including the reign of Charles II) prorogued or dissolved for years at a time. Nevertheless, the language of monarchy in the eighteenth century might still be couched in terms of hereditary right and divine sanction. The Hanoverians announced in 1714 that George I was 'ascending the throne of his ancestors', and this was technically true.[158] As Paul Monod has said, 'None of these monarchs [Charles XII, Frederick I, Joseph I, William III, Louis XIV, Peter I] . . . would have described his government in secular terms; none would have welcomed the idea that he was anything other than a Christian ruler. Yet all of them had abandoned the path of a strictly confessional, godly kingship.'[159] The most keen-sighted of contemporary observers were alert to this divergence between pretensions and actuality and understood that the superficial continuities of reverential language and the quasi-religious ceremonies of monarchical deference had been reduced to a kind of pantomime, perhaps sincere on the part of at least some of the performers but not to be pushed too far. On 25 October 1760 Hume wrote to his publisher, William Strahan, and archly commiserated with the difficult and dependent position of the new king, George III: 'I wonder how Kings dare be so free: They ought to leave that to their Betters; to Men who have no Dependance on the Mob, or the Leaders of the Mob. As to poor Kings they are obligd sometimes to retract and to deny their Writings.'[160] The condescension lying behind that phrase 'poor Kings' is an important straw in the wind.

The Divine Right of Kings ceased to have practical importance, not because its doctrines were untrue, but because its teaching had become unnecessary. The transition stage had passed. The independence of the state had been attained. Politics having made good their claim to be part of the natural order had no longer need of a theological justification' (ibid., p. 263).

158. On the survival of the dynastic idiom in the English eighteenth century, see J. C. D. Clark, *English Society 1688–1832* (Cambridge: Cambridge University Press, 1985).

159. Monod, *Power of Kings*, p. 323.

160. Hume, *Letters*, 1:336. George III had acceded to the throne on the day Hume wrote this letter.

A few years before Hume wrote that letter, Adam Smith had reflected on the disjunction between underlying political realities and the outward decencies of behaviour we observe towards kings (and even our natural, inward feelings concerning them):

> That kings are the servants of the people, to be obeyed, resisted, deposed, or punished, as the public conveniency may require, is the doctrine of reason and philosophy; but it is not the doctrine of Nature. Nature would teach us to submit to them for their own sake, to tremble and bow down before their exalted station, to regard their smile as a reward sufficient to compensate any services, and to dread their displeasure, though no other evil were to follow from it, as the severest of all mortifications.[161]

The opposition Smith reveals here between, on the one hand, reason and philosophy, and on the other, 'Nature', suggests how, after 1688, the English political nation had been refracted into a philosophical minority whose minds were strong enough to digest the bleak truths revealed by reason, and the unphilosophical majority, who were unable to relinquish the comforts provided by our natural, but groundless, customary opinions. Some, of course, might experience that division within themselves. As Bishop Berkeley had pointed out, we should speak with the vulgar but think with the learned.[162]

The substantive power of religion in relation to politics had begun to wane, although the language of politics might retain a religious character. This displacement of formal religion, however, did not herald the advent of rational utilitarianism. The place of religion was gradually being taken by a variety of proxy beliefs, none of which could withstand rational scrutiny any more than could religion itself but all of which served the purpose, previously performed by religion, of supplying social cohesion and impelling the subject to acknowledge their duty of obligation. The key term used in the seventeenth and eighteenth centuries to refer to these new quasi-creeds was 'opinion'.

Awareness of the power that opinion (whether well- or ill-grounded) might exert over human actions reaches back to at least the early seventeenth century. In Francis Bacon's essay 'Of Vaine-Glory', he had noted the curious, almost magical, creative power of opinion: 'It often falls out, that *Somewhat* is produced of *Nothing*: For Lies are sufficient to breed Opinion, and Opinion brings

161. Smith, *Sentiments*, p. 53.

162. George Berkeley, *Alciphron; or, The Minute Philosopher*, vol. 1 (1732), p. 29.

on Substance.'[163] The substantive passions that opinion could create were easily strong enough to overwhelm the comparatively mild lessons of reason, for (as Bacon observed in 'Of Death') there 'is no passion in the minde of man, so weake, but it Mates, and Masters, the Feare of *Death*.'[164] Between 1619 and 1623 Hobbes had been in contact with Bacon and had occasionally worked as his amanuensis, so it is not surprising that we also find similar perceptions concerning the power of opinion in Hobbes's works. In *Behemoth*, for example, Hobbes had pointed out that 'the power of the mighty hath no foundation but in the opinion and belief of the people'.[165] In *Leviathan*, he had asserted that 'the Actions of men proceed from their Opinions; and in the wel [*sic*] governing of Opinions, consisteth the well governing of mens Actions, in order to their Peace, and Concord.'[166]

For Bacon, as later for Hobbes, the purposes of political association were Epicurean, utilitarian, and secular, namely, to furnish all the conditions and material requirements necessary for 'commodious' living that were absent from the state of nature: 'No Culture of the Earth; no Navigation, nor use of the commodities that may be imported by Sea; no commodious Building; no Instruments of moving, and removing such things as require much force; no Knowledge of the face of the Earth; no account of Time; no Arts; no Letters; no Society.'[167] All these absences are to be made good by the commonwealth. However, the tools used by politicians to achieve these utilitarian ends can never be only those that come naturally to the hands of a rational utility-maximiser, because of the cardinal role played by opinion in shaping the behaviour of the governed. It followed that beliefs, prejudices, emotions—particularly about religion but also in other neuralgic areas—were still of vital importance and required artful management by political actors. As David Hume, here following in the footsteps of Bacon and Hobbes, would state in his essay 'Of the First Principles of Government', 'it is . . . on opinion only that government is founded'.[168] The ends prescribed by reason have to be achieved, at least in part, by manipulating non-rational instruments.

163. Bacon, *Essayes*, p. 161.
164. Bacon, *Essayes*, pp. 9–10.
165. Hobbes, *Behemoth*, p. 16.
166. Hobbes, *Leviathan*, p. 124.
167. Hobbes, *Leviathan*, p. 89.
168. Hume, *Essays*, p. 32.

It is the perception of the key importance of opinion that links the prophetic or eschatological mode of Hobbes to the deism and natural religion of Hume. Notwithstanding the immense differences of fundamental intellectual commitment that separated them, these two thinkers nevertheless shared a perception of the mischief that powerful, unscrupulous religious corporations and ungoverned or unregulated religious opinions can cause in the public sphere. But whereas Hobbes was (as we have seen) profoundly interested in the Bible, retaining an apparently firm faith in the fact of God's having acted in human history and having made promises about the future that he will keep, Hume had no such interest and no such faith. And whereas Hobbes, it seems (and despite the allegations made by his contemporary detractors), retained a lively belief in the existence of a true religion (albeit not one represented or embodied in an earthly church), Hume was not so sanguine about that possibility, although during his life-time he was outwardly and prudently reserved on the subject of religious belief (as was only reasonable, given his experience of persecution on the grounds of his suspected atheism).

For Hume, what was important in relation to opinion was social utility rather than truth. But the human ability to recognise genuine social utility was hampered by a range of customary but mischievous allegiances: allegiances, for instance, to political parties, nationalistic prejudices, or particular historical narratives. To some extent, therefore, Hume, like Hobbes, saw our ingrained beliefs as an adversary to be overcome. However, Hume also recognised that our inclination to adhere to the customary could be turned to advantage. If harmful prejudices could be abated, and their place taken by more moderate and socially useful opinions, then the human tendency to be guided by the customary could become an asset rather than a liability. The essays over which Hume laboured for more than thirty years were his attempt to mould popular opinion into just such innocuous, sociable, positive forms.[169]

Hume's awareness of the usefulness of our attachment to the customary, as the source both of stability and (if well-directed) of utility in our social arrangements, would be taken further by Edmund Burke. For all that Burke understood well the political importance of a widespread and lively sense of religion in the populace, he also knew that government was a 'contrivance of

169. Hume published the first set of what would become *Essays Moral, Political, and Literary* in 1741. He repeatedly (even obsessively) revised them until his death in 1776; and a posthumous edition embodying his ultimate revisions was published in 1777.

human wisdom to provide for human *wants*.'[170] Like Hume, therefore, Burke insisted that political opinions were not to be considered as true or false so much as harmful or salutary: 'The practical consequences of any political tenet go a great way in deciding on its value. Political problems do not primarily concern truth or falsehood. They relate to good or evil. What in the result is likely to produce evil, is politically false: that which is productive of good, politically true.'[171] And Burke's flamboyant, in some ways reckless, intellect did not stop short of embracing even prejudice as socially useful. The English, he informed C.-J.-F. Depont, 'are generally men of untaught feelings; . . . instead of casting away all our old prejudices, we cherish them to a very considerable degree, and, to take more shame to ourselves, we cherish them because they are prejudices.'[172] The utility of prejudice lay precisely in its side-stepping of conscious ratiocination:

> Prejudice is of a ready application in the emergency; it previously engages the mind in a steady course of wisdom and virtue, and does not leave the man hesitating in the moment of decision, sceptical, puzzled, and unresolved. Prejudice renders a man's virtue his habit; and not a series of unconnected acts. Through just prejudice, his duty becomes a part of his nature.[173]

Prejudice supplied a necessary anchor to withstand the destructive velocities that could be generated by the sail of abstract reason.[174]

The most explicit English analysis of the divided condition of modern politics that these developments created is to be found in Walter Bagehot's *The English Constitution*. In these essays, first published as a series in *The Fortnightly*

170. Edmund Burke, *Reflections on the Revolution in France*, in Burke, *Writings*, 8:110.

171. Edmund Burke, *Appeal from the New to the Old Whigs*, in Burke, *Writings*, 4:445.

172. Burke, *Reflections on the Revolution in France*, in Burke, *Writings*, 8:138.

173. Burke, *Reflections on the Revolution in France*, in Burke, *Writings*, 8:138.

174. 'Lastly, the theory of the Divine Right of Kings was the form in which was expressed the sense of the need of some bond of moral sentiment and conscience other than the belief in its utility to attach men to any government. Burke felt the same need and expressed it in tones which yet ring in men's ears. He knew that the influences of sentiment and tradition are stronger than the calculations of interest to bind a people's allegiance to its government, and that no constitution can be stable which makes a merely utilitarian appeal to men's assistance. He was not ashamed to say that the dead weight of custom, "prejudice," was the weapon which all states should have in their hand. For he felt that an emotional tie must add strength to the civic reason in order to make it an enduring support' (Figgis, *Divine Right*, pp. 254–55).

Review between 1865 and 1867, Bagehot analysed how in England, a utilitarian political machinery was aesthetically camouflaged, and thus enabled to operate, by the dissemination throughout the ordinary populace of carefully-nurtured opinions. These opinions amounted to a set of unexamined notions about the location and nature of political authority that guided popular conduct without engaging or arousing the conscious mind. In many ways these astringent, sometimes deliberately provocative, essays are still descriptive of the political reality we inhabit today, at least in Western democracies.

Like Hume, Bagehot was intrigued by the curious ascendancy whereby in human societies a minority had come to rule over the majority.[175] Like Hume, he realised that this ascendancy was achieved not by the power of rational argument, still less by a superiority of natural talents, but rather by adroit management amounting almost to *legerdemain*: 'the few rule by their hold, not over the reason of the multitude, but over their imaginations, and their habits; over their fancies as to distant things they do not know at all, over their customs as to near things which they know very well.'[176] Like Hume again, Bagehot realised that tradition and custom were essential to the smooth operation of society: 'Respect is traditional; it is given not to what is proved to be good, but to what is known to be old.'[177] However, this sleight of hand need not, so Bagehot suggests, be a matter of underhand manipulation on the part of the minority, although undoubtedly at some points in human history it had been that. Notwithstanding the frequent abuse of the subtle arts of government, they could be civilised and refined into an unspoken (but nevertheless real and mutually beneficial) voluntary covenant between the knowing few and the less knowing many: 'It has been thought strange, but there *are* nations in which the numerous unwiser part wishes to be ruled by the less numerous wiser part. The numerical majority—whether by custom or choice, is immaterial—is ready, is eager to delegate its power of choosing its ruler to a certain select minority.'[178] This confidingness on the part of the majority was for Bagehot a mark of civilisation, for the 'peculiar

175. David Hume, 'Of the First Principles of Government', in Hume, *Essays*, p. 32: 'Nothing appears more surprizing to those, who consider human affairs with a philosophical eye, than the easiness with which the many are governed by the few'.

176. Bagehot, *Constitution*, p. 36. Cf. Hume, *Essays*, p. 32: 'the governors have nothing to support them but opinion.'

177. Bagehot, *Constitution*, p. 36.

178. Bagehot, *Constitution*, p. 33.

marks of semi-barbarous people are diffused distrust and indiscriminate suspicion.'[179]

Bagehot viewed many of the received opinions concerning English government—for instance, that it was a system of checks and balances distributed between Crown, House of Lords, and House of Commons which produced the maximum possible amount of liberty for the governed or that the hereditary principle was compatible with rule by the most talented—with undisguised contempt. The English government was, in fact, a system of Cabinet autocracy, and the hereditary principle, in fact, seemed to produce a dearth rather than a wealth of talent:

> A constitutional sovereign must in the common course of government be a man of but common ability. I am afraid, looking to the acquired feebleness of hereditary dynasties, that we must expect him to be a man of inferior ability. Theory and experience both teach that the education of a prince can be but a poor education, and that a royal family will generally have less ability than other families.[180]

Anti-hereditary sentiments such as these seem at times to come very close to those of the republican radicals of the previous century, such as Tom Paine.[181]

179. Bagehot, *Constitution*, p. 26.

180. Bagehot, *Constitution*, p. 61. Cf. ibid., pp. 69, 90, and 166: 'We must not reckon in constitutional monarchy any more than in despotic monarchy on the permanence in the descendants of the peculiar genius which founded the race. As far as experience goes, there is no reason to expect an hereditary series of useful limited monarchs'; 'The House of Lords, being an hereditary chamber, cannot be of more than common ability'; 'An hereditary king is but an ordinary person, upon an average, at best; he is nearly sure to be badly educated for business; he is very little likely to have a taste for business; he is solicited from youth by every temptation to pleasure; he probably passed the whole of his youth in the vicious situation of the heir-apparent, who can do nothing because he has no appointed work, and who will be considered almost to outstep his function if he undertake optional work. For the most part, a constitutional king is a *damaged* common man; not forced to business by necessity as a despot often is, but yet spoiled for business by most of the temptations which spoil a despot'.

181. 'To the evil of monarchy we have added that of hereditary succession; and as the first is a degradation and lessening of ourselves, so the second, claimed as a matter of right, is an insult and imposition on posterity. For all men being originally equals, no *one* by *birth* could have a right to set up his own family in perpetual preference to all others forever, and though himself might deserve *some* decent degree of honors of his contemporaries, yet his descendants might be far too unworthy to inherit them' (Thomas Paine, *Common Sense*, in Paine, *Political Writings*, p. 11; cf. ibid., pp. 118, 124–27, 137–39, and 162–73).

Although Bagehot saw through the various fictions that had gathered round the English constitution, he was far from wanting to sweep them away. He understood that in the modern world, the nature of a 'free' government had changed. Free government was no longer a matter of either constitutional design or the purposes government was intended to serve. Free government had become simply a matter of who does the governing:

> Free government is self-government. A government of the people by the people. The best government of this sort is that which the people think best. An imposed government, a government like that of the English in India, may very possibly be better; it may represent the views of a higher race than the governed race, but it is not therefore a free government. A free government is that which the people subject to it voluntarily choose.[182]

'The best government of this sort is that which the people think best': This is truly the triumph of opinion. But opinion, and the imagination that shaped and directed it, could not be left to chance: 'The human imagination exacts keeping in government as much as in art; it will not be at all influenced by institutions which do not match with those by which it is principally influenced.'[183]

Bagehot was no more enthusiastic about the natural capacities of the people than he was about the abilities of the aristocracy or the monarchy. The 'life of labour' to which the mass of the people were condemned in an advanced economy, wrote Bagehot (echoing Adam Smith), suppressed both the intellect and the imagination: 'The fancy of the mass of men is incredibly weak; it can see nothing without a visible symbol, and there is much that it can scarcely make out with a symbol.'[184] The result was that, like the voluntarily benighted inhabitants of Plato's cave, 'most men of business love a sort of twilight.'[185]

However, this slowness of apprehension in the common people, the myopia they found comfortable, and their addiction to the visible, the tangible,

182. Bagehot, *Constitution*, p. 117.

183. Bagehot, *Constitution*, p. 99.

184. Bagehot, *Constitution*, pp. 35 and 73. Smith had rested his case for some public support for education out of the proceeds of taxation on 'the gross ignorance and stupidity which, in a civilized society, seem so frequently to benumb the understandings of all the inferior ranks of people', largely as a result of the repetitive and stunting tasks in which the division of labour obliges them to pass their days; for an 'instructed and intelligent people besides are always more decent and orderly than an ignorant and stupid one' (Smith, *Wealth*, 2:788).

185. Bagehot, *Constitution*, p. 107. Cf. Plato, *The Republic*, bk. VII, 514a–517c.

and the symbolic, could be turned to political advantage. The key to understanding how this might happen lay in Bagehot's celebrated distinction between the 'dignified' and the 'efficient' parts of the constitution:

> In such constitutions there are two parts . . . : first, those which excite and preserve the reverence of the population,—the *dignified* parts, if I may so call them; and next, the *efficient* parts,—those by which it, in fact, works and rules. There are two great objects which every constitution must attain to be successful, which every old and every celebrated one must have wonderfully achieved:—every constitution must first *gain* authority, and then *use* authority; it must first win the loyalty and confidence of mankind, and then employ that homage in the work of government.[186]

Accordingly, the 'dignified' parts of government possessed a fundamental utility:

> The dignified parts of government are those which bring it force,—which attract its motive power. The efficient parts only employ that power. The comely parts of a government have need, for they are those upon which its vital strength depends. They may not do anything definite that a simpler polity would not do better; but they are the preliminaries, the needful pre-requisites of *all* work. They raise the army, though they do not win the battle.[187]

The dignified elements of a constitution are particularly well-adapted to the needs and interests of the 'ruder sort of men', who find little to engage them in the complicated and obscure workings of the efficient parts of government:

> But this order of men are uninterested in the plain, palpable ends of government; they do not prize them; they do not in the least comprehend how they should be attained. It is very natural, therefore, that the most useful parts of the structure of government should by no means be those which excite the most reverence. The elements which excite the most easy reverence will be the theatrical elements; those which appeal to the senses, which claim to be embodiments of the greatest human ideas—which boast in some cases of far more than human origin. That which is mystic in its claims;—that which is occult in mode of action; that which is brilliant to the eye; that which is seen vividly for a moment, and then is seen no more; that

186. Bagehot, *Constitution*, p. 7.
187. Bagehot, *Constitution*, p. 7.

> which is hidden and unhidden; that which is specious, and yet interesting—palpable in its seeming, and yet professing to be more than palpable in its results;—this, howsoever its form may change, or however we may define it or describe it, is the sort of thing—the only sort which yet comes home to the mass of men. So far from the dignified parts of a constitution being necessarily the most useful, they are likely, according to outside presumption, to be the least so; for they are likely to be adjusted to the lowest orders—those likely to care least and judge worst about what *is* useful.[188]

In Bagehot's judgement, in a civilised society our lives are made efficient, 'economised', by a 'sleepy kind of habit'; and the dignified parts of a constitution minister to that side of our nature.[189]

The English constitution was fortunate in that it was replete with 'historical, complex, august, theatrical parts, which it has inherited from a long past,—which *take* the multitude,—which guide by an insensible but an omnipotent influence the associations of its subjects.'[190] Because of this rich inheritance of once efficient, now only dignified, institutions and symbols, orderly government in England depended on a kind of false consciousness concerning the mechanism of rule that was diffused throughout the population:

> The separation of principal power from principal station is a refinement which they [the populace] could not even conceive. They fancy they are governed by an hereditary queen, a queen by the grace of God, when they are really governed by a cabinet and a parliament—men like themselves, chosen by themselves. The conspicuous dignity awakens the sentiment of reverence, and men, often very undignified, seize the occasion to govern by means of it.[191]

188. Bagehot, *Constitution*, p. 9.

189. Bagehot, *Constitution*, p. 10.

190. Bagehot, *Constitution*, p. 10. Cf. ibid., p. 35: 'The apparent rulers of the English nation are like the most imposing personages of a splendid procession: it is by them the mob are influenced; it is they whom the spectators cheer. The real rulers are secreted in second-rate carriages; no one cares for them or asks about them, but they are obeyed implicitly and unconsciously by reason of the splendour of those who eclipsed and preceded them.'

191. Bagehot, *Constitution*, p. 28. Cf. Sidgwick, *Ethics*, p. 19, on the spectral afterlife of the belief in hereditary right: 'it was once held, and the doctrine still lingers, that the natural right of government in any society is vested, as a kind of heritable though not transferable property, in the persons belonging to a particular line of descent.'

In England, the chief source of this 'sentiment of reverence' was the afterlife of the once potent and functional doctrines of divine-right monarchy, for the 'popular homage clings to the line of god-descended kings.'[192] This belief was certainly a fiction, but it was nevertheless a salutary fiction:

> Mostly, the 'divinity' that surrounds a king altogether prevents anything like a steady conception of him. You fancy that the object of your loyalty is as much elevated above you by intrinsic nature as he is by extrinsic position; you deify him in sentiment, as once men deified him in doctrine. . . . They believe that there is *one* man whom by mystic right they should obey; and therefore they do obey him.[193]

Nor was it necessarily the case that the people were deluded when they believed in this sentimental ghost of formerly substantial doctrine and that the few who discounted it were knowing. In a striking passage, Bagehot presented the point of view of the philosophers as a kind of blindness, a disabling acuity that led them precisely to see *through*—and so to discard—the very thing that was in fact most worthy of their attention:

> In fact, the mass of the English people yield a deference rather to something else than to their rulers. They defer to what we may call the *theatrical show* of society. A certain state passes before them; a certain pomp of great men; a certain spectacle of beautiful women; a wonderful scene of wealth and enjoyment is displayed, and they are coerced by it. Their imagination is bowed down; they feel they are not equal to the life which is revealed to them. Courts and aristocracies have the great quality which rules the multitude, though philosophers can see nothing in it—visibility.[194]

One is put in mind of Hal's envious and melancholy remark to Poins, 'thou art a blessed fellow to think as every man thinks.'[195] For according to Bagehot the proximate danger lay not in too much credulity but rather in too much

192. Bagehot, *Constitution,* p. 179. Bagehot shrewdly notes that the durability of Jacobitism illustrates the popular attachment to indefeasible hereditary right and the mystical ideas of kingship with which it was associated: 'So strong was inbred reverence for hereditary right, that until the accession of George III the English Government was always subject to the unceasing attrition of a competitive sovereign' (ibid., p. 185).

193. Bagehot, *Constitution,* p. 28.

194. Bagehot, *Constitution,* p. 34.

195. 2 *Henry IV,* II.ii.48–49.

philosophy. After 1688, ideas of the divine authority of kingship had, it seemed, been damaged and bruised beyond substantive recovery. But by the time of Victoria, the English had somehow begun again to think in terms of 'a sacred line of sovereigns', and they 'believe they have a mystic obligation to obey her.'[196] These beliefs, no matter how ill-founded, were the lynch-pin of the English government, for the 'monarchy by its religious sanction now confirms all our political order.'[197] In consequence, the conceptual twilight in which the un-philosophical huddled together was to be carefully preserved at all costs: 'Above all things our royalty is to be reverenced, and if you begin to poke about it you cannot reverence it. When there is a select committee on the Queen, the charm of royalty will be gone. Its mystery is its life. We must not let in daylight upon magic.'[198] The brilliance of that famous formulation has perhaps distracted us from its plain but challenging meaning, namely, that the half-light of decaying religion which lends itself to successful political sleight of hand is, as a general social atmosphere, infinitely preferable to the pitiless daylight of philosophy.

Today, even in England, reverence for the monarchy has for the most part been replaced by something milder and more limited, namely, an affection for the person of Queen Elizabeth II, which was so amply demonstrated on her death in 2022. Even so, our public life, and that of all the Western democracies, still moves forward through what we might call traditional ceremonies of de-theologized solemnity: a strictly-observed calendar of events, the familiar theatre of public parades and ritual costumes, selections from a prescribed menu of musical accompaniment, the production of precious and powerful relics (such as Lincoln's Bible, on which all US presidents take the oath of office—valuable more for its contents or for its provenance?), the meticulous repetition of inherited verbal *formulae*, the composition of facial expressions into masks of impassiveness appropriate to the witnessing of, or participation in, a tremendous mystery. And that subsiding of fervour for the dignified parts of government has allowed other proxy-religions or creeds—of an ecological,

196. Bagehot, *Constitution*, p. 44.

197. Bagehot, *Constitution*, p. 44.

198. Bagehot, *Constitution*, p. 54. Cf. ibid., p. 94, and Bagehot's similar comments about the House of Lords: 'The difficulty of reforming an old institution like the House of Lords is necessarily great; its possibility rests on continuous caste and ancient deference. And if you begin to agitate about it, to bawl at meetings about it, that deference is gone, its peculiar charm lost, its reserved sanctity gone.'

sexual, racial, or political complexion and often oppositional in orientation—to mop up the surplus credulity that decaying religion can no longer absorb and engage and that is thus released once more into social circulation.

If the objects of current popular regard are nothing more than the ideological burrs on which the thistledown of our credulity happens for the time being to have snagged, then it seems that Carlyle's generalisation about authority still holds good: 'For it is most true that all available Authority is *mystic* in its conditions, and comes "by the grace of God."'[199]

The morning after the killing of Duncan, Macbeth attempts to extenuate his slaughter of the drunken grooms sleeping outside the dead king's chamber by describing the effect produced on him by the sight of Duncan's corpse:

> Who can be wise, amaz'd, temperate and furious,
> Loyal and neutral, in a moment? No man:
> Th'expedition of my violent love
> Outrun the pauser, reason.—Here lay Duncan,
> His silver skin lac'd with his golden blood;
> And his gash'd stabs look'd like a breach in nature
> For ruin's wasteful entrance: there, the murtherers
> Steep'd in the colours of their trade, their daggers
> Unmannerly breech'd with gore. Who could refrain,
> That had a heart to love, and in that heart
> Courage, to make's love known?[200]

Of what is this an image? It is a scene of king-killing, obviously enough. But, beyond that, do Macbeth's words draw back the curtain on a scene of sacrilegious outrage or on a scene of quasi-republican justice?

At first glance, that might seem to be a ridiculous question. Of all Shakespeare's plays, surely *Macbeth* is the one most deeply soaked in the language and imagery of supernatural, charismatic monarchy. This, as is well known, was the favourite political theory of the reigning monarch, James I and VI,

199. Thomas Carlyle, 'The Constitution', bk. I, ch. 1, in *The French Revolution: A History*, vol. 1 (London: Chapman and Hall, 1885), p. 249.

200. *Macbeth*, II.iii.105–14. A striking contrast would be with Warwick's description of the body of the murdered Gloucester (2 *Henry VI*, III.ii.168–78).

before whom this play, or a shortened version of it, was performed at court in 1606.[201] In *The Trew Law of Free Monarchies* (published anonymously in 1598), James had articulated in the most far-reaching and uncompromising manner the pretensions of divine-right monarchical absolutism. He defined monarchy in its opening sentence as the 'forme of gouernment, as resembling the Diuinitie, [which] approcheth nearest to perfection', a little later hyperbolically extolling monarchy as 'the trew patterne of Diuinitie', and not hesitating to call kings 'Gods . . . because they sit vpon God his Throne in the earth' and were placed in judgement over their subjects by God himself.[202] Explicating (in an ingenious but surely deeply unpersuasive way) the notorious passage from the Book of Samuel[203] in which all the manifold injustices and inconveniences that attend on monarchy are itemised, James insists that the purpose of this text is to reconcile the Israelites to the consequences of what they have demanded, 'since he that hath the only power to make him [a king], hath the onely power to vnmake him', and furthermore to demonstrate that monarchy is of divine institution, 'as beeing founded by God himselfe, who by his Oracle, and out of his owne mouth gaue the law thereof'.[204]

Macbeth contains several examples of, or allusions to, James's theory of charismatic, divine-right kingship, in which the possession of supernatural potency legitimises the exercise of an absolute authority. As the exiled Malcolm explains to Macduff, the king of England, Edward the Confessor, cures scrofula (a disease resistant to conventional medicine) with his royal touch. The Doctor's brief account is:

> There are a crew of wretched souls
> That stay his cure. Their malady convinces
> The great assay of art, but at his touch—
> Such sanctity hath heaven given his hand—
> They presently amend.[205]

201. 'There were many reasons why James I. should hold the doctrine of the Divine Right of Kings in its strictest form. His claim to the throne of England rested upon descent alone; barred by two Acts of Parliament, it could only be successfully maintained by means of the legitimist principle' (Figgis, *Divine Right*, p. 137).

202. James I and VI, *Political Writings*, pp. 63 and 64–65.

203. 1 Samuel 8:9–22.

204. James I and VI, *Political Writings*, pp. 68 and 70. On the political beliefs and writings of James I and VI, see J. P. Sommerville, *Politics and Ideology in England, 1603–1640* (London: Longman, 1986).

205. *Macbeth*, IV.iii.141–45.

This is expanded upon enthusiastically by Malcolm:

A most miraculous work in this good King,
Which often since my here-remain in England
I have seen him do. How he solicits heaven
Himself best knows; but strangely visited people,
All swoll'n and ulcerous, pitiful to the eye,
The mere despair of surgery, he cures,
Hanging a golden stamp about their necks,
Put on with holy prayers; and, 'tis spoken,
To the succeeding royalty he leaves
The healing benediction. With this strange virtue,
He hath a heavenly gift of prophecy,
And sundry blessings hang about his throne
That speak him full of grace.[206]

The same underlying belief, that kings rule by divine appointment and thus in some way participate in the nature of divinity, is more pithily present in Macduff's reference to Duncan's body as the 'Lord's anointed temple'.[207] And immediately before this, when Malcolm has been posing as a tyrant in order to discover whether Macduff may be an instrument of Macbeth's, sent 'to win me / Into his power', the catalogue of tyrannical characteristics that Malcolm pretended to have—lasciviousness towards women, avarice, an addiction to wrongdoing—shadows the list that James gave in *The Trew Law* of kingly misdemeanours (none of which, however, would justify resistance, let alone rebellion): 'tyrannizing ouer mens persons, sonnes, daughters and seruants; redacting noble houses, and men, and women of noble blood, to slauish and seruile offices; and extortion, and spoile of their lands and goods to the princes owne priuate vse and commoditie.'[208]

206. *Macbeth*, IV.iii.147–59. On the theory and practice of the royal touch, which began in the eleventh century with the Capetian dynasty in France, see Sir Raymond Crawfurd, *The King's Evil* (Oxford: Clarendon Press, 1911); and Marc Bloch, *The Royal Touch. Sacred Monarchy and Scrofula in England and France* (first published as *Les Rois thaumaturges*, Paris: Librairie Armand Colin, 1923; trans. J. E. Anderson, London: Routledge, 1973; repr., 2015). For its association with Stuart kingship, see J. C. D. Clark, *English Society 1688–1832: Ideology, Social Structure and Political Practice During the Ancien Regime* (Cambridge: Cambridge University Press, 1985), esp. pp. 161–73; Noel Woolf, *The Sovereign Remedy: Touch-Pieces and the King's Evil* (Manchester: British Association of Numismatic Societies, 1990); and Monod, *Power of Kings*, pp. 226–27, 233, 257, 312.

207. *Macbeth*, II.iii.63.

208. *Macbeth*, IV.iii.118–19; James I and VI, *Political Writings*, p. 70. Cf. *Macbeth*, IV.iii.37–114.

These ostensibly respectful glances at the theory of sacral monarchy with which James was particularly associated are reinforced in *Macbeth* by other touches of implicit Stuart panegyric or compliment, long since recognised by scholars.[209] The cardinal role allotted to the three weird sisters in the play reflects and defers to James's declared interest in, and belief in the reality of, witchcraft.[210] One of James's supposed forebears, Banquo, is an important character in the play.[211] Contrary to at least some of the play's sources, in *Macbeth*, Banquo is exonerated of any guilt in Duncan's murder.[212] The final vision Macbeth is granted when he goes to visit the weird sisters is a vision of Banquo's royal progeny. For Macbeth, the vision is terrible because it demonstrates that, as he has himself earlier feared,

> For Banquo's issue have I filed my mind,
> For them the gracious Duncan have I murdered,
> Put rancors in the vessel of my peace
> Only for them, and mine eternal jewel
> Given to the common enemy of man
> To make them kings—the seeds of Banquo kings![213]

209. Most fully set out in H. N. Paul, *The Royal Play of Macbeth* (New York: Macmillan, 1950). As Bullough summarises, 'The theme [of *Macbeth*] was chosen to please the King by referring to his ancestry, his touching for the "King's Evil", and his interest in witches and abnormal psychology' (Bullough, *Sources*, 7:427).

210. As expressed in, e.g., James's *Daemonologie* (Edinburgh, 1597), the purpose of which, as James says in 'The Preface to the Reader', is to convince his reader that '*such diuelish artes haue bene and are*' (sig. A3[r]). David Norbrook notes that the theme of witchcraft had not been emphasised by either Hector Boece or Buchanan (Norbrook, '*Macbeth*', p. 105).

211. Although their consanguinity is probably in fact fictitious: see Bullough, *Sources*, 7:433–34. Nevertheless, it was affirmed by Holinshed (Bullough, *Sources*, 7:488 and 499) and had been elaborately set out in pictorial form by John Leslie, the bishop of Ross, in his *De Origine, Moribus, et Rebus Gestis Scotorum* (Rome, 1578): see Bullough, *Sources*, vol. 7, plate 2, facing p. 517.

212. In the work of Scottish history by James's former tutor, George Buchanan, 'Mackbeth' communicates his intention to murder Duncan 'to his most intimate Friends, amongst whom *Bancho* was one' (Bullough, *Sources*, 7:513; and cf. ibid., p. 514, where 'Bancho' is said to be his 'Companion in the Kings Parricide'; quoting the 1690 English translation of Buchanan's *Rerum Scoticarum Historia* [Edinburgh, 1582]). Shakespeare's principal source, Holinshed, would follow Buchanan (Bullough, *Sources*, 7:496). The Stuart propagandist Leslie, however, had been careful to clear Banquo of involvement in the crime (Bullough, *Sources*, 7:441).

213. *Macbeth*, III.i.65–70.

However, the very details of the vision that so appalled Macbeth would by contrast have been deeply gratifying to the royal spectator in 1606:

> Thou art too like the spirit of Banquo. Down!
> Thy crown does sear mine eyeballs! And thy heir,
> Thou other gold-bound brow, is like the first.
> A third is like the former.—Filthy hags,
> Why do you show me this?—A fourth! Start, eyes!
> What, will the line stretch out to th'crack of doom?
> Another yet? A seventh! I'll see no more.
> And yet the eighth appears, who bears a glass
> Which shows me many more; and some I see
> That two-fold balls and treble scepters carry.
> Horrible sight! Now, I see 'tis true,
> For the blood-boltered Banquo smiles upon me,
> And points at them for his.[214]

'Two-fold balls and treble scepters' is a complimentary reference to the complex royal title James had acquired after his accession to the English throne in 1603 and glances at the fact of his double coronation at Scone and Westminster.

Reminded, then, of the extent of the play's engagement with the language, tropes, and history of Stuart compliment, let us return to the detail of the language in which Macbeth describes the body of the murdered king. Through its evocation of preciousness ('His silver skin lac'd with his golden blood')—indeed, through the alchemical power those words suggest that the kingly body possesses precisely to transform base violence into the preciousness of noble metals—does it speak of the power in charismatic kingship to triumph over the violence visited upon it? Does the image implicitly make the claim that the supernatural potency of the kingly body can take king-killing energies, ruinous in intention ('ruin's wasteful entrance'), and transmute them to make of its own corpse a gorgeous object which demonstrates the power in kingship to transcend the wastefulness inherent in time and nature? Is the dead Duncan even perhaps Christ-like, in this conversion of violence into the ground of his own prevailing and a demonstration of his own transcendent value?

214. *Macbeth*, IV.i.111–23. There is a suggestive parallel, possibly even a source, for this passage in Matthew Gwinn's Latin play *Vertumnus Sive Annus Recurrens*. It had been performed before James at St. John's College, Oxford, in 1605 (Bullough, *Sources*, 7:470–72).

Shakespeare's imagination was no stranger to fantasies of the benign transformation of the body of a dead king—recall Ariel's song to Ferdinand in *The Tempest,* when he wishes to mislead him that his father, Alonso, the King of Naples, has drowned and where corporal decay is re-described as enrichment:

> Full fathom five thy father lies;
> Of his bones are coral made;
> Those are pearls that were his eyes;
> Nothing of him that doth fade,
> But doth suffer a sea-change
> Into something rich and strange.[215]

Or is Macbeth's description of Duncan's corpse the reverse of that? Is it in fact a monarcho-mach image of a kingly idol rightly destroyed by justified violence? God's stern warning to the backsliding Israelites may encourage us in this train of contrary thought: 'You shall not make with me gods of silver, neither shall you make unto you gods of gold.'[216]

There are accents in the wording of the passage which point in that direction. The phrase 'Unmannerly breech'd with gore' catches our attention, in part because we notice how Shakespeare's auditory imagination has followed the 'breach in nature' with this different kind of breech. The grooms' daggers are breeched with blood because they seem to be clothed in it: the making of one kind of breach has led to another. And it is remarkable that Duncan's 'golden blood' has become, in the space of only four lines, 'gore'—a word suggestive of stubborn and untransmutable carnality. The movement from 'golden blood' to 'gore' hints that, in fewer than five lines of verse, a profound change of perspective has occurred.

That hint is amplified by the range of meaning contained in the word 'breech'd'. 'Breech' has not only the intransitive sense of 'to be clothed with breeches'. It can also be used transitively, to denote the moment in a boy's life when, for the first time, he wears man's clothing (that is to say, breeches or trousers rather than nursery clothes).[217] A boy is said to be breeched when he is moving towards the threshold of becoming a man. 'Breeching' is thus an important stage in a boy's journey out of a pre-sexual condition of nonage and towards the state of independent, virile manhood. In Milton's *Readie and Easie*

215. *The Tempest,* I.ii.395–400.
216. Exodus 20:23.
217. See *OED*, 'breech' *v.*, 1.

Way (1660), he would characterise those weaker sorts who were content to fall in with monarchy and who lacked the stomach for a republic as 'more like boyes under age then men.'[218]

Just a few years before the composition of *Macbeth,* Shakespeare had written *Julius Caesar* and had put onstage the pre-emptive killing of one who was suspected of wishing to be a king.[219] After the assassination, Brutus encourages the conspirators to

Stoop, Romans, stoop,
And let us bathe our hands in Caesar's blood
Up to the elbows and *besmear* our swords.
Then walk we forth, even to the marketplace,
And, waving our red weapons o'er our heads,
Let's all cry, "Peace, freedom and liberty!"[220]

The similarity of action is accompanied by a verbal closeness: Lady Macbeth, we recall, orders her husband to return to Duncan's chamber to '*smear* / The sleepy grooms with blood.'[221]

Shakespeare did not share Dante's view of the killing of Caesar as one of the very greatest of all human crimes—Dante, who in the *Inferno* had placed Brutus and Cassius in two of Satan's three mouths, the other being reserved for Judas Iscariot.[222] Nor, however, is *Julius Caesar* an unambiguously republican play. But nevertheless, in *Julius Caesar,* Shakespeare was undeniably interested in the possibility that republican violence may be curative, of both the state and of the individuals within it. Just before the assassination of Caesar takes place, at the end of the extraordinary, lengthy, and complicated act II, scene i, Brutus meets the patrician Ligarius, who is unwell. When Brutus says, 'Would you were not sick!', Ligarius replies, 'I am not sick, if Brutus have in hand / Any exploit worthy the name of honor.' Brutus replies that he is undertaking 'A piece of work that will make sick men whole', and the scene concludes with

218. John Milton, *The Complete Prose Works of John Milton,* vol. 7, *1659–1660,* rev. ed. (New Haven, CT: Yale University Press, 1980), pp. 362 (1st ed.) and p. 427 (2nd ed.).

219. *Julius Caesar* was probably written ca. 1599, *Macbeth* ca. 1606.

220. *Julius Caesar,* III.i.106–11: emphasis added.

221. *Macbeth,* II.ii.52–53: emphasis added.

222. Dante, *Inferno,* canto XXXIV, ll. 61–67: '"Quell' anima là su c' ha maggior pena" / disse 'l maestro, "è Giuda Scarïotto, / che 'l capo ha dentro e fuor le gambe mena. / Delli altri due c' hanno il capo di sotto, / quel che pende dal nero ceffo è Bruto /—vedi come si storce! e non fa motto!—; / e l' altro è Cassio che par si membruto."'

Ligarius exclaiming, 'with a heart new fired I follow you'.[223] Republicanism and tyrannicide, even if only in intention, here are literally invigorating.

At almost the same time that Shakespeare was writing *Julius Caesar* and entertaining at least the possibility that republican violence might be therapeutic, he was also writing *Hamlet*, in which he placed the language of divine-right monarchy in the mouth of a character of undoubted corruption. In act IV, scene ii, Laertes, at the head of a mob, bursts into Elsinore with a violence described by the messenger in language that echoes (notwithstanding the phrase 'Antiquity forgot', which perhaps admonishes us to *recollect* antiquity) a moment in *Julius Caesar*:

> Save yourself, my lord.
> The ocean, overpeering of his list,
> Eats not the flats with more impiteous haste
> Than young Laertes in a riotous head
> O'erbears your officers. The rabble call him lord
> And, as the world were now but to begin,
> Antiquity forgot, custom not known—
> The ratifiers and props of every word—
> They cry, 'Choose we: Laertes shall be king!'
> Caps, hands, and tongues applaud it to the clouds,
> 'Laertes shall be king, Laertes king!'[224]

We recall the plebeians' enthusiastic (but also politically confused) response to Brutus's speech after the assassination of Caesar:

> ALL. Live, Brutus, live, live.
> FIRST PLEBEIAN. Bring him with triumph home unto his house.
> SECOND PLEBEIAN. Give him a statue with his ancestors.
> THIRD PLEBEIAN. Let him be Caesar
> FOURTH PLEBEIAN. Caesar's better parts
> Shall be crowned in Brutus.
> FIRST PLEBEIAN. We'll bring him to his house with shouts and clamors.[225]

223. *Julius Caesar*, II.i.315, 316–17, 327, and 332.

224. *Hamlet*, IV.ii.98–108.

225. *Julius Caesar*, III.ii.44–48. Cf. ibid., I.ii.78–81 and 131–34. Note also ibid., I.ii.242–43: 'the rabblement hooted and clapped their chopped hands, and threw up their sweaty nightcaps'.

The parallel extends further than just these tumultuous would-be popular coronations. Act I, scene ii of *Julius Caesar* after this point moves into an extraordinarily naturalistic and detailed dramatisation of political seduction, as Cassius brings Brutus over to the side of the future assassins of Caesar.[226] The aftermath of the irruption of Laertes in *Hamlet* takes an exactly similar course (albeit in a different political direction), as Claudius—showing, it must be said, some personal bravery—disarms the enraged son of Polonius simply by deploying the language of divine-right monarchy:

> Let him go, Gertrude. Do not fear our person:
> There's such divinity doth hedge a king
> That treason can but peep to what it would,
> Acts little of its will.[227]

The pertinent complexity of the word 'hedge' here demands our attention. The word's primary meaning—and also the intention with which Claudius here uses it—is 'defend'.[228] But 'hedge' can also mean to constrain or restrict.[229] The word is plainly used in this sense of restriction in *Julius Caesar* (the play that, as we have seen, is a kind of sibling to *Hamlet*), where Cassius reproaches Brutus for his overbearing behaviour: 'You forget yourself / To hedge me in.'[230]

This ambivalence leads directly to the heart of what Shakespeare was doing when he placed the language of divine-right monarchy in the mouth of Claudius. For divine-right theory, like those other principles associated with early modern monarchy that sound strange to modern ears, such as the belief that the king can do no wrong or the idea that the king is *legibus solutus* or freed from the restraint of law, was never (notwithstanding modern misunderstandings of the doctrine)[231] a permission to engage in wrongdoing with impunity—what Alexander Pope, in a moment of exasperation with the Stuart dynasty to which he was nevertheless emotionally bound, would call 'The RIGHT DIVINE of Kings to govern wrong' or that Byron would still later attack as 'the

226. *Julius Caesar*, I.ii.32–299.

227. *Hamlet*, IV.ii.122–25.

228. *OED*, 'hedge,' *v.*, 1: 'to surround with a hedge or fence as a boundary, or for purposes of defence'.

229. *OED*, 'hedge,' *v.*, 5b: 'to hem in, so as to prevent escape or free movement; to confine, restrict.'

230. *Julius Caesar*, IV.iii.29–30.

231. E.g., Mary Beard in *The Guardian*, 28 September 2021, referring dismissively to Charles I and 'the "divine right of kings", or any of the other dreadful ideas for which he stood'.

blasphemy of laws / Making king's rights divine, by some Draconic clause.'[232] Rather, it imposed upon the natural man or woman a public character to the lofty level of which the incumbent was expected to raise their conduct.[233] Divine-right theory thus hedged the monarch in two senses. It both defended him and imposed upon him a standard of behaviour which limited his actions.[234] The power of divinity to restrict and guide is to the fore in the only other occurrence of the word in the play, when Hamlet reassures Horatio about the fallibility of 'our deep plots':

> Our indiscretion sometime serves us well
> When our deep plots do fall, and that should learn us
> There's a divinity that shapes our ends,
> Rough-hew them how we will.[235]

Claudius, whose corrupt understanding of kingship is bounded by nothing beyond his own desires, is alive to only one of the meanings of 'hedge' and so is subtly mocked or satirised by the other. Furthermore, as Claudius misemploys the language of divine-right monarchy, his self-interested and narrow use of the word 'hedge' in the pursuit of his entrapment of Laertes and conspiracy against Hamlet activates against him yet another meaning of 'hedge', namely, 'to go aside from the straight way; to shift, shuffle, dodge; to trim.'[236] Claudius's defectiveness as a monarch is exposed by the political language he wields with confidence but nevertheless in culpable ignorance of the fuller meanings it also possesses. His very words rebel against him.

The carefully-chosen and resonant language Shakespeare has placed in the mouth of Claudius is the prelude to Claudius's transformation of Laertes from a rebellious regicide to the murderous instrument—the 'organ'—of an incestuous usurper.[237] As was the case with Old Hamlet, Claudius's poison is administered through the 'knowing ear',[238] and over the next two scenes it corrupts a virtuous but naïve rebel into a mere assassin. So, given how it is used in *Hamlet*,

232. Alexander Pope, *The Dunciad*, IV.188; Lord Byron, *Childe Harold*, canto III, stanza lxiv.

233. See, e.g., Kantorowicz, *Two Bodies*, p. 95.

234. Cf. Sir Francis Bacon, 'Of Empire': 'All precepts concerning *Kings*, are in effect comprehended, in those two Remembrances: *Memento quod es homo*; And *Memento quod es Deus*, or *Vice Dei*. The one bridleth their Power, and the other their Will' (Bacon, *Essayes*, p. 63).

235. *Hamlet*, V.ii.8–11.

236. *OED*, 'hedge,' *v.*, 9.

237. *Hamlet*, IV.iv.68.

238. *Hamlet*, IV.iv.3.

there is little reason to believe that Shakespeare himself was any unswerving apologist for divine-right monarchy, in respect of either its language or its exponents. What Shakespeare certainly was alive to, however, was the dramatic vibrancy of that theory and its language, especially when deployed by an unlikely spokesman.

Let us return once more to the passage from *Macbeth* with which we began:

Who can be wise, amaz'd, temperate and furious,
Loyal and neutral, in a moment? No man:
Th'expedition of my violent love
Outrun the pauser, reason.—Here lay Duncan,
His silver skin lac'd with his golden blood;
And his gash'd stabs look'd like a breach in nature
For ruin's wasteful entrance: there, the murtherers,
Steep'd in the colours of their trade, their daggers
Unmannerly breech'd with gore. Who could refrain,
That had a heart to love, and in that heart
Courage, to make's love known?[239]

'Unmannerly' is also a word worth pausing over. It indicates a lack of courtesy—a lack, that is, of precisely the behaviour appropriate to royal courts. But for that very reason unmannerliness may be an appropriate reproof to, or chastisement of, royal exorbitance or folly. In *King Lear*, probably written two or three years before *Macbeth* but in any event quite close to it in date, Shakespeare would use the same word in just this sense when Kent, exasperated by Lear's unwisdom in the love-test, eventually sets aside courtly decorum and bursts out:

Be Kent unmannerly
When Lear is mad.[240]

That the ornate language of the court might conceal deceit and encourage a more general slavishness in those addicted to it was an idea that Shakespeare would have encountered, if nowhere else, then certainly in Montaigne's essays (one of which we know he would follow closely in *The Tempest*).[241] In 'Of the Arte of Conferring', Montaigne had suggested that

239. *Macbeth*, II.iii.105–14.
240. *King Lear*, I.i.342–43.
241. See above, p. 191 and n. 336.

> We should fortifie and harden our hearing, against the tendernesse of the ceremonious sound of wordes. I love a friendly society and a virile and constant familiarity: An amitie, which in the earnestnesse and vigor of it's commerce flattereth it selfe: as love in bitings and bloody scratchings. It is not sufficiently generous or vigorous, except it bee contentious and quarrelous.[242]

That unmannerliness might, in some circumstances, be the verbal sign of certain kinds of angular or difficult virtue was an idea to which Shakespeare's own day was not a stranger.

So, does the poetic language of *Macbeth* whisper to us that the killing of Duncan was, whatever else it may have been, also an act of harsh but natural and emancipatory necessity? A reminder of the possible virtue of king-killing is introduced into the play's imaginative world to startling effect when Macbeth, on his way to murder Duncan (and with what one might feel is astonishing inappropriateness), thinks of

> withered Murder,
> Alarumed by his sentinel the wolf,
> Whose howl's his watch, thus with his stealthy pace,
> With Tarquin's ravishing strides, towards his design
> Moves like a ghost.[243]

'Tarquin' is Sextus Tarquinius, the son of the last Roman king, Lucius Tarquinius Superbus, whose rape of Lucrece would provoke the transformation of early Rome from a monarchy to a republic.[244] That Macbeth should make such a long arm into early Roman history and compare his own imminent regicide

242. *Essayes Written in French by Michel Lord of Montaigne*, trans. John Florio (1613), p. 520. 'De l'Art de conferer': 'Il nous faut fortifier l'ouie et la durcir contre cette tandreur du son ceremonieux des parolles. J'ayme une societé et familiarité forte et virile, une amitié qui se flatte en l'aspreté et vigueur de son commerce, comme l'amour, és morsures et esgratigneures sanglantes' (Montaigne, *Œuvres*, p. 902). The French passages in *Henry V* (e.g., V.ii) demonstrate that Shakespeare had an adequate knowledge of French and so would not have been necessarily reliant on translations of contemporary French texts. The phrases 'comme l'amour, és morsures et esgratigneures sanglantes' perhaps show on Montaigne's part an awareness of Lucretius and of his Epicurean philosophy more generally: cf. Lucretius, *De Rerum Natura*, IV.1073–83.

243. *Macbeth*, II.i.52–56.

244. Livy, I.lvii–lx.

with the rape which led to the expulsion of kings from Rome unfolds its implications in a variety of directions.

In the first place, we should note how the repetition of 'with'—'with his stealthy pace, / With Tarquin's ravishing strides'—powerfully focuses our attention on the introduction of Tarquin by making the reference to him a parenthetic yet refining second thought, erasing and supplanting the more banal and anonymous adverbial phrase that preceded it, 'with *his* stealthy pace'. Yet the allusion is 'inappropriate', of course, because here the man about to kill a king is figured as the rapacious prince whose lust would lead to the very ejection of kings from Rome, even, indeed, to Roman self-definition as a place where kings were not and could never be tolerated and to Tarquin's own eventual merited killing in retribution for his crimes.[245] It introduces into Shakespeare's play, that is, a recollection of the moment in antiquity which had most memorably connected virtue and the resistance to monarchy. But the introduction of Tarquin is also quite appropriate, because this is a play in which 'nothing is but what is not' and where, on inspection, all things turn into their opposite.

Let us return to Macbeth's description of Duncan's corpse:

Who can be wise, amaz'd, temperate and furious,
Loyal and neutral, in a moment? No man:
Th'expedition of my violent love
Outrun the pauser, reason.—Here lay Duncan,
His silver skin lac'd with his golden blood;
And his gash'd stabs look'd like a breach in nature
For ruin's wasteful entrance: there, the murtherers,
Steep'd in the colours of their trade, their daggers
Unmannerly breech'd with gore. Who could refrain,
That had a heart to love, and in that heart
Courage, to make's love known?[246]

Macbeth begins by alleging the impossibility of holding opposites together: wisdom and amazement, temperance and fury, loyalty and neutrality. But he

245. Livy, I.lx. The complicated resonance of Macbeth's comparison of himself to Tarquin is noted also by David Norbrook (Norbrook, '*Macbeth*', p. 101). John-Mark Philo offers a deep exploration of the significance of this comparison in relation to the play's sources and their own engagement with Livyan material (Philo, *Livy*, pp. 115–41).

246. *Macbeth*, II.iii.105–14.

then follows those words with a diplopic image which nevertheless does just that: which holds together those violent antagonists, republicanism and sacral kingship, and which at different moments can be read as either monarchomach or as its reverse.

How should we make sense of this? We can begin by noting that both these political possibilities—the monarchical and the republican—are there in the play's sources and ancillary texts. They cluster around the historical issue of whether or not the Scottish monarchy was elective or hereditary (for, although both the earlier and the later Scottish kingdoms are monarchies in the sense of being 'rule by one', elective monarchy preserves something of the dynamism of a republican form in its eschewal of hereditary succession and its embracing of the principle of a more popular ratification of the monarch's title). The action of Shakespeare's play is poised on the very threshold between these political dispensations. The monarchy seems to have been elective when Duncan ascended the throne (hence the possibility of Macbeth's succeeding him, of, in Ross's words, the sovereignty 'falling' upon Macbeth).[247] But when, in act I, scene iv, Duncan makes his son Malcolm Prince of Cumberland and hence heir presumptive to the Scottish crown, it is clear that Scottish politics are moving in the direction of an hereditary title.[248] As Macbeth says to himself, 'The Prince of Cumberland! That is a step / On which I must fall down or else o'erleap.'[249]

So where do we find this political indecision in the precursor texts for Shakespeare's play? Surprisingly enough, we find it very close to James himself, that arch-apologist for charismatic kingship, in the person of the Scottish humanist George Buchanan (1508–82). Buchanan had been James's tutor from 1570 to 1578, and he wrote a Latin *History of Scotland*, the *Rerum Scoticarum Historia* (1582), some of which was incorporated into Raphael Holinshed's *Chronicle* (Shakespeare's primary source for *Macbeth*, as well as for his English history plays). In that history, Buchanan had argued that the Scottish monarchy was originally elective and had lapsed or declined into an hereditary form.[250] Three years earlier he had also published *De Jure Regni apud Scotos* (1579), a dialogue in which he had contended that the Scottish kings were

247. *Macbeth*, II.iv.30.

248. *Macbeth*, I.iv.35–42.

249. *Macbeth*, I.iv.48–49.

250. George Buchanan, *Rerum Scoticarum Historia* (Edinburgh, 1582), fols. 34 (original moderated hereditary succession) and 68 (later strict hereditary succession).

originally limited monarchs, accountable to the people, who might depose a monarch on grounds of misgovernment or tyranny.[251] The contrary view of the relation between elective and hereditary monarchies was expressed by James I himself, who in his *The Trew Law of Free Monarchies* had taken vigorous issue with the opinions of his old tutor. And in 1584, with the eighteen-year-old James VI on the throne, and notwithstanding the fact that both books had been dedicated to James, the Scottish parliament had called for all copies of Buchanan's history and the *De Jure Regni* to be handed in to the authorities, so that they could be purged of political heterodoxy.[252]

In *The Trew Law of Free Monarchies*, James (writing anonymously) had offered the following account of, firstly, the relation between elective and hereditary monarchies and, secondly, the relationship between monarch and subject:

> Since I haue so clearely prooued then out of the fundamentall lawes and practise of this country, what right & power a king hath ouer his land and subiects, it is easie to be vnderstood, what allegeance & obedience his lieges owe vnto him; I meane alwaies of such free Monarchies as our king is, and not of electiue kings, and much lesse of such sort of gouernors, as the dukes of *Venice* are, whose Aristocratick and limited gouernment, is nothing like to free Monarchies; although the malice of some writers hath not beene ashamed to mis-know any difference to be betwixt them. And if it be not lawfull to any particular Lordes tenants or vassals, vpon whatsoeuer pretext, to controll and displace their Master, and ouer-lord (as is clearer nor the Sunne by all Lawes of the world) how much lesse may the subiects and vassals of the great ouer-lord the KING controll or displace him? And since in all inferiour iudgements in the land, the people may not vpon any respects displace their Magistrates, although but subaltern: for the people of a borough, cannot displace their Prouost before the time of their election: nor in Ecclesiasticall policie the flocke can vpon any pretence displace the Pastor, nor iudge of him: yea euen the poore Schoolemaster cannot be displaced by his schollers: If these, I say (whereof some are but inferiour, subaltern, and temporall Magistrates, and none of them equall in any sort to the dignitie of a King) cannot be displaced for any occasion or pretext by them that are ruled by them: how much lesse is it lawfull vpon any pretext to controll or displace

251. George Buchanan, *De Jure Regni apud Scotos* (n.p., 1579), pp. 64–68.

252. *Oxford Dictionary of National Biography*, 'George Buchanan'.

> the great Prouost, and great Schoole-master of the whole land: except by inuerting the order of all Law and reason, the commanded may be made to command their commander, the iudged to iudge the Iudge, and they that are gouerned, to gouerne their time about their Lord and gouernour.[253]

How is this political equivocation in the play's sources and their discursive context taken up in *Macbeth*? It is addressed not directly, I think, but rather through the play's sustained opposition of two contrasting ideas of what it is to be a man.

Let us return for one final time to Macbeth's description of Duncan's corpse:

> Who can be wise, amaz'd, temperate and furious,
> Loyal and neutral, in a moment? No man:

Not 'no one' but 'no man'. In *King Lear*, the anonymous 'Captain of the Guard' who accepts Edmund's commission to kill Lear and Cordelia (without troubling to find out precisely what he will be asked to do) justifies his compliance by appealing to the notion of what it is to be a man:

> I cannot draw a cart, nor eat dried oats;
> If it be man's work, I'll do't.[254]

The Captain's rough and ready assumption of what it is to be a man runs counter to the content of the form of the play in which he exists, for it is of the nature of tragedy to uncover new potentialities in human nature, some dreadful, others uplifting. Would one have said that it was the action of a man to kill his father and sleep with his mother? But it would be ridiculous to deny to Oedipus the character of a man. So quite what 'man's work' might be is a matter on which the audience of tragedy typically grows increasingly uncertain. They are gradually estranged from the Captain's casual, unreflective certainty about what it is to be 'a man'.

Given how the tragic form is freighted with this ethical problem, it is surely important that in *Macbeth* a range of characters at different moments appeal to the concept of what it is to be a man. When Macbeth is inciting the murderers against Banquo and taunts them by asking, 'Do you find / Your patience

253. James I and VI, *Political Writings*, pp. 75–76.
254. *King Lear*, V.iii.38–39.

so predominant in your nature / That you can let this go?', and they reply, 'We are men, my liege', Macbeth retorts by mocking the baggy approximateness of a label as general as 'men':

> Ay, in the catalogue ye go for men,
> As hounds and greyhounds, mongrels, spaniels, curs,
> Shoughs, water-rugs, and demi-wolves are clept
> All by the name of dogs. The valued file
> Distinguishes the swift, the slow, the subtle,
> The housekeeper, the hunter—every one
> According to the gift which bounteous nature
> Hath in him closed, whereby he does receive
> Particular addition from the bill
> That writes them all alike; and so of men.[255]

When the ghost of Banquo appears at the banquet, Lady Macbeth berates Macbeth with the question, 'Are you a man?', to which he replies, 'Ay, and a bold one'.[256] When the ghost returns, the issue of manhood is once again to the fore:

> What man dare, I dare.
> Approach thou like the rugged Russian bear,
> The armed rhinoceros, or th'Hyrcan tiger!
> Take any shape but that, and my firm nerves
> Shall never tremble. Or be alive again,
> And dare me to the desert with thy sword.
> If trembling I inhabit then, protest me
> The baby of a girl. Hence, horrible shadow,
> Unreal mock'ry, hence! [*Exit Ghost of* BANQUO.]
>   Why, so. Being gone,
> I am a man again.[257]

And when Macduff receives news of the slaughtering of his wife and children, Malcolm urges him to 'Dispute it like a man'. Macduff's reply—'But I must also feel it as a man'—condenses into an almost stichomythic

255. *Macbeth*, III.i.86–88, 91, 92–101.
256. *Macbeth*, III.iv.59–60.
257. *Macbeth*, III.iv.101–10.

exchange the range of contending possibilities within the character of manhood at its fullest: a capacity to feel and an equal but opposite capacity to control.[258]

So the question of what it is to be a man, of what manly behaviour may embrace and must reject, recurs throughout *Macbeth*. However, the most striking instance of the theme occurs early on, when Lady Macbeth is inciting her husband to the murder of Duncan:

LADY MACBETH. Was the hope drunk,
Wherein you dressed yourself? Hath it slept since?
And wakes it now to look so green and pale
At what it did so freely? From this time
Such I account thy love. Art thou afeard
To be the same in thine own act and valour,
As thou art in desire? Wouldst thou have that
Which thou esteem'st the ornament of life,
And live a coward in thine own esteem,
Letting "I dare not" wait upon "I would,"
Like the poor cat i'th'adage?
MACBETH. Prithee, peace!
I dare do all that may become a man;
Who dares do more is none.
LADY MACBETH. What beast was't, then,
That made you break this enterprise to me?
When you durst do it, then you were a man;
And to be more than what you were, you would
Be so much more the man.[259]

Two images of manhood challenge each other here: one bounded, the other dynamic. In the former, to exceed is to cease to be a man: 'who dares do more is none'. In the latter, to exceed is to extend and further confirm your manhood: 'to be more than what you were, you would / Be so much more the man.' We can see here a translation into the realm of the human personality of Machiavelli's dilemma concerning republics. Is it better to be a static republic, like Venice, or an expansive republic, like Rome?[260]

258. *Macbeth*, IV.iii.219 and 221.
259. *Macbeth*, I.vii.35–51.
260. See Machiavelli, *Discourses*, bk. I, ch. 5.

These two images imply different conceptions of man's social existence and thus are capable of being translated into the very terms of politics that were, as we began by noting, detected by Gilbert Burnet to be in play during the Exclusion Crisis and which have, as we have seen, twisted round one another in the West and near East, in various forms, since classical antiquity. Is political society a static work of ceremonious art, dictated and handed down to men by a divinity who exacts a punctilious observation of these forms as a kind of worship? Or is it rather dynamic, existing and developing in time, and focused on the secular well-being of its citizens? Monarchy seems to have a clear affinity with the former conception of society. It seems naturally to possess stable patterns of reciprocating duties and obligations, to tend therefore towards immobility, and to extol that immobility in the language of aesthetics. It is, in Machiavellian terms, a government of stasis. Republics, however, seem naturally to be dynamic and appetitive. To use Machiavellian language, in their perfect form, they are governments of increase, or growth.[261] Their concept of virtue emphasises activity (whether military or political) rather than settledness. Republics are not timeless but exist in time (and therefore also are threatened by time: hence one of the recurrent problems in early modern politics, up to and including James Madison and the American founding, is that of how to make a republic durable).

Furthermore, republics tend to find the state of political health in terms not of harmony but rather of the clash of opposed interests. Here is Machiavelli on the tumults of the Roman republic:

> I cannot in silence pass over the tumults and commotions which hapned in *Rome* betwixt the death of the *Tarquins*, and the creation of those *Tribunes*. Nor can I forbear saying something against the opinion of many who will needs have *Rome* to have been a tumultuous Republick, so full of mutiny and confusion, that had not its good fortune and valour supplyed for its defects, it would have been inferior to any other Common-wealth whatsoever. . . . I say, those who object against the tumults betwixt the Nobles and the People, do in my opinion condemn those very things which were the first occasion of its freedom, regarding the noise and clamours which do usually follow such commotions, more than the good effects they

261. It is for this reason that Machiavelli consistently disparages or slights Venice, which although it is a republic, is a government of stasis, not growth. See Machiavelli, *Discourses*, bk. I, ch. 6.

> do commonly produce, not considering that in all Common-wealths there are two opposite humours, one of the People, the other of the Nobless; and that all Laws which are made in favour of liberty, proceed from the differences betwixt them.[262]

As Machiavelli suggests, 'confusion' ('confusione') is the word often used pejoratively by defenders of monarchy to denigrate the benign and healthful disturbances of a republic. Macduff greets the murder of Duncan by exclaiming, 'Confusion now hath made his masterpiece!'[263]

However, it is also the case that the dramatic world of *Macbeth* is organised around principles of supernatural sympathy which are deeply opposed to the more dynamic and quasi-republican details on which we have just been focusing. To clarify the point, let us contrast the world of *King Lear* with that of *Macbeth*. The storm on the heath in *King Lear* is simply a storm, despite what the maddened Lear would like to be the case. He interprets it, pathetically and misguidedly, as the reverberation in a sympathetically-organised nature of the outrage that he has suffered at the hands of two of his daughters.[264] In *Macbeth*, by contrast, the supernatural is a real and active presence in the play, as we learn not only from the witches (although their substantial power is only put beyond doubt in act IV, scene i) but also from the conversation between Ross and the Old Man, in act II, scene iv:

> ROSS. Ha, good father,
> Thou seest the heavens, as troubled with man's act,
> Threatens his bloody stage. By th'clock 'tis day,
> And yet dark night strangles the traveling lamp.
> Is't night's predominance or the day's shame,
> That darkness does the face of earth entomb
> When living light should kiss it?
> OLD MAN. 'Tis unnatural,
> Even like the deed that's done. On Tuesday last,
> A falcon, tow'ring in her pride of place,
> Was by a mousing owl hawk'd at and killed.

262. Machiavelli, *Discourses*, in Machiavelli, *Works*, p. 273.

263. *Macbeth*, II.iii.61.

264. Unlike in the source play, the *True Cronicle History*, where the equivalent storm is the expression of an affronted moral governance at work in the world (Bullough, *Sources*, 7:372–81).

ROSS. And Duncan's horses—a thing most strange and certain—
Beauteous and swift, the minions of their race,
Turned wild in nature, broke their stalls, flung out,
Contending 'gainst obedience, as they would
Make war with mankind.
OLD MAN. 'Tis said they ate each other.
ROSS. They did so, to th'amazement of mine eyes
That look'd upon't.[265]

A sympathetically-organised nature is at work here. These disturbances are, in Ross's words, heaven's response to human crime. But it is also the case that the examples of heaven's disapproval that Ross and the Old Man discuss, once looked at closely, become equivocal and shift their connotations.

The preternatural darkness that 'does the face of earth entomb' is taken by Ross as evidence that the supervising heavens are 'troubled by man's act'. Such preternatural darknesses traditionally marked the death of some great individual. The crucifixion is the most obvious instance of this.[266] But there is also Caesar's death, which was supposedly followed by a period of preternatural darkness and which had been preceded by portents.[267]

265. *Macbeth*, II.iv.4–19. For the worldly sophisticate Cardinal Pandulph, however, to see such events as prodigies is mere popular credulity and superstition (*King John*, III.iv.149–59). Similarly, the bluffly sceptical Hotspur refuses to see anything beyond the natural in the remarkable events that supposedly accompanied the birth of Glyndwr (*1 Henry IV*, III.i.12–60). In *2 Henry IV*, Gloucester and Clarence are perturbed by how unnatural events are construed by the common people but are not themselves credulous about them (*2 Henry IV*, IV.iii.121–28).

266. 'And it was now about the sixth hour, and a darkness came over the whole land until the ninth hour, the sun's light failing: and the veil of the temple was rent in the midst' (Luke 23:44–46); 'And when the sixth hour was come, there was darkness over the whole land until the ninth hour' (Mark 15:33). It is perhaps relevant that Bedford deplores the absence of a suitable darkness to signalise the death of Henry V (*1 Henry VI*, I.i.1–7); and Bedford goes on to remember the death of Caesar (ibid., I.i.55–56). This early play anticipates the conjunction in *Macbeth* of civil unrest and witchcraft (the latter introduced into the play in the person of Joan of Arc).

267. 'Among events of man's ordering, the most amazing was that which befell Cassius; for after his defeat at Philippi he slew himself with that very dagger which he had used against Caesar; and among events of divine ordering, there was the great comet, which showed itself in great splendour for seven nights after Caesar's murder, and then disappeared; also, the obscuration of the sun's rays. For during all that year its orb rose pale and without radiance, while the heat that came down from it was slight and ineffectual, so that the air in its circulation was dark and heavy owing to the feebleness of the warmth that penetrated it, and the fruits, imperfect and half ripe, withered away and shrivelled up on account of the coldness of the atmosphere'

In Shakespeare's *Julius Caesar*—the closing scenes of which seem to have been present in Shakespeare's imagination at the very end of *Macbeth*[268]—Casca superstitiously construes these prodigies as instances of a divine displeasure with men's actions:

> Either there is a civil strife in heaven,
> Or else the world, too saucy with the gods,
> Incenses them to send destruction.[269]

However, the question is, *whose* actions are offensive? The actions of Caesar, in aspiring to an extra-constitutional power, or the actions of the conspirators, in resolving to oppose him? Cassius is in no doubt:

> You are dull, Casca, and those sparks of life
> That should be in a Roman you do want,
> Or else you use not. You look pale, and gaze,
> And put on fear, and cast yourself in wonder
> To see the strange impatience of the heavens.
> But if you would consider the true cause
> Why all these fires, why all these gliding ghosts,
> Why birds and beasts from quality and kind,
> Why old men, fools, and children calculate,
> Why all these things change from their ordinance,
> Their natures, and pre-formèd faculties,
> To monstrous quality—why, you shall find
> That heaven hath infused them with these spirits
> To make them instruments of fear and warning
> Unto some monstrous state.
> Now could I, Casca, name to thee a man
> Most like this dreadful night,
> That thunders, lightens, opens graves, and roars
> As doth the lion in the Capitol;
> A man no mightier than thyself or me

(Plutarch, 'Caesar', LXIX.iii–iv). For Hobbes's dry account of such events, see *Leviathan*, ch. 37 (Hobbes, *Leviathan*, pp. 301 and 304–5).

268. 'Why should I play the Roman fool and die / On mine own sword?' (*Macbeth*, V.vii.31–32). Cf. *Julius Caesar*, V.iii (the suicide of Cassius) and V.v (the suicide of Brutus).

269. *Julius Caesar*, I.iii.11–13.

In personal action, yet prodigious grown,
And fearful, as these strange eruptions are.[270]

By which, of course, Cassius means Caesar. It is Caesar's actions, in aspiring to make himself king, that have stirred up these manifestations of disorder.[271]

There is no voice equivalent to that of Cassius in *Macbeth*, but one can see how such a voice might construe the prodigies which followed the murder of Duncan—Duncan, who is himself 'no mightier' than the generals who enact his vengeance on those who have rebelled against him and who has also been rendered 'prodigious' by the trappings of sacral monarchy. The upward transcendence of the 'mousing owl' might, in an altered scheme of value, be an image of aspiring virtue.[272] The horses 'contending 'gainst obedience' might be an image of principled resistance to a stultifying and oppressive authority. Shakespeare's imagination had already formed images of wild horses in the context of political unrest. In 2 *Henry IV*, the rebel Northumberland welcomes Lord Bardolph by emphasising the critical nature of the present moment:

The times are wild; contention, like a horse
Full of high feeding, madly hath broke loose
And bears down all before him.[273]

Later in the same scene, when news of the defeat and death of Northumberland's son at Shrewsbury has provoked him to take the field against the king, he reverts to some of the themes and language of these lines in expressing his determination to make a stand against regal authority:

270. *Julius Caesar*, I.iii.57–78.

271. Cf., as another parallel example, the Captain's relation to Salisbury of the unnatural events that 'forerun the death of kings' (*Richard II*, II.iv.8–15).

272. Cf. Richard II's invocation of the 'manage of unruly jades' and the misplaced 'night-owls shriek' in the context of monarchical overthrow (*Richard II*, III.iii.179 and 183). The exchange between Henry VI and Suffolk when out hunting also shows Shakespeare connecting the ascent of birds with political ambition (2 *Henry VI*, II.i.5–17); and Gloucester's response to his enemy Suffolk—'My lord, 'tis but a base ignoble mind / That mounts no higher than a bird can soar' (2 *Henry VI*, II.i.13–14) makes the connection between such mounting ambition and virtue. There is no evidence to suggest that Shakespeare had read Aeschylus's *Persae*, but it is nevertheless tantalising that Atossa, the mother of Xerxes and wife of Darius, has a dream, foreshadowing the Persian defeat by the Athenians, in which an eagle is killed by a falcon (Aeschylus, *Persae*, ll. 205–9).

273. 2 *Henry IV*, I.i.9–11.

Let heaven kiss earth! Now let not Nature's hand
Keep the wild flood confined! Let order die,
And let this world no longer be a stage
To feed contention in a ling'ring act; . . .[274]

Wildness, feeding, and contention would come together again a few years later in the verse of *Macbeth*, and there too they would vividly articulate—perhaps, even extenuate or defend—armed resistance to the Crown.

Moreover, the fact that Duncan's horses are referred to as 'the minions of their race' may be particularly significant. For 'minion' is a loan word and was, at this time, a comparative neologism. It was imported into English only in the early sixteenth century from the French 'mignon', a word of condescending and miniaturising affection meaning 'cute', 'sweet', or 'pretty'.[275] In the later sixteenth century the word had become associated particularly with the decadent court of the French king Henri III,[276] where it was used to refer to the group of transvestite musketeers with whom the young king amused himself and upon whom he was said to lavish expensive and sumptuous gifts. Hence, the word acquired, in the plentiful pamphlet literature published in London following events in the French Wars of Religion, connotations of a culpable monarchical voluptuousness in the realms of both material culture and sexual exorbitance.[277] It therefore acquired further connotations of court favouritism which might be strongly negative, implying that one was a pure creature of the prince. Furthermore, it became almost an axiom that only weak or effeminate princes had minions.[278] It might therefore be good for minions eventually to reject the

274. 2 *Henry IV*, I.i.153–56.

275. *OED*, 'minion', *n.* 1 and *adj.*, A, I, 1a and b.

276. Henri III (1551–89), king of France from 1574 until his assassination.

277. Christopher Marlowe, *The Massacre at Paris* (1593), sc. 14, ll. 16 and 46, sc. 17, ll. 11, 13, and 21, and sc. 21, l. 49; Geneviève Petau de Maulette, *Vertues Teares* (1597), p. 34^{v}. In the context of English history, the term was commonly applied to the favourites of Edward II: see, e.g., Samuel Daniel, *Mortimeriados* (1596), sig. E4^{v} and H2^{v}; and also Michael Drayton, *The Tragicall Legend* (1596) and *Englands Heroicall Epistles* (1597). See Louis Crompton, *Homosexuality and Civilization* (Cambridge, MA: Belknap Press of Harvard University Press, 2003), pp. 328–31. Cf. Figgis, *Divine Right*, p. 131: 'There can be no doubt that the earlier struggles of Huguenots, Leaguers, and *Politiques* all contributed to the developement [*sic*] of English political thought in the seventeenth century, whether in the direction of Divine Right or of the original compact.'

278. See, e.g., Samuel Daniel, *The Ciuile Wars* (1609): 'Minions, too great, argue a king too weake' (p. 11); 'The mighty Minions of our feeblest Kings' (p. 137). In 1 *Henry IV*, the king refers

humiliating confinements of a dependent, artificial, condition of vassalage and thereby to recover some of their natural wildness. Finally, the word 'minion' occurs twice in *Macbeth*. In the captain's narrative of the opening battle, Macbeth is styled 'valor's minion'.[279] Macbeth, too, like Duncan's horses, might reasonably wish to escape from so dependent and unmanly a condition.

If we compare the passage in Holinshed which supplied Shakespeare with the material for this conversation between Ross and the Old Man, we can see how Shakespeare blurred and smudged what he had received in a form that lacked any ambiguity:

> Monstrous sights also that were seene within the Scottish kingdome that yeere were these: horsses in Louthian, being of singular beautie and swiftnesse, did eate their owne flesh, and would in no wise taste anie other meate. In Angus there was a gentelwoman brought foorth a child without eies, nose, hand, or foot. There was a sparhawke also strangled by an owle. Neither was it anie lesse woonder that the sunne, as before is said, was continuallie couered with clouds for six moneths space. But all men vnderstood that the abhominable murther of king Duffe was the cause heereof.[280]

In Holinshed's prose, there is no doubt as to the human enormity which has created these reverberating enormities in the natural order: 'all men vnderstood that the abhominable murther of king Duffe was the cause heereof.' The language of Shakespeare's drama, however, holds in play (although it refuses explicitly to promote and defend) other possibilities.

So the language of the conversation between Ross and the Old Man carries with it undertows of meaning subversive of its primary sense. These undertows remind us that virtuous ambition can be pejoratively re-described as vicious presumption and that an overweening or despotic authority can confine and immobilise the energy of its beautiful but aestheticised creatures in 'stalls'. There these beautiful minions are tricked out with gorgeous trappings, from which their natural energy may eventually burst out with terrible but justifiable violence. These undertows remind us of all that the play's surface and overt allegiances would deny or banish, and they stir the suggestion of a

---

to Hotspur as 'sweet Fortune's minion', and Falstaff desires Hal to refer to robbers as 'minions of the moon' (*1 Henry IV*, I.i.82 and I.ii.23).

279. *Macbeth*, I.ii.19.

280. Bullough, *Sources*, 7:484.

framework of value in which Macbeth's actions would emerge as something more and other than criminal butchery.

However, in the foregoing analysis I am emphatically not trying to 'unmask' *Macbeth* as a crypto-republican play (in the manner in which, so it seems to me, Alan Sinfield and David Norbrook have tried to unmask it).[281] Rather, I wish to position *Macbeth* at the centre of Shakespeare's thoughtful and prolonged exploration of how competing considerations of religious and secular value, and of ecclesiastical and civil authority, wrestle with one another in the realm of social life. It was, as we shall see, an exploration which persisted across the whole length of Shakespeare's career as a dramatist and in which (as we should by now expect) he was concerned less to articulate a doctrine than to revolve an issue.

———

Shakespeare's earliest history plays are preoccupied by how the conjunction of religious and secular power can become calamitously defective. When in 2 *Henry VI* Warwick sees the body of the Duke of Gloucester, he gives vehement expression to his belief that Gloucester was murdered:

> As surely as my soul intends to live
> With that dread King that took our state upon him
> To free us from his Father's wrathful curse,
> I do believe that violent hands were laid
> Upon the life of this thrice-famèd duke.[282]

The theology of Warwick's periphrasis for Christ is not impeccable: the imposition of death was not a 'wrathful curse' by God but rather a matter of strict justice for undoubted transgressions. But more interesting than that is the commerce between the languages of politics and divinity that it exemplifies when it refers to Christ as 'that dread King'.[283] These early history plays are acted out against the backdrop of divine-right theory, which casts a critical

281. Alan Sinfield, '*Macbeth*: History, Ideology and Intellectuals', *Critical Quarterly* 28 (1985): 63–77; David Norbrook, '*Macbeth* and the Politics of Historiography', in *Politics of Discourse: The Literature and History of Seventeenth-Century England*, ed. Kevin Sharpe and Steven N. Zwicker (Berkeley: University of California Press, 1987), pp. 78–116.

282. 2 *Henry VI*, III.ii.153–57.

283. Cf. 'by His majesty' (2 *Henry VI*, III.ii.287) for a similar conflation of divinity and politics.

light over the action and brings the malformation of English politics at this time into relief. A preoccupation of these plays is the proper relation between throne and altar.

In 2 and 3 *Henry VI*, the religious sensibility of the king is displayed as a weakness, and its harmful consequences are unfolded onstage. Henry's speech of welcome to his wife-to-be, Margaret of Anjou, strikes a discordant note of piety that complicates with religious gratitude what should be a purely erotic and dynastic moment:

> Welcome, Queen Margaret.
> I can express no kinder sign of love
> Than this kind kiss. O Lord that lends me life,
> Lend me a heart replete with thankfulness,
> For thou hast given me in this beauteous face
> A world of earthly blessings to my soul,
> If sympathy of love unite our thoughts.[284]

The declension of 'kinder' to merely 'kind' suggests the tepidness of the emotional temperature here.

This keynote of inappropriate religious intrusion is amplified and developed in the scenes that follow. Henry's prompt and blithely unreflective—even uninterested—endorsement of the terms of the disastrous marriage contract that Suffolk has negotiated with Margaret's father ('They please us well') reveals his inattention to, or lack of concern with, the hard practicalities of rule that are necessary if he is to discharge his primary duty as king of securing the commonweal.[285] Henry's religious sensibility serves to disengage him from his monarchical responsibilities: 'Was never subject longed to be a king / As I do long and wish to be a subject.'[286] The monarch properly possesses a divine authority, but he is not therefore a priest. Indeed, the purpose of divine-right theory (as a bulwark for secular authority against the encroachments of priests, principally the pope) explicitly requires that the monarch who rules by divine right will have no 'priestly' character.

Henry's piety is not simply a matter of inward disposition. The practical disablement in the discharge of monarchical function that flows from Henry's religiosity is evident to all. As York will shortly comment, Henry's 'church-like

284. 2 *Henry VI*, i.i.17–23.
285. 2 *Henry VI*, I.i.60. Cf. ibid., I.iii.101: 'all's one to me'.
286. 2 *Henry VI*, IV.ix.5–6.

humors fits not for a crown.'[287] Margaret soon is openly contemptuous of her husband's character:

But all his mind is bent to holiness
To number Ave-Maries on his beads.
His champions are the prophets and apostles,
His weapons holy saws of sacred writ,
His study is his tilt-yard, and his loves
Are brazen images of canonizèd saints.
I would the college of the cardinals
Would choose him Pope and carry him to Rome
And set the triple crown upon his head:
That were a state fit for his holiness.[288]

It is a reproachful analysis of Henry's inadequacy as a ruler that will be echoed at the end of the play by York:

That head of thine doth not become a crown;
Thy hand is made to grasp a palmer's staff,
And not to grace an awful princely scepter.[289]

For Shakespeare's first audiences, an aggravating feature of Henry's piety would have been its strongly Catholic character.[290] Henry gullibly accepts the false miracle of the curing of Simpcox's blindness, which is presented in terms of a range of Catholic beliefs and practices that had been subject to Protestant critique in England since the 1530s: pilgrimage, the miraculous efficacy of shrines, offerings to obtain favour, intercession by saints. Henry accepts the miracle without testing it and turns it into a pretext for religious commemoration:

Poor soul, God's goodness hath been great to thee.
Let never day nor night unhallowed pass,
But still remember what the Lord hath done.[291]

287. 2 *Henry VI*, I.i.244.

288. 2 *Henry VI*, I.iii.54–63.

289. 2 *Henry VI*, V.i.96–98.

290. Henry's Catholicism, of course, is historically accurate; but that does not mean that it was not also a characteristic chosen by Shakespeare for dramatic effect. It was common on the early modern English stage for characters to undergo confessional transposition and for proto-Protestants to be created in the most unlikely places and forms. For discussion, see my *Divinity and State* (Oxford: Oxford University Press, 2012).

291. 2 *Henry VI*, II.i.82–84. This will be echoed in Henry's naïve acceptance of the outcome of the trial by combat: 'God in justice hath revealed to us / The truth and innocence of this poor

Gloucester, however, cross-examines Simpcox and uncovers the imposture. Henry's vulnerability to religious fraud, crystallised in this episode drawn from John Foxe's *Actes and Monuments*, reflects his misconception of the relation between religion and politics.

Henry's misplaced piety has both inward and outward consequences. In respect of Henry himself, it hamstrings his ability to act and ministers to a disastrous decoupling of insight from agency. Henry dwindles almost to a choric function in the plays of which he is the eponym: a diminution which reaches the point of literal clarity in *3 Henry VI*, act II, scene v. 'My thoughts do hourly prophesy', Henry says; but these prophecies never strengthen into decisive intervention.[292] Henry sees Gloucester's innocence but is unable to protect him.[293] He recognises the malignancy of Suffolk but again is unable to neutralise the threat Suffolk presents both to himself and to the realm.[294] He understands that Gloucester was murdered but is impotent to punish the crime (administration of justice being, however, one of the key regal duties and powers):

> O thou that judgest all things, stay my thoughts—
> My thoughts that labor to persuade my soul
> Some violent hands were laid on Humphrey's life.
> If my suspect be false, forgive me, God,
> For judgment only doth belong to thee.
> Fain would I go to chafe his paly lips
> With twenty thousand kisses and to drain
> Upon his face an ocean of salt tears,
> To tell my love unto his dumb deaf trunk,
> And with my fingers feel his hand, unfeeling.
> But all in vain are these mean obsequies,
> And to survey his dead and earthy image,
> What were it but to make my sorrow greater?[295]

This soliloquy is organised around a stretched internal rhyme which embodies longing without power: 'Fain' and 'all in vain'. And it ends on what is surely a note of repellent self-pity: 'And to survey his dead and earthy image, / What

---

fellow' (ibid., II.iii.95–96).

292. 2 *Henry VI*, III.ii.285.

293. 2 *Henry VI*, III.i.66–73.

294. 2 *Henry VI*, III.ii.39–55.

295. 2 *Henry VI*, III.ii.136–48.

were it but to make my sorrow greater?'[296] In one of the most striking verbal moments of the play, Henry uses the words of Christ himself: 'They know not what they do.'[297] But this biblical phrase, once it is situated in its new context, underlines the problem that Henry's misguided piety has created, namely, the separation of knowing and doing. Action by the populace is blind, and the insight of the monarch is paralysed. 'Come, wife, let's in, and learn to govern better; / For yet may England curse my wretched reign'. Awareness of defect without the power of remedy is the signature of Henry's reign.[298]

Henry's 'bookish rule' damages the commonweal not just through its enfeeblement of executive power but also because the vacancy of command it creates entices others to try to occupy that space.[299] When the relation between divinity and secular power is perverted or takes a wrong form, it creates the opportunity for disruptive ambition to take root in both prelates and peers. The repeated signature of the play is displacement (Henry's chosen pursuits as opposed to real kingly pursuits) and inversion (the ascendancy of ambitious women over their husbands). It is remarkable that, in *Richard III*, one of the stratagems that Richard employs to seize the crown is an imitation of Henry's public piety.[300] Henry's confusion of the characters of priest and king, albeit in his own case sincere, has nevertheless prepared the way for its exploitation by a tyrant.

In the first place, the wrongful ambition of prelates is encouraged. Cardinal Beaufort's complaisance[301] in the disastrous marriage contract between Henry and Margaret suggests a harmful alliance between a weak monarch and an ambitious cleric, while the antipathy between the Cardinal and Gloucester dramatises the self-interestedness of the church in propping up a weak king so that their own power should thereby be amplified. There follows a brilliantly-compressed version of a piece of stage business already familiar on the early

296. For other moments of self-pity on Henry's part, see, e.g., *3 Henry VI*, II.v.111–12 and 124.

297. *2 Henry VI*, IV.v.37. Cf. Luke 23:34.

298. *2 Henry VI*, IV.ix.47–48.

299. *2 Henry VI*, I.i.256.

300. There are frequent instances of Richard's feigning of piety, but for Richard's own statement of the strategy, see *Richard III*, I.iii.330–34. Richard's private religious position is at the very least Epicurean, possibly atheist: 'Conscience is but a word that cowards use, / Devised at first to keep the strong in awe' (*Richard III*, V.iii.307–8).

301. *2 Henry VI*, I.i.101.

modern English stage, namely, the wily prelate inducing ambitious aristocrats to do his work for him.[302]

The emboldening of prelates is followed by the enticement of powerful nobles towards rebellion. York's long, expository soliloquy at the end of act I, scene i, shows how Henry's weakness has put temptation in his way. Salisbury has just praised York for his public-spiritedness in Ireland and France, but Henry's weakness in surrendering English territory abroad motivates him to act in his own, narrower, self-interest:

> Anjou and Maine both given unto the French?
> Cold news for me: for I had hope of France
> Even as I have of fertile England's soil.
> A day will come when York shall claim his own,
> And therefore I will take the Nevilles' parts
> And make a show of love to proud Duke Humphrey,
> And when I spy advantage, claim the crown,
> For that's the golden mark I seek to hit.[303]

York's claim is not trivial, and its primogenitural basis is acknowledged in the play.[304] Nor is his analysis of the English situation wide of the mark. But what his soliloquy also reveals is how weakness on the throne perverts towards corruption and rebellion the qualities in peers that under a strong king might have taken a benign form. The later popular rebellion by Jack Cade, which York provokes and guides behind the scenes, is both the instrument of York's ambition and an episode which compromises his stature. Cade's explication of his own title to the crown stands in a relationship of uneasy parallelism with the earlier expositions we have heard of York's own claim.[305] The correspondences between the aristocratic scenes and those involving the commons do not remain securely in the relationship of authentic and parodic. Increasingly, those correspondences invite interpretation as signs of a loss of caste on the part of the aristocratic sponsors of insurrection.

The First Tetralogy's dramatisation of a misalignment between politics and religion is articulated within the apocalyptic world of vulgar anti-Catholicism.

302. 2 *Henry VI*, I.i.162–68. Cf., for an earlier and paradigmatic example, John Bale, *Kynge Johan*.

303. York's public-spiritedness: 2 *Henry VI*, I.i.191–201; ibid., I.i.233–40.

304. York's claim to the throne by birth: 2 *Henry VI*, I.i.241, I.iii.25–31, I.iii.180–84, II.ii.1–63.

305. Cade's title to the crown: 2 *Henry VI*, IV.ii.124–35.

The dying Cardinal Beaufort, tormented by guilt for the murder of Gloucester and persuaded of his own damnation, introduces a note of final judgement.[306] If *1 Henry VI* was, as some have argued, composed after 2 and *3 Henry VI*, then the explicitly supernatural framework of that play, in which Joan of Arc has commerce with demons, intensifies the atmosphere of apocalypse.[307] At one level these plays present not merely a struggle between England and France but the perennial (at least until the Second Coming) contest between true and false churches.

It is therefore very remarkable that, less than four years after Shakespeare had composed *Richard III*, he wrote two further English history plays—*Richard II* and *King John*—that, while maintaining the strong focus on the relationship between politics and religion established in the earlier history plays, were nevertheless set in a completely different political and theological universe.[308]

Richard II was the play that Ernst Kantorowicz used to introduce his classic study of medieval political theology, *The King's Two Bodies*.[309] In a *bravura* chapter that set the terms of much later criticism, Kantorowicz depicted Richard as the embodiment of a medieval legal fiction that was about to fall victim to Machiavellian *realpolitik*, as embodied in the person of Richard's kinsman Bolingbroke. *Richard II* thus became a dramatisation of (to draw on the title of another influential work of twentieth-century scholarship) the waning of the Middle Ages, and Richard's deposition was softened by nostalgia.[310] It is a reading of the play as misleading as it has been influential.

Commentary on *Richard II* has been confused by the lack of understanding amongst literary critics of the practical political function of the theory of divine-right kingship, that is to say, of the concrete and specific political objective the theory was forged to secure. Because modern critics have in general failed to understand that this theory was created to counter a rival, theocratic theory (the divine right of the pope), they have, naturally but wrongly, assumed that the divine right of kings was somehow in tension with practical secular authority—that it was, in some mysterious but fundamental way,

306. *2 Henry VI*, III.iii.

307. *1 Henry VI*, V.iii.1–29.

308. *Richard III*, composed probably in 1592; *Richard II*, composed probably in 1595 (first recorded performance in that year); *King John*, composed probably in 1596.

309. Kantorowicz, *Two Bodies*, pp. 24–41.

310. Johan Huizinga, *Herfsttij der Middeleeuwen* (Leiden, 1919).

unworldly. But nothing could be further from the truth. The divine right of kings was the most audacious statement of the independent authority of the civil magistrate that the Middle Ages and the early modern period could produce, and hence, it was the opposite of theocratic. It was the most worldly, the most secular, of political doctrines, just as it was expressed in language that was far more juristic than theological. We tend to let our attention dwell on the word 'divine', whereas in fact it should fall on the words 'right' and 'kings'.

Within the play, Richard, like many critics, is dazzled by the language of the theory and distracted from, or perhaps simply ignorant of, its practical purpose. *Richard II* is often described as staging a collision between two rival political dispensations. But in fact it is better conceived of as a collision within a single political framework: a collision, that is, between an incumbent (Richard) who misunderstands the theory of which he is the beneficiary, who is beguiled by its surface qualities of language and symbol, but who is nevertheless the legitimate monarch; and a rival (Bolingbroke) who does understand that theory but who, though very close to the throne, is not the rightful king.[311] *Richard II* is a play about a separation between legitimacy and understanding which both echoes and transposes the separation between action and insight in the *Henry VI* plays.

Richard's failure of understanding can be expressed in general terms as a concern with entitlements rather than obligations, which leads him to confuse the figural with the literal, and the ancillary with the essential. Divine-right theory, in its full development, came to rest on four cardinal pillars: first and most fundamentally, the assertion that monarchy was a divinely-ordained institution; second, that the Crown was transmitted by hereditary right; third, that kings are accountable to God alone; and fourth, that in consequence, non-resistance and passive obedience are enjoined by God.[312] The second, third, and fourth of these pillars were both logically and historically later developments of the doctrine. They are explicit formulations of positions or sub-doctrines that might be thought to be latent or implicit within the primary assertion that monarchy was divinely-ordained.[313] A striking feature of Richard's invocations of divine-right theory is that he lays emphasis heavily upon these later, derivative or secondary elements

311. For Bolingbroke's proximity to the throne, see *Richard II*, III.iii.107–8.

312. Figgis, *Divine Right*, pp. 5–6.

313. 'Passive Obedience and Indefeasible Hereditary Right were no new conceptions; they had long been in the air, and the necessity of combating Papal claims had brought about a doctrine of which they were merely the logical expansion' (Figgis, *Divine Right*, p. 144).

and ignores or fails to grasp the implications of the primary element—the divine ordination of monarchy.[314] That tendency is clear in Richard's rhetorically-resonant speech of defiance on learning of Bolingbroke's return to England:

So when this thief, this traitor Bolingbroke,
Who all this while hath reveled in the night,
Shall see us rising in our throne, the East,
His treasons will sit blushing in his face
Not able to endure the sight of day,
But, self-affrighted, tremble at his sin.
Not all the water in the rough rude sea
Can wash the balm from an anointed king.
The breath of worldly men cannot depose
The deputy elected by the Lord.
For every man that Bolingbroke hath pressed
To lift shrewd steel against our golden crown,
Heaven for His Richard hath in heavenly pay
A glorious angel. Then, if angels fight,
Weak men must fall, for heaven still guards the right.[315]

It is striking that in this speech Richard lays such emphasis on the significance of the anointing with chrism that occurs during the rite of coronation. This seems to have been a matter which the historical Richard II also regarded as of the first importance.[316] Nevertheless, when Shakespeare composed *Richard II*, it had been downgraded in the English church to a mere ceremony, as Thomas Cranmer had instructed Edward VI in 1547. The king is 'God's Anointed, not in respect of the oil which the bishop useth, but in consideration of their power which is ordained. . . . The oil, if added, is but a ceremony: if it be wanting, that king is yet a perfect monarch notwithstanding, and God's Anointed as well as if he was inoiled.'[317] That sacramental and theological

314. Richard is not alone in this; the same elevation of the secondary to the status of the primary is evident in Gaunt's rigid adherence to passive obedience: 'I may never lift / An angry arm against his minister' (*Richard II*, I.ii.40–41).

315. *Richard II*, III.ii.43–57.

316. 'We know, that until the day of his death he [Richard II] regarded himself as king by virtue of unction, despite his deposition, that he regarded this ceremony as conferring a sacramental grace, and that he directed in his will, that he should receive a royal funeral' (Figgis, *Divine Right*, p. 79).

317. Kantorowicz, *Two Bodies*, p. 318.

position would be given legal corroboration in 1609 when Edward Coke insisted that coronation was only 'a royal ornament and solemnization of the royal descent, but no part of the title.'[318] Richard's belief that the sacrament of royal unction necessarily brings with it divine protection and the promise of divine intervention is a gross politico-theological error.

That error is all the more striking because an exchange a few lines earlier between the bishop of Carlisle and Aumerle was a compressed tutorial (had Richard the ears to hear it) on the true understanding of divine-right theory. Carlisle and Aumerle offer the king instruction in what that theory promised and in what it required:

> CARLISLE. Fear not, my lord. That power that made you king
> Hath power to keep you king in spite of all.
> AUMERLE. He means, my lord, that we are too remiss,
> Whilst Bolingbroke, through our security,
> Grows strong and great in substance and in friends.[319]

Aumerle 'translates' Carlisle's orthodox divine-right language into its true meaning, namely, that political practicalities are not to be overlooked or neglected by those who claim to rule by divine right. Richard ignores Aumerle and mishears Carlisle's words as an assurance that the power that made him king *will* keep him king. That Carlisle's meaning was in fact what Aumerle said it was (namely, encouragement to take practical steps) is confirmed later in the scene, when Richard has surrendered to despondency on hearing of the executions of Bushy, Greene, and the Earl of Wiltshire. Carlisle advises him once more:

> My lord, wise men ne'er wail their present woes,
> But presently prevent the ways to wail.
> To fear the foe, since fear oppresseth strength,
> Gives in your weakness strength unto your foe.
> Fear and be slain—no worse can come to fight;
> And fight and die is death destroying death,
> Where fearing dying pays death servile breath.[320]

318. Kantorowicz, *Two Bodies*, p. 317.
319. *Richard II*, III.ii.27–31.
320. *Richard II*, III.ii.173–79.

Carlisle, who in the next act will emerge as the spokesman for divine right at its most elevated pitch,[321] nevertheless advocates practical remedies. Nor should this surprise us. Divine right does not remove the need for the king to be wise and prudent, and to believe that it does (as Richard seems to) is to indulge in magical thinking. Instead, the function of divine-right theory is precisely to enlarge the arena in which regal wisdom and prudence can operate, by pushing back against the pretensions of the pope. In the gardening scene the Gardener offers a catalogue, transposed into the language of horticulture, of the practical skills that even a divinely-appointed king cannot neglect. If such a king does neglect those skills, that reveals a scandalous disregard for the divine power that has placed him on the throne—hence those moments when one feels that Richard is edging towards blasphemy in his religious claims, language, and figurings. The veiled satiric point of this scene is that even a gardener understands divine-right theory better than does Richard.[322]

A common misunderstanding in criticism of *Richard II* is that there is a polar clash between the language of divine right deployed by Richard and the language of law, customary right, and customary taxation deployed by the disgruntled peers. But there is no conflict between these two things (that is, between divine-right theory and *realpolitik*), since the customary forms of secular authority are precisely what the doctrine of divine right was forged to defend against sacerdotal overreach. Divine-right theory was thus in some sense a *realpolitik* response on the part of the civil power to papal encroachment. But Richard simply misunderstands the theory on which he relies. He focuses on its verbal and symbolic embodiment, to the detriment of its functional tendency. He ignores the political work the theory was intended to do in the world. As we saw in the first tetralogy principally through the character of Henry VI, the cardinal political error for a prince is to misunderstand the relation between civil and ecclesiastical authority. Richard's later exchange of kingship for hermit-like piety and quasi-blasphemous self-comparisons with Christ is nothing more than an equal and opposite misunderstanding of that relationship.[323] Divine-right theory, even at its most ambitious, never asserted the identity of

321. *Richard II*, IV.i.107–43.

322. *Richard II*, III.iv.

323. *Richard II*, III.iii.143–59. Self-comparisons with Christ, e.g. ibid., IV.i.164, IV.i.232, and V.ii.6 and 30ff. These self-comparisons are another point of similarity with Henry VI (see above,

monarch and Christ. Rather, the monarch was a *persona mixta*. It is significant that James I, surely the monarch most well-informed about the doctrine, had misgivings about its thaumaturgical aspects and was reluctant to touch for scrofula. Even he did not really believe that, simply in virtue of being crowned, he had been transformed into a miracle-worker.

The mischievous tendency of Richard's misunderstandings of divine-right theory, and the encouragement those misunderstandings give to disruptive elements within the state, is made clear in the short coda to the Deposition scene.[324] Bolingbroke has left the stage, leaving behind the abbot of Westminster, the bishop of Carlisle, and the disaffected peer Aumerle. It is a menacing combination of characters that would have been familiar to the play's first audiences as boding ill to the state.[325] Their misgivings would have been immediately confirmed:

ABBOT. A woeful pageant have we here beheld.
CARLISLE. The woe's to come: he children yet unborn
Shall feel this day as sharp to them as thorn.
AUMERLE. You holy clergymen, is there no plot
To rid the realm of this pernicious blot?
ABBOT. Before I freely speak my mind herein
You shall not only take the sacrament
To bury mine intents, but also to effect
Whatever I shall happen to devise.
I see your brows are full of discontent,
Your hearts of sorrow, and your eyes of tears.
Come home with me to supper. I'll lay
A plot shall show us all a merry day.[326]

Religious oaths of alarming and unspecified amplitude ('whatever I shall happen to devise') misapplied to the furtherance of crime in an act of trespass on the

p. 276). Towards the end of the play Richard duplicates Henry's combination of insight without power in his accurate reading of Northumberland's future (ibid., V.i.55–68).

324. *Richard II*, IV.i.

325. Paradigmatically, in John Bale, *Kynge Johan*, ll. 557–626. Later examples suggest the durable appeal of this particular scenic form and its power to strike a note of political danger: see, e.g., *Sir John Oldcastle*, part I, scene ii.

326. *Richard II*, IV.i.314–26 (evident error of lineation in ll. 325–26 amended).

jurisdiction of the civil magistrate: This is precisely what Elizabethan audiences had been instructed by recent history to fear in Roman Catholicism (they would certainly recall that Henri III of France had been assassinated in 1589 by the Dominican friar Jacques Clément). York later makes clear that what had been intended was a textbook act of Roman Catholic regicide and again draws attention to the aggravating feature of the misuse of the sacrament it had involved:

> A dozen of them here have ta'en the sacrament
> And interchangeably set down their hands
> To kill the King at Oxford.[327]

This alarming conjunction of religion and regicide is the natural outcome of Richard's political misunderstandings.

If Shakespeare turned almost immediately from writing *Richard II* to writing *King John*, what might that transition tell us?[328] If *Richard II* is a dramatisation of divine-right theory misunderstood and of the calamities that such a misunderstanding draws in its wake, then *King John* is a play in which Shakespeare moved back in time to inspect the early medieval origins of the theory. In so doing, Shakespeare also showed that he possessed a very accurate understanding of how and why divine-right theory had been framed and of the practical political ends it had been intended to serve.

It is a curious fact that there are more early modern English history plays set in the comparatively brief reign of King John (1199–1216) than in the reign of any other English monarch.[329] Why should that be? Since the 1530s, and because of the conflicts that had arisen between King John and the pope over John's attempts in 1204 to tax the clergy, this reign had become a battle-ground of Reformation politics.[330] The king castigated by monkish chroniclers for his anti-papal policies (as well as for his ruinous foreign policy and oppressive domestic regime) was re-discovered by early Reformation historians and propagandists as a proto-Protestant martyr to clerical ambition. The fact that, in

327. *Richard II*, V.ii.97–99.

328. For the probable dates of these two plays, see above, p. 278, n. 308.

329. No fewer than six plays were set in John's reign: *Kynge Johan*, 1530–36; *1* and *2 Troublesome Raigne*, 1588–89; *King John*, 1592–93; *1* and *2 Robert Earl of Huntington* (1598); *King John and Matilda*, 1628–34. The next most popular reign is that of Henry VIII, with four plays.

330. On this, see Womersley, *Divinity*, pp. 115–35.

one tradition, John had met his death after being poisoned by a monk was, in this light, a very helpful circumstance.

Shakespeare was well-aware of the revisionist Protestant understanding of John's reign, since the principal source for his own play on this subject, the anonymous two-part *The Troublesome Raigne of King John* (1588–1589), displays that interpretation at full strength. At moments, *The Troublesome Raigne* seems little more than a dramatisation of the tropes of vulgar anti-Catholicism, with fornicating nuns and friars, and true kings 'shouldred out' by clerics, all set against the apocalyptic backdrop of the struggle between the true and false churches.[331] In *King John,* Shakespeare took that material but drastically lowered its ideological temperature. In particular, John's death at the hands of a monk is not the martyrdom of other, earlier dramatic treatments of his reign, for the simple reason that in Shakespeare's play, John has not been presented as a proto-Protestant defender of the national interest and civil authority against the encroachments of the pope but rather as an unprincipled and unreliable monarch interested only in self-advancement. Nor is Pandulph, the papal legate, a diabolical lieutenant of the Antichrist, as Cardinal Beaufort in *2 Henry VI* had been.[332] Rather, he is an ambitious and worldly statesman adroitly pursuing the secular interests of his master, the pope. This is made very clear in his conversation with the Dauphin in act III, scene iv, in which Pandulph emerges not as a devilish villain but rather as a subtle expert in the ways of fortune and 'this old world'.[333] *King John* is, accordingly, Shakespeare's most Hobbesian play;[334] and it is also the play in which he shows the deepest understanding of the late medieval crucible that had essentialized the most important political doctrines of his own day.

It seems to be nothing more than the most circumstantial detail when, in the play's first scene, we are told that, when king, John's brother Richard had employed the Bastard's father, Falconbridge, 'in an embassy / To Germany, there with the Emperor / To treat of high affairs touching that time'—a detail from *The Troublesome Raigne* that Shakespeare was careful to carry over into

331. 2 *Troublesome Raigne,* ll. 1091–94, in Bullough, *Sources,* 4:148.

332. See above, pp. 277–78.

333. *King John,* III.iv.107–83; quotation at l. 145.

334. For Hobbes's comments on the reign of John, see *Leviathan,* ch. 29 (Hobbes, *Leviathan,* p. 222).

his own play, notwithstanding all the rest that he was happy to discard.[335] At the most mechanical level of plot, Falconbridge's absence gives Richard the chance to seduce Lady Falconbridge and beget the Bastard. However, to specify that Falconbridge's embassy was to the emperor becomes very relevant later in the play. By retaining that detail, Shakespeare threw a Ghibelline colouring over English Plantagenet kingship.

The later encounter in act III, scene i, between Pandulph and John makes Ghibellinism (namely, affiliation to the emperor and resistance to the pope) a settled principle of Plantagenet monarchy. This is a complex scene that falls into three parts: (1) the opening exchange in which Constance berates the French king Philip for abandoning her cause and agreeing a truce with John, to be cemented by the marriage of John's niece Blanche and the Dauphin; (2) the entrance of Pandulph and his excommunication of John; (3) Philip's resiling from the marriage contract and truce and the collapse of the conference in recrimination and the resumption of violence.

The initial and final portions of the scene, in which the Bastard's relentless baiting of the Duke of Austria supplies an *obbligato* thread of comic satire, offer vivid illustrations of political duplicity, accurately analysed by Constance (whose character reprises the association between insight and impotence that Shakespeare has previously used in the character of Henry VI):

> A wicked day and not a holy day!
> What hath this day deserved? What hath it done
> That it in golden letters should be set
> Among the high tides in the calendar?
> Nay, rather turn this day out of the week,
> This day of shame, oppression, perjury.
> Or, if it must stand still, let wives with child
> Pray that their burdens may not fall this day,
> Lest that their hopes prodigiously be crossed.[336]

The keynote of unprincipled self-interest prepares the way for the central element of the scene, the exchange between Pandulph and John. Pandulph immediately charges John with invading the liberties of the church:

335. *King John*, I.i.99–101. Cf. *1 Troublesome Raigne*, ll. 161–63, in Bullough, *Sources*, 4:77.
336. *King John*, III.i.9–17.

Hail, you anointed deputies of heaven!
—To thee, King John, my holy errand is.
I Pandulph, of fair Milan Cardinal,
And from Pope Innocent the legate here,
Do in his name religiously demand
Why thou against the church, our holy mother,
So wilfully dost spurn, and force perforce
Keep Stephen Langton, chosen Archbishop
Of Canterbury, from that holy see?
This in our foresaid holy father's name,
Pope Innocent, I do demand of thee.[337]

In this speech, Shakespeare adheres closely to the equivalent speech in *The Troublesome Raigne*, with, however, one striking variant: Pandulph's greeting to John and Philip as 'Hail, you anointed deputies of heaven!'[338] It is a crucially-important addition, because it will immediately become clear that Pandulph's mission and the politico-legal basis on which it relies both strike fatally at the status of kings as God's immediate deputies. This revelation of the hypocritical contradiction between Pandulph's language and the policy that guides his mission becomes very significant as the scene develops.

John replies not with mere defiance but rather with a defiance informed by some understanding of the politico-legal issues at stake in this tussle between ecclesiastical and secular power:

What earthy name to interrogatories
Can task the free breath of a sacred king?
Thou canst not, Cardinal, devise a name
So slight, unworthy, and ridiculous
To charge me to an answer as the Pope.
Tell him this tale, and from the mouth of England
Add thus much more: that no Italian priest
Shall tithe or toll in our dominions,
But as we, under heaven, are supreme head,
So under him that great supremacy
Where we do reign, we will alone uphold

337. *King John*, III.i.62–72.
338. Cf. *1 Troublesome Raigne*, ll. 966–75, in Bullough, *Sources*, 4:97–98.

Without th'assistance of a mortal hand.
So tell the Pope, all reverence set apart
To him and his usurped authority.[339]

The contrast with the equivalent prose speech in *The Troublesome Raigne* is marked:

> And what hast thou or the Pope thy maister to doo to demaund of me, how I employ mine owne? Know sir Priest as I honour the Church and holy Churchmen, so I scorne to be subject to the greatest Prelate in the world. Tell thy Maister so from me, and say, *John* of *England* said it, that never an Italian Priest of them all, shall either have tythe, tole, or poling penie out of *England*, but as I am King, so wil I raigne next under God, supreame head both over spirituall and temrall: and hee that contradicts me in this, Ile make him hoppe headlesse.[340]

The two speeches are clearly parallel in subject matter and sequencing of material; but, equally clearly, they are separated by a very different tonality. The vivid demotic truculence shown by John in *The Troublesome Raigne* points up how Shakespeare, by contrast, has been careful to avoid the pugnacious nationalism and crudity of vulgar anti-Catholicism. In *King John*, John responds to this textbook illustration of ecclesiastical encroachment with a statement of the political doctrine that had been forged precisely to resist it, namely, the divine right of kings, which is both more precise and uncluttered by extraneous, distracting elements than the equivalent speech in *The Troublesome Raigne*. Pandulph's response confirms what would have been the expectations of the play's first audiences, aware as they would have been of the papal bull *Regnans in excelsis*, namely, that the Catholic response to monarchical resistance is to encourage regicide:

blessèd shall he be that doth revolt
From his allegiance to an heretic,
And meritorious shall that hand be called,
Canonized and worshipped as a saint,
That takes away by any secret course
Thy hateful life.[341]

339. *King John*, III.i.73–86.

340. *1 Troublesome Raigne*, ll. 73–82, in Bullough, *Sources*, 4:98.

341. *King John*, III.i.100–4. For discussion of the papal bull *Regnans in excelsis*, see above, p. 208, n. 46.

In act V, when John surrenders his crown and receives it again from ecclesiastical hands, Pandulph's words make it clear that its return is dependent on John's relinquishing of any claim to a direct title from God:

> Take again
> From this my hand, *as holding of the Pope,*
> Your sovereign greatness and authority.[342]

So in *King John,* Shakespeare shows that he understood perfectly well both the origins of the theory of the divine right of kings and also the countervailing ecclesiastical claims which that theory was intended to resist.

When *King John* is juxtaposed with *Richard II,* the two plays taken together comprise a clear-eyed but not unsympathetic analysis of divine-right theory. *King John* explores the matrix of regal and papal tension which gave birth to the theory and puts onstage its abasement at the hands of ambitious prelates. *Richard II* dramatizes the tragic consequences that ensue when the language of that theory is naïvely taken *au pied de la lettre* and hence is mistakenly assumed actually to confer the momentous sacral powers that it asserts and claims.

King John marks the end-point of a particular phase of Shakespeare's interest in the joint between the secular and the religious. That interest would continue as a shaping, but not dominant, presence in *Henry IV* and *Henry V,* where new chorographic interests are also present and where Henry V exhibits the kind of inward piety that Shakespeare had earlier attributed to the future Henry VII in *Richard III.*[343] These later history plays show Shakespeare enriching the form of the history play beyond the comparatively narrow range of politico-confessional issues that initially dominated it. The theme revives in *Macbeth* perhaps because the accession of James I, with his well-known interest in questions of political theory, had restored salience to the question of divine right, and his accession had suppressed the faint stirrings of ideas of a Parliamentary royal title that had arisen towards the end of the reign of Elizabeth.[344]

342. *King John,* V.i.2–4; emphasis added. The equivalent passage in *The Troublesome Raigne* makes John's subaltern status more explicit (2 *Troublesome Raigne,* ll. 633–37, in Bullough, *Sources,* 4:136).

343. On which, see Womersley, *Divinity,* pp. 300–356.

344. Peter Wentworth was the most prominent and colourful figure in attempts during the reign of Elizabeth to give Parliament a role in determining the succession. But note also the

At any rate, tantalizing echoes of the language of *King John* in *Macbeth* suggest that, when writing the later play, Shakespeare was also at moments imaginatively revisiting his earlier work. For instance, take the Dauphin's comparison of his world-weariness to the experience of being made to listen to something you have already heard:

There's nothing in this world can make me joy.
Life is as tedious as a twice-told tale
Vexing the dull ear of a drowsy man,
And bitter shame hath spoiled the sweet word's taste,
That it yields naught but shame and bitterness.[345]

This description seems to have supplied the hint for Macbeth's much more comprehensive and devastating evocation of the nihilism by which he has been overtaken:

Tomorrow and tomorrow and tomorrow
Creeps in this petty pace from day to day
To the last syllable of recorded time,
And all our yesterdays have lighted fools
The way to dusty death. Out, out, brief candle.
Life's but a walking shadow, a poor player
That struts and frets his hour upon the stage
And then is heard no more. It is a tale
Told by an idiot, full of sound and fury,
Signifying nothing.[346]

John's anguished reaching for metaphors of intoxication and sleep when he realises that he is unaware of important military developments—

Oh, where hath our intelligence been drunk?
Where hath it slept?[347]

is echoed in Lady Macbeth's incitement of her husband's flagging ambition:

---

memoranda in the hand of Burghley outlining how the state was to be secured in the event of Elizabeth's assassination and the decisive role that Parliament would then assume in settling the succession (J. H. Neale, 'Peter Wentworth', *English Historical Review* 39 [1924]: 180–81).

345. *King John*, III.iv.107–11.

346. *Macbeth*, V.v.19–28.

347. *King John*, IV.ii.116–17.

Was the hope drunk
Wherein you dressed yourself? Hath it slept since?[348]

These traces of shared language and metaphor remind us that *King John* and *Macbeth* are linked by a common focus on the mortification of sacral kingship. And just as Shakespeare fastidiously refuses to depict John as the proto-Protestant martyr portrayed by Bale and Foxe, so too he holds the scales with a very even hand in *Macbeth*, where both divine-right and quasi-republican perspectives find a place.

There is one final play in which Shakespeare explored once again the relationship between ecclesiastical and secular authority, albeit in a very different mood. *Henry VIII* is a play bathed not only in melancholic Tudor nostalgia but also in the light given off by the sunset of an idea and a preoccupation. The play covers historical ground that was well-adapted to the most virulent and triumphalist anti-Catholicism: the fall of Cardinal Wolsey; Henry VIII's divorce from Catharine of Aragon; the rejuvenation of the king as he disentangles himself from invasive prelates and rancorous aristocrats; the marriage to Anne Boleyn; and the birth of the saviour princess Elizabeth, who will bring to England (so Cranmer prophesies) 'a thousand thousand blessings'.[349]

Yet the expected triumphalist note is never cleanly struck. The keynote of the play, sounded in the prologue, is of the speed and ease with which 'mightiness meets misery'.[350] This conjunction of greatness and suffering has the effect of suspending or dissolving judgement in a generalised compassion. In that respect, the wonderful scene between Catharine and Griffith, her gentleman usher, in which they discuss the dead Cardinal Wolsey, is almost an epitome of the play. Catharine recounts Wolsey's faults, including the encroaching habit, familiar amongst prelates, of 'ranking / Himself with princes'.[351] Griffith responds by recalling Wolsey's virtues, principally his support of learning and the equanimity with which he met his downfall and recognised 'the blessedness of being little.'[352] There is no arbitration between these two opposing estimates. Both are allowed to stand, in a relationship more of respectful complement than challenge. Catharine praises the 'religious truth and honesty' of Griffith's account of Wolsey, in a phrase which is more broadly

348. *Macbeth*, I.vii.35–36.
349. *Henry VIII*, V.iv.19.
350. *Henry VIII*, prol., 30.
351. *Henry VIII*, IV.ii.34–35.
352. *Henry VIII*, IV.ii.66.

applicable to the play as a whole.[353] The problems towards which Catharine's words point, in this dramatic account of a momentous storm of church and state almost a century in the past, are those of how to retain the human virtues that religion and piety can activate but that churches or ecclesiastical corporations too often pervert, and of how to ally those virtues to the human ends that commonwealths were created to serve. These, surely, are problems that we have yet to solve.

353. *Henry VIII*, IV.ii.74.

4

Means and Ends

KING LEAR

The principles upon which men reason in morals are always the same; though the conclusions they draw are often very different.

—DAVID HUME[1]

Doctrines which recognise as a fact in morals the existence of conflicting considerations; which all doctrines do, that have been believed by sane persons.

—JOHN STUART MILL[2]

IT WAS, BY ALL ACCOUNTS, a spectacular occasion—according to some witnesses, 'a Political Contest, the most extraordinary, perhaps, in its nature of any on the records of Parliament.'[3]

The debate on the Quebec Bill, which occurred on 6 May 1791, was concerned with far more than the administrative arrangements of a distant and, at that time, comparatively unimportant province. For tension between the two dominant figures in the Whig party, Charles Fox and Edmund Burke, arising from their very different interpretations of recent events in France, had been growing for over a year. In a debate on the Army Estimates held on 9 February 1790, Burke had made his first public pronouncement concerning

1. Hume, *Enquiry*, p. 118
2. Mill, *Utilitarianism*, p. 36.
3. *The Oracle*, 7 May 1791; quoted in Burke, *Writings*, 4:324.

the French Revolution, and had also made it clear that, on that subject, he differed from his political ally (in the language of Parliament, 'friend') Charles Fox.[4] During that debate Burke's expressions of difference from Fox had been gently phrased: 'it was with a pain inexpressible he was obliged to have even the shadow of a difference with his friend, whose authority would always be great with him, and with all thinking people.'[5] Nevertheless, the emerging gulf between the two men was plain: one, inclined to see in the French Revolution a natural longing for liberty that was to be smiled upon to the point of 'exultation' and its excesses accordingly excused; the other, with a grim sagacity discerning within the early dynamics of French affairs a nascent threat to Europe's *ancien régime*.[6] Burke had warned that, if Fox were to pursue his policy of accommodation with the French Revolution, then he would 'abandon his best friends, and join with his worst enemies to oppose either the means or the end, and to resist all violent exertions of the spirit of innovation, so distant from all principles of true and safe reformation.'[7] Fifteen months later, that tension would come to a dramatic head, and Burke would carry out his desperate threat to secede from the party within which he had passed his political life.

The subject of the debate was the future government of Canada, and the House was supposed to be debating *seriatim* the clauses of the bill that had been laid before them. Burke, however, was determined to make this a debate about 'certain principles of government', rather than about the *minutiae* of a particular piece of legislation.[8] He had not been speaking long before he began attacking the French revolutionary constitution. He was soon called to order by members of his own party, many of whom at that stage entertained favourable views of the Revolution. Eventually Fox himself interrupted Burke and accused him of seeking 'a difference of opinion, and . . . a cause of dispute.'[9] Burke rose again and replied in terms that made it clear that a rupture between the two former friends was now in the immediate offing.

4. Burke, *Writings*, 4:287–88. Note also Burke's phrase referring to Fox, 'his *best* friend' (ibid., p. 287; emphasis added).

5. Burke, *Writings*, 4:287.

6. Burke, *Writings*, 4:287 and 301.

7. Burke, *Writings*, 4:288.

8. Burke, *Writings*, 4:325.

9. Burke, *Writings*, 4:337.

The interruptions continued, now coming from more junior members of the party as well as from its leaders. Exasperated and goaded, according to some accounts Burke now rounded on his tormentors and quoted *King Lear*:

> The little dogs and all, Tray, Blanch, and Sweetheart,
> See—they bark at me.[10]

The lines come from the trial scene on the heath, in which Lear arraigns his daughters for ingratitude. However, Burke may have been more familiar with the text of *King Lear* in Nahum Tate's revised version, which had held the stage for the past century. Tate had expunged material that he felt fell below the dignity of tragedy, and the central scenes of act III in particular show deep traces of his handiwork. In Tate's version, a significantly altered context is provided for these lines. Lear's anguished question from two scenes earlier, 'Is it the fashion that discarded fathers / Should have thus little mercy on their flesh?', in Tate's version closely precedes the pathos of his reference to the barking dogs, to which, in this revised text, it seems to be a response or an answer.[11]

Certainly, the experience of being discarded was at the centre of Burke's feelings in May 1791. Even though it was Burke who crossed to the Treasury bench and so deserted his party, he nevertheless felt (and he would set this view out at length in works such as *An Appeal from the New to the Old Whigs* [1791]) that the apostasy had more truly been on the other side. Like Abdiel amongst the seceding angels, Burke alone was

> faithful found,
> Among the faithless, faithful only hee;
> Among innumerable false, unmov'd,
> Unshak'n, unseduc'd, unterrifi'd
> His Loyaltie he kept, his Love, his Zeale;
> Nor number, nor example with him wrought
> To swerve from truth, or change his constant mind
> Though single.[12]

10. George Pellew, *The Life and Correspondence of Viscount Sidmouth*, 3 vols. (London: John Murray, 1847), 1:85; mis-lineation as in quoted text. Cf. *King Lear*, III.vi.21–22.

11. *King Lear*, III.iv.69–70; Nahum Tate, *The History of King Lear. Acted at the Duke's Theatre. Reviv'd with Alterations* (1681), pp. 30–31.

12. Milton, *Paradise Lost*, V.893–900.

So, at least, Burke's allies liked to depict him (although Burke deplored the application of these lines to himself).[13]

Those feelings of abandonment and relegation, precisely the wounding experience of being discarded, which of course are strong enough already in *King Lear*, may have been given additional definition for Burke by a recent literary use of the very lines he would quote in the House of Commons. In Henry Mackenzie's *The Man of Feeling* (1771), Harley, the 'man of feeling' of the title, is in love with his neighbour Miss Walton but is unable to declare his love because of his excessive emotional refinement. He hears that Miss Walton is being courted by Sir Harry Benson and is likely to accept him. Distracted by anguish and jealousy, Harley walks over to Miss Walton's estate:

> He went as far as a little gate, that led into a copse near Mr. Walton's house, to which that gentleman had been so obliging as to let him have a key. He had just then begun to open it, when he saw, on a terrass below, Miss Walton walking with a gentleman in riding-dress, whom he immediately guessed to be Sir Harry Benson. He stopped of a sudden; his hand shook so much that he could hardly turn the key; he opened the gate however, and advanced a few paces. The lady's lap-dog pricked up its ears, and barked: he stopped again.—
>
> —'The little dogs and all
> Tray, Blanch, and Sweetheart, see they bark at me!'
>
> His resolution failed; he slunk back, and locking the gate as softly as he could, stood on tiptoe looking over the wall till they were gone.[14]

As with Burke's quotation of the same lines in the House of Commons twenty years later, the provocation for Harley's recollection of these lines (though are

13. A few months after the break with Fox, Joshua Reynolds had published in August 1791 an engraving of Burke, based on the portrait painted by Reynolds in 1775, with these lines from *Paradise Lost* beneath the image. Burke, however, 'urged the strongest remonstrances against the application of such lines to him; and insisted, almost as the condition of continued friendship, that they should be obliterated' (James Prior, *Memoir of the Life and Character of Edmund Burke*, 2nd ed., 2 vols. [1826], 2:163–64). Notwithstanding Burke's deploring of the allusion, Milton was one of his favourite poets, and comparison between the two men was natural, culminating in Thomas Macaulay's compliment in his diary entry for 22 January 1853 that Burke was the 'greatest man since Milton' (*The Journals of Thomas Babington Macaulay*, ed. William Thomas, 5 vols. [London: Pickering and Chatto, 2008], 4:17).

14. Henry Mackenzie, *The Man of Feeling*, ed. Brian Vickers (Oxford: Oxford University Press, 2001), pp. 83–84.

they recalled by Harley—or by the narrator?—the ownership of the words is suggestively ambiguous) is the apprehension of being discarded or supplanted, of being substituted and replaced. It seems, then, that these words from *King Lear* are, in the late eighteenth century, an objective correlative for the arrival of the distressing information that one is fungible; that is (to use Kantian language) the unwelcome realisation that one has a price, rather than a dignity.[15]

I begin with these late eighteenth-century applications of lines from *King Lear* because I find that, in these quotations, both Burke and Mackenzie have responded very directly to the ethical core of the play from which they are taken. At the heart of *King Lear* is the pain of substitution: that is, the pain of realising that one is discardable, that one does not hold an unchallengeable place in the regard of others. It is a play which puts before us a whole series of substitutions and their consequences, from Lear's spurning of Cordelia in favour of Goneril and Regan to Gloucester's adultery (the substitution of a mistress for his wife), which produces Edmund, to the kinds of equivalence which are both entertained and rejected in the various parallelisms that exist between the main plot and the sub-plot.

But if *King Lear* tells us in one breath about the terrible things that can arise from a casual assumption of substitutability, then in the next it also confronts us with the pain that arises from the denial or impossibility of finding a substitute. On the one hand, we are shown the cascade into suffering and moral savagery evoked by Samuel Johnson in his general note on the play: 'that villainy is never at a stop, that crimes lead to crimes and at last terminate in ruin.'[16] These calamities are the consequence of viewing people as interchangeable, in the way that (as we will see presently) Edmund does. But the impossibility of substitution may also bring pain. When Lear, holding the corpse of Cordelia at the end of the play, cries, 'Why should a dog, a horse, a rat have life, / And thou no breath at all?', he is tormented by his new understanding that a substitute for Cordelia is unavailable and, even if a substitute were available, would be as grotesquely inadequate as equating his daughter with a horse or a rat or even a dog—even, perhaps, those little dogs Tray, Blanch, and Sweetheart, whose sudden hostility had earlier caused Lear such a pang.[17]

There are, as is so often the case in tragedy, griefs both ways: both in the ease and in the impossibility of replacement. And, in this instance, that

15. Kant, *Metaphysics*, p. 53. This distinction is discussed more fully on pp. 319–22 and 338.

16. Johnson, *Shakespeare*, p. 222.

17. *King Lear*, V.iii.282–83.

ambivalence of pain gathers around a perennial line of tension within the Western ethical tradition.

The section that follows has two objectives. In the first place, I want to identify and trace a recurrent feature of arguments in Western moral philosophy from Plato to John Rawls: namely, that, although the arguments of Western moral philosophers tend to begin either by elevating the *utile* (or expedient) above the *honestum* (or right), or conversely by elevating the *honestum* over the *utile,* in practice whichever initial move is made, the banished or relegated term always returns towards the end of the argument, either deliberately smuggled in to do important work of argumentative closure or perhaps unconsciously relied upon. This may be philosophically scandalous (or, rather, it may be uncomfortable for practising philosophers). But for the rest of us, this is just part of our daily experience as moral beings of goodwill trying to do the right thing in equivocal circumstances. In such cases, both the *utile* and *honestum* have an undeniable and legitimate, but incomplete, purchase on our reflections and actions. And in due course I will hope to show that what is scandalous for the philosopher is useful for the dramatist.

Secondly, and more briefly, I will explore the affinity of a major branch of that tradition of moral philosophy—namely, moral theories that are consequentialist or utilitarian in character—to one of the cardinal elements in the mode of drama as an art-form, namely, personation, or one person taking the part of another. My purpose in pursuing this excursion into the *longue durée* of Western moral philosophy is to prepare the ground for an exploration of how these fundamental questions of morals are taken up in Shakespeare's plays. For I will argue that, in certain plays of Shakespeare, these two things exist in very close proximity. That is to say, Shakespeare's dramatisations of the entwinings and collisions between the *utile* and the *honestum* tend to involve patterns of action that are strongly marked by personal substitutions. I will go on to explore this in a discussion of three plays: *King Lear, Measure for Measure,* and *The Two Noble Kinsmen.*

In Book II of *The Republic* Glaucon relates a legend the implications of which have resonated throughout the moral philosophy of the West. Glaucon wishes to provoke Socrates into censuring injustice and praising justice.[18] To

18. Plato, *The Republic,* 358d.

do so, he himself advances a sceptical account of justice, arguing that, far from being a disinterested adherence to what is right, at the heart of justice lies not principle but rather a wary and prudential bargain struck between people who are driven into the pursuit of narrow self-interest because they have been cowed by those who are stronger:

> You see, people do say that to commit an injustice is naturally good, while to be the victim of it is bad. Yet being wronged is much more of a bad thing than committing wrong is a good thing. The result of this is that whenever people wrong each other and are also victims of wrong and have a taste of both sides, those who are unable to avoid the one or achieve the other believe that it is in their interest to make a mutual agreement with each other not to do anything wrong to each other. From this basis they begin to make laws and covenants with each other, and they give the terms legal and just to what is laid down by the law. This is indeed the origin and essence of justice, lying between what is best: to commit wrong with impunity, and what is worst: not being able to get revenge when wronged. So justice, being midway between these two, is welcomed not as a good thing, but is valued through our being too weak to commit an injustice.[19]

Glaucon insists that anyone who could commit injustice with impunity would do so, and to illustrate that tendency in human nature, he relates the parable of the Ring of Gyges.[20] Gyges (or, in Glaucon's version, an unnamed ancestor of Gyges) was a Lydian shepherd who chanced upon a ring that had the power to make the wearer invisible. He quickly grasped what he could do with this magical power:

> He pondered this and experimented with the ring to see if it actually had this power, and he found that this was the case: if he turned the setting inward he became invisible, outward and he became visible again. As soon as he became aware of this, he immediately arranged to become one of the messengers who went to the king, and when he got there he seduced his

19. Plato, *The Republic*, 358e–359a.

20. The earliest version of the story of Gyges that has come down to us is in Herodotus (I.viii–xiv), where, however, there are important differences of detail from the account given by Glaucon. In particular Herodotus makes no mention of a magic ring; his account of Gyges's seizure of the throne is entirely naturalistic.

> wife and with her help attacked the king, killed him and took possession of his kingdom.[21]

Glaucon draws the following conclusion:

> There is far more personal profit in injustice than in justice is what every man believes, and rightly so, as the person putting forward this sort of argument will maintain, because if a person who had this sort of opportunity within his grasp should be unwilling ever to behave unjustly or seize the possessions of others, he would be regarded as most wretched and foolish by those who observed him, although in front of each other they would commend him, deceiving one another for fear of being treated unjustly themselves.[22]

Against Glaucon, Socrates will argue that, although the ring seems to give the wearer power, in fact it enslaves him to his own passions.[23] According to Socrates, only the just man is also a free man.

The afterlife of this wonderful parable flows in two streams, one more imaginative, the other more strictly philosophical. In Glaucon's story and Socrates's reply we can discern the seed of those later myths or stories of rings which bestow upon the wearer supernatural powers but which also destroy them—stories such as Wagner's *Der Ring des Nibelungen* and Tolkien's *The Lord of the Rings*. These fables address our common awareness that not infrequently what we most crave does us mortal harm. Philosophers, on the other hand, have responded less to the concrete personal predicaments and exhilarations that might result from possessing the ring of Gyges and more to the general ethical issues Glaucon's story raises: namely, whether one should pursue either what is advantageous or what is right, and furthermore what may be the relationship between what is right and what is advantageous.

Cicero in the *De Officiis* made three notable contributions to this ethical conversation. In the first place, he gave prominence to the Latin terms (*utile* and *honestum*) that have since tended to be used as a form of shorthand for the ostensible alternatives in this debate. Secondly, Cicero initiated the argumentative move that would, in various shapes and forms, be duplicated by

21. Plato, *The Republic*, 360a–b.

22. Plato, *The Republic*, 360d.

23. 'Haven't we instead discovered that justice is the best thing for the soul itself and that it ought to perform just deeds, whether it has Gyges' ring or not, and in addition Hades' magic helmet?' (Plato, *The Republic*, bk. X, 612b).

many later philosophers who addressed this question. Cicero sought to defuse the apparent dilemma by denying that the *utile* and the *honestum*, when properly understood, could ever truly be set in opposition to each other.

The *De Officiis* begins with a ringing assertion of the importance of moral philosophy to the right conduct of life: 'For no phase of life, whether public or private, whether in business or in the home, whether one is working on what concerns oneself alone or dealing with another, can be without its moral duty; on the discharge of such duties depends all that is morally right, and on their neglect all that is morally wrong in life.'[24] However, this important field of moral reflection has been corrupted by a pernicious and false doctrine, which asserts that the *utile* and the *honestum* are separable: 'The usage of this word [*utile*] has been corrupted and perverted and has gradually come to the point where, separating moral rectitude from expediency, it is accepted that a thing may be morally right without being expedient, and expedient without being morally right. No more pernicious doctrine than this could be introduced into human life.'[25] Men are misled into believing that the *utile* can be separated from the *honestum* because they entertain shallow and inadequate ideas of the *utile*, confusing it with what seems most immediately to gratify their desires or to promote a vulgar notion of their well-being.

For Cicero, however, the *honestum* is always really the *utile*, and there is nothing truly *utile* which is not also *honestum*: 'To conclude, then, it is never expedient to do wrong, because wrong is always immoral; and it is always expedient to be good, because goodness is always moral.'[26] The argument culminates in a simple, single emphasis: 'But for all cases we have one rule, with which I desire you to be perfectly familiar: that which seems expedient must not be morally wrong; or, if it is morally wrong, it must not seem expedient.'[27]

I have referred to Cicero's exposition of this important topic in moral philosophy as an 'argument'. But in some respects, that term mis-describes what Cicero offers us in this text, at least if we think of an argument as a series of propositions bound together sequentially in a structure of logical entailment. For what Cicero does in the *De Officiis* is rather different from that. Cicero makes it clear that he is following in the footsteps of an earlier Stoic philosopher, Panaetius of Rhodes, who had written a work in Greek with the

24. Cicero, *De Officiis*, I.ii.4.
25. Cicero, *De Officiis*, I.iii.9.
26. Cicero, *De Officiis*, III.xv.64.
27. Cicero, *De Officiis*, III.xx.81.

same title (*mutatis mutandis*) as Cicero's, which is now substantially lost.[28] Cicero explains his own relation to Panaetius towards the end of the *De Officiis*:

> Panaetius, then, has given us what is unquestionably the most thorough discussion of moral duties that we have, and I have followed him in the main—but with slight modifications. He classifies under three general heads the ethical problems which people are accustomed to consider and weigh: first, the question whether the matter in hand is morally right or morally wrong; second, whether it is expedient or inexpedient; third, how a decision ought to be reached, in case that which has the appearance of being morally right clashes with that which seems to be expedient.[29]

However, Panaetius had unaccountably failed to compose the third, most important, part of his treatise, 'especially, as he states that there is no other topic in the whole range of philosophy so essentially important as this'.[30] But nevertheless, Cicero knew what Panaetius had thought on that subject:

> In the first place, I must undertake the defence of Panaetius on this point; for he has said, not that the truly expedient could under certain circumstances clash with the morally right (for he could not have said that conscientiously), but only that what seemed expedient could do so. For he often bears witness to the fact that nothing is really expedient that is not at the same time morally right, and nothing morally right that is not at the same time expedient; and he says that no greater curse has ever assailed human life than the doctrine of those who have separated these two conceptions.[31]

But both the justifications for the identity of the *utile* and the *honestum* that Cicero proceeds to offer are weak. One is nakedly a matter of wishful thinking about nature: 'But if there is nothing so repugnant to Nature as immorality (for Nature demands right and harmony and consistency and abhors their opposites), and if nothing is so thoroughly in accord with Nature as

28. Panaetius of Rhodes (ca. 185–ca. 110 BC), Stoic philosopher, *protégé* of Scipio Æmilianus, author of 'On Duties' ('Περί του Καθήκοντος'). A fragment of Panaetius's book is preserved in the *Noctes Atticae* of Aulus Gellius.

29. Cicero, *De Officiis*, III.ii.7.

30. Cicero, *De Officiis*, III.ii.7.

31. Cicero, *De Officiis*, III.vii.34.

expediency, then surely expediency and immorality cannot coexist in one and the same object.'[32] The second justification is merely an argument from authority:

> Again: if we are born for moral rectitude and if that is either the only thing worth seeking, as Zeno thought, or at least to be esteemed as infinitely outweighing everything else, as Aristotle holds, then it necessarily follows that the morally right is either the sole good or the supreme good. Now, that which is good is certainly expedient; consequently, that which is morally right is also expedient.[33]

But what if nature can in fact accommodate both immorality and expediency and is indifferent to the ethical distinctions drawn by men? And what if Zeno and Aristotle were mistaken?

My intention here is not to score points off Cicero but rather to suggest that his extolling of the *honestum* above the *utile* is in fact governed by a higher-level attentiveness to the *utile*. In the end, the *De Officiis* has no stronger claim on our agreement than that it would be inconvenient—that is to say, it would not be *utile*—were the *utile* not to be either identical with or subsumable within the *honestum*. Thus, ultimately Cicero's appeal to his reader in the *De Officiis* is made on consequentialist grounds. And this surreptitious return of the rejected term, in a position of unacknowledged but effective mastery, is the third paradigmatic element in Cicero's treatment of the topic of the *utile* and the *honestum* that we will find in the writings of later thinkers on this question.

The advent of Christianity saw Cicero's conflation of the *utile* and the *honestum* revived, re-shaped, and re-purposed. An early Church Father of Stoic inclinations, such as St. Ambrose, took much from the *De Officiis* and adapted it to the doctrinal ends of the new religion.[34] In particular, it was the Christian promise of eternal life for the saved that re-configured the relation between the *utile* and the *honestum*. In Ambrose's *De Officiis Ministrorum*, the identity of the *utile* and the *honestum* was again proclaimed, although the grounds of that identity were quite unlike those offered by Cicero: 'We posit the rule that nothing is fitting or right [*honestum*] unless it is oriented toward future goods more than to present ones; and we state that nothing is useful [*utile*] unless it

32. Cicero, *De Officiis*, III.viii.35.

33. Cicero, *De Officiis*, III.viii.35.

34. Note Sidgwick's observation that Stoicism is 'a transitional link between ancient and modern ethics' (Sidgwick, *Ethics*, p. 99).

directs us to the grace of that life eternal, and not to the enjoyment of the present.'[35] So for Ambrose, our every-day distinction between the right and the expedient disappears. What could be more for our self-interest, what could be more *utile*, than to secure eternal life?[36] And what could be more right, what could be more *honestum*, than the imitation and service of Christ that leads us to eternal life?[37] The result is an account of the *utile* and the *honestum* which, while being recognisably modelled on that of Cicero, nevertheless re-orders Cicero's priorities: 'The result of Cicero's reformulation of the *honestum* and the *utile* is to assimilate the *honestum* to the *utile*; the result of Ambrose's handling of the same topic is exactly the reverse. Instead of bringing the Stoic sage down to earth, . . . Ambrose seeks to bring the Stoic sage into the fullness of being through Christian redemption.'[38] And this patristic understanding of the relation between the *utile* and the *honestum* was substantially adopted by the humanist writers of the early modern period, upon whom Cicero was a dominant influence.

It was Machiavelli who decisively broke with this humanist consensus. In Book I, chapter 3 of *The Discourses*, Machiavelli had stated plainly that politicians should act on the assumption that all men will pursue their expedient self-interest if they can do so with impunity: 'According to the judgment of all Authors who have written of Civil Government, and the examples of all History, it is necessary to who-ever would establish a Government, and prescribe

35. St. Ambrose, *De Officiis Ministrorum*, I.ix.28. On the adaptations of classical Stoicism by a range of early church fathers, see Marcia L. Colish, *The Stoic Tradition from Antiquity to the Early Middle Ages: Stoicism in Christian Latin Thought Through the Sixth Century*, 2nd ed. (Leiden: Brill, 1990).

36. 'In the ages of Christian faith, it has been still more obvious and natural to hold . . . that the realization of Virtue is essentially an enlightened and far-seeing pursuit of Happiness for the agent' (Sidgwick, *Ethics*, p. 108).

37. 'None the less, what he [Ambrose] actually does in his own second book is to turn Cicero inside out. This he accomplishes not merely by redefining the *summum bonum* in Christian terms but by altering the relationship that Cicero had posited between the *honestum* and the *utile*. In a sense both authors redefine the *honestum* as the *utile*, Cicero by obliterating the idea of virtue as an end in itself and Ambrose by presenting the *honestum*, like the *utile*, as a means to eternal life. But at the same time Ambrose reclassifies the *utile* as a species of the *honestum* by taking it out of the sphere of worldly advantage altogether and by associating it, along with the *honestum*, with man's redemption' (Colish, *Stoic Tradition*, p. 67).

38. Colish, *Stoic Tradition*, pp. 69–70. On Ambrose's likely influence on Augustine's thinking about the *honestum* and the *utile*, see ibid., p. 233.

Laws to it, to presuppose all men naturally bad, and that they will shew and exert that natural malignity as often as they have occasion to do it securely.'[39]

However, in chapters 16 and 17 of *The Prince*, Machiavelli went further. There he provocatively explained how, for a ruler, the *utile* and the *honestum* might be irreconcilable, and that therefore in many instances an astute ruler would deliberately choose the *utile* over the *honestum*. Concerning liberality and parsimony, for example, which is the subject of chapter 16 of *The Prince*, Machiavelli begins by conceding that liberality is a princely virtue and to that extent is *honestum*. But he then goes on to set out how liberality, if unwisely pursued, can draw disaster in its wake:

> It would be advantageous to be accounted liberal; nevertheless liberality so used as not to render you formidable, does but injure you, for if it be used virtuously, and as it ought to be, it will not be known, nor secure you from the imputation of its contrary: To keep up therefore the name of liberal amongst men, it is necessary that no kind of luxury be omitted, so that a Prince of that disposition will consume his revenue in those kind of expences, and be obliged at last, if he would preserve that reputation, to become grievous, and a great exactor upon the people, and do whatever is practicable for the getting of Money, which will cause him to be hated, of his Subjects, and despised by every body else, when he once comes to be poor, so that offending many with his liberality, and rewarding but few, he becomes sensible of the first disaster, and runs great hazard of being ruined, the first time he is in danger; which when afterwards he discovers, he desires to remedy; he runs into the other extream, and grows as odious for his avarice.

The result is that parsimony emerges as the preferred rule of conduct for all rulers whose means are not unlimited (which in practice means all rulers):

> So then if a Prince cannot exercise this virtue of liberality, so as to be publickly known, without detriment to himself, he ought if he be wise, not to dread the imputation of being covetous, for in time he shall be esteemed liberal when it is discovered that by his parsimony he has increased his revenue to a Condition of defending him against any Invasion, and to enterprize upon other people, without oppressing them; so that he shall be accounted Noble to all from whom he takes nothing away, which are an

39. Machiavelli, *Discourses*, in Machiavelli, *Works*, p. 272.

> infinite number; and near and parsimonious only to such few as he gives nothing to.[40]

It is clear that Machiavelli's advocacy of the *utile* over the *honestum* is entirely consequentialist in character. But it is also clear, when Machiavelli refers to 'all from whom he takes nothing away, which are an infinite number,' that the *utile* is being subtly re-defined in a direction which makes the elevation of the *utile* over the *honestum* less affronting to traditional morality.

Going back to Glaucon's parable of the Ring of Gyges in Plato's *Republic,* the expedient actions that the ring made possible for its wearer are all to do with personal and immediate gratification: that is to say, sexual conquest and the sudden acquisition of power and wealth. In the *De Officiis* Marius's seizure of the consulship, Cicero's climactic example of a politician putting the *utile* before the *honestum,* is again an instance where narrow personal advantage was culpably given precedence over the broader public good.[41] But in *The Prince,* what is *utile* for the ruler begins to converge with what is *utile* also for his subjects. This convergence becomes clear at the end of chapter 18, where Machiavelli considers whether or not a prince should always keep his word:

> A Prince then is to have particular care that nothing falls from his mouth, but what is full of the five qualities aforesaid [i.e., the *honestum*], and that to see, and to hear him, he appears all goodness, integrity, humanity, and religion, which last he ought to pretend to more than ordinarily, because more men do judge by the eye, than by the touch, for every body sees, but few understand; every body sees how you appear, but few know what in reality you are, and those few dare not oppose the opinion of the multitude who have the Majesty of their Prince to defend them; and in the actions of all men, especially Princes, where no man has power to judge, every one looks to the end. Let a Prince therefore do what he can to preserve his life, and continue his Supremacy, the means which he uses shall be thought honorable, and be commended by every body; because the people are always taken with the appearance, and event of things, and the greatest part of the world consists of the people: Those few who are wise, taking place when the multitude has nothing else to relye upon.[42]

40. Machiavelli, *The Prince,* in Machiavelli, *Works,* p. 220.
41. Cicero, *De Officiis,* III.xx.79 and 81.
42. Machiavelli, *The Prince,* in Machiavelli, *Works,* p. 223.

This convergence will later be characterised as a movement from egoistic hedonism to universalistic hedonism.[43] It represents a significant convergence between the *utile* and the *honestum*; and it shows Machiavelli, notwithstanding his provocative elevation of the expedient over the right, silently acknowledging and deferring to the claims of the *honestum* over our conduct.

The rupture represented by the work of Machiavelli was developed and systematised in the Counter-Reformation doctrine of *ragion di stato* (reason of state) that became influential in the later sixteenth and earlier seventeenth centuries.[44] Although it was the purpose of 'reason of state' to account for princely deeds that seemed to flout commonly-accepted religious and moral precepts, the Counter-Reformation 'reason of state' theorists (Botero, de Ribadeneyra, Venturi, Frachetta) aimed to show that 'various forms of apparent immorality and deception were compatible with their overall moral programme'.[45] This was plainly another attempt to show that the ostensible conflict between the *utile* and the *honestum* was more apparent than real. That conciliatory purpose was unmistakable in the thought of, for instance, Justus Lipsius, who attempted to create a 'mixed prudence' in which both the *utile* and the *honestum* had a part to play: 'vtilia honestis miscere'.[46] Lipsius's follower Robert Dallington made the strategy explicit:

> All Moralists hold nothing profitable that is not honest. Some Politicks haue inuerted this order, and peruerted the sense, by transposing the tearmes in the proposition: holding nothing honest that is not profitable. Howsoeuer those former may seeme too straight laced, these surely are too

43. 'The two systems which make Happiness an ultimate end it will be convenient to distinguish as Egoistic and Universalistic Hedonism: and as it is the latter of these, as taught by Bentham and his successors, that is more generally understood under the term Utilitarianism, I shall always restrict that word to this signification. For Egoistic Hedonism it is somewhat hard to find a single perfectly appropriate term. I shall often call this simple Egoism: but it may sometimes be convenient to call it Epicureanism: for though this name more properly denotes a particular historical system, it has come to be commonly used in the wider sense in which I wish to employ it' (Sidgwick, *Ethics*, p. 9).

44. On which, see Friedrich Meinecke, *Die Idee der Staatsräson* (Munich: R. Oldenbourg, 1924); and Noel Malcolm, *Reason of State, Propaganda, and the Thirty Years' War: An Unknown Translation by Thomas Hobbes* (Oxford: Clarendon Press, 2007).

45. Malcolm, *Reason of State*, p. 99.

46. J. Lipsius, *Politicorum sive civilis doctrinae libri sex* (Leiden, 1589), p. 203. Quoted in Malcolm, *Reason of State*, p. 101.

loose. For there is a middle way betweene both which a right Statesman must take.[47]

The political philosophy of Hobbes has some limited points of contact with this school of thought. Like the *ragion di stato* theorists, Hobbes was willing to defend some unpalatable princely actions (the various practices of absolutism) on the grounds of a broader utility (the preservation of peace and the securing of property). Where Hobbes parted company with the *ragion di stato* theorists, however, was in his insistence that his political philosophy rested upon scientific foundations, rather than being a mere digest of the tricks of the political trade practised by experienced insiders.[48]

The turmoil of the English mid-seventeenth century, and the political and religious *revanchism* of the Carolean Restoration in which those tumults eventuated, had the effect of bestowing once more a transient authority on the most traditional precepts of conduct (at least for subjects, if not always in practice for their rulers). But by the mid-eighteenth century, social, moral, and political conditions had altered sufficiently so that an intrepid thinker such as David Hume might venture to re-open the question of the *utile* and the *honestum*. Hume's moral philosophy was furiously denounced by the orthodox, who saw (probably correctly) that it constituted an attempt to separate human ethics from divine authority.[49] Nevertheless, and despite the contumely that was heaped upon it by some contemporaries, Hume's thought forms two important links with later moral philosophy: one with the Kantian ethics which launched themselves by repudiating it and the other with the utilitarian ethics which to some degree followed and developed it.

However, we must begin not with the links between Hume's philosophy and what came after it but rather with its links with what preceded it. Hume, although he had little time for Machiavelli's virtue-politics, nevertheless acknowledged that Machiavelli was 'certainly a great genius';[50] and Hume had

47. Robert Dallington, *Aphorismes Civill and Militarie* (1613), bk. V, aphorism 19, p. 314. Quoted in Malcolm, *Reason of State*, pp. 101–2.

48. Malcolm, *Reason of State*, pp. 114–18.

49. For instance, James Balfour (Hume, *Enquiry*, p. lxvii).

50. David Hume, 'Of Civil Liberty', in Hume, *Essays*, p. 88. 'Hume has virtually no affinities with the Machiavellian moralists and corruption mongers of his age' (Forbes, *Politics*, p. 225).

unquestionably read the entirety of Machiavelli's works with close attention.[51] So it is a plausible inference that Hume's comments on the inutility of the customary virtue of liberality in princes contains a silent reference back to chapter 16 of *The Prince*: 'Liberality in princes is regarded as a mark of beneficence: But when it occurs, that the homely bread of the honest and industrious is often thereby converted into delicious cates for the idle and the prodigal, we soon retract our heedless praises.'[52] Hume's quiet nod to Machiavelli serves to situate the philosophy of his *An Enquiry Concerning the Principles of Morals* (first published, 1751; substantially drafted, 1749–1750) within the broadly utilitarian tradition to which Machiavelli had given an early impetus.

In *An Enquiry Concerning the Principles of Morals*, which re-packaged elements from the earlier, and less engaging, *Treatise of Human Nature* (1739), Hume set out in quest of the 'true origin of morals.'[53] He explained the method he would follow: 'As this is a question of fact, not of abstract science, we can only expect success, by following the experimental method, and deducing general maxims from a comparison of particular instances.'[54] And he elaborated the merits of this empirical approach in terms which would, later in the century, provoke Kant into a powerful and sweeping *riposte*:

> Men are now cured of their passion for hypotheses and systems in natural philosophy [i.e., science], and will hearken to no arguments but those which are derived from experience. It is full time they should attempt a like reformation in all moral disquisitions; and reject every system of ethics, however subtile or ingenious, which is not founded on fact and observation.[55]

When Hume reflected on our moral experience, what did he find? In the first place, he set out a general contention about the way in which our feelings and our reasonings collaborate in conditioning our moral life. Neither unaided feelings nor unaided reason could create an adequate moral sense:

51. Note the entry in Hume's 'Early Memoranda': 'There is not a Word of Trade in *all Matchiavel*, which is strange considering that Florence rose only by Trade' (MS 23159, item 14, p. 16, NLS; emphasis added).

52. Hume, *Enquiry*, p. 11.

53. Hume, *Enquiry*, p. 6.

54. Hume, *Enquiry*, p. 6.

55. Hume, *Enquiry*, p. 7.

> I am apt to suspect . . . that *reason* and *sentiment* concur in almost all moral determinations and conclusions. The final sentence, it is probable, which pronounces characters and actions amiable or odious, praise-worthy or blameable; that which stamps on them the mark of honour or infamy, approbation or censure; that which renders morality an active principle, and constitutes virtue our happiness, and vice our misery: It is probable, I say, that this final sentence depends on some internal sense or feeling, which nature has made universal in the whole species. For what else can have an influence of this nature? But in order to pave the way for such a sentiment, and give a proper discernment of its object, it is often necessary, we find, that much reasoning should precede, that nice distinctions be made, just conclusions drawn, distant comparisons formed, complicated reasons examined, and general facts fixed and ascertained.[56]

But which of the two, feeling or reason, is *primary* in the formation of our moral sense? For Hume, feeling is primary, and reason, although in practice indispensable, is secondary in the development of our moral natures: 'moral beauty . . . demands the *assistance* of our intellectual faculties, in order to give it a suitable influence on the human mind'.[57] But our sensitivity to moral beauty does not originate in our reason, which has only a subsequent and ancillary role. As Hume will eventually conclude, 'morality is determined by sentiment'.[58]

If our perceptions of moral beauty originate in our feelings, rather than in our reason, what experiences or sensations give rise to those perceptions? Hume is adamant that these perceptions are associated with utility, for 'the UTILITY, resulting from the social virtues, forms, at least, a part of their merit, and is one source of that approbation and regard so universally paid to them': 'The eye is pleased with the prospect of corn-fields and loaded vineyards; horses grazing, and flocks pasturing: But flies the view of briars and brambles,

56. Hume, *Enquiry*, p. 5. Cf. ibid., p. 82: 'One principal foundation of moral praise being supposed to lie in the usefulness of any quality or action; it is evident, that *reason* must enter for a considerable share in all decisions of this kind; since nothing but that faculty can instruct us in the tendency of qualities and actions, and point out their beneficial consequences to society and to their possessor.'

57. Hume, *Enquiry*, p. 6; emphasis added. Cf. Sidgwick: 'it is an essential characteristic of a moral feeling that it is bound up with an apparent cognition of something more than mere feeling' (Sidgwick, *Ethics*, p. 63).

58. Hume, *Enquiry*, p. 85.

affording shelter to wolves and serpents . . . what praise is implied in the simple epithet *useful*! What reproach in the contrary!'[59] The later eighteenth-century vogue for the sublime and the picturesque suggests that in this passage Hume may not have taken the full measure of the range of natural objects, even amongst his contemporaries, from which the human aesthetic sense can derive pleasure.[60]

Hume nevertheless shows great imagination and argumentative finesse in tracing the moral aspects of our ideas of justice, of property, and of sexual morality back to the key principle of utility.[61] But he is also keen to separate his idea of the utility that informs our moral sense from any narrow avidity for what we find personally gratifying:

> Usefulness is agreeable, and engages our approbation. This is a matter of fact, confirmed by daily observation. But, *useful*? For what? For some body's interest, surely. Whose interest then? Not our own only: For our approbation frequently extends farther. It must, therefore, be the interest of those, who are served by the character or action approved of; and these we may conclude, however remote, are not totally indifferent to us. By

59. Hume, *Enquiry*, p. 10.

60. And, conversely, cf. Sidgwick: 'many useful things we do not think beautiful' (Sidgwick, *Ethics*, p. 99).

61. Justice (Hume, *Enquiry*, p. 13): 'public utility is the *sole* origin of justice, and that reflections on the beneficial consequences of this virtue are the *sole* foundation of its merit.' Cf. also ibid., p. 27, and the following passage from 'Of Passive Obedience': 'When the execution of justice would be attended with very pernicious consequences, that virtue must be suspended, and give place to public utility, in such extraordinary and such pressing emergencies. The maxim, *fiat Justitia & ruat Cœlum*, let justice be performed, though the universe be destroyed, is apparently false, and by sacrificing the end to the means, shews a preposterous idea of the subordination of duties. What governor of a town makes any scruple of burning the suburbs, when they facilitate the approaches of the enemy? Or what general abstains from plundering a neutral country, when the necessities of war require it, and he cannot otherwise subsist his army?' (Hume, *Essays*, p. 489). Property (Hume, *Enquiry*, p. 16): 'the ideas of property become necessary in all civil society: Hence justice derives its usefulness to the public: And hence alone arises its merit and moral obligation.' Sexual morality (Hume, *Enquiry*, p. 30). One might think, however, that there was a public utility in the vulgar belief in the principle of 'fiat iustitia & ruat cœlum'. The useful habit of abiding by law in the general populace might be strengthened were they to believe that justice was administered without regard to consequences (which they might acutely suspect were the special interests of the rich and powerful in disguise).

> opening up this principle, we shall discover one great source of moral distinctions.[62]

Hume then reviews the earlier sceptical ethical tradition that resolved all apparently altruistic behaviour into modifications of the deeper principle of self-love but rejects it: 'we must renounce the theory, which accounts for every moral sentiment by the principle of self-love.'[63]

With egoism rejected, the way is clear for Hume to place utility at the centre of our moral life in all its various aspects:

> It appears to be matter of fact, that the circumstance of *utility*, in all subjects, is a source of praise and approbation: That it is constantly appealed to in all moral decisions concerning the merit and demerit of actions: That it is the *sole* source of that high regard paid to justice, fidelity, honour, allegiance, and chastity: That it is inseparable from all the other social virtues, humanity, generosity, charity, affability, lenity, mercy, and moderation: And, in a word, that it is a foundation of the chief part of morals, which has a reference to mankind and our fellow-creatures.[64]

And so it follows that the *utile* is expanded into a general benevolence: 'in our general approbation of characters and manners, the useful tendency of the social virtues moves us not by any regards to self-interest, but has a tendency much more universal and extensive.'[65] The existence of moral sympathy is demonstrated by the fact that 'qualities, which tend only to the utility of their possessor, without any reference to us, or to the community, are yet esteemed and valued'.[66] It is on the fact of sympathy that Hume's expansion of the *utile* into a general benevolence turns.

Thus, in Hume's moral thought the *utile* becomes virtually co-extensive with the purest altruism. One can see this either as the conquest of the *honestum* by the *utile* or as the tribute that the *utile* is obliged to pay to the *honestum*. Either way, the impossibility of finally doing away with either of those principles is re-affirmed by, and enacted within, Hume's moral philosophy.

62. Hume, *Enquiry*, p. 37.
63. Hume, *Enquiry*, p. 37.
64. Hume, *Enquiry*, p. 45. Note Sidgwick's endorsement (Sidgwick, *Ethics*, pp. 97 and 453).
65. Hume, *Enquiry*, p. 45.
66. Hume, *Enquiry*, p. 54.

Hume claimed that his idea of virtue required of its devotees only 'just calculation, and a steady preference of the greater happiness.'[67] Those words 'the greater happiness', as they fall on our ears at least, point forward to the utilitarians of the nineteenth century and their 'cumbrous phrase' the 'greatest happiness of the greatest number'.[68] Bentham was the principal originator of this school of moral philosophy, but (as later thinkers such as John Rawls have observed)[69] utilitarianism as a creed is more conveniently studied in the works of those who followed Bentham and who clarified utilitarianism's doctrinal precepts. I will consider in the first place (and very briefly) John Stuart Mill and secondly (and with interesting complications) Henry Sidgwick.

Mill's *Utilitarianism* (1863) begins with some extremely acute criticisms of Kant's moral philosophy, to which we will turn shortly when we consider Kant's brilliant critique of the tradition of moral philosophy which he himself had inherited. Concerning the positive arguments that Mill advances in *Utilitarianism*, I have only a few, very short, observations to make. In the first place, we should note that Mill follows Hume in expanding the principle of utility so that it encompasses a general benevolence. Mill devotes considerable time and care to separating utility from mere, or selfish, expediency.[70] The point of this separation of the utility that Mill feels should be the object of our moral actions from selfish expediency is that it allows him to characterise utilitarianism as a form of universal hedonism: 'the happiness which forms the utilitarian standard of what is right in conduct, is not the agent's own happiness, but that of all concerned.'[71] But there is also a turbulence in Mill's philosophy towards which he himself appears to direct us when he comments approvingly on 'doctrines which recognise as a fact in morals the existence of conflicting considerations; which all doctrines do, that have been believed by sane persons.'[72] For in Mill's own case, we can see once more the endless tug between the *utile* and the *honestum*. While Mill's subscription to universal hedonism shows (as it did also in Hume) the gravitational pull exerted by the *honestum* over a philosophy

67. Hume, *Enquiry*, p. 79.

68. The disparaging adjective is Henry Sidgwick's (Sidgwick, *Ethics*, p. viii).

69. 'I shall take Henry Sidgwick's *The Methods of Ethics*, 7th ed. (London, 1907), as summarizing the development of utilitarian moral theory' (Rawls, *Justice*, p. 20, n. 9).

70. Mill, *Utilitarianism*, pp. 31–33.

71. Mill, *Utilitarianism*, p. 24.

72. Mill, *Utilitarianism*, p. 36.

which proclaims that its principal loyalty has been given to the *utile*, Mill's concluding analysis of justice as a province in the 'field of General Expediency,' which culminates in the generalisation that 'all cases of justice are also cases of expediency,' demonstrates the secure, but counter-vailing, anchoring of his moral thinking in the *utile*.[73]

Henry Sidgwick is often taken to be a utilitarian (for instance, by John Rawls, as we have seen).[74] But this is not how Sidgwick himself viewed the tendency of his work. Rather, Sidgwick thought that the achievement of *The Methods of Ethics* (first published, 1874; 7th ed., 1907) was that its arguments transcended 'the commonly received antithesis between Intuitionists and Utilitarians.'[75] Why did Sidgwick believe that he had achieved this? Sidgwick had traced the implications of the intuitionist Kant's duty of benevolence and found that finally these implications converged with the purest utilitarianism:

> He [Kant] regards it as evident *à priori* that each rational agent is bound to aim at the happiness of all other rational beings no less than its own: nay, in his view, it can only be stated as *duty* for me to seek my happiness in so far as I consider it a part of Universal Happiness.
>
> Here then we have arrived, in our search for really clear and certain ethical intuitions, at the fundamental maxim of Utilitarianism.[76]

Accordingly, for Sidgwick, 'Utilitarianism thus appears as the final form into which a really scientific Intuitionism tends to pass,' and 'the Intuitional method rigorously applied yields as its final result the doctrine of pure Universalistic Hedonism.'[77] Intuitionists, such as Kant, emerge in Sidgwick's account as unconscious utilitarians, struggling against the principles on which their own philosophy ultimately depends: 'the present argument does not aim at proving an exact coincidence between Utilitarian inferences and the intuitions of

73. Mill, *Utilitarianism*, pp. 62 and 94.

74. Above, p. 313, n. 69.

75. Sidgwick, *Ethics*, p. xii. By 'Intuitionists', Sidgwick refers to those, such as Kant, who believe that 'certain kinds of conduct are prescribed absolutely, without reference to their ulterior consequences' (ibid., p. 287); and Intuitionism as a philosophy Sidgwick defines as 'the complete observance of certain absolute rules of Duty, intuitively known' and as 'the method which recognises rightness as a quality belonging to actions independently of their conduciveness to any ulterior end' (ibid., pp. 9 and 85).

76. Sidgwick, *Ethics*, p. 360.

77. Sidgwick, *Ethics*, pp. 361 and 373.

Common Sense, but rather seeks to represent the latter as inchoately and imperfectly Utilitarian.'[78] Sidgwick's conclusion is clear: 'We have found that the common antithesis between Intuitionists and Utilitarians must be entirely discarded: since such abstract moral principles as we can admit to be really self-evident are not only not incompatible with a Utilitarian system, but even seem required to furnish a rational basis for such a system.'[79]

Sidgwick argues in a similar way concerning moral sense or commonsense ethics. In these moral theories, too, he discovers a 'latent Utilitarianism' operative, to the point where he can speak of 'the unconscious Utilitarianism of Common Sense' and of 'the general Utilitarian basis of the Morality of Common Sense', concluding that 'there seems to be no fundamental difference between Utilitarianism and Common Sense. The Utilitarian only performs somewhat more consistently and systematically the reasoning processes which are generally admitted to be properly decisive of the questions that this pursuit raises.'[80] Sidgwick's point is to emphasise that neither intuitionism nor moral, or common, sense gets us further forward in our quest for an adequate moral philosophy than does utilitarianism. He shows repeatedly how intuitionist and commonsense arguments result in a position that can be characterised as utilitarian (even though they are of course not presented in such terms by those who advance them). Thus, to some extent it is correct to say (as Sidgwick himself says) that *The Methods of Ethics* offers a synthesis of utilitarianism and intuitionism in that it repeatedly shows how the precepts of those two philosophical schools converge. But it would be closer to the truth to say that Sidgwick hopes to show that utilitarianism *comprises* both intuitionism and moral or commonsense ethics. To that extent, it may be more true to say (as was said for many years) that *The Methods of Ethics* is a demonstration of the superiority of utilitarianism, understood as universal hedonism, over all its philosophical rivals.

Even though Sidgwick's eirenic language of convergence and reconciliation might be better described as a language of stealthy conquest, in one respect at least his comprehensive understanding of the general field of ethics from antiquity onwards does give his work a distinctive quality. Although it seems to me that, finally, Sidgwick is an advocate for utilitarianism, he nevertheless is no blinkered combatant. He understands that our human nature resonates, to

78. Sidgwick, *Ethics*, p. 395.

79. Sidgwick, *Ethics*, p. 456.

80. Sidgwick, *Ethics*, pp. 406, 421, 424, and 437. Cf. also ibid., p. 392.

differing degrees and at various moments, to *all* the various ethical theories that have over the centuries been put forward. Egoism or Epicureanism, intuitionism, common or moral sense, and the various shades of hedonism that have at different times supported utilitarianism—all these different philosophical schools respond to, and find an echo in, the different elements in our complex human nature. Otherwise, they would never have been advanced in the first place:

> All moral principles that have ever been put forward . . . find a response in our nature: their fundamental assumptions are all such as we are disposed to accept, and such as we find to govern to a certain extent our habitual conduct. . . . We admit the necessity, when they conflict, of making this choice, and that it is irrational to let sometimes one principle prevail and sometimes another; but the necessity is a painful one.[81]

The practical consequence of this is that a 'loose combination or confusion of methods is the most common type of actual moral reasoning.'[82] And this state of confusion may even be desirable: 'it may be best on the whole that there should be conflicting codes of morality in a given society at a certain stage of its development.'[83] Different areas of human life demand ethical systems of different complexions: 'Utilitarianism seems to be commonly accepted in Politics to a much greater extent than it is in the sphere of private conduct: many who recognize absolute rules of private duty, to be obeyed without regard to consequences, still hold that it is a question of expediency what actions and abstinences morally right or allowable should be made compulsory under legal penalties; and similarly that the right form of government for any society is to be determined on grounds of expediency only.'[84] In the case of Sidgwick's own philosophy, this amalgam of discrepant codes expresses itself (as Thomas Baldwin has observed) in his 'observation that a utilitarian account of obligation, which he endorsed, needs to be supplemented by an intuitionist specification of the ideal ends of action.'[85]

It is at this late stage of the argument that the conventional precepts of morality, embodied in our customary sense of the *honestum*, return to the

81. Sidgwick, *Ethics*, p. 12.
82. Sidgwick, *Ethics*, p. 91.
83. Sidgwick, *Ethics*, p. 450.
84. Sidgwick, *Ethics*, p. 18.
85. Thomas Baldwin, 'Introduction', in Moore, *Principia*, p. xiv.

centre of Sidgwick's argument, dressed as familiar intuitionist notions of the ends of moral action. Sidgwick is careful to suggest that utilitarianism implies no sharp break with the existing fabric of our moral behaviour: 'It should be observed, however, that a great part of the reform in popular morality, which a consistent Utilitarian will try to introduce, will probably lie not so much in establishing new rules (whether conflicting with the old or merely supplementary) as in enforcing old ones.' Utilitarianism thus demands no root and branch overhaul of our moral conduct, only a clearer understanding of the abiding considerations that have immemorially shaped that conduct: 'we do not require the promulgation of any new moral doctrine, but merely a bracing and sharpening of the moral sentiments of society, to bring them into harmony with the greater comprehensiveness of view and the more impartial concern for human happiness which characterize the Utilitarian system.'[86] We shall see this again in the thought of Kant and John Rawls. Like the moral theories of Kant and Rawls, Sidgwick's philosophy resembles a chimera, in which the monstrous hinder parts are the result of a radical critique of existing philosophical systems executed in a spirit of pitiless utilitarianism, but the head and forequarters present to us the docile appearance of the moral values and practices to which we are accustomed—the *honestum* in its most comfortable form.

We have traced the tradition of moral thought, in which the *utile* is ostensibly elevated above the *honestum*, from Machiavelli to Sidgwick. We must now turn to the rival tradition, in which the *utile* is ostensibly rejected in favour of the *honestum*, as it is represented in the thought of Kant and John Rawls, by way of an interesting diversion to take in the subtle (but no less conflicted) ethics of G. E. Moore. And just as in the former tradition we saw that the principle of the *honestum* could not be entirely extirpated but continued to exercise a gravitational pull over the argument, so we will see in the latter that the *utile*, though often disparaged and even at moments dismissed with contempt, proves impossible thoroughly to uproot.

Kant's moral philosophy can be sampled in two works published over ten years apart: the *Groundwork of the Metaphysics of Morals* (1785) and its later counterpart, *Metaphysics of Morals* (1797).[87]

86. Sidgwick, *Ethics*, p. 444.

87. Immanuel Kant, *Grundlegung zur Metaphysik der Sitten* (Riga, 1785); Immanuel Kant, *Die Metaphysik der Sitten* (Königsberg, 1797).

The *Groundwork of the Metaphysics of Morals* was written in a spirit of adamant hostility to the prevailing ethical conversation in western Europe. As we have seen, Hume's moral philosophy was avowedly empirical, being premised on the conviction that nowadays men will 'hearken to no arguments but those which are derived from experience.'[88] The moral philosophy of Hume's friend Adam Smith, although it varied from Hume's ideas in a number of important particulars, was similarly empirical in its mode of proceeding. Kant, however, sweeps this entire empirical tradition aside. His own work aspires to unravel 'the concept of morality generally in vogue', which he characterises as 'a disgusting mish-mash of gleaned observations and half-rationalizing principles, which dreary pates savor because it is quite useful for everyday chatter, while men of insight feel confused, and discontented.'[89] For this popular philosophy, which he dismisses contemptuously as a mere 'groping by means of examples', Kant has no time.[90]

Kant's own moral philosophy, by contrast, will be 'carefully cleansed of everything empirical.'[91] The unworthiness of empiricism and example to influence our moral philosophy is a point to which Kant returns many times in this quite short text to enforce his view that moral imperatives 'cannot be made out by any example, and hence empirically':

> Imitation has no place at all in moral matters, and examples serve for encouragement only, i.e. they put beyond doubt the feasibility of what the law commands, they make intuitive what the practical rule expresses more generally, but they can never entitle us to set aside their true original, which lies in reason, and to go by examples.
>
> . . . The principles of morality . . . are to be found completely a priori, free from all that is empirical, simply in pure rational concepts and nowhere else, not even in the least part. . . .
>
> . . . All moral concepts have their seat and origin completely a priori in reason, and indeed in the commonest human reason. . . .
>
> Thus everything that is empirical is not only quite unfit to be added to the principle of morality, it is also most disadvantageous to the purity of morals themselves, in which the actual worth of a will absolutely good and

88. Hume, *Enquiry*, p. 7.
89. Kant, *Groundwork*, pp. 55 and 24.
90. Kant, *Groundwork*, p. 26.
91. Kant, *Groundwork*, p. 4.

elevated above any price consists precisely in this: that the principle of action is free from all influences of contingent grounds, which only experience can furnish.

Empirical principles are not fit to be the foundation of moral laws at all.[92]

Kant's rejection of experience allows him to re-conceptualise moral law, and in the process to separate it from practical maxims of conduct. The former is the product of pure reason, while the latter are shaped by experience.[93] For Kant, only those actions performed out of a sense of consciously and rationally apprehended duty are truly moral; and he defines duty as '*the necessity of an action from respect for the law*'.[94]

Kant then proceeds to spell out the implications of this metaphysical stance in two famous formulations. The first formulation describes a formal property of moral rules, namely, that they should be capable of being universalised without generating awkward or disabling contradictions. This is the so-called 'categorical imperative': 'There is therefore only a single categorical imperative, and it is this: *act only according to that maxim through which you can at the same time will that it become a universal law*.'[95] The second formulation prescribes the stance that rational moral agents should adopt towards other rational moral agents (the 'formula of humanity'): '*A rational nature exists as an end in itself*. . . . The practical imperative will thus be the following: *So act that you use humanity, in your own person as well as in the person of any other, always at the same time as an end, never merely as a means*.'[96] Kant then goes on to indicate how these two formulations are interdependent: 'every rational being, as an end in itself, must be able to view itself as at the same time universally legislating with regard to any law whatsoever to which it may be subject, because it is just this fittingness of its maxims for universal legislation that marks it out as an end in itself'.[97]

92. Kant, *Groundwork*, pp. 32, 23, 24, 25, 38, 53.

93. Kant, *Groundwork*, p. 5.

94. Kant, *Groundwork*, p. 16.

95. Kant, *Groundwork*, p. 34. Cf. also ibid., p. 17: 'I ought never to proceed except in such a way *that I could also will that my maxim should become a universal law*.'

96. Kant, *Groundwork*, p. 41; cf. ibid., p. 11.

97. Kant, *Groundwork*, p. 49. Cf. also Kant, *Metaphysics*, p. 168: 'The supreme principle of the doctrine of virtue is: act in accordance with a maxim of *ends* that it can be a universal law for everyone to have.—In accordance with this principle a human being is an end for himself as well as for others, and it is not enough that he is not authorized to use either himself or others

These formulations are severe, lofty, and (in all senses of the word) idealistic. In their denial that the categorical imperative can be derived from 'some *particular property of human nature*', they firmly shut the door in the face of the moral sense school, whose most recent spokesmen had been Hume and Adam Smith.[98] For, according to Kant, what merit is there in simply following the inclination of your nature? In Kant's eyes, moral sense philosophy runs the risk of reducing the moral law to reflexive self-gratification, like scratching an itch.[99] Even if good things arise from such reflexive actions, even if they are in themselves identical with the actions that a truly moral person would perform, they nevertheless fall short of being in the fullest sense moral: 'though much may be done that *conforms* with what *duty* commands, still it is always doubtful whether it is actually done *from duty* and thus has a moral worth.'[100]

Kant's views of moral philosophy are similarly incompatible with any kind of consequentialism: 'Now, to be truthful from duty is something quite different from being truthful from dread of adverse consequences; as in the first case, the concept of the action in itself already contains a law for me, whereas in the second I must first look around elsewhere to see what effects on me this might involve.'[101] For Kant, any attention towards consequences is just a distraction, and moreover a potentially fatal distraction, because to fall into consequentialism may tempt us further into what Kant shrewdly identifies as the most common source of human moral failings, namely, our tendency to hunt for comfortable exceptions to the austere and impersonal stringencies of the moral law.[102] Kant wants us, as moral beings, to focus on the 'form and principle' which dictates a moral action, not on what may or may not happen as a result of performing it: '[The categorical imperative] concerns not the matter of the action or what is to result from it, but the form and principle from which it does itself follow; and the essential good in it consists in the disposition, let

merely as means (since he could then still be indifferent to them); it is in itself his duty to make the human being as such his end.'

98. Kant, *Groundwork*, p. 37.

99. For Kant, the problem with moral sense philosophy, and indeed with all ethics that possesses no metaphysical grounding, is that it is 'not dictated by reason but would be taken to be a duty only instinctively, and hence blindly' (Kant, *Metaphysics*, p. 152).

100. Kant, *Groundwork*, p. 21.

101. Kant, *Groundwork*, p. 18. Cf. ibid., p. 28: 'The categorical imperative would be the one that represented an action as objectively necessary by itself, without reference to another end.'

102. Kant, *Groundwork*, pp. 36–37.

the result be what it may.'[103] 'Let the result be what it may'—this is surely a silent *riposte* to Hume's critique of the classical maxim 'fiat iustitia et ruat coelum': 'The maxim, *fiat Justitia & ruat Cœlum,* let justice be performed, though the universe be destroyed, is apparently false, and by sacrificing the end to the means, shews a preposterous idea of the subordination of duties.'[104] For Kant, the moral law must be quarantined from counsels of prudence.[105]

Furthermore, the principle of hedonism, whether egoistic or universal, is also for Kant a snare and a delusion:

> We do find that the more a cultivated reason engages with the purpose of enjoying life and with happiness, so much the further does a human being stray from true contentment; and from this there arises in many, and indeed in those who are most experienced in its use, if only they are sincere enough to admit, a certain degree of *misology,* i.e. hatred of reason.[106]

Not only is the achievement of happiness not the true goal of moral action, but to focus on the attainment of happiness may have the further unfortunate effect of alienating us from reason and hence making it harder for us to perceive and follow the true (and reason-dictated) moral law. Hedonism poisons the well of moral action.

Surely never before in the history of philosophy had the *honestum* been so extolled, the *utile* so banished and abjected. These are exhilarating, radical, even at moments utopian arguments.[107] They whet our appetite for the next stage in the explanation of Kant's moral philosophy, when he will make what he calls a turn to 'anthropology' and will derive maxims of practical conduct from this metaphysics.[108] Given what Kant has told us about the deceptive appearances that abound in the field of human moral action ('though much may be done that *conforms* with what *duty* commands, still it is always doubtful whether it is actually done *from duty* and thus has a moral worth'), we naturally

103. Kant, *Groundwork,* p. 30.

104. David Hume, 'Of Passive Obedience', in Hume, *Essays,* p. 489. For Moore's comments on this classical maxim, see Moore, *Principia,* p. 197.

105. Kant, *Groundwork,* p. 32.

106. Kant, *Groundwork,* p. 11.

107. Kant's utopianism is detectable in his rejection of empiricism and blossoms towards the end of the *Groundwork* when Kant introduces the concept of the ideal 'kingdom of ends' (Kant, *Groundwork,* pp. 45 and 71). Cf. also ibid., p. 50: 'every rational being must so act as if through its maxims it were at all times a legislating member of the universal kingdom of ends'.

108. Kant, *Groundwork,* p. 26.

expect that this morality will embody a thorough overhauling of our customary maxims, just as Kant has wrought creative devastation in the realm of the metaphysics of moral philosophy.[109]

Kant executed this anthropological turn twelve years later, in his *Metaphysics of Morals* (1797), where he repeats his point that 'a metaphysics of morals cannot be based upon anthropology but can still be applied to it.'[110] The opening sections of this longer and more complicated text are devoted to creating a measure of continuity with the positions staked out in the earlier *Groundwork of the Metaphysics of Morals* (1785). So Kant re-states the formulations of the categorical imperative and the 'formula of humanity' which are familiar to us from the earlier work.[111] He reminds us of the nullity of the moral sense school of philosophy and insists once more on the rational, rather than empirical or affective, basis of the moral law.[112]

However, it is in the very execution of the anthropological turn (that is, in the application of Kant's *a priori* insights to practical conduct) that problems arise. For Kant erects a very familiar and indeed conventional morality on the foundations of what is, even in his own estimation, a revolutionary *a priori* basis.[113] Consider, for instance, Kant's defences of a completely traditional sexual morality or of the existing, very restricted, political franchise, or his denial of a popular right to resist oppressive authority, or his support of the death penalty for even offences less grave than murder, or his adamant resistance to constitutional change.[114] At moments such as these we can sense

109. Kant, *Groundwork*, p. 21.

110. Kant, *Metaphysics*, pp. 13 and 32. Cf. Kant, *Groundwork*, p. 26.

111. Kant, *Metaphysics*, p. 21. On their relation, see Kant, *Metaphysics*, p. 168.

112. Kant, *Metaphysics*, pp. 23 and 26.

113. See Kant's own remarks in the preface to the second, 1787, edition of the *Critique of Pure Reason* suggesting some analogy between his innovations in moral philosophy and the innovations of Copernicus in cosmology: 'Hence let us once try whether we do not get farther with the problems of metaphysics by assuming that the objects must conform to our cognition, which would agree better with the requested possibility of an *a priori* cognition of them, which is to establish something about objects before they are given to us. This would be just like the first thoughts of Copernicus, who, when he did not make good progress in the explanation of the celestial motions if he assumed that the entire celestial host revolves around the observer, tried to see if he might not have greater success if he made the observer revolve and left the stars at rest' (Kant, *Critique*, p. 110). Cf. Norwood Russell Hanson, 'Copernicus' Role in Kant's Revolution', *Journal of the History of Ideas* 20, no. 2 (1959): 274–81.

114. Sexual morality: Kant, *Metaphysics*, pp. 67–68 and 191–93. The existing franchise: ibid., p. 100. Denial of the right of resistance: ibid., p. 105. Death penalty: ibid., p. 116 (and note the contemptuous treatment of Beccaria, ibid., p. 117). Constitutional change: ibid., p. 121.

the hand of the man raised in conditions of modest pietism in northern Prussia guiding the pen and directing the arguments of his alter ego, the rational philosopher. And, as the Prussian pietist exerts this powerful but silent influence, in the same moment the *utile*, banished with such contumely from the realm of moral philosophy in the *Groundwork of the Metaphysics of Morals*, makes its stealthy and customary return and resumes its position alongside the conceptual companion from whom yet again it has proved impossible finally to separate it: namely, the *honestum*.[115] It is for this reason that Kant's moral philosophy, in which the *utile* is banished at the outset, is both so inspiring and so pointless. An audacious metaphysics is harnessed, once the descent to what Kant dismissively calls 'anthropology' has been made, to the most conforming, and in certain respects repressive, set of practical rules for living.[116] This is surely a very anti-climactic outcome for a philosophical endeavour that announced itself as a cleansing of the Augean stables of Enlightenment moral philosophy. Kant seems to have fallen into the trap that Sidgwick said awaited the intuitionist, namely, that of failing to distinguish 'real intuitions of rightness from the blind sense of obligation arising out of mere custom.'[117]

To follow this swift survey of Kant's moral philosophy with an examination of G. E. Moore's *Principia Ethica* is to be reminded of how common it is for philosophers to lack insight into their own work, even though this is the work that they might be supposed to know best. For, although Moore treats Kant with affectionate condescension, we will see that the argumentative structure of *Principia Ethica* is in fact a mirror image (i.e., identical but inverted) of Kant's; and furthermore, we will see that this unacknowledged proximity to Kant's work is bound up with the particular form that the recurrent inextricability of the *utile* and the *honestum* takes in Moore's philosophy.

Like Sidgwick, Moore begins *Principia Ethica* by surveying the inadequacies of the various schools of ethical philosophy that have hitherto found advocates, in order to clear the ground for the aesthetic egoism in which his ethical philosophy will, notoriously, conclude.[118] But this opening survey is no

115. Cf. Sidgwick: 'even moralists . . . who are most strongly opposed to Utilitarianism have, in attempting to exhibit the "necessity" of moral rules, been led to dwell on utilitarian considerations' (Sidgwick, *Ethics*, p. 74).

116. Cf. Roger Scruton: 'Kant's passionate defence of his passionless morality is one of the marvels of philosophy, deriving the finest psychological distinctions and the highest aspirations with an equal logic from the idea of an impartial and emotionless law' (Scruton, *Parsifal*, p. 112).

117. Sidgwick, *Ethics*, p. 216.

118. E.g., 'By far the most valuable things, which we know or can imagine, are certain states of consciousness, which may be roughly described as the pleasures of human intercourse and the

disinterested consideration of the field, since Moore's review of the various ethical systems available to him is in fact a series of implicit defences of what will emerge as the central contention of his own moral philosophy, namely, that the good (towards which moral action should tend) is undefinable. The good, according to Moore, is not the same as the natural, not the same as evolution, not the same as pleasure, and certainly not the same as utility.

Moore treats two ethical systems with particular asperity: that of Kant and that of the utilitarians (here represented by J. S. Mill). In the case of Kant, Moore dismisses Kant's decision 'to base Ethics on Metaphysics', asserting that this is 'solely due to confusion.'[119] He rejects Kant's view that the moral law is an imperative (namely, that 'this ought to be' means 'this is commanded').[120] And the text of *Principia Ethica* is peppered with incidental sniping remarks at Kant's expense.[121] As Thomas Baldwin says, 'In his early writings, the philosopher whom he [Moore] criticises most strenuously, and yet takes most seriously, is Kant; Moore develops his own ethical theory (and his early metaphysics) precisely by making up his mind about where Kant was mistaken.'[122]

Baldwin's genealogical account of the relationship between Kant's philosophy and that of Moore, satisfactory as it may be in its own terms, nevertheless leaves an important question unposed: namely, what can explain the particular *animus* that Moore seems to have towards Kant? We perhaps find a clue in Moore's attacks on what he calls the 'naturalist fallacy' (i.e., the view that the good is an analytic concept that may be resolved into something more fundamental, such as pleasure or utility). For Moore, on the other hand, 'Anything which is good as an end must be admitted to be good without proof.'[123] And this position to some extent pushes him into the arms, and requires him to use

---

enjoyment of beautiful objects. . . . It is only for the sake of these things—in order that as much of them as possible may at some time exist—that any one can be justified in performing any public or private duty; . . . they are the *raison d'être* of virtue; . . . it is they—these complex wholes *themselves*, and not any constituent or characteristic of them—that form the rational ultimate end of human action and the sole criterion of social progress: these appear to be truths which have been generally overlooked. . . . Personal affections and aesthetic enjoyments include *all* the greatest, and *by far* the greatest, goods we can imagine' (Moore, *Principia*, pp. 237–38).

119. Moore, *Principia*, p. 169.

120. Moore, *Principia*, p. 178.

121. E.g., Moore, *Principia*, p. 223.

122. Baldwin, 'Introduction', in Moore, *Principia*, pp. xxxvi–xxxvii.

123. Moore, *Principia*, p. 117.

the distinctive language, of Kant: 'it follows from the meaning of good and bad, that such propositions are all of them, in Kant's phrase, "synthetic": they all must rest in the end upon some proposition which must be simply accepted or rejected, which cannot be logically deduced from any other proposition.'[124] However, Moore's exploration of the synthetic nature of the good develops in a direction that would have appalled Kant. For upon that insight Moore erects what looks like the most thorough-going moral scepticism: 'No sufficient reason has ever yet been found for considering one action more right or more wrong than another.'[125] This startling assertion turns, as will be immediately understood, on the very high bar that is implicitly set by the phrase 'sufficient reason'. Nevertheless, one can see how statements such as these (which may be unassailably true at the level of philosophical technique), if placed before the un-adept, could seem to open the door to a complete, antinomian, freedom of conduct. (Though it must be admitted that the likelihood of someone so intellectually vulnerable picking up *Principia Ethica* and fighting their way through its argumentative thickets to reach and awaken the sleeping beauty of these sceptical formulations is not a prospect that should keep us awake at night.) But even amongst those with strong enough minds to take the measure of Moore's philosophy, these conclusions will surely tend to make our attachment to the precepts of conventional morality thinner—more a matter of a provisional compliance that might easily (or even lightly) be withdrawn, rather than of an irrefragable duty. Nor does Moore soft-pedal the tendency of his exposition. Rather, he seems to take pleasure in depicting its implications in the most alarming language: 'We can secure no title to assert that obedience to such commands as "Thou shalt not lie," or even "Thou shalt do no murder," is *universally* better than the alternatives of lying and murder.'[126] The reasons Moore offers for this scepticism can be characterised as a kind of hyper-consequentialism:

> It is plain, then, that we are not soon likely to know more than that one kind of action will *generally* produce better effects than another; and that more than this has certainly never been proved. In no two cases will *all* the effects of any kind of action be precisely the same, because in each case some of the circumstances will differ; and although the effects, that are important

124. Moore, *Principia*, p. 193.
125. Moore, *Principia*, pp. 201–2.
126. Moore, *Principia*, p. 204.

> for good or evil, may be generally the same, it is extremely unlikely that they will always be so.[127]

It follows that established moral rules enjoy no impregnable authority: 'Since, as I have tried to shew, it is impossible to establish that any kind of action will produce a better total result than its alternative *in all cases*, it follows that in some cases the neglect of an established rule will probably be the best course of action possible.'[128]

Yet it is surely very surprising to find Moore drawing on consequentialist arguments, since earlier in the *Principia Ethica*, he has shown almost as little patience with utilitarianism as with Kant. Moore dismisses Mill's philosophy as 'contemptible nonsense' and sneers at the broad acceptability of utilitarianism's guidance for the practical conduct of life as just a kind of lucky shot:

> It may well be that the *practical* conclusions at which Utilitarians do arrive, and even those at which they ought logically to arrive, are not far from the truth. But in so far as their *reason* for holding these conclusions to be true is that "Pleasure alone is good as an end," they are *absolutely* wrong: and it is with *reasons* that we are chiefly concerned in any scientific Ethics. . . .
>
> The most that can be said for it [Utilitarianism] is that it does not seriously mislead in its practical conclusions, on the ground that, as an

127. Moore, *Principia*, p. 205.

128. Moore, *Principia*, p. 211. Note, however, on the following page Moore's cautious drawing back from this position: 'Our judgment will generally be biassed by the fact that we strongly desire one of the results which we hope to obtain by breaking the rule. It seems, then, that with regard to any rule which is *generally* useful, we may assert that it ought *always* to be observed, not on the ground that in *every* particular case it will be useful, but on the ground that in *any* particular case the probability of its being so is greater than that of our being like to decide rightly that we have before us an instance of its disutility. In short, though we may be sure that there are cases where the rule should be broken, we can never know which those cases are, and ought, therefore, never to break it' (ibid., p. 212). By then, however, the ethical damage has already occurred. Cf. the comments of Thomas Baldwin on this move from scepticism to conformity in Moore's philosophy: '[Moore] argues, concerning most of the rules of conventional morality, "On any view commonly taken, it seems certain that the preservation of civilised society, which these rules are necessary to effect, is necessary for the existence, in any great degree, of anything which may be held to be good in itself" (§ 95). So Moore moves from a sweeping moral scepticism to a rather unquestioning moral conservatism; the line of thought is paradoxical, though not unfamiliar in the sceptical tradition' (Baldwin, 'Introduction', in Moore, *Principia*, p. xxviii).

> empirical fact, the method of acting which brings most good on the whole does also bring most pleasure.[129]

However, these critiques of utilitarianism camouflage the presence of consequentialism at the heart of Moore's philosophy. As Baldwin has observed, 'It may be felt that . . . an important ethical presumption has slipped in, namely a utilitarian account of obligation, which threatens to restrict the scope of Moore's thesis concerning the unanalysability of ethical value to utilitarian theories. . . . There is no doubt that Moore himself conducts his discussion within a broadly utilitarian perspective.'[130] Once one has been sensitized to their existence, one sees that statements of a consequentialist complexion abound in *Principia Ethica*:

> In short, to assert that a certain line of conduct is, at a given time, absolutely right or obligatory, is obviously to assert that more good or less evil will exist in the world, if it be adopted than if anything else be done instead.
>
> By what means shall we be able to make what exists in the world as good as possible?
>
> In any actual choice we should have to consider the possible effects of our action upon conscious beings.
>
> Metaphysics, then, will have a bearing upon practical Ethics—upon the question what we ought to do—if it can tell us anything about the future consequences of our actions beyond what can be established by ordinary inductive reasoning.
>
> To ask what kind of actions we ought to perform, or what kind of conduct is right, is to ask what kind of effects such action and conduct will produce. . . . All moral laws, I wish to shew, are merely statements that certain kinds of actions will have good effects.
>
> Our 'duty,' therefore, can only be defined as that action, which will cause more good to exist in the Universe than any possible alternative.[131]

129. Moore, *Principia*, pp. 123, 141, and 159.

130. Baldwin, 'Introduction', in Moore, *Principia*, p. xvii. Cf. ibid., p. xxvi: 'Moore's account of obligation is fundamentally utilitarian (or "consequentialist"): in any situation, the action which will produce the best state of the universe is that which we *ought* to perform (or is the *right* action, or is our *duty*—Moore does not distinguish between these concepts).'

131. Moore, *Principia*, pp. 77, 89, 135, 168, 196, and 198.

In part, the antinomian poses struck by Moore were surely provocative acts of self-individuation from the sanctimonious morality of the Victorian age. (It is no wonder that Lytton Strachey, that flail of the Victorians, was such an enthusiast for Moore's philosophy; and this may also explain Moore's sharp and, one might think, ungrateful attitude towards Sidgwick, who had been Moore's teacher and who for many years was his senior colleague in the fellowship at Trinity College, Cambridge.)[132] But eye-catching statements such as those also make Moore a curious inverse of Kant. As we have seen, the pietistic Kant allowed (with what degree of self-awareness is unclear) the consequentialism he had initially repudiated to direct his practical moral recommendations towards the conventional morality he found congenial (and, as we shall see in a moment, Rawls will repeat this Kantian conservative swerve). The aesthete Moore draws on the consequentialism he has earlier seemed to disavow in order to mount a destructive and Pyrrhonistic argument, to the effect that no practical ethical recommendation can ever be entitled to our reasonable obedience (though we may nevertheless for various prudential reasons comply with them), since the infinite consequences of any such recommendation will always exceed our ability to calculate them. Thus, *Principia Ethica* is the kind of book we can imagine Kant writing, had he enjoyed the bad (or maybe good) fortune to have been raised by an amoral aesthete, such as Huysman's Des Esseintes, rather than being brought up (as in fact he was) in the austere religious and moral traditions of northern German Protestantism.

Hence, perhaps, Moore's ungenerous criticisms of Kant: for he might easily have been uncomfortably aware of the structural common ground shared by their respective moral philosophies. And if Moore was indeed a strange *doppelgänger* of Kant, it will surprise us less to discover that in Moore's philosophy no less than in that of Kant, the *utile* and the *honestum* come together. Moore explicitly denies that the *utile* and the *honestum* can be made to quarrel with each other:

> 'The right' and 'the useful' have been supposed to be at least *capable* of conflicting with one another, and, at all events, to be essentially distinct. It has been characteristic of a certain school of moralists, as of moral common sense, to declare that the end will never justify the means. What I wish first to point out is that 'right' does and can mean nothing but 'cause of a good result,' and is thus identical with 'useful'; whence it follows that the end will

132. For Strachey's enthusiasm, see Moore, *Principia*, p. xi.

> always justify the means, and that no action which is not justified by its results can be right.[133]

Moore's argument for this familiar insistence on the identity of the *utile* and the *honestum* is, however, original. According to Moore, the traditional verbal distinction between the *utile* and the *honestum* (which, as we have seen, reaches back to Cicero) points not to any ontological difference but rather to a sluggishness in the moral constitution of men which needs to be overcome by rhetoric: 'We may then roughly distinguish "duties" from expedient actions, as actions with regard to which there is a moral sentiment, which we are often tempted to omit, and of which the most obvious effects are effects upon others than the agent.'[134] Moore then goes on to deny that the performance of duties, so defined, necessarily makes for good to a greater extent than does the performance of expedient actions: 'the question whether an action is a duty or merely expedient, is one which has no bearing on the ethical question whether we ought to do it.'[135] It follows that the 'true distinction between duties and expedient actions is not that the former are actions which it is in any sense more useful or obligatory or better to perform, but that they are actions which it is more useful to praise and to enforce by sanctions, since they are actions which there is a temptation to omit.'[136] This particular convergence of the *utile* and the *honestum* had been foreshadowed in an apparently innocent move Moore had made quite early in the *Principia*, when he had identified the good rather than the right as the object towards which moral actions should tend. For this replacement of the right by the good opened up a path that leads towards both the aestheticizing of moral action and the denial of any essential difference between the *utile* and the *honestum*.

John Rawls's *A Theory of Justice*, first published in 1971 and then revised in 1999, contains fewer than a handful of references to Moore. This is perhaps not surprising, given how little echo would have been returned to Rawls's moral earnestness by *Principia Ethica*.[137] Notwithstanding that lofty negligence, Rawls's work is beyond question the most influential work of moral philosophy of the later twentieth century. It is therefore interesting that *A Theory of Justice* is no

133. Moore, *Principia*, p. 196.

134. Moore, *Principia*, p. 218.

135. Moore, *Principia*, p. 218.

136. Moore, *Principia*, p. 219.

137. For Rawls's glancing references to Moore, see Rawls, *Justice*, pp. 30, n. 18; 35; and 287, n. 51.

more successful than are the works of any of Rawls's predecessors when it comes to untying the stubborn entanglement of the *utile* and the *honestum*.

Rawls was clear about where he thought his own work stood in relation to the philosophical conversation when he became a participant. At the outset of the book, he stated his opposition to the utilitarian tradition: 'I wanted to work out a conception of justice that provides a reasonably systematic alternative to utilitarianism, which in one form or another has long dominated the Anglo-Saxon tradition of political thought.'[138] Why did Rawls wish to push back against utilitarianism? Again, he states his reasons plainly and quickly: 'I do not believe that utilitarianism can provide a satisfactory account of the basic rights and liberties of citizens as free and equal persons, a requirement of absolutely first importance for an account of democratic institutions.'[139] A further shortcoming in utilitarianism, according to Rawls, is that it lacks 'an independent definition of the good'.[140] This lack of an ethical anchor in utilitarianism makes possible an alarming moral drift:

> Whenever a society sets out to maximize the sum of intrinsic value or the net balance of the satisfaction of interests, it is liable to find that the denial of liberty for some is justified in the name of this single end. The liberties of equal citizenship are insecure when founded upon teleological principles. The argument for them relies upon precarious calculations as well as controversial and uncertain premises.[141]

Against this, Rawls advances the anti-utilitarian position that he will be championing:

> Each person possesses an inviolability founded on justice that even the welfare of society as a whole cannot override. For this reason, justice denies that the loss of freedom for some is made right by a greater good shared by others. It does not allow that the sacrifices imposed on a few are outweighed by the larger sum of advantages enjoyed by many.[142]

138. Rawls, *Justice*, p. xi. Cf. ibid., p. 20: 'My aim is to work out a theory of justice that represents an alternative to utilitarian thought generally.'

139. Rawls, *Justice*, p. xii.

140. Rawls, *Justice*, p. 22.

141. Rawls, *Justice*, p. 185. Cf. ibid., p. 135: 'it has sometimes been held that under some conditions the utility principle . . . justifies, if not slavery or serfdom, at any rate serious infractions of liberty for the sake of greater social benefits.'

142. Rawls, *Justice*, p. 3.

'Justice as fairness' (the slogan in which Rawls encapsulated his moral philosophy) entails a prioritising of the right over the good. In utilitarianism, on the other hand, the production of the good determines what is right.

What are the intellectual roots of this contrasting position that Rawls erects against the dominant utilitarian consensus? Rawls himself characterised his philosophy as an attempt 'to generalize and carry to a higher order of abstraction the traditional theory of the social contract as represented by Locke, Rousseau, and Kant.'[143] But of these three great forebears, Rawls singled out one above all others as exerting a particularly powerful influence over the character of his own thought. For (as Rawls himself says) the 'theory that results [from his combative engagement with utilitarianism] is highly Kantian in nature.'[144]

In what sense is *A Theory of Justice* 'highly Kantian'?[145] Certainly Rawls is Kantian when he insists that moral principles should be the result of rational choice.[146] However, the famous 'two principles' that Rawls says people would naturally choose in what he calls 'the initial situation' (more of this in a moment) are not, when closely inspected, particularly Kantian:

> The persons in the initial situation would choose two rather different principles: the first requires equality in the assignment of basic rights and duties, which the second holds that social and economic inequalities, for example inequalities of wealth and authority, are just only if they result in compensating benefits for everyone, and in particular for the least advantaged members of society.[147]

143. Rawls, *Justice*, p. xviii. Here it is helpful to distinguish two traditions of contractualism: on the one hand, an historical, constitutionalist, and legal tradition in which the fundamental contracts are actual events and undertakings (such as a coronation oath) or documents (such as Magna Carta); on the other, a philosophical tradition in which fundamental contracts are hypothetical. Rawls's contractualism is plainly of this second kind, as he states explicitly: 'this original position is purely hypothetical' (ibid., p. 19). On the twin traditions of contractualism, see Martyn P. Thompson, 'Significant Silences in Locke's *Two Treatises of Government*: Constitutional History, Contract and Law', *The Historical Journal* 31, no. 2 (1987): 275–94.

144. Rawls, *Justice*, p. xviii. Cf. Stefan Eich, who notes that Rawls's theory was quickly seen as 'a daring exercise in Kantian idealism that set out a neo-Kantian "regulative ideal." What had started out as a postwar attempt to locate the rational in the actual came to be seen as an articulation of the actual in the rational' (Stefan Eich, 'The Theodicy of Growth: John Rawls, Political Economy, and Reasonable Faith', *Modern Intellectual History* 18 [2021]: 990).

145. For Rawls's own answer to this question, see Rawls, *Justice*, pp. 221–27.

146. Rawls, *Justice*, p. 221.

147. Rawls, *Justice*, p. 13. Cf. ibid., pp. 53 and 132–33.

Equality was certainly important to Kant. But for him equality had little to do with the material conditions of existence, which are at the forefront of Rawls's mind. Kant's idea of equality was rather more lofty and abstract, being a matter of 'independence from being bound by others to more than one can in turn bind them.'[148] Moreover, the beneficiaries of Kantian equality were also closely defined, consisting only of what he called active citizens, as opposed to passive citizens. Of those who comprised this under-class, from whom equality would be withheld or to whom it would be unavailable, Kant provided a handy check-list:

> An apprentice in the service of a merchant or artisan; a domestic servant (as distinguished from a civil servant); a minor (*naturaliter vel civiliter*); all women and, in general, anyone whose preservation in existence (his being fed and protected) depends not on his management of his own business but on arrangements made by another (except the state). All these people lack civil personality and their existence is, as it were, only inherence.[149]

This looks very like the kind of equality that obtained in, say, ancient Athens, where only adult male citizens could exercise political authority.[150] It seems safe to say that when Rawls spoke of equality he had in mind something more comprehensive than this.

However, Rawls comes closer to Kant when we consider one of the striking features of the 'initial situation', namely, the 'veil of ignorance' behind which Rawls requires us to select the principles around which a just society will be organised. Rawls explains the need for the 'veil of ignorance' in terms of men's inveterate tendency to prefer the *utile* to the *honestum* and hence to seek their own narrow advantage to the detriment of others:

> Somehow we must nullify the effects of special contingencies which put men at odds and tempt them to exploit social and natural circumstances to their own advantage. Now in order to do this I assume that the parties are situated behind a veil of ignorance. They do not know how the various alternatives will affect their own particular case and they are obliged to evaluate principles solely on the basis of general considerations.[151]

148. Kant, *Metaphysics*, p. 34.

149. Kant, *Metaphysics*, p. 100.

150. Paul Cartledge, 'Review Article on "Democracy"', *History of Political Thought* 43, no. 3 (2022): 408.

151. Rawls, *Justice*, p. 118.

So the Kantian role played by the veil of ignorance is that it prevents people from choosing (as Rawls puts it) 'heteronomously'.[152] Rawls's quest is for the principles of justice that emerge once 'those aspects of the social world that seem arbitrary from a moral point of view' are set to one side, and the veil of ignorance is the device he comes up with to attain that goal.[153] The point of the veil of ignorance is to try to ensure that distracting considerations of the *utile* do not influence our choice of the *honestum* (i.e., our society's structural principles of justice); and it achieves this by masking from us precisely what would be *utile* to us personally. So the veil of ignorance nullifies the 'effects of special contingencies which put men at odds and tempt them to exploit social and natural circumstances to their own advantage.'[154] The veil of ignorance thus helps bring it about that men will select their principles of justice on grounds other than the private hope that they may personally benefit from them disproportionately; for behind the veil of ignorance, one could not make such a calculation. Behind the veil of ignorance, 'parties have no basis for bargaining in the usual sense. No one knows his situation in society nor his natural assets, and therefore no one is in a position to tailor principles to his advantage.'[155] Rawls is nowhere more Kantian than in this determination to banish all awareness of the *utile* from the 'initial situation'.[156]

However, Rawls would be no more successful than Kant in extricating himself from the toils of the *utile*. At the end of *A Theory of Justice*, Rawls makes an unguarded claim for the theory he has just elaborated:

> Thus to see our place in society from this perspective of this position ['the original position'] is to see it *sub specie aeternitatis*: it is to regard the human situation not only from all social but also from all temporal points of view. The perspective of eternity is not a perspective from a certain place beyond the world, nor the point of view of a transcendent being; rather it is a certain form of thought and feeling that rational persons can adopt within the world.[157]

But is it really the case that Rawls has managed to step outside history, in the way that this passage claims? Has he really delivered a timeless theory to us

152. Rawls, *Justice*, p. 222.
153. Rawls, *Justice*, p. 14.
154. Rawls, *Justice*, p. 118.
155. Rawls, *Justice*, pp. 120–21.
156. For Kant's explicit abjection of the *utile*, see above, pp. 320–22.
157. Rawls, *Justice*, p. 514.

from a position '*sub specie aeternitatis*'? If so, it is surely surprising that the practical recommendations of *A Theory of Justice* so closely follow what a highly-educated East Coast Democrat might be expected to prefer as the best solutions for the problems faced by the United States in the 1970s, as economic growth weakened and social tensions strengthened.

A very interesting passage immediately follows Rawls's statement of the two principles.[158] Rawls is explaining how these two principles secure the ends of justice:

> These principles rule out justifying institutions on the grounds that the hardships of some are offset by a greater good in the aggregate [i.e., the utilitarian position]. It may be expedient but it is not just that some should have less in order that others may prosper. But there is no injustice in the greater benefits earned by a few provided that the situation of persons not so fortunate is thereby improved. The intuitive idea is that since everyone's well-being depends upon a scheme of cooperation without which no one could have a satisfactory life, the division of advantages should be such as to draw forth the willing cooperation of everyone taking part in it, including those less well situated. The two principles mentioned seem to be a fair basis on which those better endowed, or more fortunate in their social position, neither of which we can be said to deserve, could expect the willing cooperation of others when some workable scheme is a necessary condition of the welfare of all.[159]

This passage seems to reveal that, at a practical level, the undeclared tendency of Rawls's argument is to secure 'the willing cooperation' of the less fortunate in society. In other words, Rawls's theory seems in part to be driven by a practical desire to avert social unrest or to neutralise or dissipate the energies that might fuel such unrest—that is to say, to preserve social orderliness, while at the same time tipping its cap respectfully towards the goal of social justice. It is hard not to believe that some unconscious calculus was at work here, trying to assess the minimum amount of the latter (social justice) that would be necessary to secure an acceptable amount of the former (social order). Allan Bloom, in an acute but uncharitable review, sensed this: 'This correspondence, unique in the history of political philosophy, between what is wanted by many

158. See above, p. 331.

159. Rawls, *Justice*, pp. 13–14.

for current political practice and the conclusions of abstract, rigorous political philosophy would be most remarkable if one did not suspect that Rawls began from what is wanted here and now and then looked for the principles that would rationalize it.'[160] This is surely too harsh and crude, and (given the evident decency and honesty of Rawls's proceeding) psychologically unpersuasive. Rawls was not some cheap intellectual prestidigitator, knowingly trying to pass off his premises as his conclusions. But one may nevertheless suspect that, in the deep recesses of thought, an unconscious but strong desire laid hold upon the conduct of the argument and directed it towards the least uncomfortable destination. Such is the revenge exacted by the *utile* upon those who openly renounce it. Rawls's theory is (like the moral metaphysics of Kant) replete with radical implications and possibilities. But these radical implications are not allowed unfettered expression in Rawls's practical recommendations. They are curbed and muted. And in that curbing, one can detect the *utile* exerting itself over the *honestum*.

Part of the difficulty in which Rawls found himself is that he was trying to discover an unconflicted and rational basis in theory for a set of 'natural' or 'intuited' moral attitudes or principles that, in fact, are a heavily-sedimented product of an historical process that has lasted for millennia and in which (to take only the Western tradition) ethical streams of very different characters (for example, those of classical antiquity, of Christianity, and of modern liberalism) have left significant but conflicting deposits. For instance, Rawls cites 'civil disobedience and conscientious refusal' as if they were moral principles that have been universally recognised, rather than what they certainly are, namely, historically-conditioned attitudes that have arisen in particular places and times and may yet in time pass away from general acceptance even in the regions where they are currently cherished. Neither of them, for instance, was conspicuously championed by Rawls's chosen mentor in philosophy, Kant.

160. Allan Bloom, 'Justice: John Rawls vs. the Tradition of Political Philosophy', *American Political Science Review* 49, no. 2 (1975): 649. Cf. also ibid., p. 657: 'He constantly returns to our common wishes and familiar experiences to make his undemonstrated conclusions appear convincing. He is persuasive because he supports familiar contemporary beliefs, not because he provides rational grounds for them.' A similar point has more recently been made by Charles Mills, who has characterised Rawls's philosophy as an idealizing portrayal intended to shore up reasonable faith in existing institutions (Charles Mills, 'Ideal Theory as Ideology', *Hypatia* 20, no. 4 [2005]: 165–84).

Or, to take another example, consider Rawls's statement that 'the state upholds moral and religious liberty.'[161] Once again, this is precisely the position that a highly-educated, once Christian, East Coast Democrat would hope to find endorsed from the farther side of the veil of ignorance. But one would have more confidence in the impartiality of Rawls's deductions if, instead of this familiar and reassuring verdict, the recommendation emerging from beyond the veil of ignorance was (to choose a provocative example) for the adoption of Sharia law. In its own terms, that would be a deeply unwelcome outcome. But it would at least be an outcome invulnerable to the suspicion that Rawls's thumb had surreptitiously tilted the scales of his deduction.

The reliance on, or guidance of, Rawls's analysis by a series of 'curbing' or limiting considerations, appealed to in phrases such as 'our considered judgments' or 'our intuitive judgments' or 'our common sense convictions' or 'a short list of traditional and familiar principles' or 'the limits imposed by the circumstances of human life' or 'the facts which everyone recognizes', aligns his work with that of many political philosophers (including Hobbes, Locke, and Hume, as well as Kant), whose project was to find new and hopefully more secure foundations for political and moral positions that were then widely if not universally accepted (passive obedience, the right to resist, etc.).[162] But if you are willing to accept these positions as immoveable givens, how wide then is the scope for the remedial action of rational political or moral philosophy? It seems that the real, if undeclared, purpose of Rawls's theory was to make the hegemonic class in the late twentieth-century United States mildly uncomfortable and hence willing to accept moderate reforms to the US social and political order in the direction of social justice. But Rawls's intention was certainly not to alarm that hegemonic class by articulating a theory that demanded wholesale or deep change. Thus, there was an unavowed pragmatism silently at work in *A Theory of Justice*, just as we saw that a similar tendency had been active in the political and moral theory of Kant. In a moment of almost irritated candour, Rawls seems to admit as much when he concedes, notwithstanding his opposition to utilitarianism, that 'all ethical doctrines worth our attention take consequences into account in judging rightness. One which did not would simply be irrational, crazy.'[163]

161. Rawls, *Justice*, p. 186.

162. Rawls, *Justice*, pp. 214, 262, 292, 294, 312, and 356.

163. Rawls, *Justice*, p. 26. Perhaps an unconscious echo of Sidgwick: 'no morality ever existed which did not consider consequences' (Sidgwick, *Ethics*, p. 85)?

My intention in pointing this out is not to disparage Rawls but rather to show how (as was the case also with Kant), even in moral theories which set out to banish considerations of the *utile*, the presence of the *utile* will nevertheless be detectable in the final mix. It would, in particular, be wrong to attack Rawls, given the evident fairness and goodwill evident in his way of proceeding. Justice as fairness was not a concept he explored in its social or political dimension alone; it was also a principle he seems to have applied to his own writing, in which good intentions and a kind of plain dealing are unmistakable. Nevertheless, both Kant and Rawls end up recommending rules of conduct that are precisely what we would expect them to recommend, given their backgrounds, dispositions, and historical setting (Rawls's deeply Augustinian view of the frailty of human nature is especially interesting here). In both their cases, the *utile* returned in the form of the congenial, the familiar, the not-too-disruptive—to the point where, in Rawls's case, one may be led to question precisely how impenetrable the veil of ignorance in fact was. (The problem, of course, does not arise in utilitarianism, where the *utile* [the good] is prior to the *honestum* [the right]. Utilitarians are embarrassed by the mirror image of the problem that faced Kant and Rawls; that is to say, they are embarrassed by vestigial and involuntary attachments to the *honestum* which limit their willingness in practice to follow the lead given by the *utile*.) Nor would Rawls himself have been surprised by this criticism, though he might naturally have been disappointed. For he himself became anxiously aware that political philosophy can be silently *parti-pris* and amount to nothing more than a defence of a state of affairs in which the hegemonic class feels relatively at ease:

> Political philosophy is always in danger of being used corruptly as a defense of an unjust and unworthy status quo, and thus of being ideological in Marx's sense. From time to time we must ask whether justice as fairness, or any other view, is ideological in this way; and if not, why not? Are the very basic ideas it uses ideological? How can we show they are not?[164]

These are excellent questions. Moreover, they are questions which—as we have seen—might have been put to all the major thinkers in the Western tradition of moral philosophy since Cicero.

If Rawls was in some respects confused or conflicted in respect of his own philosophy, he was nevertheless an extremely acute reader of the utilitarian

164. John Rawls, *Justice as Fairness* (Cambridge, MA: Harvard University Press, 2001), p. 4, n. 4.

tradition against which he ranged himself, and I will begin the next, much shorter, phase of this chapter with a piercing remark made by Rawls concerning his philosophical adversaries: 'Utilitarianism does not take seriously the distinction between persons.'[165] Because utilitarianism is indifferent about the precise distribution of the good (however defined) amongst the individuals of society, it follows that it is disposed to view those individuals under the horizon of a principle of interchangeability. The happiness of a saint, in the utilitarian view, is equivalent to the similar degree of happiness of the most abandoned sinner, since a 'classical utilitarian . . . is indifferent as to how a constant sum of benefits is distributed.'[166] That is to say, to a utilitarian, the benefit *x* enjoyed by person *y* is indistinguishable (and, indeed, should not be distinguished from) the identical benefit *x* enjoyed by person *z*. Persons are perfectly interchangeable or fungible within the felicific calculus, since for a utilitarian, 'persons are of equal intrinsic value'.[167] There is a paradox here, since the exponents of utilitarianism were to a man individualists (perhaps because they found in utilitarianism a useful solvent of the stifling customary morality of Victorian society—this certainly seems to have been part of the appeal of the doctrine for Mill). But as a moral doctrine, utilitarianism is not in the fullest sense individualistic (although it may seem to minister to a high degree of personal freedom), since (to quote Rawls again) it necessarily refuses to 'take seriously the plurality and distinctness of individuals'.[168] In pursuing this critique of utilitarianism, it may be that Rawls was influenced by Kant's distinction between those things which have a price (and hence are fungible) and those different things which have a dignity: 'Everything has either a *price* or a *dignity*. Whatever has a price can be replaced by something else as its equivalent; on the other hand, whatever is above all price, and therefore admits of no equivalent, has a dignity. But that which constitutes the condition under which alone something can be an end in itself does not have mere relative worth, i.e., price, but an intrinsic worth, i.e., a dignity'.[169] For Kant, the principal example of something that has a dignity rather than a price is the human individual. For

165. Rawls, *Justice*, p. 24. Cf. ibid., p. 163.

166. Rawls, *Justice*, p. 67.

167. Rawls, *Justice*, p. 185.

168. Rawls, *Justice*, p. 26.

169. Kant, *Metaphysics*, p. 53.

'being of absolute value, human beings should not sacrifice themselves or one another for merely relatively valuable ends.'[170]

Rawls identified this feature of utilitarianism with commendable clarity, but it was an insight that we can detect tugging also at the minds of some of his predecessors. G. E. Moore came close to a similar perception when he observed of utilitarianism that the 'Utilitarians tend to regard everything as a mere means, neglecting the fact that some things which are good as means are also good as ends.'[171] For the interchangeability of individuals in utilitarianism flows from considering them as means towards the end of maximising the felicific product. Sidgwick, too, reflected on the significance of Bentham's pithy utilitarian maxim, 'everybody to count for one, and nobody for more than one', and concluded that 'it must be reasonable to treat any one man in the same way as any other, if there be no reason apparent for treating him differently.'[172] But Sidgwick also turned the utilitarian assumption of the interchangeability of individuals, which Rawls would view as kind of moral coarseness, in the direction of sympathy and altruism: 'The Utilitarian doctrine, as we have seen, is that each man ought to consider the happiness of any other as *theoretically* of equal importance with his own, and only of less importance *practically*, in so far as he is better able to realize the latter.'[173] Here Sidgwick was following Mill, who had located the basis of the utilitarian understanding of the human faculty of sympathy in the assumption of the commensurability of individuals.[174] This positive presentation of utilitarian interchangeability reached its height when Mill aligned it with the moral teachings of the Gospel: 'In the golden rule of Jesus of Nazareth, we read the complete spirit of the ethics of utility. To do as you would be done by, and to love your neighbour as yourself, constitute the ideal perfection of utilitarian morality.'[175] The impeccable provenance of these moral principles should not disguise from us the point of personal interchangeability (neighbour = self) upon which they turn.

However, Mill's redirection of the utilitarian principle of commensurability in an altruistic and sympathetic direction was not mere window-dressing. For

170. Kant, *Groundwork*, p. xxv.

171. Moore, *Principia*, pp. 157–58.

172. Sidgwick, *Ethics*, p. 385. Cf. Mill, *Utilitarianism*, p. 91.

173. Sidgwick, *Ethics*, pp. 221–22.

174. Mill, *Utilitarianism*, p. 47.

175. Mill, *Utilitarianism*, pp. 24–25.

the principle of interchangeability or commensurability between individuals does seem to be ambivalent. It is able to further both self-interested, manipulative substitutions and high-minded, self-denying sacrifices. For Roger Scruton, the instrumentality that is enabled by the fungibility of individuals marks an effacement of our moral lives:

> There is a temptation to rewrite human relations in the language of deals, and indeed this is one legacy of the Enlightenment, which aimed to replace hierarchies and inherited authorities with freely chosen laws. Taken to its extreme the 'social contract' vision points to the 'commodification' of human relations. . . . Human relations could become defeasible and renegotiable as in a market. In the world of markets existential ties, which change the nature and condition of those whom they join, would be increasingly eroded as the contractual worldview expands. All would become a matter of free choice among options, undertaken by self-contained and autonomous individuals within a legally established framework, itself no more than a summary of human agreements.[176]

And as his example of the impoverished realm of human interactions this might produce, Scruton cited the 'trivial promiscuity' of the flower-maidens of Klingsor's castle (in Wagner's *Parsifal*), 'for whom the object of lust can always be exchanged for a better one.'[177] But equally, the interchangeability of persons can minister to self-sacrifice. The Christian doctrine of the Atonement is the most tremendous example of this positive side of interchangeability.[178] Yet Kant would be adamant that making yourself a means to serve the ends of others was just as bad as treating others as a means to serve your own ends: 'The practical imperative will thus be the following: *So act that you use humanity, in your own person as well as in the person of any other, always at the same time as an end, never merely as a means.*'[179]

176. Scruton, *Parsifal*, p. 15.

177. Scruton, *Parsifal*, p. 84.

178. Though possibly not an action of which Kant would have approved: 'Rightful honor [*honestas iuridica*] consists in asserting one's worth as a human being in relation to others, a duty expressed by the saying, "Do not make yourself a mere means for others but be at the same time an end for them"' (Kant, *Metaphysics*, p. 32).

179. Kant, *Groundwork*, p. 41. Cf. Kant, *Metaphysics*, p. 225: 'a human being cannot be used merely as a means by any human being (either by others or even by himself) but must always be used at the same time as an end.'

But how easy is it in fact to sift means from ends in cases of self-sacrifice? To take the place of another can involve the ultimate sacrifice; but, at the same time, it clearly indicates the levelling possibility of equivalence (you and another were exchangeable). It is a gesture conferring paramountcy on the recipient, while at the same time necessarily and implicitly claiming that you can in some sense take their place. So it involves at the same time both self-denial and self-assertion. Leaving aside the Atonement as in so many respects a special case, what (for instance) should we make of the actions of Sydney Carton at the end of *A Tale of Two Cities*? In so arranging it that he is executed in the place of Charles Darnay, Carton in one sense surely makes himself a means to serve the end of the happiness of Darnay and Lucie. Yet at the same time he achieves the end of his own moral redemption and furthermore makes the transition from agitated cynicism to calm principle, as his famous final words affirm: 'It is a far, far better thing that I do, than I have ever done; it is a far, far better rest that I go to than I have ever known.'[180] Here it seems impossible finally to separate means from ends, as individual actions may present themselves as either one or the other, depending on the standpoint from which they are viewed. To offer yourself for another makes of them an end but of yourself a means; unless, of course, it is an end for you so to offer yourself, in which case they are the means, even though at first glance they may seem to be the beneficiaries of your action. So such an action cannot be said to adhere to the Kantian principle that human beings should always be ends and never means because (however you choose to look at it), in either case, it treats a human being (either oneself or the beneficiary) precisely as a means.

Even in more mundane and quotidian contexts, ends and means exist in what for a Kantian must be a disconcerting proximity. Kant seems to have had a wary respect for Adam Smith. He must have regarded the moral theory of *The Theory of Moral Sentiments* as almost everything that a moral theory should not be (i.e., empirical, affective, consequentialist). And although Kant quotes Smith's definitions of money with apparent endorsement in *The Metaphysics of Morals*, he must also have found Smith's vision of how our practical economic interactions build up the social fabric a challenge to his own more austere morality.[181] For, as *The Wealth of Nations* lays out in both normative and empirical terms, our ends of well-being and thriving can be achieved only by

180. Charles Dickens, *A Tale of Two Cities*, ed. Andrew Sanders, Oxford World's Classics (Oxford: Oxford University Press, 2008), p. 361.

181. Kant, *Metaphysics*, pp. 76 and 77.

making ourselves the means of the well-being and thriving of others: we 'are mutually the servants of one another'.[182] Human society, in this view, is little more than an immense web of reciprocal substitutions.

Dramas of substitution, of which Shakespeare was understandably so fond, spanned the entire length of his career as a playwright. However, substitution for Shakespeare was not merely a source of amusing stage business. He was aware of the deep dramas of moral ambiguity that episodes of personal interchangeability could set in motion. And Shakespeare also understood how interchangeability had the power to give dramatic life and shape to the great ethical theme of the relationship between the expedient and the right.

Examples of substitution can be found from Shakespeare's earliest plays to his latest. The comedies are, as one would expect, full of apposite instances. *The Comedy of Errors* is a series of variations on confusions of identity, producing inexplicable misery for some and equally inexplicable felicity for others. In *A Midsummer Night's Dream* the power of the love-juice creates confusions of persons that might be grotesque, or painful, or releasing. The bed-tricks of *All's Well That Ends Well* and *Measure for Measure* can be either entrapments or solutions, depending on where you stand. In *The Merchant of Venice* taking the place of another can be noble service (although we perhaps feel a trace of Kantian disapproval at the way Antonio so unreservedly—even servilely—makes himself a means to serve the ends of Bassanio). In *Twelfth Night* the resolution of the plot turns, precariously, on the ability of Sebastian perfectly to take the place of Viola, though we may feel troubled by Orsino's readiness immediately to fall in with and profit from this new and sudden disposition of persons: 'I shall have share in this most happy wrack.'[183] In *Much Ado About Nothing* Borachio's scheme to have Margaret mistaken for Hero threatens to 'misuse the Prince, to vex Claudio, to undo Hero, and kill Leonato.'[184] But plasticity of personhood is also the means whereby the play swerves back towards its promised, comic, ending:

HERO. And when I lived I was your other wife,
And when you loved you were my other husband.
CLAUDIO. Another Hero?
HERO. Nothing certainer.

182. Adam Smith, *Wealth of Nations*, III.i.77, in Smith, *Wealth*, 1:378.

183. *Twelfth Night*, V.i.156.

184. *Much Ado About Nothing*, II.ii.24–25.

One Hero died defiled, but I do live,
And surely as I live, I am a maid.
PEDRO. The former Hero? Hero that is dead?[185]

The history plays also offer memorable instances. The deposition scene in *Richard II* raises the question of whether or not Bolingbroke truly can take the place of Richard and if so, how.[186] In *1 Henry IV* the rehearsal scene puts before the audience a politically-bewildering series of equivalences, just as in the battle with the rebels, Douglas is deceived by the 'many marching in his coats' that Henry IV has cunningly distributed amongst his forces.[187] In *Cymbeline* Imogen's readiness to take Cloten's headless body for that of Posthumus is a perturbing confirmation of Cloten's mistaken confidence that there is nothing to choose between him and his rival: 'the lines of my body are as well drawn as his: no less young, more strong, not beneath him in fortunes, beyond him in the advantage of the time, above him in birth, alike conversant in general services, and more remarkable in single oppositions.'[188]

I say that Shakespeare was 'understandably so fond' of dramas of substitution because substitution is more than just a subject matter for drama, as deception, or murder, or rebellion, or adultery might be subject matter. Substitution resonates more powerfully within drama than do those other subjects because it has a deep affinity with the very mode of drama, which involves one person (the actor) taking the part of another (the character). We think of 'doubling' (that is, when a single actor plays more than one part) as an instance of conspicuous thespian virtuosity. But Jaques's famous speech on the seven ages of man in *As You Like It* suggests that in this respect art is easily eclipsed by life:

All the world's a stage,
And all the men and women merely players.
They have their exits and their entrances,
And one man in his time plays many parts,
His acts being seven ages.[189]

185. *Much Ado About Nothing*, V.iv.60–65. Shakespeare will revisit and rework this for the ending of *The Winter's Tale*.

186. *Richard II*, IV.i.

187. *1 Henry IV*, II.iv and V.iii.25.

188. *Cymbeline*, IV.ii.294–331 and IV.i.8–12.

189. *As You Like It*, II.vii.139–43.

Living is a hyper-complicated performance, in which we not only double but 'septuple'. We all play the same seven parts, in the same order. When mode and matter chime in this way, then extraordinarily powerful effects can result. Think, perhaps, of the exhilarations and mortifications of interchangeability that Da Ponte and Mozart put before us in *Così fan tutte* or the dire consequences of similar exchanges—Gunther for Siegfried, Gutrune for Brünnhilde—in *Götterdämmerung*, an opera in which the material of a comic opera is grimly quoted with ultimately apocalyptic effects.[190]

One might think therefore that an affinity with utilitarian modes of ethical thought is somehow ingrained in drama, given their common investment in personal interchangeability. Yet drama—perhaps because of that intrinsic pull towards the utilitarian—has also been from the first fascinated by that great antagonist of the utilitarian way of thinking about moral life, namely, an adherence to an intuited conviction of what is right, maintained in the teeth of the most dreadful consequences. Frequently it is a woman who embodies this intransigent refusal to strike a compromise with what the world calls prudence and who insists on this rejection of an identity the world would force upon her by compelling her to act as something other than what she is.

Sophocles's *Antigone* supplies the paradigm. Early in that play, Ismene pleads with her sister to keep consequences in mind:

> Woe! Think, sister, of how our father perished hated and ill-famed, through the crimes he had himself detected, after striking both his eyes himself, with his own hand! And then his mother and his wife, two names in one, did violence to her life with twisted noose; and, thirdly, our two brothers, on one day killing each other, did themselves both to death at one another's hands. And now consider how much the worse will be the fate of us two, who are left alone, if in despite of the law we flout the decision of the ruler or his power. Why, we must remember that we are women, who cannot fight against men, and then that we are ruled by those whose power is greater, so that we must consent to this and to other things even more painful! So I shall beg those beneath the earth to be understanding, since I act under constraint, but I shall obey those in authority; for there is no sense in actions that exceed our powers.[191]

190. See below, p. 356 and n. 223.

191. Sophocles, *Antigone*, ll. 49–68.

Antigone's reply comes from an entirely different, and profoundly Kantian, moral universe, in which what is intuited to be right should never be abandoned in the teeth of adverse consequences and in which personal identity is neither flexible nor negotiable:

> I would not tell you to do it, and even if you were willing to act after all I would not be content for you to act with me! Do you be the kind of person you have decided to be, but I shall bury him! It is honourable [καλόν] for me to do this and die. I am his own and I shall lie with him who is my own, having committed a crime that is holy, for there will be a longer span of time for me to please those below than there will be to please those here; for there I shall lie forever. As for you, if it is your pleasure, dishonour what the gods honour![192]

Later, Antigone explains to Creon why she defied his order to leave Polynices unburied:

> It was not Zeus who made this proclamation, nor was it Justice who lives with the gods below that established such laws among men, nor did I think your proclamations strong enough to have power to overrule, mortal as they were, the unwritten and unfailing ordinances of the gods. For these have life, not simply today and yesterday, but for ever, and no one knows how long ago they were revealed.[193]

Creon, however, is contemptuous of these immemorial intuitions, this 'woman's law', as he calls it.[194] His own moral outlook and his technique of governing turn on the willingness of people to take consequences into account and to be either induced or intimidated by them: 'even those who are bold try to escape, when they see Hades already near to their lives.'[195] It is therefore a great irony when this inveterate consequentialist proves to be blind to the inescapable consequences of his own overbearing rule, despite being warned about them by the literally blind priest, Tiresias.

This clash between those who speak for the expedient and those who defend the intuited is repeated frequently in Western drama. We witness it again, for instance, in Hedda Gabler's refusal to fall in with the snares of that

192. Sophocles, *Antigone*, ll. 69–77.

193. Sophocles, *Antigone*, ll. 450–57.

194. 'ἐμοῦ δὲ ζῶντος οὐκ ἄρξει γυνή' (Sophocles, *Antigone*, l. 525).

195. Sophocles, *Antigone*, ll. 580–81.

arch-consequentialist Judge Brack. And in *King Lear*, we see it vividly in the very first scene of the play.

———

Shakespeare raises palpably Kantian moral scenery before us in the opening scene of *King Lear* where, in a setting of ethical conflict and debate, two Kantians (Cordelia and Kent) clash with a phalanx of utilitarians.

King Lear begins by evoking an atmosphere in which worth and merit are unclear or undecidable:

> KENT. I thought the King had more affected the Duke of Albany than Cornwall.
>
> GLOUCESTER It did always seem so to us. But now, in the division of the kingdom, it appears not which of the Dukes he values most, for qualities are so weighed that curiosity in neither can make choise of either's moiety.[196]

That keynote of equivalence and hence interchangeability is reinforced when, a little later, Lear speaks of 'our no-less-loving son of Albany'.[197]

Lear's love-test has the 'darker purpose' of disrupting this moral climate of equivalence:

> Tell me, my daughters,
> Since now we will divest us both of rule,
> Interest of territory, cares of state,
> Which of you shall we say doth love us *most*,
> That we our *largest* bounty may extend
> Where nature doth with merit challenge?[198]

It is clear that Lear expects to bestow this 'largest bounty' on Cordelia. On Goneril he bestows a portion 'With shadowy forests and with champaigns riched / With plenteous rivers and wide-skirted meads', and to Regan he gives a portion 'No less in space, validity, and pleasure / Than that conferred on

196. *King Lear*, I.i.1–6.

197. *King Lear*, I.i.40.

198. *King Lear*, I.i.46–51; emphases added.

Goneril', while for Cordelia he has provisionally reserved a 'third more opulent than your sisters.'[199]

The question that is designed to differentiate the three sisters seems disarmingly simple: 'Which of you shall we say doth love us most?'[200] Yet Lear's question contains an ambiguity which comes into focus if we reflect on what kind of answer Lear would find adequate. For two kinds of answer to this question are possible, each of which is a response to a subtly different interrogation. The first possibility is that Lear is asking, 'Which of you three loves me more than the other two?' In other words, it is an attempt to quantify the *amount* of love for Lear in each of his daughters and then to place his daughters in an order by reference to those amounts. In this understanding of the words, the answer to Lear's question is some kind of volume (or, in Kantian terms, a price). The second possibility is that Lear is asking, 'Which of you three loves me most of anything in the world?' In this version of Lear's question, he is inquiring into the *position* he holds in the affections of each of his daughters. The answer in this case is a ranking, rather than a volume (or, in Kantian terms, a dignity).[201] This is not an ambiguity which exists in the earlier play on the story of King Lear, the *True Chronicle Historie of King Leir* (performed 1594; printed 1605). There, Leir's question is to discover 'which of my daughters loves me best', and he imagines that they will 'contend / Eche to exceed the other in their love'.[202] In other words, in the *True Chronicle Historie*, Leir's question is unmistakably a volume question, not a ranking question.

In *King Lear*, Goneril and Regan interpret Lear's question as a volume question. Regan seeks to overtop Goneril's response by drawing attention to her own superfluity of emotion:

> I am made of that self-mettle as my sister
> And prize me at her worth. In my true heart
> I find she names my very deed of love,
> Only she comes too short, . . .[203]

For Cordelia, however, Lear's question is rather a matter of ranking, which is why she retorts upon her sisters the fact of their having husbands:

199. *King Lear*, I.i.62–63, 79–80, and 84.

200. *King Lear*, I.i.49.

201. For a discussion of the Kantian distinction between price and dignity, see above, p. 338.

202. *True Chronicle Historie*, ll.79, 81–82, in Bullough, *Sources*, 7:339.

203. *King Lear*, I.i.67–70.

Why have my sisters husbands if they say
They love you all?[204]

Only if Lear's is a ranking question does the fact of being married create difficulties, since if it were a volume question, it would be possible for Goneril and Regan to exceed each other and Cordelia in love for Lear and yet still to love their husbands more. But when Cordelia winds up by contrasting the implications of her own response with that of her sisters—

Sure, I shall never marry like my sisters,
To love my father all.

it is clear that, for her, the love which is owed to a father is of a different kind from the love which is owed to a husband. Husbands and fathers have different dignities, and consequently the different loves that each properly attracts cannot be measured against one another. They are different things. To think otherwise is to be blind to the difference between dignities and prices and hence to be open to the interchangeableness that is characteristic of utilitarianism.

Lear's question thus indeed divides and fragments his family, albeit not in quite the way he intended. Instead of arranging them in a hierarchy of love for him, it splits them into two moral camps: on the one hand, the proto-utilitarians Goneril and Regan; on the other, the proto-Kantian Cordelia. And this ethical division immediately spreads through the court. When Lear offers Cordelia to Burgundy without a dowry, the language he uses to justify this change is significant: 'now her price is fall'n.'[205] Burgundy's response had been couched in the language of trade: 'I crave no more than hath your highness offered, / Nor will you tender less.'[206] But the king of France's response, which again turns on the language of worth and price, expresses the view that what is without a price can nevertheless be worth most: 'Not all the dukes of wat'rish Burgundy / Can buy this unprized, precious maid of me.'[207]

In the person of Kent we see how Lear's question provokes defiant resistance to what he eventually denounces as 'evil' (rather than the milder word, 'folly', that he had initially used). It is a movement up the scale of wrongdoing sufficient to jolt Kent out of his initial courtesy into the 'unmannerly'

204. *King Lear*, I.i.97–98.
205. *King Lear*, I.i.195.
206. *King Lear*, I.i.192–93.
207. *King Lear*, I.i.256–57.

language he will eventually use towards Lear.[208] And just as Cordelia, in refusing to give Lear the answer he wanted, was unmoved by a consideration of the consequences of her silence, so too is Kent unconcerned by Lear's threats of retribution:

> My life I never held but as a pawn
> To wage against thine enemies; ne'er fear to lose it,
> Thy safety being motive.[209]

The scene ends with Lear's court ethically fractured as well as politically divided and geographically dispersed, as Kent shapes his 'old course in a country new' and Cordelia departs for France.[210]

The sudden disorientation dramatized onstage would have been shared by the play's first audiences had they been familiar with the *True Chronicle Historie of King Leir*. Shakespeare took over much material from that earlier play. But he also altered freely what he took, and he did so with a consistent intention, especially in this first scene, which compresses no fewer than the first seven scenes of the *True Chronicle Historie*. The character of Lear/Leir was changed in particularly significant ways. Shakespeare omitted the references to the recent past and the justification for the love-test carefully set out by the earlier playwright in the first speech of the play, spoken by Leir himself:

> Thus to our griefe the obsequies performd
> Of our (too late) deceast and dearest Queen,
> Whose soule I hope, possest of heavenly joyes,
> Doth ride in triumph 'mongst the Cherubins;
> Let us request your grave advice, my Lords,
> For the disposing of our princely daughters,
> For whom our care is specially imployd,
> As nature bindeth to advaunce their states,
> In royall marriage with some princely mates:
> For wanting now their mothers good advice,
> Under whose government they have receyved
> A perfit patterne of a vertuous life:
> Lest as it were a ship without a sterne,

208. *King Lear*, I.i.164. Cf. ibid., I.i.147, I.i.142.
209. *King Lear*, I.i.153–55.
210. *King Lear*, I.i.185.

Or silly sheepe without a Pastors care;
Although our selves doe dearely tender them,
Yet are we ignorant of their affayres:
For fathers best do know to governe sonnes;
But daughters steps the mothers counsell turnes.[211]

Immediately one notices three important changes Shakespeare made to this inherited material. Firstly, he eliminated the Christian setting of the play which Leir invokes when referring to his dead queen (I will discuss the significance of this erasure of Christianity in a moment). Secondly, he almost completely suppressed any reference to Lear's queen (there is only one line in *King Lear* which glances at her past existence, which is perhaps the result of inadvertence on Shakespeare's part).[212] Thirdly, whereas all Leir's daughters are unmarried when the *True Chronicle Historie* begins, in *King Lear* Goneril and Regan were married before the beginning of the action.

The second and third of the changes made by Shakespeare have the effect of making Lear's actions inscrutable. In the *True Chronicle Historie,* a clear reason for the division of the kingdom is implied. The play begins in a moment of natural change for the state, with the death of the queen and the need for the daughters to marry. We are given a coherent and rational (if, in the event, misguided) political motivation for the events which set the action of the play in motion. In *King Lear,* by contrast, we hear only the rumour and surmise of Kent and Gloucester in the opening lines and Lear's enigmatic and, as we have seen, ambiguous 'darker purpose'.

This sense of significant difference and revision is sustained if we compare Leir/Lear's motives for stepping aside from the throne. Leir is motivated by exhaustion and piety:

The world of me, I of the world am weary,
And I would fayne resigne these earthly cares,
And thinke upon the welfare of my soule:
Which by no better meanes may be effected,
Then by resigning up the Crowne from me,
In equal dowry to my daughters three.[213]

211. *True Chronicle Historie,* ll. 1–20, in Bullough, *Sources,* 7:337.

212. See *King Lear,* II.iv.124–25.

213. *True Chronicle Historie,* ll. 27–31, in Bullough, *Sources,* 7:337–38.

This may be unwise, but it would be harsh to criticise it as, at least in intention, indifferent to the public good. Compare the triviality and self-indulgence of the considerations which motivate Lear's decision:

> and 'tis our fast intent
> To shake all cares and business from our age,
> Conferring them on younger strengths, while we
> Unburthen'd crawl toward death. . . .
> Only we shall retain
> The name, and all th'addition to a king; the sway,
> Revenue, execution of the rest,
> Beloved sons, be yours: . . .[214]

The gap between these two justifications for retirement is evident if we reflect on how improbable it is that Lear, at the beginning of the play and when so intoxicated with himself, would ever have entertained Leir's insight that 'The world of me [is] weary.'

The tendency of Shakespeare's revisions to the character of Leir/Lear is amplified and strengthened by how he altered the purpose of the love-test. In the *True Chronicle Historie*, the love test serves a practical purpose, related to Leir's public-spirited anxiety to secure the state. Cordella has refused to marry any of the 'divers Peeres' by whom she has been solicited, but Leir comes up with a plan to outmanoeuvre her resistance:

> I am resolv'd, and even now my mind
> Doth meditate a sudden stratagem,
> To try which of my daughters loves me best:
> Which till I know, I cannot be in rest.
> This graunted, when they joyntly shall contend,
> Eche to exceed the other in their love:
> Then at the vantage will I take *Cordella*,
> Even as she doth protest she loves me best,
> Ile say, Then, daughter, graunt me one request,
> To shew thou lovest me as thy sisters doe,
> Accept a husband, whom my selfe will woo.
> This sayd, she cannot well deny my sute,
> Although (poore soule) her sences will be mute:

214. *King Lear*, I.i.36–39 and 127–30.

Then will I tryumph in my policy,
And match her with a King of Brittany.[215]

This again is very different from what we are given in *King Lear*, where Lear bribes his daughters to make protestations of love by dangling in front of them the possibility of a larger share of the kingdom:

Tell me, my daughters,
Since now we will divest us both of rule,
Interest of territory, cares of state,
Which of you shall we say doth love us most,
That we our largest bounty may extend
Where nature doth with merit challenge?[216]

The Leir of the *True Chronicle Historie* is certainly misguided, but he is also undeniably well-intentioned. The same cannot be said for the sly, childish, and vain old man of *King Lear*.

So far, then, Shakespeare's changes to the opening of the received dramatic version of the 'King Lear' story show him making the character of Lear less admirable, less disinterested, more capricious, and more selfish. The last change Shakespeare made that I want to examine fits in well with this revision of the character of Lear, in that it seems to be part of the same coherent plan which governed Shakespeare's recasting of the opening of the play.

In the *True Chronicle Historie*, a corrupt courtier, Skalliger, tells Gonorill and Ragan that Leir is going to ask them to declare their love.[217] They therefore have an opportunity to prepare extravagant speeches beforehand, as they explicitly state to the audience:

GON. I will so flatter with my doting father,
As he was ne're so flattred in his life.
Nay, I will say, that if it be his pleasure,
To match me to a begger, I will yeeld:
For why, I know what ever I do say,
He meanes to match me with the Cornwall King.
RAG. Ile say the like: for I am well assured,
What e're I say to please the old man's mind,

215. *True Chronicle Historie*, ll. 78–91, in Bullough, *Sources*, 7:339.
216. *King Lear*, I.i.46–51.
217. *True Chronicle Historie*, ll. 133–68, in Bullough, *Sources*, 7:340–41.

Who dotes, as if he were a child agayne,
I shall injoy the noble Cambrian Prince:
Only, to feed his humour, will suffice,
To say, I am content with any one
Whom heele appoynt me; this will please him more,
Then e're *Apolloes* musike pleased Jove.[218]

But in *King Lear*, no one has any warning of what Lear intends. Goneril and Regan are presumably as taken aback as anyone else when their father suddenly starts playing the terribly unfair, but also terribly dangerous, game of the love-test. The consequence is that, whereas in the *True Chronicle Historie*, Gonorill and Ragan are unmasked as scheming villains from the outset, in *King Lear*, at least in the first scene, the moral colouring of the characters of Goneril and Regan is not made explicit and unmistakable for us in the same way. And this is sustained to some extent beyond the first scene. So, in the *True Chronicle Historie*, Gonorill complains bitterly to Skalliger about her father's reproofs of her self-indulgence and extravagance:

GON. I prithy, *Skalliger*, tell me what thou thinkst:
Could any woman of our dignity
Endure such quips and peremptory taunts,
As I do daily from my doting father?
Doth't not suffice that I him keepe of almes,
Who is not able for to Keepe himselfe?
But as if he were our better, he should thinke
To check and snap me up at every word.
I cannot make me a new fashioned gowne,
And set it forth with more then common cost;
But his old doting doltish withered wit,
Is sure to give a sencelesse check for it.
I cannot make a banquet extraordinary,
To grace my selfe, and spread my name abroad,
But he, old foole, is captious by and by,
And sayth, the cost would well suffice for twice.
Judge then, I pray, what reason ist, that I
Should stand alone charg'd with his vaine expence,
And that my sister *Ragan* should go free,

218. *True Chronicle Historie*, ll. 173–86, in Bullough, *Sources*, 7:341.

To whom he gave as much, as unto me?
I prithy, *Skalliger*, tell me, if thou know,
By any meanes to rid me of this woe.[219]

The equivalent, much shorter, speech in *King Lear* lays the emphasis elsewhere:

By day and night he wrongs me; every hour
He flashes into one gross crime or other
That sets us all at odds. I'll not endure it:
His knights grow riotous, and himself upbraids us
On every trifle.[220]

After the adjustments to the received account to which the audience has been exposed in the first scene, it would not be hard for them to extend at least a measure of credibility towards this portrait of a peevish and captious old man. Shakespeare's audience is not, from the outset, alienated from Goneril and Regan as was the audience of the *True Chronicle Historie*.

Why should Shakespeare have chosen so to recast the opening of *King Lear* so that one of the characters with whom he will eventually wish us to feel at least a measure of sympathy—Lear—emerges as less admirable and sympathetic than the play's first audience were probably expecting him to be, and two of the characters whom he will eventually lead us to repudiate as morally bankrupt—Goneril and Regan—command in the first scene a degree of sympathy, and perhaps even a trace of admiration, from the audience?

King Lear is remarkable for the number of characters the play contains about whom the audience has drastically revised its initial moral assessments by the end of act V. On the one hand, there are a number of characters from whom we feel a measure of early estrangement but who in the end we recognise have a stronger claim on our sympathies than we had originally allowed: Lear himself, Cordelia, Albany, Edgar. On the other hand, there are characters from whom we feel obliged steadily to distance ourselves as the action proceeds: Goneril, Regan, Oswald, and principally Edmund. And as we have seen by comparing the first scene of *King Lear* with the equivalent material in the *True Chronicle Historie*, Shakespeare seems to have adjusted his sources so as deliberately to accentuate this effect of moral revision.

219. *True Chronicle Historie*, ll.774–95, in Bullough, *Sources*, 7:356.
220. *King Lear*, I.iii.3–7.

Edmund is perhaps the character about whom we revise our moral estimation most sharply. And this revision of judgement is particularly salient, since Shakespeare seems to have gone out of his way to make this character attractive to us when the audience first meets him for any length of time in act I, scene ii. This is a long and complex scene, falling into five distinct parts: (1) the invocation of 'Nature'; (2) the entry of Gloucester and his deception by use of the forged letter; (3) Edmund's mockery of Gloucester's superstitions about astrology; (4) the entry of Edgar and his deception by Edmund; and (5) Edmund's final gleeful resolve to have lands by wit, if not by birth. So Edmund is onstage throughout, beginning and ending this predominantly prose scene with two verse soliloquies. Another way of describing the structure of the scene would be to say that it consists of two episodes of trickery, each framed by direct addresses from Edmund to the audience. So Edmund here commandingly but also improvisationally shapes the action as he chooses and comments on it amusingly to the audience. He is presented to us as a character in the mould of others whom Shakespeare's first audiences would have trusted and liked: in particular the sceptical, disengaged, witty choric figures of the comedies—Berowne in *Love's Labour's Lost*, Benedick in *Much Ado About Nothing*, even perhaps Rosalind in *As You Like It*. Edmund's dramatic profile and stage signature encourage the audience, at this early stage of the play, to like and to trust him.

The question of comedy arises within the scene itself. Edgar comes onstage just as Edmund is speaking of him: 'Pat, he comes like the catastrophe of the old comedy.'[221] This is more than just a casual jibe, because the whole shape and tone of this scene is comic, to the point where we might almost call it a scene extracted from a comedy and inserted into a tragedy. Edmund has some of the characteristics of a stock comic figure, the trickster or clever servant. Moreover, the deceiving of the old and foolish by the young, irreverent, and freethinking is a comic paradigm which Shakespeare has used in earlier comedies: for instance, in the gulling of Malvolio by Maria and Feste in *Twelfth Night* or the discomfiting of Shylock by Portia in *Merchant of Venice*. We are tempted, then, initially to misread this scene as an instance of the comic, and therefore finally benign, defeating of age and credulity by wit, youth, and presence of mind. Moreover, this scene makes it clear that Edmund is another proto-utilitarian. His defiant declaration, 'All with me's meet that I can fashion fit', makes clear that he can see no difference between the expedient ('fit') and the

221. *King Lear*, I.ii.121–22.

right ('meet'). For Edmund the expedient and the right are equivalent, just as he can see no difference between baseness and legitimacy.[222] Whereas Cicero had maintained that the *utile* had no existence outside the bounds of the *honestum*, for Edmund the *honestum* is entirely contained within the *utile*.

Only later in the play, when we have seen what is produced from this episode of high-spirited invention, do we form a more severe judgement of the moral stance that Shakespeare here seems to have deliberately made so alluring to us. Such inappropriate or 'off-key' intrusions of the comic into the realm of tragedy can have a baleful yet powerful effect. A much later example would be the dreadful exchange between Gutrune and Siegfried, in which Siegfried describes how he wooed Brünnhilde on Gunther's behalf. In Wagner's annotation of the score used for the inaugural performance, he specified how he wanted this *ecphrasis* of the hinge of the tragedy of *Götterdämmerung* to be sung: 'The whole thing must always be a "lively conversation", delivered in the manner of a comic opera.'[223] Something similar to this artful but gruesome Wagnerian moment occurs towards the end of *King Lear* in Goneril's sarcastic response, 'An interlude!', to Albany's bitter translation of the erotic entanglements of Edmund, Regan, and Goneril into the complicated yet superficial patterns of a farce:

> For your claim, fair sister,
> I bar it in the interest of my wife.
> 'Tis she is subcontracted to this lord,
> And I her husband contradict your banns.
> If you will marry, make your loves to me:
> My lady is bespoke.[224]

However, the ethical unfixedness with which Shakespeare confronts us in *King Lear* is quite different from the moral world of the *True Chronicle Historie*, where we are never called upon to revise or reopen a moral judgement we have

222. *King Lear*, I.ii.162. Cf. 'Edmund the base / Shall to the legitimate' (ibid., I.ii.20–21).

223. Wagner, *Götterdämmerung*, II.ii.953–99. 'Das Ganze ist immer als "lebhafte Conversation", "im Stile der komischen Oper" zu halten' (recorded in Heinrich Porges's 1876 publication of the annotated scores: quoted in Richard Wagner, *The Ring of the Nibelung*, trans. and ed. John Deathridge [London: Penguin Classics, 2018], pp. 623 and 744). Pierre Boulez noted that the relationship of Siegfried and Gutrune was studded with trivialising recollections of *opéra comique*, particularly of Daniel Auber's *La muette de Portici*—Auber, whom Wagner both disparaged as heartless and admired as a genius.

224. *King Lear*, V.iii.78–83.

passed on a character. In the earlier play, everyone remains statically 'in character' from the beginning to the end.

There are, I think, two reasons why Shakespeare crafted the action of *King Lear* so as to produce this effect of ethical unfixedness. In the first place, it ensures that the audience of *King Lear* enjoys no impregnable superiority of moral insight over that bestowed on the characters. Lear, Gloucester, and Edgar all make errors of moral judgement, and so do we, insofar as we respond sensitively to the early scenes of the play. The audience cannot congratulate itself on any greater perceptiveness than that possessed by the main characters, and this is in the end a way of enlisting our sympathy all the more strongly in favour of characters who, had the play been differently organised (or had it been a comedy), we might have been tempted to dismiss as simply stupid or impercipient. Secondly, Shakespeare suggests that our moral identities are not fixed and that we do not enter the world with a moral character which then remains unchanged whatever we happen to do. Rather, we create our own moral characters through our actions, which somehow remain within us and become constitutive of our selves. We become the people who possess the moral characters we have acted out.

This perhaps makes *King Lear* seem rather sceptical, even relativistic, about moral values. The play presents us with a shifting surface of moral instability, in which our perceptions of the probity of individual characters can change with disorienting results. But in the midst of this flux, Shakespeare also repeatedly shows us characters taking moral stands against what they instinctively see as wrong. These characters are moved to act in defiance of all learnt behaviour, and at severe cost to themselves, to oppose what they intuitively perceive to be outrageous actions. Cordelia and Kent are two such characters. But another example would be the anonymous servant in act III, scene vii, who, despite being (as we later learn) 'bred' in the service of Cornwall, is so outraged by the blinding of Gloucester that he turns on his master, in defiance of the habits of his whole life and in reckless disregard of the consequences:

> Hold your hand, my Lord.
> I have serv'd you ever since I was a child,
> But better service have I never done you
> Than now to bid you hold.[225]

225. *King Lear*, IV.ii.43 and III.vii.71–74.

The messenger uses a striking word, employed neither beforehand nor afterwards by Shakespeare, when he reports these events to Albany:

> A servant that he bred, *thrilled* with remorse,
> Opposed the act, . . .[226]

Today 'thrilled' has become purely metaphorical and means something like 'deeply and pleasurably excited'. But the fundamental and literal meaning of the word, and still the primary meaning in Shakespeare's day, is 'pierced'.[227] So used, the word denotes a certainly intense but not necessarily pleasant experience; moreover, an experience in some way visceral, physical, and also unintended and unsummoned by the one who suffers it. This sense of the word is echoed twice later in act IV: firstly, when Kent asks the Gentleman, 'Did your letters pierce the Queen to any demonstration of grief?', and secondly, when Edgar, on seeing the distracted King Lear, exclaims, 'O thou side-piercing sight!'[228] This idiom of physical penetration is a language of moral affect used exclusively by proto-Kantians in *King Lear,* and it is powerfully suggestive of the nature of their moral behaviour, in which an intuitive perception of right or wrong is followed by a deliberate decision to adhere to the right, no matter how inexpedient the consequences for them personally.[229] Against characters such as these, Shakespeare places the 'serviceable villain[s]'[230] whose moral judgement is limited to an inclination towards their own advantage: characters such as Oswald or the anonymous Officer in act V, scene iii who, when asked by Edmund to carry out the orders contained in the note he has just given him without being told what the orders are, replies simply and terribly, 'I'll do't, my Lord.'[231]

So the fundamental moral question in *King Lear* is not 'What is the right thing to do?', since even corrupt characters seem able to distinguish good and evil accurately, as we can see from some of Edmund's last words:

> I pant for life; some *good* I mean to do
> Despite of my own nature.[232]

226. *King Lear,* IV.ii.43–44; emphasis added.

227. *OED*, 'thrill' *v.*, I.1.a.

228. *King Lear,* IV.iii.9 and IV.vi.87.

229. Other instances come from the lips of Lear (*King Lear,* I.iv.271 and IV.vi.167) and Albany (ibid., I.iv.317).

230. *King Lear,* IV.vi.243.

231. *King Lear,* V.iii.35.

232. *King Lear,* V.iii.218–19; emphasis added.

Once the *utile* is out of reach, even Edmund will incline towards the *honestum*. Rather, in this play the essential moral question is, 'Will we have the courage to do what we judge intuitively to be right, despite all the temptations we face to ignore the promptings of our moral reason and pursue our own advantage?' Repeatedly in *King Lear*, Shakespeare dramatizes this Kantian moment of deliberate moral choice.

Some characters come through that moment of moral trial while others fail. What Shakespeare insists on in *King Lear*, however, is that it is a free choice. Once again, the *True Chronicle Historie* provides a telling contrast. A long, central scene in the earlier play shows Leir and his loyal counsellor, Perillus, accosted by an anonymous Messenger, who embodies aspects of both Shakespeare's Oswald and Edmund.[233] The Messenger has been sent by Ragan to kill them but runs away when it thunders just as he is about to commit the murders. 'O, heavens be thanked', says Leir as the Messenger drops the dagger he was about to use on Perillus, and Perillus replies in kind when the Messenger also drops the dagger he was about to use on Leir:

> Oh, happy sight! he meanes to save my Lord.
> The King of heaven continue this good mind.[234]

But in the world of Shakespeare's play, nature will neither dissuade us from evil nor encourage us in virtue. It is a morally neutral backdrop to men's actions, and not the least pathetic aspect of Lear on the heath is his egotistical desire to see in the storm some projection on the vast stage of nature of his own inner turmoil.[235] In Shakespeare's play, the storm is just a storm, not a nudging sign to men from an offended, interventionist, and morally-sensible deity. It is here that Shakespeare's stripping out of the explicitly Christian colouring of the earlier play (in which the virtuous Cordella is a Protestant and the vicious Gonorill and Ragan are Catholics) is so decisive.[236] In the pre-Christian world of *King Lear* there are no supernatural sanctions for our moral values and also no supernatural safety-net to protect us from those who would do us harm.

233. *True Chronicle Historie,* sc. xix, ll. 1431–1790, in Bullough, *Sources,* vol. 7:372–81.

234. *True Chronicle Historie,* ll. 1741 and 1743–44, in Bullough, *Sources,* 7:379–80.

235. Cf. Sonnet 29, l. 3: 'trouble deaf heaven with my bootless cries.'

236. In Shakespeare's play this confessional colouring survives only in Kent's incidental declaration that he will eat no fish (i.e., is not a Roman Catholic; *King Lear,* I.iv.15).

I began by discussing how Shakespeare re-modelled the beginning of *King Lear* so as to create a measure of moral bewilderment in his audience. I now want to move towards a close by discussing how Shakespeare handled the end of the play, where again we can see him playing against expectations in pursuit of a certain ethical impact.

The greatest comment on the ending of *King Lear* remains that of Samuel Johnson, which is so impressive in the way it brings together literary discernment and moral sensitivity:

> But though this moral [that villainy is never at a stop and that crimes lead to crimes] be incidentally enforced, Shakespeare has suffered the virtue of Cordelia to perish in a just cause, contrary to the natural ideas of justice, to the hope of the reader, and, what is yet more strange, to the faith of chronicles. . . . A play in which the wicked prosper and the virtuous miscarry may doubtless be good, because it is a just representation of the common events of human life: but since all reasonable beings naturally love justice, I cannot easily be persuaded that the observation of justice makes a play worse; or that if other excellencies are equal the audience will not always rise better pleased from the final triumph of persecuted virtue.
>
> In the present case the public has decided. Cordelia from the time of Tate has always retired with victory and felicity. And if my sensations could add anything to the general suffrage, I might relate that I was many years ago so shocked by Cordelia's death that I know not whether I ever endured to read again the last scenes of the play till I undertook to revise them as an editor.[237]

Johnson is certainly correct that most earlier versions of the story of King Lear conclude with the triumph of Cordelia and the restoration of her father. This is the 'promised end' we find in Geoffrey of Monmouth's *Historia Anglicana*, the *Mirror for Magistrates*, William Warner's *Albion's England*, Holinshed's *Chronicles*, and Spenser's *Faerie Queene*, as well as in the *True Chronicle Historie*.[238] Of course, the Lear story in Shakespeare's day had an uncertain status. It was not quite accredited history in the manner of the fifteenth-century material Shakespeare had quarried for his history plays, since its factuality had been vigorously questioned (for instance, by Polydore Vergil). But equally it had

237. Johnson, *Shakespeare*, pp. 222–23. In 1681, Nahum Tate had freely revised *King Lear* for the Restoration stage. See above, p. 295 and n. 11.

238. *King Lear*, V.iii.237.

not yet passed fully into the status of myth. It therefore occupied a space in the no-man's-land between ascertained fact and acknowledged fiction. Nevertheless, Johnson was right to observe that the great majority of the versions of the Lear story that have come down to us conclude in victory and restoration for Cordelia and Lear.

But Shakespeare does not follow these precedents, and we must ask the question why he once again challenged the expectations of his audience. For Shakespeare seems not to proceed in utter forgetfulness or disregard of how the Lear story had been told before. Rather, in the final act of the play he repeatedly (but, as it transpires, only teasingly) suggests that he will keep faith with the play's 'promised end' in the successful restoration of Lear by the forces of Cordelia and his son-in-law.

At several points in the protracted final act of *King Lear* the play seems indeed to be heading towards the customary destination of this story. In the *True Chronicle Historie* the final battle is a non-event, since the forces of Gonorill and Ragan promptly desert to the invading French army. So, to the first audiences of *King Lear*, Edgar's lines to Gloucester early in act V must have been startling:

Away, old man, give me thy hand, away!
King Lear hath lost, he and his daughter ta'en.
Give me thy hand. Come on.[239]

Perhaps it was a little like one might feel today watching a recording of a sporting fixture in which, in the last quarter of an hour, and in defiance of ascertained fact, the known result is reversed.

Nevertheless, the expected happy ending seems to come within reach once more when Edgar defeats Edmund in single combat and when Edmund reveals the existence of the order to have Lear and Cordelia killed. Even when Lear re-enters almost immediately holding the body of Cordelia, all hope is not extinguished, since to Lear's eyes, at least, Cordelia may still be breathing:

Howl, howl, howl! Oh, you are men of stones!
Had I your tongues and eyes, I'd use them so
That heaven's vault should crack. She's gone forever.
I know when one is dead and when one lives;

239. *King Lear*, V.ii.5–7.

She's dead as earth. Lend me a looking glass,
If that her breath will mist or stain the stone,
Why, then, she lives.[240]

Then, in a few lines, we are given the arrival of cruel hope, with its extravagant promise:

This feather stirs. She lives! If it be so,
It is a chance which does redeem all sorrows
That ever I have felt.[241]

Even the ambiguous exclamations Lear utters at the point of death do not quite close off, either for him or for the audience, the torturing hope that Cordelia still lives:

And my poor fool is hanged. No, no, no life?
Why should a dog, a horse, a rat have life,
And thou no breath at all? Thou'lt come no more,
Never, never, never, never, never!
Pray you, undo this button. Thank you, sir.
Do you see this? Look on her! Look, her lips,
Look there. Look there![242]

The textual history of this passage suggests that, in the revisions Shakespeare made to the quarto text for the version published in the folio, he added one further twist to this spiral of alternating hope and despair. The 1608 'Pied Bull' quarto ends, more simply, with these words, which lack the final upswelling of what may be ungrounded hope that we find in the folio:

And my poor fool is hanged. No, no life.
Why should a dog, a horse, a rat have life,
And thou no breath at all? O, thou wilt come no more.
Never, never, never. Pray you, undo
This button. Thank you, sir. O, O, O, O![243]

240. *King Lear*, V.iii.231–37.
241. *King Lear*, V.iii.239–41.
242. *King Lear*, V.iii.281–87.
243. *King Lear*, Q1608, V.iii.297–301.

Johnson, as we have seen, found these passages unendurable. Shakespeare, however, when he came to revise these lines, was sufficiently self-controlled to add a further grace-note to the orchestration of false hope (both onstage and in the audience) that seems to have been his governing intention when he wrote the final scenes of *King Lear*.

In both the quarto and folio versions, *King Lear* swerves away from the promised, happy ending. Yet in the end it is the freedom of life, its unconstrained nature, which is affirmed in the play's concluding tableau of loss and waste, for the 'unaccommodated' state of man from which that tableau arises is a state of mortal danger and yet also moral dignity. That such things can happen is terrible; but the human liability to tragedy is not as devastating morally speaking as it would be if we were defended against tragedy. Then we would be living in the world of the *True Chronicle Historie*, where all the characters, whether vicious or virtuous, exist in a state of ethical nonage, acting out moral characters which they have not chosen and which they are powerless to change. The familiar phrase 'tragic necessity' does not refer simply to the entailing of events within the tragic process. It also reminds us that tragedy is itself a necessity because of its power paradoxically to underwrite the human dignity which is frequently trampled upon in the actions it requires us to contemplate.

At the end of act V, scene i, Edmund soliloquizes on the complicated state of his erotic life:

> To both these sisters have I sworn my love,
> Each jealous of the other, as the stung
> Are of the adder. Which of them shall I take?
> Both? One? Or neither? Neither can be enjoyed
> If both remain alive. To take the widow
> Exasperates, makes mad, her sister Goneril,
> And hardly shall I carry out my side,
> Her husband being alive.[244]

As is so often the case with Edmund's speeches, what we have here is a speech from a comedy delivered in a tragedy—in this case, a speech by a roguish seducer debating which of two women to have. Edmund sees the two sisters as interchangeable, and he speaks from the standpoint of easy indifference as to

244. *King Lear*, V.i.47–54.

which of them he enjoys: 'Both? One? Or neither?' Against this assumption of equivalence and interchangeability, proto-Kantian characters such as Kent are committed to difference; and it is no accident that Shakespeare uses the words 'difference' and 'differences' almost twice as often in *King Lear* than in any other play.[245] When Kent threatens Oswald by saying, 'I'll teach you differences', he means not just differences of rank, to which Oswald has shown himself to be *in*different by referring to Lear as 'My lady's father', but also more generally everything that challenges the proto-utilitarian indifference to persons. For such characters—for Regan, say, and her husband, Cornwall—'differences' means simply quarrels or disputes.[246] They are deaf to the word's deeper meanings, which resist the principle of interchangeability that is central to their moral stance. But when Kent refers to Lear's daughters as the 'different issues' of 'one self mate and make', he is talking about a distinction in the moral character of persons that makes them quite un-interchangeable. And when he reveals to Lear that he 'from your first of difference and decay / Have followed your sad steps', he uses 'difference' to refer to Lear's descent into moral blindness.

If Edmund had been, say, Bertram in *All's Well That Ends Well*, he might have been unconcerned to have the bed-trick played upon him. But in *King Lear* Shakespeare presents that relaxed indifference as the gateway to a catastrophic collapse into a general equivalence: 'A man may see how this world goes with no eyes. Look with thine ears. See how yond justice rails upon yond simple thief. Hark in thine ear. Change places, and handy-dandy, which is the justice, which is the thief?'[247] The climax of villainy in *King Lear* is the weird monstrosity of a triple death which is also a triple marriage:

I was contracted to them both; all three
Now marry in an instant.[248]

In these lines the ultimate deformity of the principle of interchangeability is unmasked. The moral coolness of substitution in *King Lear* points towards an

245. Seven occurrences of the two words taken together in *King Lear*; four in *Merchant of Venice*; three in *Richard II, Hamlet, Henry VIII,* and *King John*; two in *As You Like It, All's Well That Ends Well, Winter's Tale, 1 Henry IV, Antony and Cleopatra, Cymbeline, Two Noble Kinsmen,* and *Coriolanus*; one in *Two Gentlemen of Verona, Merry Wives of Windsor, Much Ado About Nothing, Titus Andronicus, Julius Caesar, Othello,* and *Pericles*.

246. 'Our father, he hath writ, so hath our sister / Of differences' (*King Lear*, II.i.126); 'What is your difference?' (ibid., II.ii.45).

247. *King Lear*, IV.vi.146–50.

248. *King Lear*, V.iii.203–4.

indifferent world in which materialism, hedonism, and violence cascade through the play. As Johnson said, 'crimes lead to crimes'.[249]

That is why the subtle crux of whether Lear is posing a ranking or a volume question when he asks, 'Which of you shall we say doth love us most?', is so important, although its importance is brought home to us only in retrospect.[250] In this play, healthy moral attitudes, we eventually are made to see, are founded on a resistance to the utilitarian principle of interchangeability. Without the ethical anchor furnished by believing that people should be regarded as ends rather than as means and should be recognised to possess dignities rather than to have prices, in *King Lear* the indifferent drift into casual inhumanities is irresistible. So Lear's question acts like moral litmus paper. The various responses it provokes divide the three sisters into two groups, and the action of the play unfolds to us the typical consequences of those different moral positions as they spread through the other characters of the play.

———

Measure for Measure was composed during the winter of 1604 for performance at court on 26 December of that year. It is therefore almost exactly contemporary with *King Lear*, which was also probably written during the winter of 1604–1605. The two plays share many pre-occupations: justice, law and sex, rule and the relinquishing of rule. But in one important way, the two plays are perfectly opposed. *King Lear* is ultimately a Kantian play, where intuited right must be done, no matter what the consequences. The *honestum* takes precedence over the *utile*. *Measure for Measure* is ultimately a utilitarian play in which what is legally and morally right must yield to what is good, judged by consequences. The *utile* takes precedence over the *honestum*. So, like *Antony and Cleopatra* and *Coriolanus*, or *Timon of Athens* and *The Tempest*, *King Lear* and *Measure for Measure* form one of those pairs of plays, composed close to each other or maybe even concurrently, in which Shakespeare demonstrated his intellectual freedom by writing on both sides of a question.[251]

Both *King Lear* and *Measure for Measure* begin with an act of renunciation of rule, and in both plays this qualified abdication (both Lear and the Duke abdicate only with reservation) has the effect of unmasking moral deformities

249. Johnson, *Shakespeare*, p. 222.

250. *King Lear*, I.i.49.

251. See the 'Introduction' above, pp. 11–12.

that had previously lain concealed, if not entirely unsuspected. But whereas in *King Lear* moral deformity is discovered in proto-utilitarianism and the principle of interchangeability or indifference of persons with which that moral preference is associated, in *Measure for Measure* it is precisely that principle of the interchangeability of persons which supplies the sought-for remedy.[252] Both plays begin by dramatizing how the utilitarian and the Kantian or intuitionist, the *utile* and the *honestum*, co-exist and collide (and these collisions of principle can occur both between and within characters). Both plays move towards a conclusion in which one or other of these moral positions prevails. But, at that point, the two plays diverge, since in each case it is the adherents of a different moral position who are left in moral possession of the stage at the end of act V: the Kantians in *King Lear*, the utilitarians (whether acknowledged by themselves to be so or not) in *Measure for Measure*.

The paradigmatic form of action in *Measure for Measure* is substitution. To confine ourselves for the moment to only literal, rather than imaginative, substitutions: the plot is set in motion when Angelo substitutes for the Duke; the Duke substitutes himself for a friar; Angelo tries to substitute Isabella for Claudio when he suggests that she sleep with him in return for Claudio's life; Pompey substitutes for Abhorson's assistant; Ragozine's head substitutes for Barnardine's head, which was itself to have substituted for Claudio's head; Mariana substitutes for Isabella in the bed-trick. The connotations of substitution in *Measure for Measure* are complex, and much of that complexity is produced in the extraordinary final act, which is as protracted, and as replete with misleading indications, as the final act of *King Lear*. But at least part of what the prevalence of substitution in *Measure for Measure* eventually creates in act V is a flexible climate of moral accommodation which is palpable, if not proclaimed, a region of ethical *détente* in which one person may stand for another, not only without loss but even with benefit. This vision of human life is by no means uncontested within the play. In particular, it is to begin with anathema to the Duke (although he is not above availing himself of it, when it suits him).

252. Once again, the words to which Shakespeare returns in a play hint at the play's centre of interest. The word 'remedy' is used eight times in *Measure for Measure*, twice the frequency we find in any other Shakespearean play: four times in *Merry Wives of Windsor*, *All's Well That Ends Well*, *Twelfth Night*, *1 Henry VI*, and *A Midsummer Night's Dream*; three times in *As You Like It*, *Romeo and Juliet*, and *A Winter's Tale*; twice in *Much Ado About Nothing*, *Henry VIII*, *Troilus and Cressida*, *Titus Andronicus*, *Cymbeline*, *Two Noble Kinsmen*, and *The Taming of the Shrew*; once in *Two Gentlemen of Verona*, *2 Henry IV*, *2 Henry VI*, *Coriolanus*, *Macbeth*, *Hamlet*, *King Lear*, *Othello*, and *King John*.

But arguably, although the Duke prevails in *Measure for Measure* and is able in the last act to impose his own will upon the action, the vision of human life with which he begins the play does not emerge unscathed or unmodified. The Duke has been discomfited in the eyes of the audience in ways which his own conceit prevents him from noticing. Lucio, who wryly observes of lechery that 'it is impossible to extirp it quite, Friar, till eating and drinking be put down', and who is a follower, in utilitarian vein, of the 'unshunned consequence', is the principal spokesman for this more forgiving view of human failing and human appetite.[253]

The very title of *Measure for Measure* evokes a conflict of ethical and legal dispensations. As has long been recognised, on the one hand the phrase alludes to a passage in the Sermon on the Mount:

> Judge not, that ye be not judged. For with what judgment ye judge, ye shall be judged: and with what measure ye mete, it shall be measured to you again. And why beholdest thou the mote that is in thy brother's eye, but considerest not the beam that is in thine own eye. . . . Thou hypocrite, first cast out the beam out of thine own eye; and then shalt thou see clearly to cast out the mote out of thy brother's eye.[254]

The relevance of these words to the play is beyond question, particularly in what they say about hypocrisy and the retorting of a judgement on the person who initially passed it. But Shakespeare had used the phrase 'measure for measure' once before, and the circumstances of that earlier usage are also relevant to the later play, although they point in a different direction. In *3 Henry VI*, Warwick orders that York's head be taken down and replaced with the head of Clifford:

> From off the gates of York fetch down the head,
> Your father's head, which Clifford placèd there;
> Instead whereof let this supply the room.
> Measure for measure must be answerèd.[255]

Warwick's application of the phrase reveals its ambivalence. Whereas in the New Testament Christ drew upon the idea of measure to teach the need for mercy when we judge, as Warwick uses the phrase 'measure for measure', it

253. *Measure for Measure*, III.i.348–49 and 311–12.
254. Matthew 7:1–5. Cf. Mark 4:24 and Luke 6:38.
255. 3 *Henry VI*, II.vi.51–54.

refers rather to the unforgiving *lex talionis* of the Old Testament that Christ's teaching was intended to supplant and that had been articulated in a series of propositions all taking the form '*x* for *x*': 'But if any mischief follow, then thou shalt give life for life, eye for eye, tooth for tooth, hand for hand, foot for foot, burning for burning, wound for wound, stripe for stripe.'[256] So the phrase 'measure for measure' echoes both the old severe law of precise retribution and the more flexible law of grace and forgiveness that Christ offers as a substitute for it.

That hint of ethical contest, present in the very title of the play, is reinforced by the play's setting. The principal source play for *Measure for Measure*, George Whetstone's *Promos and Cassandra* (1578), was also set in Mitteleuropa, in the realm of Corvinus, king of Hungary, in the (fictional?) city of 'Julio'. So too was another possible source, Cinthio's *Epitia*, of which Shakespeare may also have been aware: Cinthio's work was set in Innsbruck. But in *Measure for Measure* Shakespeare placed the action in Vienna. Why might he have done so?

In the 1590s, Vienna had seen a number of attempts by civic authority to uphold standards of public behaviour and repress immorality. On 6 October 1592, the city authorities in Vienna had tried to reform public conduct in the city:

> In the present grievous times, with death rampant, wars, disunion and tribulations, the perversion and decay of the land and the people as well as the shedding of Christian blood wax ever more disastrous. The monstrous undertakings of the Arch-Enemy of the name of Christ show that the prayers we have been offering up for the averting of these dangers and misfortunes do not suffice. It therefore behoves and well befits every one of us, as it is only meet that all should abstain from all worldly luxuries and joy. It

256. Exodus 21:23–25. For contemporary instances of the phrase being used to encapsulate the Old Testament principle of exact retribution visited on the wicked, see Edward Topsell, *The Revvard of Religion* (1596), p. 77; and Luis de Granada, *A Memoriall of a Christian Life* (1599), p. 82. For a contemporary instance of the phrase being used, on the contrary, to recommend a merciful abstention from strict justice, see Gervase Babington, *Comfortable Notes vpon the Bookes of Exodus and Leuiticus* (1604): 'So teaching *all Gouernours* patience and long suffering, not to followe with rigour & extremitie all wrongs, not setting power against folly, and yéelding measure for measure in full recompence of ill deserts, but according to the Course of *God* here doing good for euill, euen to men of bitter *tongues* and naughtie *hearts* against vs, to men forgetfull of the good wee haue done them, and euery way deseruing euill of vs' (p. 283).

> is therefore my command that at the very earliest moment you should affix in my name . . . mandates on all the church doors with the sexton's seal thereon, forbidding most forcibly, at the risk of chastisement, all public festivities, such as singing, whistling, dancing, masques, promenading in the streets and other worldly merry-making.

In the summer of 1597, the city elders had launched another moral crusade. The Viennese had been forbidden to go 'walking, riding or driving on Sundays, holidays and other days to Enzersdorf, Vösendorf, Rodaun and other such like places to hear the sectarian, seductive preachers.'[257] News of these developments in Vienna had been spread through the major cities of Europe by means of the correspondents of the great trading houses, such as the house of Fugger. The avidity shown by characters within *Measure for Measure* for news ('What news abroad, Friar? What news?', asks Lucio; 'What news abroad i'th'world?', asks Escalus) reflects these informal early modern mechanisms for the wider sharing of topical information.[258] Thanks to such networks Vienna had acquired a reputation as a site of repeated collisions between authoritarian severity and public dissoluteness; and this reputation may have influenced Shakespeare's choice of setting for his play.

These hints of a contest of moral dispensations in both the title and the setting of *Measure for Measure* are amplified and focused in the play's early scenes, where the audience is presented with a series of collisions between the *utile* and the *honestum*. The Duke assures Angelo that 'Your scope is as mine own':

> So as to enforce or qualify the laws
> As to your *soul* seems good.[259]

The word 'soul' implies that it is an intuitionist idea of moral principle that the Duke recommends to Angelo, and this reinforces an earlier remark:

> Mortality and mercy in Vienna
> Live in thy *tongue* and *heart*.[260]

257. *Fugger*, pp. 173–74 and 207. I owe my awareness of these passages to Paul Monod.

258. *Measure for Measure*, III.i.331–32 and 453. Cf. also ibid., III.i.335 and 460–61, IV.i.25, IV.ii.110, and IV.iii.34.

259. *Measure for Measure*, I.i.64–66; emphasis added.

260. *Measure for Measure*, I.i.44–45: emphases added. Claudio will attribute a similar intuitive concept of law and justice to God (ibid., I.ii.111–12). Cf. Romans 9:15.

But this intuitionist idea of law and justice is set to work in a society which is thoroughly utilitarian and consequentialist in its thinking. Nor is this division simply a reflection of different social fractions. To Friar Thomas the Duke reveals the motivation behind his temporary abdication:

Sith 'twas my fault to give the people scope,
'Twould be my tyranny to strike and gall them
For what I bid them do. For we bid this be done,
When evil deeds have their permissive pass
And not the punishment. Therefore indeed, my father,
I have on Angelo imposed the office,
Who may in th'ambush of my name strike home,
And yet my nature never in the fight
To do in slander.[261]

It is clear that the temporary bestowal of authority on Angelo is a matter of expediency. It is *utile* rather than strictly *honestum*. The right course of action would have been for the Duke to correct the disorder that his own neglect had created, as Friar Thomas points out: 'It rested in your grace / To unloose this tied-up justice when you pleased'.[262] The Duke is using a utilitarian strategy to reinvigorate an intuitive or Kantian ideal of law and justice. Not for the last time in this play, the *utile* is being deployed to assist the *honestum*.

This division within the Duke, who is outwardly committed to the *honestum* but adept in expediency and inwardly motivated by the *utile*, is quickly replicated both between individual characters and in Viennese society as a whole. Isabella's demand of the nun Francisca for a 'more strict restraint' marks her out as (at least ostensibly) another Kantian moral intuitionist like the Duke: that is to say, someone who wishes to universalise to the greatest extent possible the moral law they discover within themselves.[263] Almost at once, she finds herself in conversation with Lucio, whose warmly appreciative lines on Julietta's pregnancy are an ode to the utility of fecundity. Lucio's agricultural metaphor presents Julietta's pregnancy not just as an instance of human flourishing but also as an expression of what sustains human well-being:

261. *Measure for Measure*, I.iii.35–43.
262. *Measure for Measure*, I.iii.31–32.
263. *Measure for Measure*, I.iv.4.

Your brother and his lover have embraced.
As those that feed, grow full; as blossoming time
That from the seedness the bare fallow brings
To teeming foison; even so her plenteous womb
Expresseth his full tilth and husbandry.[264]

Lucio then explains the recent revolution in the government of Vienna, which he characterises as the replacement of one moral dispensation by another. Angelo,

to give fear to use and liberty,
Which have for long run by the hideous law
As mice by lions, hath picked out an act
Under whose heavy sense your brother's life
Falls into forfeit.[265]

We should pause over the multiple meanings of 'use', which, in Shakespeare's day as in ours, could refer to both custom and utility, as well as also to sexual use.[266] The anti-utilitarian nature of the provisions against what the law sees as sexual irregularity (fornication and brothels) that Angelo has decided suddenly to enforce, his desire to attack utility, is economically touched on in the rich semantic field of this word.

Lucio goes on to give a pithy sketch of a quite different understanding of law from the implicit definitions of it that have been deployed in earlier scenes, when he speaks of 'the hideous law' evaded by common humanity as nimble mice can evade the ponderous power of a lion. The relation between law and wrongdoing is represented not as a matter of the salutary imposition of the dictates of the moral law, of the *honestum*, but rather as a game of intermittent and lazy predatoriness met by agile evasion. Law and justice, those supposedly sophisticated and advanced elements of social organisation, are re-imagined as an unregulated encounter between different kinds of wild animal, in which the *utile* is everything and the *honestum* nothing.

This ethical clash between the *utile* and the *honestum* is sustained in the following scene, which opens with the Duke's deputy, Angelo, in conversation

264. *Measure for Measure*, I.iv.41–45.

265. *Measure for Measure*, I.iv.63–67.

266. *OED*, 'use' *n.*, I 1 c (sexual use); II 7 a and d, and II 10 (customary practice); III 14 b and 15 a (utility or benefit). All these senses of 'use' were available in 1604.

with his fellow judge, Escalus. Although both men are magistrates, their discussion of Claudio's case reveals that they have very different ideas both of what the law is and of how it should be implemented. Both men can see that the law is only very imperfectly observed and enforced. As Escalus says,

> Well, heaven forgive him, and forgive us all!
> Some rise by sin, and some by virtue fall.
> Some run from brakes of vice, and answer none,
> And some condemnèd for a fault alone.[267]

For Escalus this situation of moral confusion arising from imperfect justice warns the magistrate to show flexibility and breadth of consideration, but for Angelo it is an encouragement towards ever-greater inflexibility and narrowness of focus. For Escalus utility is to be borne in mind when passing judgement:

> Let us be keen, and rather cut a little
> Than fall and bruise to death.[268]

But for Angelo the law is to be applied peremptorily and irrespective of consequences or wider reflections: 'What's open made to justice, / That justice seizes.'[269]

The entry of the constable Elbow and those he has arrested, Pompey and Froth, transforms the scene from a private conversation between magistrates to a court of law. It is significant that Angelo is unable to endure the incompetence of Elbow and the filibustering of Pompey and leaves them to Escalus. Here the brittleness of Angelo's uncompromising stance towards law and justice is made clear. Left to dispense sole justice, Escalus reveals how a keen sense of the *utile* governs his deliberations. Although he is in no doubt that Pompey makes his living unlawfully, Escalus also understands that no broader good would be satisfied by punishing the bawd. Hence, Pompey is to 'continue in his courses', a verdict that, with ludicrous triumphalism, Elbow brandishes before him: 'Thou seest, thou wicked varlet now, what's come upon thee. Thou art to continue now, thou varlet, thou art to continue.'[270] In the case of Froth, the affluent *habitué* of taverns and brothels, Escalus again shows the utilitarian cast of his understanding of justice by pointing out to Froth the likely

267. *Measure for Measure*, II.i.37–40.
268. *Measure for Measure*, II.i.5–6.
269. *Measure for Measure*, II.i.21–22.
270. *Measure for Measure*, II.i.171–72 and 173–75.

consequences should he not reform: 'Come hither to me, Master Froth. Master Froth, I would not have you acquainted with tapsters. They will draw you, Master Froth, and you will hang them. Get you gone, and let me hear no more of you.'[271] After Froth has been dismissed, Escalus engages in a lengthy conversation with Pompey, which we can characterise as a conversation between two utilitarians, one moderate (Escalus) and the other radical (Pompey), in which the malefactor educates the magistrate about the implications of the ethical position they both broadly share. As we have seen, on the heath, Lear had cried out, 'See how yond justice rails upon yond simple thief. Hark in thine ear. Change places, and handy-dandy, which is the justice, which is the thief?'[272] Elbow's malapropisms have just provoked Escalus to say something similar, albeit in a key of rueful dismay rather than anguish: 'Which is the wiser here, Justice or Iniquity?'[273] This exchange between Pompey and Escalus lies close to the heart of *Measure for Measure*'s concerns about law and morality and illustrates (in a way that perhaps would have surprised Escalus) the truth of that recent observation about the difficulty of distinguishing degrees of wisdom and the imperfection with which insight is correlated with probity.

Pompey's radicalism is clear in his nominalist conception of law. When asked if his trade is lawful, he replies, 'If the law would allow it, sir'.[274] This is law understood not as the transcription of an intuited moral sense but rather a series of inherited social rules that are often neglected and only sometimes enforced and that may also be quite arbitrary. We see that radical utilitarianism again in Pompey's vividly consequentialist imagination, evident in his awareness of what Angelo's austerity will bring in its wake:

> If you head and hang all that offend that way but for ten year together, you'll be glad to give out a commission for more heads. If this law hold in Vienna ten year, I'll rent the fairest house in it after threepence a bay. If you live to see this come to pass, say Pompey told you so.[275]

271. *Measure for Measure*, II.i.186–89. Froth has a comfortable income of £80 a year (ibid., II.i.113 and 178). A benchmark working wage at this time would have been in the region of £10 a year (William Ingram, 'The Economics of Playing', in *A Companion to Shakespeare*, ed. David Scott Kastan [Oxford: Blackwell, 1999], pp. 313–27). A rural clergyman might earn up to £20, as might a well-established actor in one of the London companies.

272. *King Lear*, IV.vi.147–50.

273. *Measure for Measure*, II.i.158.

274. *Measure for Measure*, II.i.206.

275. *Measure for Measure*, II.i.217–21.

However Angelo's revival of Vienna's moral law may serve the *honestum*, it will (as Pompey understands) do a grave disservice to the *utile*. Escalus's administration of justice is broadly utilitarian in character, but he seems to have a weaker grasp of what such a position entails than does Pompey—or, perhaps, he flinches from its full implications.

The following scene, act II, scene ii, in which Isabella pleads for Claudio's life before Angelo, presents the audience with another variation on the complicated dance (which is of course another meaning of the word 'measure') between the *utile* and the *honestum* that has so far occupied the stage.[276] The scene begins as a collision between two Kantians who happen to be divided over a certain issue (the death sentence passed on Claudio). What happens is that we see the undermining of the dispassionate Kantian (Angelo) by the interested Kantian (Isabella), who increasingly deploys arguments which are ever more utilitarian in character (stressing consequences; invoking the interchangeability of persons); and she does so goaded, provoked, and guided by asides from the arch-utilitarian, Lucio. The yielding of Angelo is not so much a case of the weakness of principle before desire as of the vulnerability of the Kantian before the utilitarian. And in act II, scene iv, when Angelo and Isabella meet again, the direction of influence is reversed, with Angelo using utilitarian arguments to unsettle Isabella. Whereas in *Lear* Shakespeare had dramatised the defiant resoluteness of Kantianism, in *Measure* he dramatised its vulnerability in the persons of both Isabella and Angelo. At the end of their first interview Angelo reflects ruefully on his moral precariousness:

> Most dangerous
> Is that temptation that doth goad us on
> To sin in *loving* virtue.[277]

This is a bitter and belated recognition of a Kantian insight by one who has fallen away from that lofty moral creed. One of Kant's shrewdest perceptions about our moral nature is that, if our attachment to moral law is a matter of affection rather than reason—if, that is to say, it is a matter of loving virtue rather than of rationally discerning both it and the reasons for observing it—then even that innocent attachment can be perverted into a pathway towards vicious conduct. And the utilitarian character of the lapsed Angelo is later

276. *OED*, 'measure' *n.*, III 15 a.

277. *Measure for Measure*, II.ii.183–85; emphasis added.

reinforced when he soliloquizes on why (as he thinks has happened) he had Claudio executed:

He should have lived,
Save that his riotous youth with dangerous sense
Might in the times to come have ta'en revenge
By so receiving a dishonored life
With ransom of such shame.[278]

It is a sharpened sense of probable consequences that tempts the neophyte utilitarian Angelo to commit a shameful and dishonest action. The extreme point of Angelo's descent comes in act V, when he attempts to persuade the Duke to disregard Isabella's cry for justice:

My lord, her wits I fear me are not firm.
She hath been a suitor to me for her brother
Cut off by course of justice.[279]

This is a re-working, in a very different key, of Falstaff's wonderful deflection of the Hostess's similar appeal to the Lord Chief Justice in 2 *Henry IV*: 'My lord, this is a poor mad soul, and she says up and down the town that her eldest son is like you. She hath been in good case, and the truth is poverty hath distracted her. But for these foolish officers, I beseech you I may have redress against them.'[280] Falstaff's inventive effrontery—his sublime resistance to being abashed—is re-imagined a few years later as the desperate expedient of a lost and bewildered Kantian, clumsily seeking to avail himself of the *utile* while still tethered to the *honestum*.

So, given the frailty of Kantianism and the seductiveness of utilitarianism, the audience of *Measure for Measure* is unlikely to be optimistic about Isabella's chances with Claudio when she resolves to inform him of what Angelo has proposed and to persuade him to reject the shameful bargain to exchange her virginity for his life:

I'll to my brother.
Though he hath fallen by prompture of the blood,
Yet hath he in him such a mind of honor

278. *Measure for Measure*, IV.iv.26–30.
279. *Measure for Measure*, V.i.36–38.
280. 2 *Henry IV*, II.i.90–94.

That had he twenty heads to tender down
On twenty bloody blocks, he'd yield them up
Before his sister should her body stoop
To such abhorred pollution.[281]

The fragility of such a Kantian willingness to do right, irrespective of the consequences, when confronted by utilitarian arguments and inducements has just been demonstrated twice over and is about to be demonstrated once more.

The ensuing conversation between brother and sister is a perfect illustration of the conflict between those ethical siblings, the *utile* and the *honestum*, with Claudio preoccupied with consequences and Isabella focused instead on an intuited sense of wrongdoing:

CLAUDIO. Death is a fearful thing.
ISABELLA. And shamèd life a hateful.[282]

And it is Claudio's vivid sense of consequences that, from his point of view, overpowers any other consideration. In the first instance, the consequences that absorb him are the consequences for himself, which he imagines with great intensity:

Ay, but to die, and go we know not where,
To lie in cold obstruction and to rot,
This sensible warm motion to become
A kneaded clod; and the delighted spirit
To bathe in fiery floods or to reside
In thrilling region of thick-ribbèd ice,
To be imprisoned in the viewless winds
And blown with restless violence round about
The pendent world, or to be worse than worst
Of those that lawless and incertain thought
Imagine howling—'tis too horrible!
The weariest and most loathed worldly life
That age, ache, penury, and imprisonment
Can lay on nature, is a paradise
To what we fear of death.[283]

281. *Measure for Measure*, II.iv.174–80.
282. *Measure for Measure*, III.i.116–17.
283. *Measure for Measure*, III.i.118–32.

It is striking that the verb which in *King Lear* has been associated with an intuited sense of right and wrong—namely, 'thrill'—in *Measure for Measure* has migrated to being a term in the vocabulary of the consequentialist imaginary, as Claudio's apprehension dwells on the 'thrilling region of thick-ribbèd ice' that is one of the terrifying possibilities of what awaits him after execution.

But then, to persuade his sister, Claudio goes on to deploy consequentialism in a more subtle way. If an action is to be judged by its consequences, rather than by its intrinsic nature, then for Isabella to fall in with Angelo's demands would be no sin:

> What sin you do to save a brother's life,
> Nature dispenses with the deed so far
> That it becomes a virtue.[284]

But in response, Isabella escalates the debate further with a protestation of an even more extremely Kantian nature. She refuses point-blank to infringe what she perceives to be the moral law, no matter what the consequences of her refusal. At the same time she refuses to allow herself to serve as a means, rather than exist as an end:

> O you beast!
> O faithless coward, O dishonest wretch!
> Wilt thou be made a man out of my vice?
> Is't not a kind of incest to take life
> From thine own sister's shame? What should I think?
> Heaven shield my mother played my father fair,
> For such a warpèd slip of wilderness
> Ne'er issued from his blood. Take my defiance;
> Die, perish! Might but my bending down
> Reprieve thee from thy fate, it should proceed.
> I'll pray a thousand prayers for thy death,
> No word to save thee.[285]

This histrionic Kantianism is echoed when, after the Duke has outlined to Isabella in general terms his solution to her and Claudio's predicament, she declares, 'I have spirit to do anything that appears not foul in the truth of my

284. *Measure for Measure*, III.i.134–36.
285. *Measure for Measure*, III.i.136–47.

spirit.'[286] But after the Duke has explained the bed-trick in detail and defended the deception upon which it turns on consequentialist grounds ('the doubleness of the benefit defends the deceit from reproof'), Isabella's moral position alters from the almost hyperbolical Kantianism she has demonstrated towards her brother. Now, she embraces a mild consequentialism.[287] She thanks the Duke for the 'comfort' he has brought her and greets his scheme with an approval couched in consequentialist terms: 'The image of it gives me content already, and I trust it will grow to a most prosperous perfection.'[288] The language of the expedient good—'comfort', 'content', 'prosperous'—has taken the place of her earlier language of intuited right and wrong.[289]

The rich confusions of moral stance that Shakespeare has dramatised in the first three acts of *Measure for Measure* are sustained in act IV, albeit in a different key. For instance, the radical utilitarian Pompey, when obliged to become the executioner Abhorson's assistant, suddenly becomes a Kantian, albeit a half-hearted and unpersuasive one. His invitation to Barnardine to be executed—'You must be so good, sir, to rise and be put to death'—seems naïvely to expect a willing and spontaneous compliance with the moral law, in the spirit of Kantian ethics.[290] This may be metaphysically irreproachable, but it shows a very poor understanding of the character of Barnardine.

However, it is in act V that the entanglement of the *utile* and the *honestum* reaches its climax, as those former Kantians, the Duke, Angelo, and Isabella, frame and benefit from an expedient solution to the play's apparently intractable complications of plot. It is a solution which makes lavish use of that characteristic feature of utilitarian thought, the interchangeability of persons. The bed-trick has required a bodily interchange of persons, but before the remedy it promises can be achieved, that literal act of substitution has to be followed by a series of imaginative substitutions. Mariana's climactic plea to Isabella is a request that Isabella should now put herself imaginatively in Mariana's position, just as Mariana has physically put herself in Isabella's position in the bed-trick:

286. *Measure for Measure,* III.i.200–201.

287. *Measure for Measure,* III.i.245–46.

288. *Measure for Measure,* III.i.256 and 248–49.

289. Shakespeare seems to have been careful not to activate any distracting memory of the biblical precedents for the bed-trick: see Genesis 29:21–24 and 38:14–26.

290. *Measure for Measure,* IV.iii.24–25.

Sweet Isabel, *take my part.*
Lend me your knees, and all my life to come
I'll lend you all my life to do you service.[291]

Imaginative interchangeability (phrased, interestingly, in terms as much theatrical as anything else: 'take my part') here emerges as a technique for generating forgiveness.

This is the culmination of a thread of instances of figurative substitutions of persons that runs through the play as a counterpart to the literal substitutions that sustain the plot. The thread begins in Escalus's appeal to Angelo to show mercy to Claudio:

Let but your honor know—
Whom I believe to be most strait in virtue—
That in the working of your own affections,
Had time cohered with place, or place with wishing,
Or that the resolute acting of your blood
Could have attained th'effect of your own purpose,
Whether you had not sometime in your life
Erred in this point which now you censure him,
And pulled the law upon you.[292]

Angelo responds with a different kind of substitution, common on the early modern English stage, in which a character is invited to give a verdict while functioning as a judge which they are later obliged to accept themselves when they are revealed to be guilty of the identical misdemeanour:

You may not so extenuate his offense
For I have had such faults; but rather tell me
When I, that censure him, do so offend,
Let mine own judgment pattern out my death,
And nothing come in partial.[293]

291. *Measure for Measure,* V.i.433–35; emphasis added.

292. *Measure for Measure,* II.i.8–16.

293. *Measure for Measure,* II.i.27–31. For other examples of this trope of action in late sixteenth-century English drama, see, for instance, *Henry V,* II.ii (Henry tempts the conspirators to show no mercy to 'the man . . . That railed' against the king, and then shows the same severity to them: 'The mercy that was quick in us but late / By your own counsel is suppressed and killed'; ll. 40–41 and 77–78); and *The Booke of Sir Thomas More,* the episode of the lifting of

This is precisely what the Duke's scheme brings about, in that Angelo, pre-contracted to Mariana, commits exactly the same offence as Claudio, who is pre-contracted to Juliet. The Duke's apparently jocular reassurance to Angelo in act V cements the point:

> Do you not smile at this, Lord Angelo?
> O heaven, the vanity of wretched fools.
> Give us some seats. Come, cousin Angelo,
> In this I'll be impartial; be you judge
> Of your own cause.[294]

Again, there is a teasing point of contact with act V of *King Lear,* where pre-contracts are also unexpectedly to the fore. Albany points out that Goneril 'is subcontracted to this lord', meaning Edmund, and a little later Edmund himself confirms the existence of yet another contract, to Regan: 'I was contracted to them both.'[295] The means of remedy in *Measure for Measure* is an index to depravity in *King Lear.*

Is it surprising that the Duke should be the architect of so utilitarian, so expedient a resolution of the action? (A resolution which, it must be said, leaves the problematic public morality of Vienna precisely where it was at the beginning of the play.)[296] In one sense, yes, for the Duke, as we have seen, bestows authority on Angelo in moral language which is thoroughly intuitionist.[297] But once the Duke forsakes 'the life removed' that he has hitherto led and wanders in disguise through Vienna (a feature of the plot of *Measure for Measure* that is not present in Whetstone's *Promos and Cassandra,* where King Corvinus is genuinely absent until he returns to dispense justice), the moral complexion of his actions undergoes a transformation. He becomes the play's most adept artist in the utilitarian skills of personal interchangeability, in respect both of himself and of others. Yet at the same time the Duke remains vestigially wedded to moral ideas that smack of Kantian, or even Rawlsian, intuition. When he conceals from Claudio that he intends to save his life, and

---

Suresby's purse (again, the magistrate Suresby expresses a harsh judgement which More, by means of some adroit stage business, obliges him to apply to himself).

294. *Measure for Measure,* V.i.168–72.

295. *King Lear,* V.iii.80 and 203.

296. As Coleridge noted: 'Our feelings of justice are grossly wounded in Angelo's escape' (Coleridge, *Table Talk,* p. 13).

297. Above, pp. 369–70.

still more when in act V he conceals from Isabella that Claudio is in fact alive, is he not constructing a Rawlsian 'veil of ignorance' to test how their moral natures will respond when the idea of any advantage to themselves seems to have been removed? Yet he represents these deceptions to himself in language that quarrels with this reading of them. To himself he represents the purpose of his deception of Isabella in utilitarian terms, focusing on questions of expediency ('comfort') rather than rightness:

> But I will keep her ignorant of her good,
> To make her heavenly comforts of despair
> When it is least expected.[298]

The confusions in the Duke's self-understanding and self-awareness lend both pathos and comedy to Escalus's summary of the Duke's character, as a man 'that above all other strifes contended especially to know himself'.[299] For instance, the Duke describes himself to Angelo and Escalus as one who shuns the theatre of power and mistrusts those who revel in it:

> I love the people,
> But do not like to stage me to their eyes.
> Though it do well, I do not relish well
> Their loud applause and aves vehement,
> Nor do I think the man of safe discretion
> That does affect it.[300]

Yet what is act V if not justice re-presented as public theatre (the Duke has insisted that Escalus and Angelo meet him in public, 'at the gates')?[301] Again, the Duke describes laws as the 'needful bits and curbs to headstrong jades'; but who has been more of a headstrong jade than the Duke himself, pursuing his own interests and neglecting the duties of rule?[302]

So it is hard to accept the accuracy of Escalus's account of the Duke as an accomplished practitioner of the classic precept 'cognosce te ipsum'. That cannot be an accurate description of the conflicted man we see, who in fact is much closer to Lucio's acute sketch of 'the old fantastical Duke of dark

298. *Measure for Measure*, IV.iii.102–4.
299. *Measure for Measure*, III.i.463–64.
300. *Measure for Measure*, I.i.67–72.
301. *Measure for Measure*, IV.iv.4.
302. *Measure for Measure*, I.iii.20.

corners.'[303] Once again, Escalus's rueful question, 'Which is the wiser here, Justice or Iniquity?', seems to the point.[304] And in the Duke's final lines, the emphasis again falls on the good, the *utile*, rather than on the right or *honestum*, accompanied by a promise of the interchangeability of personal effects:

> Dear Isabel,
> I have a motion much imports your *good*,
> Whereto if you'll a willing ear incline,
> What's mine is yours, and what is yours is mine.[305]

On the other hand, Angelo's final words in the play show a reversion to the Kantianism from which he had fallen and which as a moral position entertains the willing acceptance of punishment as a satisfying acting-out of the moral law, to be embraced no matter what its consequences for the individual:

> I am sorry that such sorrow I procure,
> And so deep sticks it in my penitent heart
> That I crave death more willingly than mercy.
> 'Tis my deserving, and I do entreat it.[306]

Angelo has had an expedient solution forced upon him, and he complies with it notwithstanding the insult it inflicts on his re-discovered Kantian moral character. This is why, at the end of the play, Angelo is such an isolated character, despite having acquired a wife. He is an apostate Kantian, surrounded by contented and comforted utilitarians. For even Lucio has managed to elude the severe punishments of whipping and hanging with which he was threatened.

In act II, scene ii of *Measure for Measure*, the Provost reminds Angelo of the perils of passing judgement. Later circumstances, he points out, can unmask what at the time seemed to be rectitude as in fact rashness or harshness:

> Under your good correction, I have seen
> When after execution, judgment hath
> Repented o'er his doom.[307]

303. *Measure for Measure*, IV.iii.150.
304. *Measure for Measure*, II.i.158.
305. *Measure for Measure*, V.i.537–40; emphasis added.
306. *Measure for Measure*, V.i.478–81.
307. *Measure for Measure*, II.ii.11–13.

Some ten years later, Shakespeare collaborated with John Fletcher to write a play, *The Two Noble Kinsmen,* in which this imagined peril very nearly comes to pass. Palamon, having lost the fight with his kinsman Arcite to decide who will marry Emilia, is condemned to suffer the fate of execution that was prescribed for the loser of the combat. His head is on the block when a messenger enters, to say that Arcite has suffered an accidental fall from his horse and is likely to die and that Palamon is therefore reprieved and the way lies clear for him to marry Emilia. *The Two Noble Kinsmen* is based on a Chaucerian predecessor, *The Knight's Tale;* but this near-mortal near-miss is unique to Shakespeare and Fletcher's play, for in *The Knight's Tale,* the losers in the fight for Emelye's hand were not to be sentenced to death.[308] And other important elements of both *King Lear* and *Measure for Measure* are reworked in *The Two Noble Kinsmen.* For example, Lear's love-test is recalled by Palamon and Arcite's disputes about which of them loves Emilia more, while Mariana's pleading for Isabella to intercede with the Duke is revisited in Emilia's pleading with Hippolyta to intercede with Theseus.[309]

The Two Noble Kinsmen is a play that challenges many Romantic and post-Romantic assertions about the literary work of art. An instance of strikingly successful collaboration, it poses a question for Romantic notions of the poem as an intimate expression of the complexities of the single, poetic character.[310] A play which is saturated with significant and functional intertexts (both Shakespearean and non-Shakespearean), it declines to associate itself with mid-twentieth-century assumptions about the literary work as a self-sufficient verbal icon.[311] So to describe *The Two Noble Kinsmen* may seem to be the first step in an argument that will describe it as an immovably early modern text, trapped in a particular historical set of attitudes. In part, the play surely is that. But it is also possible to consider *The Two Noble Kinsmen* in a less constrained way, as a work in which the preoccupation with the *utile* and the *honestum* which we have traced in *King Lear* and *Measure for Measure* is picked up once more and taken in a new and surprising direction. As in those two earlier plays,

308. Chaucer, *The Knight's Tale,* ll. 1829–69, in Chaucer, *The Works of Geoffrey Chaucer,* ed. F. N. Robinson, 2nd ed. (London: Oxford University Press, 1968), p. 35.

309. *Two Noble Kinsmen,* III.vi.188 ff.

310. 'What is poetry? is so nearly the same question with, what is a poet?, that the answer to the one is involved in the solution of the other' (Coleridge, *Biographia,* 2:15).

311. See, as classic examples of this way of considering poetry, Cleanth Brooks, *The Well Wrought Urn: Studies in the Structure of Poetry* (London: Dennis Dobson, 1949); and W. K. Wimsatt, *The Verbal Icon: Studies in the Meaning of Poetry* (London: Methuen, 1970).

a plot with questions of personal interchangeability and substitution at its heart supplies the dramatic language through which ethical concerns are sustained and interrogated. If in *King Lear* Shakespeare put onstage the discomfiting of the utilitarian, and if in *Measure for Measure* he dramatised both the fragility of Kantianism and the remedial powers of utilitarianism, in *The Two Noble Kinsmen* he and Fletcher together crafted a play that puts onstage an action in which the stand-off between those two rival philosophies is unexpectedly dissolved.

The Two Noble Kinsmen begins with a prologue which draws attention to the play's relationship to Chaucer:

For I am sure
It has a noble breeder and a pure,
A learnèd, and a poet never went
More famous yet twixt Po and silver Trent.
Chaucer—of all admired—the story gives;
There, constant to eternity, it lives.[312]

Chaucer is praised as unsurpassable, and in consequence, *The Knight's Tale* is irreplaceable. It is 'there', and there alone, that the story of Palamon and Arcite truly and perpetually 'lives'. This denial of the possibility of substitution introduces a play which nevertheless will substitute for its Chaucerian predecessor, which was itself a substitution for an earlier version of the story in Boccaccio's *Teseida*.[313] Furthermore, the prologue also serves as introduction to a play in which this very theme—the simultaneous impossibility and necessity of substitution—supplies the marrow of the plot. The characters in the play recoil from such substitutions and yet are obliged to embrace them, albeit out of compassion rather than naked expediency.

The play's intertext with Chaucer, then, is presented to us in the prologue with a measure of knowingness, as offering a foretaste of the tension between the competing claims of uniqueness and replaceability that will be developed at greater length in the main action of the play. The early scenes place before us another important intertext, this time with classical mythology. The prehistory of the plot of *The Two Noble Kinsmen* involves the mythological history of Thebes and thus draws upon the same material which Sophocles had used

312. *Two Noble Kinsmen*, 'Prologue', 9–15.

313. Giovanni Boccaccio, *Teseida della nozze d'Emilia* (comp. 1340–1341). There is a critical edition by Edvige Agostinelli and William Coleman (Edizioni del Galluzzo, 2015).

in *Antigone*. Creon's tyrannical refusal to allow burial to his enemies is the subject of the First Queen's complaint to Theseus:

> We are three queens, whose sovereigns fell before
> The wrath of cruel Creon; who endured
> The beaks of ravens, talons of the kites,
> And pecks of crows in the foul fields of Thebes.
> He will not suffer us to burn their bones,
> To urn their ashes, nor to take th'offense
> Of mortal loathsomeness from the blessed eye
> Of holy Phoebus, but infects the winds
> With stench of our slain lords.[314]

As we have seen, Antigone's response to this instance of Creon's tyranny was to attempt the remedy herself, and jealously to share the responsibility for it with no one else, not even her sister.[315] The First Queen, however, pleads with Theseus to assist her and to make it possible for her and the two other widowed queens to perform the proper rites on their husbands' corpses:

> Oh pity, Duke,
> Thou purger of the earth; draw thy feared sword
> That does good turns to th'world; give us the bones
> Of our dead kings, that we may chapel them; . . .[316]

These words bring the matter of *Antigone* into *The Two Noble Kinsmen*. That paradigmatic moment of drama's enduring fascination with those who recoil from the flexibility of interchangeability and from the options created by consequentialist calculation that are offered by a utilitarian morality is recalled in the first scene of *The Two Noble Kinsmen*, a play which will refuse finally to choose between intuitionism and utilitarianism and which will exploit accident to escape from the harsh necessity of choice. Emilia's condition of being 'guiltless of election' is eventually made generally true.[317]

The ferocity displayed by Antigone in pursuing her intuited sense of the *honestum* is, however, not absent from *The Two Noble Kinsmen*, although it is significantly displaced. Kant was adamant that for centuries men and women

314. *Two Noble Kinsmen*, I.i.39–47.
315. See above, pp. 344–45.
316. *Two Noble Kinsmen*, I.i.47–50.
317. *Two Noble Kinsmen*, V.i.154.

had been misled by Aristotle's identification of virtue with moderation. For Kant, moral rectitude was nothing to do with following a mean between extremes:

> The distinction between virtue and vice can never be sought in the *degree* to which one follows certain maxims; it must rather be sought only in the specific *quality* of the maxims (their relation to the law). In other words, the well-known principle (Aristotle's) which locates virtue in the *mean* between two vices is false. Let good management, for instance, consist in the *mean* between two vices, prodigality and avarice: as a virtue, it cannot be represented as arising either from a gradual diminution of prodigality (by saving) or from an increase of spending on the miser's part—as if these two vices, moving in opposite directions, met in good management. Instead, each of them has its distinctive maxim, which necessarily contradicts the maxim of the other.[318]

The uncompromising purity of an intuited sense of what is right is evident in the character of Antigone. In *The Two Noble Kinsmen,* it is transposed into the violent absoluteness demonstrated particularly by Palamon, but also to a lesser degree by Arcite and the Jailer's daughter, towards questions of erotic attachment.

Palamon has revealed the absoluteness of his character very early on, when he describes himself to Arcite in these words:

> Either I am
> The fore-horse in the team or I am none
> That draw i'th'sequent trace.[319]

So, when the sight of Emilia has suddenly engaged the affections of both men, Palamon's intransigent insistence on exclusivity of possession is not entirely unexpected:

> PALAMON. I saw her first.
> ARCITE. That's nothing—
> PALAMON. But it shall be.
> ARCITE. I saw her too.
> PALAMON. Yes, but you must not love her.

318. Kant, *Metaphysics*, pp. 174–75.
319. *Two Noble Kinsmen*, I.ii.58–60.

ARCITE. I will not, as you do, to worship her
As she is heavenly and a blessèd goddess;
I love her as a woman, to enjoy her.
So both may love.
PALAMON. You shall not love at all.
ARCITE. Not love at all! Who shall deny me?
PALAMON. I that first saw her; I that took possession
First with mine eye of all those beauties
In her revealed to mankind. If thou lov'st her,
Or entertain'st a hope to blast my wishes,
Thou art a traitor, Arcite, and a fellow
False as thy title to her. Friendship, blood,
And all the ties between us I disclaim,
If thou once think upon her.
ARCITE. Yes, I love her
And if the lives of all my name lay on it,
I must do so; I love her with my soul.
If that will lose ye, farewell, Palamon.
I say again I love, and, in loving her, maintain
I am as worthy and as free a lover
And have as just a title to her beauty,
As any Palamon or any living
That is a man's son.[320]

In this dialogue we see Arcite becoming infected in his turn by the ferocious possessiveness to which Palamon had immediately succumbed. Under the pressure of this sudden erotic attachment, the behaviour of both men becomes grotesquely incoherent. They are at the same time 'twins of honor'[321] and antagonists, both solicitous for one another's welfare, 'twined together', and also eager to kill one another.[322] A commitment to exclusivity, it seems, breeds these patterns of contradictory inhumanity. So whereas *Lear* shows tragically how interchangeability leads to moral savagery, and *Measure* dramatizes, but finally in a comic mode, how interchangeability can supply solutions to the terrible

320. *Two Noble Kinsmen*, II.ii.160–83.

321. *Two Noble Kinsmen*, II.ii.18.

322. *Two Noble Kinsmen*, II.ii.64. See, e.g., the abrupt alternations between care and aggression ibid., III.vi.

impasses created by moral absolutism, *The Two Noble Kinsmen* takes a middle path. The later play explores sympathetically the pathos of exclusive attachment as well as revealing its moral grotesqueness.

Is such extreme behaviour truly noble? Arcite suggests that a jealous exclusiveness of attachment, to 'love alone', is 'unlike a noble kinsman'.[323] This is the 'tyrannous' nature of love, which in the world of this play recalls the cruel severity of the tyrant Creon.[324] Alternatively, we may think that, for better or worse, this preternatural vigilance over precedence and priority is not unlike the amplified alertness to abstruse points of honour that, in the world of chivalry, was deemed incumbent on those of high birth. Such extravagance was recognised even at the time as a marker of nobility (an extreme sensitivity to personal honour that might produce exorbitant behaviour). But equally there was a sceptical strain of analysis that dismissed extreme chivalry as just the social code of a particular caste which bore no relation to genuine virtue. Certainly *The Two Noble Kinsmen* is not inclined to take the moral hyperboles of nobility entirely at face value. Just before Emilia enters the garden, and thereby innocently drives a wedge between Palamon and Arcite, Palamon asks Arcite,

> Is there record of any two that loved
> Better than we do, Arcite?[325]

The dramatic irony requires no underlining. Nobility of birth, it is clear, confers no special clarity of moral insight.[326]

So when Palamon says

> I love Emilia, and in that I'll bury
> Thee and all crosses else.[327]

we perhaps hear an echo of the reckless wildness of Laertes, returned to Elsinore to exact revenge:

323. *Two Noble Kinsmen*, II.ii.193–94.

324. *Two Noble Kinsmen*, IV.ii.146.

325. *Two Noble Kinsmen*, II.ii.112–13.

326. For an account of Shakespeare's Late Plays that challenges the usual arguments that they as a group are sympathetic to the pretensions of birth and to assertions of intrinsic nobility, see Simon Palfrey, *Late Shakespeare: A New World of Words* (Oxford: Clarendon Press, 1997).

327. *Two Noble Kinsmen*, III.vi.126–27.

To hell, allegiance! Vows to the blackest devil!
Conscience and grace to the profoundest pit!
I dare damnation. To this point I stand,
That both the worlds I give to negligence,
Let come what comes; . . .[328]

It is not just the ambivalence of 'crosses' (referring to both 'obstacles' and the Christian symbol of atonement) that brings these words of Laertes to mind. It is also the terrifying indifference to consequences that Laertes and Palamon share and that marks them out as occupying an extreme point on the spectrum of possible moral positions. When Palamon and Arcite are discovered duelling in the woods by Theseus, Palamon (recalling the apostate Kantian Angelo in act V of *Measure for Measure*) pleads not for mercy but for severity:

Stop,
As thou art just, thy noble ear against us[329]

This desire for a judgement delivered, in Kantian fashion, without a view to consequences finds an echo in the conditions Theseus imposes on the trial by combat that will end the dispute:

He [the victor] shall enjoy her; the other lose his head,
And all his friends. Nor shall he grudge to fall,
Nor think he dies with interest in this lady.
Will this content ye?[330]

Theseus specifies an absolute victory and an absolute defeat, accompanied by a complete renunciation of all consequences on the part of the loser. Hence the use of the unexpected word 'interest' and the requirement to forsake all—surely natural—'grudge'. This is to be a hyper-Kantian encounter.

It is here that the most important of Shakespeare and Fletcher's additions to Chaucer is so revealing. In *The Knight's Tale* Palamoun escapes from prison by 'helpyng of a freend' and by drugging his jailer.[331] In *The Two Noble Kinsmen* Palamon escapes from jail thanks to the assistance of the (un-named) Jailer's

328. *Hamlet*, IV.v.131–36.
329. *Two Noble Kinsmen*, III.vi.173–74.
330. *Two Noble Kinsmen*, III.vi.297–300.
331. Chaucer, *The Knight's Tale*, ll. 1470–74.

daughter. She has fallen in love with Palamon with a violent exclusivity to match his own love for Emilia, notwithstanding (as she admits) the equal attractiveness of Arcite:

> And yet he had a cousin, fair as he, too;
> But in my heart was Palamon and there,
> Lord, what a coil he keeps![332]

As she later says, 'but for one thing, / I care for nothing—and that's Palamon.'[333] Her madness, appropriately enough, takes the form of fantasies of impossible promiscuity on the part of Palamon—'All the young maids / Of our town are in love with him'. Thoughts such as these are most proper to torment someone tethered to the ideal of an exclusive relationship. When the Jailer's daughter exclaims, 'Dissolve, my life!', we see again what we have seen also in the exchanges between Palamon and Arcite, namely, the self-destructiveness that lies in wait for those who refuse to accept, in a spirit of more relaxed accommodation, the possibility of a substitute.[334] When she longs for 'An end, and that is all', this expresses, of course, a longing for death. But, in a sense that the Jailer's daughter does not suspect, these words also express the harmful exclusiveness and singularity of her attachment—'*An* end'. The desire for death and the impossibility of accepting a substitute are the two sides to the ambiguity of this line, in which the Jailer's daughter's predicament is crystallised. This singular focus on 'an end' has to yield, if life is to continue, to a more plural focus on means.

This strand of plot introduced by Shakespeare and Fletcher to the material they inherited from Chaucer is transformative, adding a perspective on the themes of the 'noble' plot that challenges its emphases and priorities—indeed, its whole implicit moral philosophy. If in one sense the love of the Jailer's daughter for Palamon is the mirror image of Palamon's love for Emilia, albeit transposed from a high to a low social station, it nevertheless follows a very different course. For the Jailer's daughter has a Wooer (also un-named) whose love for the Jailer's daughter leads him to seek a cure for her distraction from a Doctor. Whereas the remedy prescribed for the noble kinsmen is an elaborate trial by combat, the Doctor has a different prescription for the Jailer's daughter:

332. *Two Noble Kinsmen*, II.iv.16–18.
333. *Two Noble Kinsmen*, III.ii.5–6.
334. *Two Noble Kinsmen*, III.ii.29.

> This you must do: confine her to a place where the light may rather seem to steal in than be permitted; take upon you [gesturing to Wooer]—young sir, her friend—the name of Palamon; say you come to eat with her and to commune of love. This will catch her attention, for this her mind beats upon; . . . Sing to her such green songs of love as she says Palamon hath sung in prison. . . . All this shall become Palamon, for Palamon can sing, and Palamon is sweet and ev'ry good thing. Desire to eat with her, crave her, drink to her, and, still among, intermingle your petition of grace and acceptance into her favor. Learn what maids have been her companions and play-feres, and let them repair to her with 'Palamon' in their mouths and appear with tokens, as if they suggested for him. It is a falsehood she is in, which is with falsehoods to be combated.[335]

This impersonation is to be taken to extremes: 'Lie with her if she ask you . . . in the way of cure.'[336] This is the bed-trick of *Measure for Measure*, but pursued as medicinal remedy rather than as entrapping ruse. The Doctor goes on to explain,

> if you perceive
> Her mood inclining that way that I spoke of,
> *Videlicet*, the way of flesh—you have me? . . .
> Please her appetite,
> And do it home; it cures her.[337]

When the Jailer objects to this unusual prescription, the Doctor replies, with a significant choice of word: 'Ne'er cast your child away for *honesty*.'[338] While the noble characters are trapped in a ceremony of extreme complexity, the mechanicals can take comfort in a solution that disregards the *honestum* and pursues the *utile* in a spirit of humane, if robustly practical, compassion.

The Jailer's daughter is to be deceived out of her delusion and tricked into accepting a substitute for the man she believes she loves. Emilia's experience is both parallel to that of the Jailer's daughter and the inverse of it. Emilia too will have to accept a substitute, but she must do so knowingly and notwithstanding the principle of exclusivity that, in this play at least, hangs around noble erotic attachment. This contradiction or flaw is announced when

335. *Two Noble Kinsmen*, IV.iii.66–85.

336. *Two Noble Kinsmen*, V.ii.18–19.

337. *Two Noble Kinsmen*, V.ii.33–37.

338. *Two Noble Kinsmen*, V.ii.21; emphasis added.

Theseus explains the implications of the trial by combat for Emilia, implications in which the principles of both exclusivity and substitution are involved:

> Say, Emilia,
> If one of them were dead, as one must, are you
> Content to take th'other as your husband?
> They cannot both enjoy you. They are princes
> As goodly as your own eyes and as noble
> As ever fame yet spoke of. Look upon 'em
> And, if you can love, end this difference—
> I give consent. Are you content too, princes?[339]

'End this difference': Theseus uses that significantly Kantian word to command a transcendence of a Kantian dilemma.[340] It is the co-existence of the rival principles of equivalence ('They are princes / As goodly as your own eyes') and exclusivity ('They cannot both enjoy you') that makes this so disorienting a prospect for Emilia. That disorientation—the simultaneity of needing to accept one and being at the same time ready to accept either—is caught in another altered recollection of an earlier Shakespearean moment. Hamlet had confronted Gertrude with portraits of Old Hamlet and Claudius, the better to make her understand the impossibility of comparison between the two men:

> Look here upon this picture, and on this—
> The counterfeit presentment of two brothers.
> . . . Have you eyes?
> Could you on this fair mountain leave to feed
> And batten on this moor? Ha, have you eyes?[341]

But when Emilia considers the portraits of Palamon and Arcite, her powers of decision are disarmed:

> Stand both together. Now, come ask me, brother;
> Alas, I know not. Ask me now, sweet sister;
> I may go look. What a mere child is Fancy,

339. *Two Noble Kinsmen*, III.vi.272–79.

340. Cf. above, pp. 319 and 364.

341. *Hamlet*, III.iv.53–54, 65–67.

That having two fair gauds of equal sweetness
Cannot distinguish, but must cry for both![342]

Emilia's deepest predicament is not that she is being fought over by Palamon and Arcite but rather that she finds herself at the point where the two competing moral dispensations of the play—the one asserting the necessity, the other the impossibility, of substitution—meet. While Palamon and Arcite are both afforded the luxury of exclusivity in their erotic attachments, Emilia is forced to accept the principle of the interchangeability of persons, even though in this soliloquy, she struggles against it. 'You must love one of them', insists Theseus.[343] 'I have no choice', pleads Emilia, meaning that she is unable to choose.[344] She will revert to this theme in the final act:

I am bride-habited,
But maiden-hearted; a husband I have 'pointed,
But do not know him. Out of two, I should
Choose one and pray for his success, but I
Am guiltless of election. Of mine eyes,
Were I to lose one, they are equal precious;
I could doom neither—that which perished should
Go to't unsentenced. Therefore, most modest queen,
He of the two pretenders that best loves me
And has the truest title in't, let him
Take off my wheaten garland, or else grant
The file and quality I hold I may
Continue in thy band.[345]

But in fact it will be the fate of Emilia, like that of the Jailer's daughter, to be denied choice.

Accident intervenes to draw, to some extent, the sting of this dilemma. In *The Knight's Tale*, the victorious Arcite dies when malevolent Saturne intervenes:

Out of the ground a furie infernal sterte,
From Pluto sent at requeste of Saturne,

342. *Two Noble Kinsmen*, IV.ii.50–54.

343. *Two Noble Kinsmen*, IV.ii.68.

344. *Two Noble Kinsmen*, IV.ii.35.

345. *Two Noble Kinsmen*, V.i.150–62.

For which his hors for fere gan to turne,
And leep aside, and foundred as he leep;
And er that Arcite may taken keep,
He pighte hym on the pomel of his heed,
That in the place he lay as he were deed,
His brest tobrosten with his sadel-bowe.[346]

In *The Two Noble Kinsmen*, in another significant deviation from the Chaucerian source, this literal supernatural intervention becomes metaphorical:

As he thus went counting
The flinty pavement, dancing as 'twere to th'music
His own hoofs made—for, as they say, from iron
Came music's origin—what envious flint,
Cold as old Saturn and, like him, possessed
With fire malevolent, darted a spark
Or what fierce sulfur else to the end made,
I comment not.[347]

That the solution in *The Two Noble Kinsmen* is produced by accident, rather than by supernatural malevolence, alters how we respond to the outcome of the play, because it rescues the protagonists from the state of victimhood within which they are trapped in *The Knight's Tale*. In *The Two Noble Kinsmen*, as Theseus says, the 'gods have been most equal' (that is to say, impartial).[348] The removal of supernatural agency bestows—strangely perhaps, in a story so saturated with the tropes of chivalric romance—a measure of ethical naturalism over the ending. A willingness to bend to the principle of interchangeability and to be open to the possibility of substitution becomes a humane and chosen response to mischance, rather than a slavish posture compelled by exogenous mischief. It becomes elective rather than inflicted and so acquires a greater moral dignity. 'Never Fortune / Did play a subtler game', says Theseus, acknowledging the crucial role of accident in shaping the play's outcome.[349]

346. Chaucer, *The Knight's Tale*, ll. 2684–91.

347. *Two Noble Kinsmen*, V.iv.58–65. For a classical parallel, see Aeschylus, *The Persians*, ll. 353–54.

348. *Two Noble Kinsmen*, V.iv.115.

349. *Two Noble Kinsmen*, V.iv.112–13.

Divine intervention, at least from the vindictive and amoral gods of pagan antiquity, reduces human life to puppetry:

> As flies to wanton boys are we to th'gods:
> They kill us for their sport.[350]

Gloucester's words, although a profound misreading of the world of the play within which they are uttered, are nevertheless true as a general principle. The blind and random operation of Fortune, however, unlike the childish and irresponsible meddling of wanton gods, does not demean us to the level of flies; and the subtlety of the game that Fortune has played in *The Two Noble Kinsmen* emerges when we realise how, with a finesse that has eluded all the most powerful philosophical intellects of western Europe, in act V of this play she has managed to engineer a kind of equilibrium between the *utile* and the *honestum*.

Two striking features of the language of *The Two Noble Kinsmen* guide our understanding of the play's conclusion. The first is a fact about the play's vocabulary. The word 'end' is used more times in this play than in any other by Shakespeare.[351] The second is a thread of nautical imagery. It is initiated in the 'Prologue', in the context of the difficulty of having a literary predecessor of the stature of Chaucer:

> This is the fear we bring;
> For to say truth, it were an endless thing
> And too ambitious to aspire to him,
> Weak as we are, and almost breathless swim
> In this deep water. Do but you hold out
> Your helping hands, and we shall tack about
> And something do to save us: . . .[352]

350. *King Lear*, IV.i.38–39.

351. Nineteen occurrences. Seventeen: *Coriolanus*; sixteen: *Cymbeline, Hamlet, Comedy of Errors*; fourteen: *Richard III, 2 Henry IV*; thirteen: *Henry VIII, Love's Labour's Lost*; ten: *As You Like It*; nine: *Henry V, 1 Henry IV, Richard II*; eight: *Romeo and Juliet, Merchant of Venice*; seven: *Antony and Cleopatra, Julius Caesar, Troilus and Cressida, 2 Henry VI, Twelfth Night*; six: *Pericles, Titus Andronicus, 3 Henry VI, Winter's Tale, All's Well That Ends Well, Taming of the Shrew, Midsummer Night's Dream, Much Ado About Nothing, Merry Wives of Windsor, Two Gentlemen of Verona, Tempest*; four: *King Lear, 1 Henry VI, Measure for Measure*; three: *Macbeth, Timon of Athens, King John*; two: *Othello*.

352. *Two Noble Kinsmen*, 'Prologue', 21–27.

Arising in the context of the simultaneous irreplaceability of Chaucer, and yet the countervailing necessity to do 'something', metaphors of sailing recur as the plot advances and as the rival imperatives of both reaching the proposed end and availing oneself of fortuitous expedients are translated from the level of metadrama to the action itself. Theseus encourages Palamon and Arcite to 'hold your course'.[353] The Jailer's daughter, in her delirium, figures the remedy for her affliction in terms of skilful seamanship:

JAILER'S DAUGHTER. You are master of a ship?
JAILER. Yes.
JAILER'S DAUGHTER. Where's your compass?
JAILER. Here.
JAILER'S DAUGHTER. Set it to th' north.
And now direct your course to th' wood, where Palamon
Lies longing for me. For the tackling,
Let me alone. Come, weigh, my hearts, cheerily!
ALL. Ugh, ugh, ugh!
'Tis up! The wind's fair! Top the bowline!
Out with the mainsail!—Where's your whistle, master?
JAILER'S BROTHER. Let's get her in.
JAILER. Up to the top, boy.
JAILER'S BROTHER. Where's the pilot?
FIRST FRIEND. Here—
JAILER'S DAUGHTER. What kenn'st thou?
SECOND FRIEND. A fair wood.
JAILER'S DAUGHTER. Bear for it, master.
Tack about![354]

Before the combat begins, Arcite also reaches for seafaring imagery:

So hoist we
The sails that must these vessels port, even where
The heavenly limiter pleases.[355]

Finally, as Arcite lies dying, Pirithous also turns to the sea to evoke his situation:

353. *Two Noble Kinsmen*, III.vi.305.

354. *Two Noble Kinsmen*, IV.i.142–54.

355. *Two Noble Kinsmen*, V.i.28–30.

Yet is he living,
But such a vessel 'tis that floats but for
The surge that next approaches.[356]

The desire for the end ('port'), the need to take advantage of the fortuitous and variable ('tack'), the danger of miscarriage: These seafaring risks, skills, and imperatives work strongly and metaphorically through the plot of *The Two Noble Kinsmen.*

In *King Lear* (a Kantian tragedy), exclusivity and pre-eminence make for nobility and humanity. In *Measure for Measure* (a utilitarian comedy) the inhumanity of absoluteness is revealed, and the more positive side of the moral outlook that had opened the door to cruelty and bloodshed in *King Lear* prevails. In *The Two Noble Kinsmen* (a tragi-comedy in which intuitionist and utilitarian moral perspectives manage fortuitously to co-exist), the two positions co-habit without achieving resolution—and the absence of resolution is caught in the atmosphere of melancholy that overshadows the end of the play. Theseus affirms that 'due justice' has been done, but what does that mean?[357] The spread of signification in the word 'due' (capable of meaning not only 'exact' but also 'sufficient') keeps both moral positions in play to the very end.[358] Is the outcome of *The Two Noble Kinsmen* the perfection of justice, or (more practically) does it supply just enough justice to suffice?

The Two Noble Kinsmen is a romance, and its other-worldliness is in many ways very clear. Yet it may be that it responds to the full range of our moral lives more faithfully than do either *King Lear* or *Measure for Measure,* where the siren-song of the elimination of either the *utile* or the *honestum,* by which so many philosophers have been ship-wrecked, can be plainly heard.

356. *Two Noble Kinsmen,* V.iv.82–84.

357. *Two Noble Kinsmen,* V.iv.109.

358. *OED,* 'due', *adj. and adv.,* A 3 c ('sufficient') and B 1 ('exact')—this latter nautical meaning activated by the thread of seafaring language and metaphors in the play, noted above, pp. 395–97.

Coda

JONSON ON SHAKESPEARE

BEN JONSON CONTRIBUTED TWO POEMS to the first folio of Shakespeare's plays, *Mr. William Shakespeare's Comedies, Histories, and Tragedies* (1623). The shorter of the two (little more than an epigram) was printed on the verso facing the Droeshout portrait that served as the volume's frontispiece. The second, and much longer poem, entitled 'To the memory of my beloued, / The AVTHOR / MR. WILLIAM SHAKESPEARE: / AND / what he hath left vs.', was published as the first of the four longer commendatory poems that were printed before the text of the plays.[1] Jonson's poem is today chiefly remembered as the source of the (misleading) information that Shakespeare had 'small *Latine*, and lesse *Greeke*', and as containing a famous exclamation about Shakespeare's timelessness: 'He was not of an age, but for all time!'[2] Yet on closer inspection, this poem has much more to offer us in the way of guidance about how to read Shakespeare and about the nature of his extraordinary achievement.

The first sixteen lines of the poem are a *captatio benevolentiae* which takes the form of a series of reflections on the complexity and difficulty of the act of praise. For how easily the desire to praise can miscarry! Jonson begins by striking a note of diffidence. Is he capable of praising Shakespeare?

> To draw no enuy (*Shakespeare*) on thy name,
>   Am I thus ample to thy Booke, and Fame:
> While I confesse thy writings to be such,
>   As neither *Man*, nor *Muse*, can praise too much.[3]

1. Shakespeare, *Mr. William Shakespeare's Comedies, Histories, and Tragedies* (1623), sigs. A4^{r-v}. Quotations are taken from the text printed in Jonson, *Works*, 8:390–92.

2. Jonson, *Works*, 8:391, ll. 31 and 43.

3. Jonson, *Works*, 8:390, ll. 1–4.

But praise from the ignorant or shallow might harm its intended beneficiary. Merely to praise what is by all accounts praiseworthy is to do nothing: 'seeliest Ignorance', 'blinde Affection', and even 'crafty Malice' might do as much.[4]

Once these false, ineffectual, or disingenuous forms of praise have been identified and dismissed, Jonson launches himself on his own panegyric of Shakespeare in the next section of the poem (ll. 17–40). This section begins with a compliment that will eventually be retracted and enlarged. Jonson praises Shakespeare as the 'Soule of the Age!', before going on to assert that Shakespeare still lives for as long as we know how to read him:

> Thou art a Moniment, without a tombe,
> And art aliue still, while thy Booke doth liue,
> And we haue wits to read, . . .[5]

It is on Jonson's adequacy as a reader of Shakespeare—as one who has 'wits to read'—that the effectiveness of his tribute will depend.

Jonson compares Shakespeare to his advantage with his contemporaries (Lyly, Kyd, and Marlowe) and with the great dramatists of antiquity (Aeschylus, Euripides, Sophocles, Pacuvius, Accius, and Seneca). But then, at l. 41, the poem pivots, and in the next fourteen lines (ll. 41–54), Jonson addresses '*Britaine*' rather than Shakespeare himself (who in this section is referred to in the third rather than the second person). This new apostrophe precipitates a disruptive insight, which cancels and amplifies the earlier tribute that Shakespeare was the 'Soule of the Age!', for now we are told, 'He was not of an age, but for all time!'[6] Jonson rests this bold assertion of Shakespeare's timelessness on two claims. The first is that Shakespeare's subject matter was 'Nature her selfe':

> Nature her selfe was proud of his designes,
> And ioy'd to weare the dressing of his lines!
> Which were so richly spun, and wouen so fit,
> As, since, she will vouchsafe no other Wit.[7]

The second, however, is the art with which Shakespeare handled the 'matter' of Nature, and at this point in the poem, Jonson turns away from '*Britaine*' and once more addresses Shakespeare directly:

4. Jonson, *Works*, 8:390–91, ll. 7, 9, and 11.
5. Jonson, *Works*, 8:391, ll. 17 and 22–24.
6. Jonson, *Works*, 8:391, l. 43.
7. Jonson, *Works*, 8:392, ll. 47–50.

Yet must I not giue Nature all: Thy Art,
My gentle *Shakespeare*, must enioy a part.
For though the *Poets* matter, Nature be,
His Art doth giue the fashion. And, that he,
Who casts to write a liuing line, must sweat,
(Such as thine are) and strike the second heat
Vpon the *Muses* anuile: turne the same,
(And himselfe with it) that he thinkes to frame:
Or for the lawrell, he may gaine a scorne,
For a good *Poet's* made, as well as borne.[8]

It is perhaps a commonplace to emphasise the effort which is demanded by art and which successful art manages to conceal. But even so, Jonson's precise evocation of Shakespeare's artful efforts transforms the commonplace. Usually to speak of lines being 'turned' is a reference to the art of lineation, the line-break being the 'volta' or turn, usually between the octave and the sestet in a Petrarchan sonnet; or it may refer to different parts of a poem, as the 'strophe' and 'antistrophe' of a Greek chorus mean 'turn' and 'counter-turn'. But when Jonson writes 'turne the same, / (And himselfe with it)', the familiar expression (soon to be recalled and revived in the phrase 'well torned . . . lines') is given a new resonance, through an allusion which is activated by the extension of the metaphor of turning from the lines or sections of the poem to include also the poet. Horace had emphasised in his *Epistles* the critical labour that a poet must undergo in order to create a true poem:

at qui legitimum cupiet fecisse poema,
cum tabulis animum censoris sumet honesti[9]

And he goes on to compare this poetic labour to the contortions of a mime artist:

ludentis speciem dabit et torquebitur, ut qui
nunc Satyrum, nunc agrestem Cyclopa movetur[10]

8. Jonson, *Works*, 8:392, ll. 55–64.

9. 'But the man whose aim is to have wrought a poem true to Art's rules, when he takes his tablets, will take also the spirit of an honest censor' (Horace, *Epistles*, II.ii.109–10).

10. 'Wear the look of being at play, and yet be on the rack, like a dancer who plays now a Satyr, and now a clownish Cyclops' (Horace, *Epistles*, II.ii.124–25).

It is Horace's 'torquebitur' that prompts Jonson's extension of the metaphor of turning from the movement of the poet's lines to the flexible posture demanded of the poet himself by the act of composition; and this self-turning is further associated with a versatility of representation and a plasticity of self and creation—the ability, precisely, to represent now a satyr and now a Cyclops.

With this insight into the nature of Shakespeare's distinctive literary art and the grounds of his achievement, Jonson vindicated his own 'ample' sufficiency to praise Shakespeare without running the risk of inadvertently disparaging him. At the same time, Jonson offered a supportive anticipation of the argument of this book, which has also traced the presence of general nature in Shakespeare's plays and which has sought to relate the durable interest of Shakespeare's handling of that general nature to a versatility of mind and imagination which protected him, like Horace's mime artist, from being trapped in a single posture or character.

INDEX

A NOTE ON THE TYPE

This book has been composed in Arno, an Old-style serif typeface in the classic Venetian tradition, designed by Robert Slimbach at Adobe.